CW00684643

# ¡Zapatistas!

## Documents of the New Mexican Revolution

### (December 31, 1993–June 12, 1994)

# ¡Zapatistas!

## Documents of the New Mexican Revolution

### (December 31, 1993–June 12, 1994)

Autonomedia

Text anti-copyright @ 1994 Autonomedia, editors, and contributors.
This book may be freely pirated and quoted for non-commercial purposes,
provided that a portion of any income derived thereby returns to
the Indigenous and campesino communities of Southern Mexico.
Please inform the editors and publishers at:

Autonomedia
POB 568 Williamsburg Station
Brooklyn, New York 11211-0568 USA

Phone and Fax: (718) 963-2603

Printed in the United States of America

All photos are © 1994 by Joshua Schwartz. All rights reserved.

A portion of the proceeds from the publication of this book
will be donated to the Zapatistas.

ISBN: 1-57027-014-7

# CONTENTS

# PREFACE

We put this book together because we believe that the Zapatistas should be heard in their own words. In their hurry to analyze the Zapatistas many have ignored the analyses that the Zapatistas themselves have developed through years of struggle. As far as we know, this book is the largest collection of their communiqués, letters, and interviews in any language anywhere in the world. We think that people wishing to understand the Zapatistas should listen to *them*.

This book was produced through the donated labor of a large number of people around the US and Mexico working in solidarity with the EZLN. All of the people who worked on this book believe in the justice of the EZLN's demands and the legitimacy of their struggle. The efforts that helped to make this project a reality are greatly appreciated.

Not everyone has the time or the desire to read every word of a 350-page book. If you aren't going to read all of the material here, you can get a fairly good idea about who the Zapatistas are by reading:

The Introduction, The Southeast in Two Winds, *El Despertador Mexicano*, Responses to Government Lies, What Are They Going to Forgive Us For?, On Misunderstandings about the EZLN and the Real First Uprising, Interview with Major Ana María, On the Outcome of the Dialogue, Professionals in Hope, We Are Surrounded, To the Workers of the Republic, Interview with Subcommander Marcos (Chapter 11), Second Declaration from the Lacandona Jungle, and the Responses to the Peace Accord Proposal.

**Translators:**

Eugenio Aguilera, Peter B., Elizabeth Bright, Paul Coltrin, Shelly Feiner, Robin Flinchum, Christine Halvorson, Huasipungo, Selene Pinti Jaramillo, Susan Marsh, Matt Miscreant, Javier Ortega, Michael Pearlman, Barbara Pillsbury, Todd Prane, Leopoldo Rodríguez, Pablo Salazar Devereaux, The Subaltern Studies Collective of the University of Maryland, Ruth Warner

**The Copyediting and Proofing Army:**

Matt Black, Elizabeth Bright, Sara Brodzinsky, Mitchel Cohen, Dema Crassy, Christine Halvorson, Bazooka Joe, Tommy Lawless, Todd, Rachel Rinaldo, Joshua Schwartz, Michael Ulrich, Bill Weinberg

**Book and Cover Design:**

Matt Black, Jim Fleming, Joshua Schwartz, and the Editorial Collective

**Photos:**

Joshua Schwartz

**The Editorial Collective:**

This book project was conceived of and coordinated by the Editorial Collective. We are Zapatista solidarity activists, revolutionaries, workers, dreamers. We work for wages and we also work for ourselves. We pay too much rent and don't get enough sleep. We are inspired by the vision of the Zapatistas because we, too, dream of a better world.

Dema, Eugenio, Matt B., Matt M., Pablo, Sara, Todd

**Nothing for themselves, so that we would have everything:**

Sara and Todd

**A note on translation:**

We have done our best to create a book that is both easy to read for English speakers and true to the original Spanish. There are several language and translation issues that make this difficult. This book was translated by a large number of volunteers. This effort made the publication of this book possible, but it made consistency in the translations difficult. We think that it is important that the same words be translated in the same way each time, and all of the translations have been checked thoroughly for consistency. Another difficulty in translation was the original Spanish. Most of the Zapatistas are not native Spanish speakers. Their Spanish is sometimes awkward, and the concepts that they use are not always clearly expressed in Spanish, and are even harder to translate into English. Readers should be aware that there are many possible translations for some words, and should keep this in mind as they read the text.

**A note on sources:**

We have tried to authenticate all the materials in this book. We have been able to trace nearly all the materials to their first publication, either by the EZLN or by the media. We have included the original sources when we were able. Many materials came from the book *La palabra de los armados de verdad y fuego*, a documentary anthology of the EZLN published in Mexico.

We hope that this book is a useful resource.

Hope lives in our heart,
The Editorial Collective

# INTRODUCTION

BY HARRY CLEAVER

The time of revolution has not passed. Despite celebrating the collapse of Soviet-style communism and promising yet another social and economic renaissance, the world capitalist system is in deep trouble: East and West, North and South.

If you listen carefully to the celebrating voices, those of the rich and the powerful in their corporate offices and government buildings, you can pick up a nervous undertone. If you watch the policy-makers closely, you may notice that the smiles are often thin and the hands that hold champagne glasses sometimes twitch, involuntarily.

If you listen even more carefully, you can discover why. In the background you can hear another set of voices—those from below—far, far more numerous. These are voices the powerful do not want to hear, but they are having a harder and harder time ignoring them. Some of these voices are quiet and determined, talking together in bare tenements. Some are singing and reciting poetry in the plazas, or stirring young hearts with old tales deep in the forests. Some are discussing, planning their future, inventing new worlds. Many are angry, increasingly impatient, sometimes shouting on picket lines or chanting in the streets. All are talking about revolution, whether they use that term or not. The policy-makers of capitalism have good reasons to worry.

## GLOBAL CRISIS

Throughout the North, the old Second and First Worlds are both in deep crisis. In the East the imposition of Western-backed austerity has brought ever-wider unemployment and the destruction of social protections. Factories are closing; beggars haunt the streets. The budding "free" market is in the hands of Western carpetbaggers and local organized crime. Opportunistic politicians are fanning smoldering economic unrest into the flames of ethnic and racial hatred.

In the West—which ex-communist countries are supposed to emulate—all-time high unemployment, vicious attacks on wages and welfare benefits, and experiments

11

with economic and social restructuring have failed to produce a new cycle of growth. There, too, factories rust, homelessness spreads, and politicians channel discontent into racism and the fear of others, especially immigrants. The capitalist societies of the North, in short, are reeling, and can no longer offer attractive models for the South.

The situation in the South, in turn, is even more dramatic. A decade of debt crisis, austerity, famine, soaring unemployment and spreading disease has spawned only a few isolated pockets of profits and growth. Here and there multinational corporations have reopened their runaway plants, taking advantage of cheap wages guaranteed by police-state repression (e.g., Mexico, China). But for the most part the postwar development project is a fading memory, and talk of "sustainable growth" has the ring of fantasy to it. The smiling "human face" of capitalist development—the rising tide that lifts all boats—has been replaced by the ugly snarl of "international competition," underdevelopment, racism, ethnic cleansing and mass murder.

The grimness of these days is that of a historical impasse. For over 20 years the very survival of capitalism has been threatened; its ugliness grows out of its desperation. For over 20 years the voices in the background have multiplied and grown louder. Protests, strikes, guerrilla war and cultural revolution threw Western capitalism (North and South) into crisis back in the 1960s and early 1970s, as new desires joined old to outstrip the ability of the system to cope. Persistent and pervasive passive resistance produced rigidity and technological stagnation in the East, bringing crisis in the 1970s and 1980s. Perestroika—the last desperate effort of the old regime to cope—was swept aside by the vast, popular uprising in Eastern Europe.

For over two decades people have been demanding change and better lives. Instead, capitalist policymakers have responded with superficial political reform, monetarist austerity, sacrifice and the imposition of ever more work. Squeezed by this reaction people have grown angrier, but also more self-reliant. When business is unable or unwilling to provide acceptable jobs at acceptable wages, when government is unable or unwilling to ensure the well-being of its citizens, people turn away; they begin to listen to the voices of their own desires, and to each other, to find their own paths into the future. Such is the genesis of revolution.

Who are those with desires not met, those increasingly inventing their own solutions, their own ways of meeting their needs? They are diverse and can be found throughout society. The simple antagonisms of the 19th and early 20th centuries between factory labor and industrial capital have fragmented and become more complex. The colonization of the whole of society by business and the state has generalized both the alienating constraints of capitalism and the antagonism to them—throughout the globe.

## LISTENING

Everywhere voices can be heard—if we will only take the time to listen. They are voices from up and down the hierarchy of capitalist society, throughout the world. They are the voices of all kinds of people, both better and worse off, the relatively powerful and the sorely exploited, those who would live better and those who hope only to survive. And listen we must, because these voices are talking about the impasse in today's society, and discussing ways out.

The conversations are numberless, and their content as varied. Please note: I am not talking about the familiar debates of the Cold War. Neither of the old choices—between some variation of Western capitalism or Eastern socialism—is appealing, with both in crisis. There are, of course, institutionalized pundits still stuck in the past. But for growing numbers of people the old words have grown stale. And as they reject the old words, they are searching for new ones. They are rethinking not only their vocabulary, but the world.

But learning to listen is not always easy, even today. To clear the way, we have to learn to cut through the "noise" of official discourse, to recognize and avoid debates over how to "solve" the crisis within the old frameworks. We have to learn to decode the official jargon, to cut through the euphemisms that cloak the "business as usual" of subordinating desire to investment and growth, to corporate profits and state power. We have to recognize that adding an adjective to an old concept really changes nothing, e.g., "sustainable" development is still "development," and that project has failed.

The very diversity of alternative dialogues is daunting. There are many voices, of many people in many lands. They have many cultural roots and speak many languages. At the same time, desires and needs are not only multiple but cut across time, space and daily life. Nevertheless, whatever our diversity, we all share a common antagonism—the constraints that business and the state seek to impose on us—and in our common seeking for alternatives there are infinite possibilities of sharing and learning from each other. Conversation is not only possible in the absence of universal truth, it can be endless and fruitful.

Will we learn to listen? This book provides a vital and important opportunity for just such learning. In it you will hear new voices, voices "from the mountains of the Mexican Southeast" that have only been speaking to the world for a very short time. Yet, as you will learn, these voices have been talking among themselves for much longer.

Draw close and listen well, for the voices in this book are multiple and complex, direct and filtered, deadly serious and sometimes very funny. They are the voices of people in struggle.

## THE ZAPATISTAS

The voices and writings collected here come primarily from the Zapatista National Liberation Army (EZLN), the army that woke up the world on January 1, 1994 by seizing four towns in Chiapas, the southern-most state of Mexico.

The EZLN has organized itself among some of the most dispossessed people of the world. Its composition is almost as diverse as the outside world to which it speaks. Its soldiers are drawn from the forests, mountains and small towns of the region, both from the Indigenous and linguistically diverse Mayan population, and from immigrants from Central and Northern Mexico. Its soldiers have been subsistence cultivators and landless wage-laborers; they have grown and marketed their own export crops and they have worked on the plantations and ranches of others. They have cultivated their *milpas* (corn plots) on rocky hillsides and sought temporary manual work in the towns. They have toiled as unskilled laborers and skilled artisans. A very few are intellectuals drawn to the area over a decade ago by their ideals and hopes.

For those of us outside this movement, these de-professionalized intellectuals serve as mediators to help us understand the larger political processes out of which the EZLN has emerged, and within which it continues to operate. They have drafted many of the communiqués and served as the public voice for both the Army and the wider community. They speak our language and speak to us in words that are familiar. We can understand them easily because we all share the forms of discourse common to Western political traditions.

But, the words they speak, and the way they speak them, are translations of other words and discourses rooted in other, much less familiar languages and ways of being— the diverse Mayan cultures of the region. Fortunately for us, the Zapatistas are very self-conscious speakers, and often speak to us about their own speaking, so that we will understand the words that come to us through their mouths. They are the words of those who have gone before us to the people of Chiapas; they are the voices of people who have learned to listen.

As some of the statements you will find in this book make clear, the spokespersons who speak to us today are different from the urban intellectuals who went into the mountains years ago. Those intellectuals carried with them a whole left-wing baggage of theoretical and political preconceptions which proved totally inadequate for communicating with the local population.

In the confrontation of those preconceptions (which they now call "undemocratic and authoritarian") with the collective decision-making traditions of the people living in Indigenous communities, those intellectuals were transformed (as were, undoubtedly, the locals). In these documents we only get glimpses of this transformation, but it seems to have been remarkable—one in which the authoritarian relations of the Zapatista Army came to be subordinated to the democratic processes of the communities. In the process the interlopers seem to have learned to see things with new eyes, to do politics in new ways.

Along the way they seem to have acquired a simple, vernacular way of speaking which makes reading their communiqués and their interviews refreshing in comparison with the familiar, jargon-laden political diatribes of old-left guerrilla groups. It is probably this quality which has made the motivations, hopes and aspirations of the EZLN and the Chiapanecos so accessible to the wider Mexican community and beyond. The Mexican state's efforts to portray the EZLN as a group of outside agitators, of "professionals in violence," quickly collapsed in the face of the obvious: Theirs were not old voices but new voices, and their language was not that of ideology but of frustrated desires, urgent needs and committed determination.

Their words, the spokespersons tell us quite explicitly, come from the collectivity, not just the individuals. This, they say, is one reason why they wear ski-masks—so our reception of their voice can be divorced from the face, the personality of the individual.

14

The desire to avoid *caudillismo* (someone being singled out, or even putting themselves forward, as "the leader" of the revolution) is quite explicit. This approach, of course, is primarily symbolic, as the individualities of the speakers inevitably do come through, as in the best-known case of Subcommander Marcos.

Thus formed through a political process of dialogue and collective struggle, the voices in this book articulate two fundamental messages. First, they explain why they reject the current institutions and development projects of Mexican business and government. Second, they explain their own new political synthesis and their own political proposal for the future of Mexico. Let us examine the content of these two messages.

## THE REFUSAL OF DEVELOPMENT

In the North we come across the use of the term "development" rarely, usually in regard to plans to restructure the relationships between poor communities and the larger economy (e.g., community development, urban development). But in the South "development" has been the accepted framework ever since the defeat of overt colonialism. An essential ingredient of the Cold War debates was competing strategies of "development," of how "underdeveloped" regions or countries could "develop" to the point of becoming part of the "developed world."

Since the beginning of the EZLN offensive, considerable commentary from both the state and a variety of independent writers has used the language of "two nations" to talk about the situation in Chiapas. The two nations, of course, are that Mexico whose growth will be spurred by the North American Free Trade Agreement (NAFTA), and "*el otro México*," which is backward and left behind. The solution proposed, as always, is "development." Within a month of the EZLN offensive, and following the political defeat of its military counter-attack, the Mexican government created a "National Commission for Integral Development and Social Justice for Indigenous People," and promised more development aid to the area to expand the investments made through its previous development project, Solidaridad. On January 27 it was also announced that these regional development efforts (and others in similar "backward" states) would be buttressed by World Bank loans of some $400 million—loans that will increase the already-staggering international debt that has been at the heart of class struggle in Mexico since the early 1980s.

The EZLN's responses to these proposals have articulated the experience of Mexico's campesino and Indigenous populations—they have denounced these development plans as another step in their cultural assimilation and economic annihilation. They point out that there have never been "two nations"; Chiapanecos have labored for 500 years within the framework of capitalist development—they have simply been held at the bottom.

In their initial declaration of war, the EZLN wrote "We use black and red in our uniform as our symbol of our working people on strike." In other words, the Zapatista refusal of development quite consciously articulates a refusal of capitalist imposed work. (Not surprisingly, the state's negotiator, Manuel Camacho Solís, early on called not only for an end to hostilities but for a "return to work.")

The Indigenous also know that further "development" means a continuation of their expulsion from the land, which has gone on during economic booms (e.g., oil/hydroelectric boom of the 1970s) as well as busts (e.g., the debt-crisis/austerity of the 1980s). Reduced to wage earners, they have sometimes benefited from economic upturns financed by government expenditures, and have also discovered how transitory those benefits can be as they were subsequently devastated in downturns.

At the best of times rising income is differentially distributed, accentuating inequalities to the point of splitting communities. Even worse, "development" can mean a role well known to Native Americans in the US: attractions within the tourist industry—a strategy for areas with "primitive" peoples that takes advantage of their "comparative advantage" in exotic culture. The government, one EZLN spokesperson has said, sees the Indigenous "as nothing more than anthropological objects, tourist curiosities, or part of a 'Jurassic Park.'"

But Salinas and Clinton have promised that NAFTA will open US markets to Mexican exports; Mexico will develop faster. This, too, the EZLN understands all too well. Chiapas is already an export-oriented economy; it always has been: "Chiapas loses blood through many veins: through oil and gas ducts, electric lines, train cars, bank accounts, trucks and vans, boats and planes, through clandestine paths, gaps and forest trails."

The EZLN has also understood how NAFTA opens Mexico to US exports, and how the most threatening of these is corn, the basic food crop of the Indigenous population and an important source of cash income. Already they are suffering from low prices for coffee, another cash crop, due to the government's elimination of financial support for that production. Like all Chiapanecos they also know that export development means ecological destruction, especially deforestation. Their antagonism to development, therefore, springs not from an overactive imagination or sterile ideology, but from bitter experience.

## THE EZLN PROPOSAL

The second EZLN message concerns the conclusions they have drawn from their political experience, and their political proposal for the future of Mexico. Whereas their detailed condemnations of development have a familiar ring, their positive proposals are both novel and fascinating. Their "wind from below" carries new ideas for us to consider, a true gift in this period when the usual politicos demonstrate a total lack of imagination, as little on the Left as on the Right.

First, in terms of their own political character, at the very start of its offensive the EZLN sharply differentiated itself from the previous guerrilla movements of Central America (e.g., the Sandinistas or the URNG) and elsewhere (e.g., the Tupamaros), and explicitly rejected the traditional Leninist objectives of "taking power," "the dictatorship of the proletariat," "international communism" and "all that."

Listen to Major Benjamin: "We are not Maoists or Marxists, sir. We are a group of campesinos, workers and students for whom the government has left no other path than arms to resolve our ancestral problems." Listen to Marcos: "In the movement of the EZLN there is no perfectly defined ideology, in the sense of communist or Marxist-Leninist." "It is not a nucleus that has come, not a guerrilla *foco*; what has come is something you have never in your life dreamed of: this is the truth."

Although their Army has a typical hierarchical command structure, the Zapatistas appear to have achieved a new political synthesis that subordinates its actions to frameworks of collective and democratic decision-making developed out of local traditions. Strategic issues are not left to the Army, but must be decided at the community level.

The Zapatista communiqués are generally signed by the "Clandestine Revolutionary Indigenous Committee-General Command" (CCRI-CG)—apparently a council of Indigenous leaders. But behind that "General Command" are an unknown number of Clandestine Committees (apparently four Committees representing four ethnic groups sent delegates to the peace negotiations); and behind them are the communities.

As the conclusion of the first round of negotiations between the EZLN and the Mexican government made clear, on basic strategic issues the EZLN reports back to the local communities for collective consultation and discussion about how to proceed. According to EZLN spokespersons, this consultation is extensive; it includes everyone so that all will consider the outcome a valid expression of their communal desires. The EZLN seems to truly embrace its own words: "The will of the majority is the path on which those who command should walk. If they separate their step from the path of the will of the people, the heart that commands should be changed for another that obeys."

Second, such democratic political processes have given rise to a new political project: AUTONOMY—a democratic autonomy for all levels of Mexican society, for regions, for Indigenous peoples, for campesino groups, for workers, for students, for women, for townships, for regional governments and so on. There is no utopian blueprint for the construction of such autonomy; the proposal is one of principle, of the direction of movement. "This new voice...is conspiring for a new world, so new that it is barely an intuition in the collective heart that inspires it." But: "When the storm calms, when rain and fire again leave the country in peace, the world will no longer be the world, but something better."

Some of what this means is clear enough in the EZLN's demands. They call for the dismissal of corrupt local governments and the installation of democratically elected leaders. Their "Agrarian Law" orders the return of cultivable land to the Indigenous and poor campesinos so that they can have the material basis for organizing their own lives and cultures. It also orders forests, rivers, lakes, oceans and sub-soil minerals liberated from capitalist corporations and government monopolies and restored to the keeping of the local populations (partly for use, partly for ecological preservation—yes, they are explicit about this). They demand the right of those who have been forced out of their communities (e.g., religious exiles) to return unhindered to live in their own ways. They support the local use of Indigenous languages and the reorganization of education (e.g., bilingualism) and health organizations (e.g., prevention of disease and respect for Indigenous practices). Their "autonomy" appears to be a complex but real pluralism rather than either the pseudo-pluralism we know so well in the North or any kind of secessionist separatism.

17

Such demands are rooted in the self-activity of the Indigenous peoples and communities who form the EZLN. They have resisted the lure of capitalism's "universal values" (work, money, the market) in favor of clear, though evolving, concepts of who they are and how they want to live. The direct democracy of their collective decision-making is part of this, but there is much more.

Most obvious, because frequently repeated, is that these people want to be rooted in the land. They want land not just as a "resource" to grow export crops, but because their *milpas*, the work of their cultivation and the food they provide, have provided the pivot of their culture for a thousand years.

Because the EZLN representatives are not sociologists and anthropologists, they do not give us anything like exhaustive portrayals of the various Indigenous cultures, much less detailed analyses of the complex communities of economic, political and religious immigrants in recently colonized areas. But they do tell us enough that we can understand that these communities are not stagnant "cultural survivals" from a traditional past. On the contrary, their commitment to autonomy also seems to be strong where people are fighting for change and struggling to create new identities. An example of this commitment can be found in the EZLN's support for women's struggles against traditional patterns of patriarchy.

The patriarchal character of Mexican society is well known; that of campesino and Indigenous communities less recognized but often no less real. In terms of family decision-making, men have generally commanded money income and ruled, sometimes with physical force. Women have often had few or no choices about who they marry, how many children they will have or how much domestic work they must do without help from men.

But these conditions make strong women—if they don't kill them—and such women have challenged the traditional roles. This challenge has found support in the EZLN. Not only are women encouraged to join the EZLN, but they are treated as equals to the point that many women have officer status and men and women are expected to carry the burdens of work and fighting equally.

Queried about the politics of gender in the organization and in the communities in which it is based, Marcos has affirmed the EZLN's official support for women's struggles against patriarchy. This involves not only a redistribution of responsibilities and work and the defense of women against men's abuse, but also material support for women's health and birth control. The EZLN has organized sex-education classes to teach about hygiene and disease—especially women's diseases (e.g., urinary tract infections) that men do not understand and misinterpret. The organization also teaches about contraceptives and supports their use. Moreover: "The *compañera* not only has the right to terminate pregnancy," Marcos has stated, "but the organization also has the obligation to provide the means for her to do it with total safety."

When Indigenous women organized in dozens of communities to produce a code of women's rights, the EZLN leadership—the CCRI-CG—adopted the code unanimously. The "Women's Law" included the rights of all women to such things as control over their own bodies, wages, political participation, health care, and freedom from violence and rape. According to one report, when one of the male committee members quipped, "The good part is that my wife doesn't understand Spanish," an EZLN officer told him:

"You're fucked, because we're going to translate it into all the [Indigenous] languages." Clearly, the passage of this Bill of Rights demonstrates the EZLN's commitment to meaningful gender autonomy within the diverse Indigenous cultures of Chiapas.

When asked about the problems and rights of gays, Marcos has said that the position of the EZLN is the same as that on women and other "minorities". As they too begin to say "Enough is Enough!" and fight for their rights, they will be supported by the organization. What is unusual and exciting about this pattern is how these struggles are not being marginalized or subordinated to "class interests," but are being accepted as integral parts of the overall project of political autonomy. Among the 34 points presented by the EZLN to the government during the first stage of negotiations, the longest was the "Indigenous Women's Petition" detailing the specific demands of women.

Third and last, and perhaps the clearest indication of the seriousness with which they take their notion of autonomy, they present their proposal as only one among many that they hope to see emerge throughout Mexican society. They reject the notion that they should have all the answers, should be able to figure out all the solutions to all the problems.

Listen: "What we have made clear, and what we will always explain, is that we cannot lead a process that will solve all of Mexico's problems." Thus their repeated and insistent demand that politics be stripped from the state and the political parties and reborn in the community as a whole.

## THE PATH FROM HERE TO THERE

The EZLN clearly believes that the construction of autonomy in every sphere of life will involve diverse processes, and for the moment is primarily interested in clearing a path toward that goal. Clearing the path involves nothing less than the revolutionary transformation of the Mexican political system. The path to the autonomy of "*Tierra*" is political "*Libertad.*"

"We are proposing a space," Marcos has said in an interview, "an equilibrium between the different political forces in order that each position has the same opportunity to influence the political direction of this country... The rest of the country shouldn't be spectators... The people have to decide what proposal to accept, and it's the people who you have to convince that your opinion is correct. This will radically change the concept of revolution, of who the revolutionary class is, of what a revolutionary organization is.... The Zapatista revolution isn't proposing the taking of power... We are saying 'Let's destroy this State, this State system. Let's open up this space and confront the people with ideas, not weapons.' " What he is describing seems to be nothing less than a generalization, locally and to the country as a whole, of the political processes of direct democracy that have been developed within the mountains of Chiapas.

As a first step in this transformation, the EZLN called in early January for the resignation (or overthrow) of the present, undemocratic PRI government and its replacement by a transitional government "of people of prestige outside the parties, who have the moral authority to lead the country." This call was reiterated in the EZLN's June communiqués rejecting the government's position after the first round of negotiations.

Elaborating their initial proposal, they have called on Mexican civil society to organize a "National Dialogue on Democracy, Freedom and Justice." Local discussions "in every *ejido*, settlement, school and factory," they suggest, can be followed by the formation of committees to collect proposals for a new constitution and for the policies of a new government. These local committees, in turn, could organize a "revolutionary National Democratic Convention" to create the transitional government and a new constitution. The EZLN even offers itself as the nucleus of a new army "to guarantee that the people's will is carried out"!

Needless to say such proposals have been rejected outright by the central government. But, at the same time, the EZLN uprising and their audacious demands have generated a whirlwind of political discussion in Mexico and challenges to the existing system as have not been seen since the Revolution of 1910.

## The Government Backs Down

Given the radicalness of their demands and the military character of their uprising, the Mexican government's response to the EZLN challenge has been surprising. With startling rapidity the state shifted from a truly massive military repression (over 15,000 troops dispatched to Chiapas, aerial bombings of villages, summary torture and execution of captives) to a cease-fire and high-level negotiations with the rebels, mediated by progressive representatives of the Catholic Church. Why?

Conventional political pundits attribute the change to the government's fear of international scrutiny of its behavior in the wake of the implementation of NAFTA and in the light of its new pretensions to First World status. Not only did the Zapatistas attack NAFTA in their very first declaration, but their uprising threatened multinational capitalist estimates of the risks of investing in Mexico. Thus, better to quiet things down quickly, to use the velvet glove of co-optation rather than the mailed fist of repression.

But this hypothesis of "sensitivity" to international opinion does not explain why the government judged that such opinions might turn negative or influential enough to affect foreign investment. To explain why it was worried we have to turn from the government's reactions per se to those of Mexico as a whole, and to those of the world beyond.

## The Circulation of Struggle

An examination of popular reaction to the Chiapas uprising, both in Mexico and elsewhere, makes it very clear why the Mexican government changed its way of dealing with the situation. Its fears were based on the extremely rapid spread of popular support for the EZLN and for the communities they represent.

From the very first day, when news of the uprising went out through the media and details began to circulate through computer networks, people listened to the words of the EZLN Declaration of War, sympathized with them, and began to mobilize to block the government's repressive moves. Even as the Mexican Army poured into Chiapas, so too did representatives of human rights organizations, of other Indigenous peoples and of free-lance and foreign journalism which the Mexican government could not control. Within days these observers reported Army atrocities and repression. Others mobilized protest demonstrations all across North America, and even in Europe, to denounce the Mexican government. These actions tremendously strengthened the hand of the Zapatistas, and forced the government to withdraw to the negotiating table.

In turn, this tremendous outpouring of popular support and willingness to take action in support of this uprising, must themselves be explained. As indicated above, the world is rife with antagonism and conflict; there have been many uprisings that have failed to provoke this kind of response. What was different about Chiapas?

The answer, I think, is two-fold. First, an international network capable and primed to respond was already in place as a result of the last few years of organizing against NAFTA. Second, the uprising in Chiapas was by no means as isolated in Mexico as it seemed.

The fight against NAFTA took the form of growing coalitions of grassroots groups in Canada, the United States and Mexico. In each country a broad coalition, such as the Mexican Action Network on Free Trade, was constituted by knitting together several hundred groups opposed to the trade pact. That knitting was accomplished partly through joint discussions and actions and partly through the sharing of information and analysis about the meaning and implications of the agreement. Increasingly, computer communications became a basic political tool for extremely rapid sharing among groups and individuals.

The same processes of communication linked the coalitions in each country in a manner never before seen in the Western Hemisphere. The result, both locally and internationally, was a new organizational form—a multiplicity of rhizomatically linked autonomous groups—connecting all kinds of struggles throughout North America that had previously been disconnected and separate.

The obviously concerned (US workers threatened with losing their jobs as plants were relocated to Mexico, Mexicans concerned with the invasion of US capital) linked with a wide variety of others who could see indirect threats in this capitalist reorganization of trade relations, e.g., ecological activists, women's groups, human rights organizations and yes, organizations of Indigenous groups throughout the continent. Although the anti-NAFTA movement was unable to block ratification of the agreement, it has continued to monitor the impact of the agreement in order to facilitate struggle against it and ultimately to get it canceled.

So when the Zapatista Army marched into San Cristóbal and the other towns of Chiapas, not only did those already concerned with the struggles of Indigenous peoples react quickly, but so did the much more extensive organizational connections of anti-NAFTA struggles. Already in place were the computer conferences and lists of the anti-NAFTA alliances. For many, the first information on their struggles came in the regular postings of the NAFTA Monitor on "trade.news" or "trade.strategy" either on Peacenet or through the Internet. Even if EZLN spokespeople had not explicitly damned NAFTA and timed their offensive to coincide with the first day of its operation in Mexico, the connections would have been made and understood throughout the anti-NAFTA network.

Besides this, there was another whole area of self-organized networking in Mexico that only partly overlapped the anti-NAFTA movement: that of campesinos and Indigenous peoples.

Outside the EZLN, far beyond Chiapas, they too had been developing networks of cooperation to fight for the things they need: schools, clean water, the return of their lands, freedom from state repression (police and Army torture, jailings and murders), and so on. Given the fierce autonomy of the participating communities—sometimes based on traditional ethnic culture and language—these networks have been shaped like the electronic web described above: in a horizontal, non-hierarchical manner.

This process has been accelerating for several years, not only in Mexico, but throughout the Americas and beyond. Partly inspired by the example of the Black Civil Rights Movement in North America as early as the mid-1960s (e.g., the rise of the American Indian Movement) and partly forced into action by continuing state-backed assaults on their land in South and Central America (e.g., the enclosure of the Amazon), Indigenous peoples have been overcoming the spatial and political divisions that have isolated and weakened them.

In 1990 a First Continental Encounter of Indigenous Peoples was organized in Quito, Ecuador. Delegates from over 200 Indigenous nations launched a movement to achieve continental unity. To sustain the process a Continental Coordinating Commission of Indigenous Nations and Organizations (CONIC) was formed at a subsequent meeting in Panama in 1991. The unity sought, as in the Zapatista movement, was not the unity of the political party or trade union—solidified and perpetuated through a central controlling body—but rather a unity of communication and mutual aid among autonomous nations and peoples.

A second Continental Encounter was organized in October of 1993 at Temoaya, Mexico. One of the hosting groups at that meeting was the Frente Independiente de Pueblos Indios (FIPI) and one of the members of FIPI was the Coordinadora de Organizaciones en Lucha del Pueblo Maya para su Liberación from San Cristóbal, Chiapas.

Faced with the violence of the Mexican military's counter-offensive, the FIPI sent out a call to CONIC requesting that other Indians in the network come to Chiapas as observers to help constrain state violence. CONIC responded immediately by organizing international delegations to the battle zones. When they arrived in Chiapas they were received by the local offices of the Consejo Estatal de Organizaciones Indígenas y Campesinas—made up of 280 Indigenous and campesino organizations throughout the state.

So, we begin to understand how it was possible that such a small uprising in such an isolated part of Mexico could generate so much popular support and force unheard-of concessions from an unwilling government and political elite. A more complete understanding, of course, would require an investigation into the backgrounds of all of those who mobilized, not just the Indigenous and the anti-NAFTA militants. Whatever explains the sensitivity of these various listeners whose reactions circulated this struggle, we have witnessed a fascinating process through which the voices of a relative small number of very creative and dedicated revolutionaries have been amplified again and again until they can be heard around the world.

## SOME EARLY LESSONS

What can we learn by listening to the voices of the Chiapas uprising? They offer political proposals for us to consider, not a specific model to be imitated. The new organizational forms we see in action are not substitutes for old formulas—Leninist or social democratic. They provide something different: inspiring examples of workable solutions to the post-socialist problem of revolutionary organization and struggle.

The efforts of the Zapatistas in Chiapas, like the anti-NAFTA and Indigenous networks that laid the groundwork for their circulation, demonstrate how organization can proceed locally, regionally and internationally through a diversity of forms. That diversity can be effective precisely to the degree that organizers weave a fabric of cooperation to achieve the (often quite different) concrete material projects of the various participants.

We have known for some time that a particular organization can be substituted for the processes of organization only at great peril. It is a lesson we have learned the hard way in struggle for, and then against, trade unions, and social democratic and revolutionary parties. What we hear from the Zapatistas, and what we see in their interaction with other groups, is a fabric of cooperation among the most diverse kinds of people throughout the international wage and income hierarchy. That fabric has not appeared suddenly, out of the blue; it has been woven over a period of years. And in its weaving many threads have certainly been broken and been retied, or new knots have been designed to replace those that could not hold.

The spokespersons of the EZLN have given us glimpses of their part in this work. Hopefully more of the story will be told over time. We also need to examine what others have contributed and how.

Today, the social equivalent of an earthquake is rumbling through Mexican society. Every day brings reports of people moving to action. Campesinos and Indigenous peoples completely independent of the EZLN are taking up its battle cries and occupying municipal government buildings, blockading banks, seizing lands and demanding "*Libertad.*" Students and workers are being inspired not just to "support the campesinos" but to launch their own strikes throughout the Mexican social factory.

You hold in your hands a collection of the words that have set all this movement in action. Read it well. Listen to the voices. And then do not be afraid to add your own to the growing tumult. If these voices from the mountains of the Mexican Southeast tell us nothing else, it is that a multiplicity of voices can achieve coherence, and with coherence—action that can change the world.

Austin, Texas
June 22, 1994

# Chiapas: The Southeast in Two Winds

## A Storm and a Prophecy

*[This essay by Insurgent Subcommander Marcos of the Zapatista National Liberation Army was written in August of 1992. Although it was not released publicly until January 27, 1994, we have placed it first because it puts the Zapatista uprising in context.]*

## The First Wind: The One From Above

### Chapter One

*This chapter tells how the supreme government was affected by the poverty of the Indigenous peoples of Chiapas and endowed the area with hotels, prisons, barracks, and a military airport. It also tells how the beast feeds on the blood of the people, as well as other miserable and unfortunate happenings.*

Suppose that you live in the North, Center, or West of this country. Suppose that you heed the old SECOTUR (Department of Tourism) slogan, "Get to know Mexico first." Suppose that you decide to visit the Southeast of your country and that in the Southeast you choose to visit the state of Chiapas. Suppose that you drive there (getting there by airplane is not only expensive but unlikely, a mere fantasy: There are only two "civilian" airports and one military one). Suppose that you take the Transistémica Highway. Suppose that you pay no attention to the Army barracks located at Matías Romero and that you continue on to Ventosa. Suppose that you don't notice the Department of Government's immigration checkpoint near there (the checkpoint makes you think that you are leaving one country and entering another). Suppose that you decide to take a left and head towards Chiapas. Several kilometers further on you will leave the state of Oaxaca and you will see a big sign that reads, "WELCOME TO CHIAPAS." Have you found it? Good, suppose you have. You have entered by one of the three existing roads into Chiapas: The road into the northern part of the state, the road along the Pacific coast, and the road you entered by are the three ways to get to this Southeastern corner of the country by land. But the state's natural wealth doesn't leave only by way of these three roads. Chiapas loses blood through many veins: Through oil and gas ducts, electric lines, railways, through bank accounts, trucks, vans, boats and planes, through clandestine paths, gaps, and forest trails. This land continues to pay tribute to the imperialists: petroleum, electricity, cattle, money, coffee, banana, honey, corn, cacao, tobacco, sugar, soy, melon, sorghum, mamey, mango, tamarind, avocado, and Chiapaneco blood flows as a result of the thousand teeth sunk into the throat of the Mexican Southeast. These raw materials, thousands of millions of tons of them, flow to Mexican ports and railroads, air and truck transportation centers. From there they are sent to different parts of the world: The United States, Canada, Holland, Germany, Italy, Japan, but with the same fate—to feed imperialism. The fee that capitalism imposes on the Southeastern part of this country oozes, as it has since from the beginning, blood and mud.

A handful of businesses, one of which is the Mexican State, take all the wealth out of Chiapas and in exchange leave behind their mortal and pestilent mark: in 1989 these businesses took 1,222,669,000,000 pesos from Chiapas and only left behind 616,340,000,000 pesos worth of credit and public works. More than 600,000,000,000 pesos went to the belly of the beast.

In Chiapas, Pemex [the national oil company] has 86 teeth clenched in the townships of Estación Juárez, Reforma, Ostuacán, Pichucalco, and Ocosingo. Every day they suck out 92,000 barrels of petroleum and 517,000,000,000 cubic feet of gas. They take away the petroleum and gas, and in exchange leave behind the mark of capitalism: ecological destruction, agricultural plunder, hyperinflation, alcoholism, prostitution, and poverty. The beast is still not satisfied and has extended its tentacles to the Lacandona jungle: eight petroleum deposits are under exploration. The paths are made with machetes by the same campesinos who are left without land by the insatiable beast. The trees fall and dynamite explodes on land where campesinos are not allowed to cut down trees to cultivate. Every tree that is cut down costs them a fine that is 10 times the minimum wage, and a jail sentence. The poor cannot cut down trees, but the petroleum beast can, a beast that every day falls more and more into foreign hands. The campesinos cut them down to survive, the beast to plunder.

Chiapas also bleeds coffee. Thirty-five percent of the coffee produced in Mexico comes from this area. The industry employs 87,000 people. Forty-seven percent of the coffee is for national consumption and 53% is exported abroad, mainly to the United States and Europe. More than 100,000 tons of coffee are taken from this state to fatten the beast's bank accounts: in 1988 a kilo of pergamino coffee was sold abroad for 8,000 pesos. The Chiapaneco producers were paid 2,500 pesos or less.

The second most important plunder, after coffee, is beef. Three million head of cattle wait for middle-men and a small group of businessmen to take them away to fill refrigerators in Arriaga, Villahermosa, and Mexico City. The cattle are sold for 400

pesos per kilo by the poor farmers and resold by the middle-men and businessmen for up to ten times the price they paid for them.

The tribute that capitalism demands from Chiapas has no historical parallel. Fifty-five percent of national hydroelectric energy comes from this state, along with 20% of Mexico's total electricity. However, only a third of the homes in Chiapas have electricity. Where do the 12,907 kilowatts produced annually by hydroelectric plants in Chiapas go?

In spite of the current trend toward ecological awareness, the plunder of wood continues in Chiapas's forests. Between 1981 and 1989, 2,444,777 cubic meters of precious woods, conifers, and tropical trees were taken from Chiapas. They were taken to Mexico City, Puebla, Veracruz, and Quintana Roo. In 1988 wood exports brought a revenue of 23,900,000,000 pesos, 6,000% more than in 1980.

The honey that is produced in 79,000 beehives in Chiapas goes entirely to US and European markets. The 2,756 tons of honey produced annually in the Chiapaneco countryside is converted into dollars which the people of Chiapas never see.

Of the corn produced in Chiapas, more than half goes to the domestic market. Chiapas is one of the largest corn producers in the country. Sorghum grown in Chiapas goes to Tabasco. Ninety percent of the tamarind goes to Mexico City and other states. Two-thirds of the avocados and all of the mameys are sold outside of the state. Sixty-nine percent of the cacao goes to the national market, and 31% is exported to the US, Holland, Japan, and Italy. The majority of the bananas produced are exported.

What does the beast leave behind in exchange for all it takes away?

Chiapas has a total area of 75,634.4 square kilometers, some 7.5 million hectares. It is the eighth largest state and is divided into 111 townships organized, for the purposes of looting, into nine economic regions. Forty percent of the nation's plant varieties, 36% of its mammal species, 34% of its reptiles and amphibians, 66% of its bird species, 20% of its fresh-water fish, and 80% of its butterfly species are found in Chiapas. Seven percent of the total national rainfall falls in Chiapas. But its greatest wealth is the 3.5 million people of Chiapas, two-thirds of whom live and die in rural communities. Half of them don't have potable water and two-thirds have no sewage service. Ninety percent of the rural population pay little or no taxes.

Communication in Chiapas is a grotesque joke for a state that produces petroleum, electricity, coffee, wood, and cattle for the hungry beast. Only two-thirds of the municipal seats have paved-road access. Twelve thousand communities have no other means of transport and communication than mountain trails. Since the days of Porfirio Díaz, the railroad lines have serviced capitalism rather than the people. The railroad line that follows the coast (there are only two lines: the other crosses the northern part of the state) dates back to the turn of the century, and its tonnage is limited by the old bridges that cross the canyons of the Southeast. The only port in Chiapas, Puerto Madero, is just one more way for the beast to extract the state's resources.

Education? The worst in the country. At the elementary school level, 72 out of every 100 children don't finish the first grade. More than half of the schools only offer up to a third grade education and half of the schools only have one teacher for all the courses offered. There are statistics, although they are kept secret of course, that show that many

Indigenous children are forced to drop out of school due to their families' need to incorporate them into the system of exploitation. In any Indigenous community it is common to see children carrying corn and wood, cooking, or washing clothes during school hours. Of the 16,058 classrooms in 1989, only 96 were in Indigenous zones.

Industry? Look, 40% of Chiapas's "industry" consists of Nixtamal mills, tortillas, and wood furniture mills. Large companies (petroleum and electricity), 0.2% of the total industry, belong to the Mexican government (and soon to foreigners). Medium-sized industry, 0.4% of the total industry, is made up of sugar refineries and fish, seafood, flour, milk, and coffee processing plants. Of the state's industry, 94% of the area's industry is micro-industry.

The health conditions of the people of Chiapas are a clear example of the capitalist imprint: One-and-a-half million people have no medical services at their disposal. There are 0.2 clinics for every 1,000 inhabitants, one-fifth of the national average. There are 0.3 hospital beds for every 1,000 Chiapanecos, one third the amount in the rest of Mexico. There is one operating room per 100,000 inhabitants, one half of the amount in the rest of Mexico. There are 0.5 doctors and 0.4 nurses per 1,000 people, one-half of the national average.

Health and nutrition go hand in hand in poverty. Fifty-four percent of the population of Chiapas suffer from malnutrition, and in the highlands and forest this percentage increases to 80%. A campesino's average diet consists of coffee, corn, tortillas, and beans.

This is what capitalism leaves as payment for everything that it takes away...

This part of the Mexican territory, which willingly annexed itself to the young independent republic in 1824, appeared in national geography when the petroleum boom reminded the country that there was a Southeast (82% of Pemex's petrochemical plants are in the Southeast; in 1990 two-thirds of public investment in the Southeast was in energy). Chiapas's experience of exploitation goes back for centuries. In times past, wood, fruits, animals, and men went to the metropolis through the veins of exploitation, just as they do today. Like the banana republics, but at the peak of neoliberalism and "libertarian revolutions," the Southeast continues to export raw materials, just as it did 500 years ago. It continues to import capitalism's principal product: death and misery.

One million Indigenous people live in these lands and share a disorienting nightmare with mestizos and *ladinos*: their only option, 500 years after the "Meeting of Two Worlds," is to die of poverty or repression. The programs to improve the conditions of poverty, a small bit of social democracy which the Mexican state throws about and which, under the regime of Salinas de Gortari carries the name Pronasol, are a joke that brings bloody tears to those who live under the rain and sun.

Welcome! You have arrived in the poorest state in the country: Chiapas.

Suppose that you drive on to Ocosocoatla and from there down to Tuxtla Gutierrez, the state capital. You don't stay long. Tuxtla Gutierrez is only a large warehouse which stores products from other parts of the state. Here you find some of the wealth which will be sent to whatever destinations the capitalists decide. You don't stay long, you have just barely touched the lips of the wild beast's bloody jaws. You go on to Chiapas de Corzo without noticing the Nestlé factory that is there, and you begin to

climb up into the mountains. What do you see? One thing is certain, you have entered another world, an Indigenous world. Another world, but the same as that in which millions of people in the rest of the country live.

Three hundred thousand Tzotziles, 120,000 Choles, 90,000 Zoques, and 70,000 Tojolabales inhabit this Indigenous world. The supreme government recognizes that "only" half of these 1,000,000 Indigenous people are illiterate.

Continue along the mountain road and you arrive in the region known as the Chiapaneco highlands. Here, more than 500 years ago, Indigenous people were the majority, masters and owners of land and water. Now they are only the majority in population and in poverty. Drive on until you reach San Cristóbal de las Casas, which 100 years ago was the state capital (disagreements among the bourgeoisie robbed it of the dubious honor of being the capital of the poorest state in Mexico). No, don't linger. If Tuxtla Gutierrez is a large warehouse, San Cristóbal is a large market. From many different routes the Tzotziles, Tzeltales, Choles, Tojolabales, and Zoques bring the Indigenous tribute to capitalism. Each brings something different: wood, coffee, cloth, handicrafts, fruits, vegetables, corn. Everyone brings something: sickness, ignorance, jeers, and death. This is the poorest region of the poorest state in the country. Welcome to San Cristóbal de las Casas, a "Colonial City" according to the history books, although the majority of the population is Indigenous. Welcome to Pronasol's huge market. Here you can buy or sell anything except Indigenous dignity. Here everything is expensive except death. But don't stay too long, continue along the road, the proud result of the tourist infrastructure. In 1988 there were 6,270 hotel rooms, 139 restaurants, and 42 travel agencies in this state. This year, 1,058,098 tourists visited Chiapas and left 250,000,000,000 pesos in the hands of restaurant and hotel owners.

Have you calculated the numbers? Yes, you're right: there are seven hotel rooms for every 1,000 tourists while there are only 0.3 hospital beds per 1,000 Chiapaneco citizens. Leave the calculations behind and drive on, noticing the three police officials in berets jogging along the shoulder of the road. Drive by the Public Security station and continue on passing hotels, restaurants, large stores and heading towards the exit to Comitán. Leaving San Cristóbal behind you will see the famous San Cristóbal caves surrounded by leafy forest. Do you see the sign? No, you are not mistaken, this natural park is administered by...the Army! Without leaving your uncertainty behind, drive on...Do you see them? Modern buildings, nice homes, paved roads...Is it a university? Workers' housing? No, look at the sign next to the cannons closely and read: "General Army Barracks of the 31st Military Zone." With the olive-green image still in your eyes, drive on to the intersection and decide not to go to Comitán so that you will avoid the pain of seeing that, a few meters ahead, on the hill that is called the Foreigner, North American military personnel are operating, and teaching their Mexican counterparts to operate radar. Decide that it is better to go to Ocosingo since ecology and all that nonsense is very fashionable. Look at the trees, breath deeply...Do you feel better? Yes? Then be sure to keep looking to your left, because if you don't you will see, seven kilometers ahead, another magnificent construction with the noble symbol of SOLIDARIDAD on the facade. Don't look. I tell you, look the other way. You don't notice that this new building is...a jail (evil tongues say that

this is a benefit of Pronasol; now campesinos won't have to go all the way to Cerro Hueco, the prison in the state capital). No brother, don't lose heart, the worst is always hidden: Excessive poverty discourages tourism. Continue on, down to Huixtán, up to Oxchuc, look at the beautiful waterfall where the Jatate river, whose waters cross the Lacandona Jungle, begins. Pass by Cuxulja and instead of following the detour to Altami-rano drive on till you reach Ocosingo: "The Door to the Lacandona Jungle..."

Good, stay a while. Take a quick tour around the city... Principal points of interest? The two large constructions at the entrance to the city are brothels, next door is a jail, the building further beyond, a church, this other one is a beef-processing plant, that other one, Army barracks, over there is the court, the Municipal building, and way over there is Pemex. The rest are small piled-up houses which crumble when the huge Pemex trucks and ranch pick-up trucks pass by.

What does it look like? A Porfirista-type large-landed estate? But that ended 75 years ago! No, don't follow the road that goes to San Quintín, in front of the Montes Azules Reserve. Don't go to where the Jatate and Perlas rivers join, don't go down there, don't walk for three eight-hour days, don't go to San Martín and see that it is a very poor and small community, don't approach that shed that is falling to pieces. What is it? A sometimes church, school, meeting room. Now it is a school. It is 11 a.m.. No, don't go closer, don't look in, don't look at the four groups of children rid-dled with tapeworms and lice, half-naked, don't look at the four young Indigenous teachers who work for miserable pay for which they have to walk three days, the same three days that you just walked, to collect. Don't notice that the only division between the classrooms is a small hall. Up to what grade do they teach here? Third. No, don't look at the posters which are the only thing that the government has sent to these chil-dren. Don't look at them: They are posters about AIDS prevention.

Better for us to move on, let's return to the paved roads. Yes, I know that it is in bad condition. Let's leave Ocosingo, continue to admire the countryside... The owners? Yes, ranch owners. What is produced? Cattle, coffee, corn... Did you see the National Indigenous Institute? Yes, the one as you leave the city. Did you see those pickup trucks? They are given on credit to Indigenous campesinos. They only take unleaded gas because it's better for the environment... There is no unleaded gas in Ocosingo? Well, that's not a big thing... Yes, you are right, the government is worried about the campesinos. Of course evil tongues say that there are guerrillas in these mountains and that the government's financial aid is really to buy Indigenous people's loyalty, but these are rumors, surely they are just trying to undermine Pronasol... What? The Citi-zen's Defense Committee? Oh yes! It consists of a group of "heroic" ranchers, traders, and corrupt union bosses who organize small guards to threaten the people. No, I already told you that the Porfirista large-landed estate was done away with 75 years ago... It would be better for us to move on...At the next intersection take a left. No, don't go towards Palenque. Let's go to Chilón... Pretty, no? Yes.

Yajalon...it's very modern, it even has a gas station... Look, there's a bank, the municipal building, the courthouse, over there the Army... It looks like another hacien-da? Let's go and you won't see those other large, modern buildings on the outskirts of

town, along the road to Tila and Sabanilla with their big beautiful SOLIDARIDAD signs, you won't see that it is...a jail.

Good, we have arrived at the intersection. Now to Ocosingo...Palenque? Are you sure? Okay, let's go. Yes, the countryside is beautiful. Are those ranches? You're correct: they produce cattle, coffee, wood. Look, we're already at Palenque. A quick tour of the city? Okay. Those are hotels, over there restaurants, the municipal building, the courthouse, those are the Army barracks, and over there... What? No, I already know what you're going to tell me... Don't say it... Tired? Okay, we'll stop for a bit. You don't want to see the pyramids? No? Okay. Xi'Nich? Ah...an Indigenous march. Yes, it's going to Mexico City. How far? 1,106 kilometers. Results? The government receives their petitions. Yes, that's all. Are you still tired? More? Let's wait... To Bonampak? The road is very bad. Okay, let's go. Yes, the panoramic route...This is the Federal Military Reserve, that other one belongs to the Navy, the one over there belongs to the Department of Government... Is it always like this? No, sometimes they top it off with a campesinos' protest march. Tired? Do you want to go back? Okay. Other places? Different places? In what country? Mexico? You will see the same. The colors will change, the languages, the countryside, the names, but the people, the exploitation, the poverty and death are the same. Just look closely in any state in the Republic. Well, good luck...And if you need a tourist guide please be sure to let me know. I'm at your service. Oh! One more thing. It will not always be this way. Another Mexico? No, the same...I am talking about something else, about other winds beginning to blow, as if another wind is picking up...

## CHAPTER TWO

*This chapter tells the story of the Governor, an apprentice to the viceroy, and his heroic fight against the progressive clergy and his adventures with the feudal cattle, coffee and business lords. It also tells other equally fantastic tales.*

Once upon a time there was a viceroy made of chocolate with a peanut for a nose. The viceroy's apprentice, Governor Patrocinio González Garrido, in the manner of the old monarchs who were put in power by the Spanish crown during the Conquest, has re-organized the geography of Chiapas. The assignment of spaces to the urban and rural categories is a somewhat sophisticated exercise of power but when directed by Mr. González Garrido's denseness, it has reached exquisite levels of stupidity. The viceroy decided that cities with services and benefits should be for those who already have everything. And he decided, the viceroy that is, that the masses are fine out in the open, exposed to wind and rough weather, and that they only deserve space in the jails, which never cease to be uncomfortable. Because of this, the viceroy decided to construct jails in the outskirts of the cities so that the proximity of the undesirable and delinquent masses would not disturb the rich. Jails and Army barracks are the principal works promoted by this governor in Chiapas. His friendship with ranchers and powerful businessmen is a secret to no one. Neither is his animosity for the three dioceses which regulate the state's Catholic life. The Diocese of San Cristóbal, headed by Bishop Samuel Ruiz, is a constant menace to González

Garrido's reorganizing project. Hoping to modernize the absurd system of exploitation and extraction which prevails in Chiapas, Patrocinio González comes up against the stubbornness of religious and secular figures who support and preach Catholicism's option for the poor.

With the hypocritical applause of Aguirre Franco, the Bishop of Tuxtla Gutierrez, and the mute approval of the Bishop of Tapachula, González Garrido sustains and gives new life to the "heroic" conspiracies of ranchers and businessmen against the members of the Diocese of San Cristóbal. "Don Samuel's teams," as they are called by some, are not made up of inexperienced believers: Before Patrocinio González Garrido had even dreamed of being state governor, the Diocese of San Cristóbal de las Casas preached the right to freedom and justice. For one of the country's most backward bourgeoisie, the agricultural bourgeoisie, this could only mean one thing: rebellion. These rancher and business "patriots" and "believers" know how to prevent rebellion: the existence of privately financed, armed paramilitary groups trained by members of the Federal Army, Public Security police and state law is well known by the campesinos who suffer from their threats, torture and gunshots.

A few months ago, Father Joel Padrón from the parish of Simojovel was arrested. Accused by the region's ranchers of initiating and taking part in land take-overs, Father Joel was arrested by state authorities and held in the Cerro Hueco Jail in the state capital. The mobilization of the members of the Diocese of San Cristóbal (those of Tuxtla Gutierrez and Tapachula were conspicuous in their absence) and a federal compromise succeeded in obtaining the parish priest Padrón's freedom.

While thousands of campesinos marched in Tuxtla Gutierrez to demand Padrón's freedom, ranchers in Ocosingo sent their paramilitary forces to clear out property-owning campesinos. Four hundred men, armed by the ranchers, destroyed and burned houses, beat Indigenous women and murdered a campesino, Juan, by shooting him in the face. After the expulsion, the paramilitary forces–composed mostly of workers from local ranches and small-property owners proud of partaking in raids with the young ranchers–drove along the region's roads in pickup trucks provided by their masters. Ostentatiously displaying their arms, drunk and intoxicated, they shouted: "Ranchers are number one!" and warned everyone that it was only the beginning. Undaunted, municipal authorities in Ocosingo and soldiers stationed in the region looked passively on the gunmen's triumphant parade.

In Tuxtla Gutierrez, almost 10,000 campesinos marched in favor of Father Padrón's release. In a corner of Ocosingo, Juan's widow buried her husband, victim of the proud ranchers. There was no march or protest petition for Juan's death. This is Chiapas.

Recently, Viceroy González Garrido was the protagonist of a new scandal, which was uncovered because the press reported the story. With the viceroy's approval, Ocosingo's feudal lords organized the Committee for Citizen Defense, a blatant attempt to institutionalize their neo-Porfirista paramilitary forces that keep order in the countryside of Chiapas. Surely nothing would have happened had it not been for the discovery of a plot to assassinate the parish priest Pablo Ibarren and the nun María del Carmen, along with Samuel Ruiz, the Bishop of San Cristóbal. The plot was reported by the honest Chiapaneco press, which even now exists, and reached national forums. There were retractions and denials; the viceroy declared that he maintains good relations with the Church and named a special committee to investigate the case. The investigation yielded no results, and the waters returned to their course.

During the same days, government agencies made some horrifying statistics known: in Chiapas 14,500 people die every year, the highest mortality rate in the country. The causes? Curable diseases such as respiratory infections, enteritis, parasites, amoebas, malaria, salmonella, scabies, dengue, pulmonary tuberculosis, trachoma, typhus, cholera and measles. Many say that the figure is actually over 15,000 because deaths in marginalized zones, the majority of the state, are not reported... During Patrocinio González Garrido's four-year term more than 60,000 Chiapanecos have died, most of them poor. The war against the people, directed by the viceroy and commanded by the feudal lords, consists of methods more subtle than bombardments. There is no mention in the press of this murderous plot which costs lives and land as in the days of the Conquest.

The Committee for Citizen Defense continues to carry out its proselytizing work, holding meetings to convince the rich and poor of the city of Ocosingo that they should organize and arm themselves so that the campesinos won't enter the city because they will destroy everything, without respecting the rich or the poor. The viceroy smiles with approval.

## CHAPTER THREE

*This chapter tells how the viceroy had a brilliant idea and put this idea into practice. It also tells how the Empire decreed the death of socialism, and then put itself to the task of carrying out this decree to the great joy of the powerful, the distress of the weak and the indifference of the majority. It tells of Zapata and how he is said to be still be alive. It also tells of other disconcerting events.*

The viceroy is worried. The campesinos refuse to applaud the institutional pillage written into the new Article 27 of the Constitution. The viceroy is enraged. The poor aren't happy with being exploited. They refuse to humbly accept the charity that Pronasol spreads around the Chiapaneco countryside. The viceroy is desperate. He consults his advisors. His advisors tell him an old truth: Jails and military bases aren't enough to ensure continued domination. It is also necessary to control people's thoughts. The viceroy is disturbed. He paces his palace. Then he stops and smiles.

XEOCH: Rap and lies for the campesinos.

In Ocosingo and Palenque, Cancue and Chilón, Altamirano and Yajalón, the Indigenous people are celebrating. A new gift from the supreme government has made life a little happier for the peons, small landowners, landless campesinos and impoverished inhabitants of the *ejidos*. They have been given a local radio station that reaches the most isolated corners of eastern Chiapas. The station's programming is fitting: Marimbas and rap music proclaim the good news. The Chiapaneco countryside is being modernized. XEOCH transmits from the township of Ocosingo and can be found at 600 Mhz AM from four in the morning till 10 at night. Its news shows abound with lies. They tell of the "disorientation" that "subversive" lay-workers spread among the peasantry, the abundance of aid credits that are never received by the Indigenous communities, and the existence of public works that have never been built. The viceroy is also given time on the air so that he can remind the

population with threats that not all is lies and rap music; there are also jails and military bases and a penal code which is the most repressive in the Republic. The penal code punishes any expression of discontent. The laws against demonstrations, rebellion, inciting to riot, etc., demonstrate that the viceroy is careful to maintain everything in order.

There isn't any reason to fight. Socialism has died. Long live conformity and reform and the modern world and capitalism and all of the cruelties that are associated with them! The viceroy and the feudal lords dance and smile euphorically in their palaces. Their joy is disconcerting for the few free-thinkers who live in the area. Even they are incapable of understanding. They are without hope. It is true that one must fight, but the balance of forces isn't favorable, now isn't the time. We must wait longer, maybe years. We must be alert against the adventurers. We must make sure that nothing happens in the cities or in the countryside, that everything continues as always. Socialism has died. Long live capitalism! Radio, the print media, and television proclaim it. It is repeated by some ex-socialists who are now sensationally changed.

Not everyone hears the voices of hopelessness and conformity. Not everyone is carried away by hopelessness. There are millions of people who continue on without hearing the voices of the powerful and the indifferent. They can't hear; they are deafened by the crying and blood that death and poverty are shouting in their ears. But, when there is a moment of rest, they hear another voice. They don't hear the voice that comes from above; they hear the voice that is carried to them by the wind from below, a voice that is born in the Indigenous heart of the mountains. This voice speaks to them about justice and freedom, it speaks to them about socialism, about hope...the only hope that exists in the world. The oldest of the old in the Indigenous communities say that there once was a man named Zapata who rose up with his people and sang out, "Land and Freedom!" These old campesinos say that Zapata didn't die, that he must return. These old campesinos also say that the wind and the rain and the sun tell the campesinos when to cultivate the land, when to plant and when to harvest. They say that hope is also planted and harvested. They also say that the wind and the rain and the sun are now saying something different: that with so much poverty, the time has come to harvest rebellion instead of death. That is what the old campesinos say. The powerful don't hear; they can't hear, they are deafened by the brutality that the Empire shouts in their ears. "Zapata," insists the wind, the wind from below, our wind.

# THE SECOND WIND: THE WIND FROM BELOW

## CHAPTER FOUR

*This chapter tells how dignity and defiance joined hands in the Southeast, and how Jacinto Pérez's phantoms run through the Chiapaneco highlands. It also tells of a patience that has run out and of other happenings which have been ignored but have major consequences.*

These people were born dignified and rebellious, brothers and sisters to the rest of Mexico's exploited people. They are not just the product of the Annexation Act of 1824,

41

but of a long chain of ignominious acts and rebellions. From the time when cassock and armor conquered this land, dignity and defiance have lived and spread under these rains.

Collective work, democratic thinking, and subjection to the decisions of the majority are more than just traditions in Indigenous zones. They have been the only means of survival, resistance, dignity, and defiance. These "evil ideas," as they are seen by landholders and businessmen, go against the capitalist precept of "a lot in the hands of a few."

It has mistakenly been said that the Chiapas rebellion has no counterpart, that it is outside the national experience. This is a lie. The exploited Chiapaneco's specialty is the same as that of exploited people from Durango, Veracruz, or the plateau of northern Mexico: to fight and to lose. If the voices of those who write history speak excessively, it is because the voice of the oppressed does not speak...yet. There is no historic, national, or regional calendar that has documented each and every rebellion against this system that is imposed and maintained with blood and fire throughout the national territory. In Chiapas, this rebel voice is only heard when it shakes the world of the landowners and businesspeople. Indeed, the phantom of Indigenous barbarism strikes government-building walls and gains access with the help of revolution, trickery, and threats. If the rebellion in the Southeast loses, as the rebellions lost in the North, Center, and West, it is not the result of bad timing, it is because wind is the fruit of the land; it comes in time and ripens in the breasts of those who have nothing but dignity and rebelliousness. And this wind from below, that of rebellion and dignity, is not just an answer to the wind from above. It is not just an angry response or the destruction of an unjust and arbitrary system. Rather it carries with it a new proposal, a hope of converting rebellion and dignity into freedom and dignity.

How will this new voice make itself heard in these lands and across the country? How will this hidden wind blow, this wind which now blows only in the mountains and canyons without yet descending to the valleys where money rules and lies govern? This wind will come from the mountains. It is already being born under the trees and is conspiring for a new world, so new that it is barely an intuition in the collective heart that inspires it...

# CHAPTER FIVE

*This chapter tells how the dignity of the Indigenous people tried to make itself heard, but its voice only lasted a little while. It also tell how voices that spoke before are speaking again today and that the Indians are walking forward once again but this time with firm footsteps. They are walking together with other dispossessed peoples to take what belongs to them. The music of death that now plays only for those who have nothing will now play for everyone. It also tells of other frightful things which have happened and, they say, must happen.*

The Indigenous march to Xi'Nich, composed of campesinos from Palenque, Ocosingo, and Salto de Agua, demonstrates the system's absurdity. These Indigenous people had to walk 1,106 kilometers to make themselves heard. They had to go to the capital of the Republic in order for the central power to arrange a meeting with the viceroy. They arrived in Mexico City when capitalism was painting a frightful tragedy

across the skies of Jalisco. They arrived at the capital of old New Spain, now Mexico, exactly 500 years after the foreign nightmare imposed itself in the night of this land. They arrived and all the honest and noble people, of which there are still some, listened to them and the voices that oppress them today in the Southeast, North, Center and West of the country also listened to them. They walked back, another 1,106 kilometers, their bags filled with promises. Again, nothing came of it....

In the municipal seat of Simojovel campesinos belonging to the CIOAC organization were attacked by people paid by local ranchers. The campesinos in Simojovel have decided to stop being silent and to respond to the ranchers threats. Campesinos surround the municipal seat. Nothing and no one enters or leaves without their consent. The Federal Army withdraws to its barracks, the police retreat, and the state's feudal lords demand arms in an attempt to restore order and respect. Negotiating commissions come and go. The conflict appears to have resolved itself. But the causes persist. With the same outward appearances everything returns to calm.

In the town of Betania, in the outskirts of San Cristóbal de las Casas, Indigenous people are regularly detained and harassed by judicial agents for cutting firewood for their homes. The judicial agents say that they are only doing this to protect the environment. The Indigenous people decide to stop being silent and kidnap three judicial officials. They take the Panamerican highway and cut off communications to the east of San Cristóbal. At the intersection between Ocosingo and Comitán, campesinos are holding the judiciaries and they demand to speak to the viceroy before they will agree to unblock the road. Business comes to a halt, tourism collapses. Negotiating commissions come and go. The conflict appears to resolve itself but the causes persist. With the same outward appearances, everything returns to calm.

In Marqués de Comillas, in the township of Ocosingo, campesinos cut wood to survive. The judicial officials arrest them and confiscate the wood for their commander. The Indigenous people decide to stop being silent and they take the agents' vehicles and kidnap the agents. The Governor sends Public Security police who are kidnapped in the same way. The Indigenous people hold on to the trucks, the wood and the prisoners. They let the prisoners go. There is no response. They march to Palenque to demand solutions and the Army oppresses them and kidnaps their leaders. They hold on to the vehicles. Negotiating commissions come and go. The government lets the leaders go, the campesinos return the vehicles. The conflict appears to resolve itself but the causes persist. With the same outward appearance everything returns to calm.

In the municipal seat of Ocosingo, 4,000 Indigenous campesinos from the organization ANCIEZ march from different points of the city. Three marches converge in front of the Municipal building. The municipal president doesn't know what it's all about and flees. On the floor of his office is a calendar indicating the date: April 10, 1992. Outside Indigenous campesinos from Ocosingo, Oxchuc, Huixtán, Chilón, Yajalon, Sabanilla, Salto de Agua, Palenque, Altamirano, Margaritas, San Cristóbal, San Andrés and Cancuc dance in front of a giant image of Zapata painted by one of them, recite poetry, sing, and speak. Only they are listening. The landowners, businessmen, and judicial officials are closed up in their homes and shops, the federal garrison appears

deserted. The campesinos shout that Zapata lives and the struggle continues. One of them reads a letter addressed to Carlos Salinas de Gortari [President of Mexico, 1988—present] in which they accuse him of having brought all of the Agrarian Reform gains made under Zapata to an end, of selling the country with the North American Free Trade Agreement and of bringing Mexico back to the times of Porfirio Díaz. They declare forcefully that they will not recognize Salinas' reforms to Article 27 of the Political Constitution. At two o'clock in the afternoon the demonstration disperses, in apparent order, but the causes persist. With the same outward appearances everything returns to calm.

Abasolo is an *ejido* in the township of Ocosingo. For years, campesinos took land that legally belonged to them. Three of this community's leaders have been put in jail and tortured by the Governor. The Indigenous people decide to stop being silent and they take the San Cristóbal-Ocosingo highway. Negotiating commissions come and go. The leaders are freed. The conflict appears to resolve itself but the causes persist. With the same outward appearance everything returns to calm.

Antonio dreams of owning the land he works on, he dreams that his sweat is paid for with justice and truth, he dreams that there is a school to cure ignorance and medicine to scare away death, he dreams of having electricity in his home and that his table is full, he dreams that his country is free and that this is the result of its people governing themselves, and he dreams that he is at peace with himself and with the world. He dreams that he must fight to obtain this dream, he dreams that there must be death in order to gain life. Antonio dreams and then he awakens... Now he knows what to do and he sees his wife crouching by the fire, hears his son crying. He looks at the sun rising in the East, and, smiling, grabs his machete.

The wind picks up, he rises and walks to meet others. Something has told him that his dream is that of many and he goes to find them.

The viceroy dreams that his land is agitated by a terrible wind that rouses everything, he dreams that all he has stolen is taken from him, that his house is destroyed, and that his reign is brought down. He dreams and he doesn't sleep. The viceroy goes to the feudal lords and they tell him that they have been having the same dream. The viceroy cannot rest. So he goes to his doctor and together they decide that it is some sort of Indian witchcraft and that they will only be freed from this dream with blood. The viceroy orders killings and kidnappings and he builds more jails and Army barracks. But the dream continues and keeps him tossing and turning and unable to sleep.

Everyone is dreaming in this country. Now it is time to wake up...

The storm is here. From the clash of these two winds the storm will be born, its time has arrived. Now the wind from above rules, but the wind from below is coming...

The prophecy is here. When the storm calms, when rain and fire again leave the country in peace, the world will no longer be the world but something better.

The Lacandona Jungle, August 1992

# 1. THE REVOLT

*[The Mexican Awakener [El Despertador Mexicano] is the newspaper of the EZLN, issued on January 1 in conjunction with the uprising. It was the first document released by the Zapatistas. It contains their Declaration of War, an editorial, and the revolutionary laws.]*

## EL DESPERTADOR MEXICANO

### DECLARATION OF WAR

[from a photocopy of the original]
Lacandona Jungle, December 31, 1993

TODAY WE SAY ENOUGH IS ENOUGH!
TO THE PEOPLE OF MEXICO:
MEXICAN BROTHERS AND SISTERS:

We are the product of 500 years of struggle: first against slavery, then during the War of Independence against Spain led by insurgents, then to avoid being absorbed by North American imperialism, then to promulgate our constitution and expel the French Empire from our soil, and later the dictatorship of Porfirio Díaz denied us the just application of the Reform Laws, and the people rebelled and leaders like Villa and Zapata emerged, poor people just like us. We have been denied the most elemental preparation so that they can use us as cannon fodder and pillage the wealth of our country. They don't care that we have nothing, absolutely nothing, not even a roof over our heads: no land, no work, no health care, no food, no education. Nor are we able to freely and democratically elect our political representatives, nor is there independence from foreigners, nor is there peace nor justice for ourselves and our children.

But today, we say ENOUGH IS ENOUGH. We are the inheritors of the true builders of our nation. The dispossessed, we are millions, and we thereby call upon our brothers and sisters to join this struggle as the only path, so that we will not die of

49

hunger due to the insatiable ambition of a 70-year dictatorship led by a clique of traitors who represent the most conservative and sell-out groups. They are the same ones who opposed Hidalgo and Morelos, the same ones who betrayed Vincente Guerrero, the same ones who sold half our country to the foreign invader, the same ones who imported a European prince to rule our country, the same ones who formed the "scientific" Porfirista dictatorship, the same ones who opposed the Petroleum Expropriation, the same ones who massacred the railroad workers in 1958 and the students in 1968, the same ones who today take everything from us, absolutely everything.

To prevent the continuation of the above, and as our last hope, after having tried to utilize all legal means based on our Constitution, we go to our Constitution, to apply Article 39, which says:

"National Sovereignty essentially and originally resides in the people. All political power emanates from the people and its purpose is to help the people. The people have, at all times, the inalienable right to alter or modify their form of government."

Therefore, according to our Constitution, we declare the following to the Mexican Federal Army, the pillar of the Mexican dictatorship that we suffer from, monopolized by a one-party system and led by Carlos Salinas de Gortari, the supreme and illegitimate federal executive who today holds power.

According to this Declaration of War, we ask that other powers of the nation advocate to restore the legitimacy and the stability of the nation by overthrowing the dictator.

We also ask that international organizations and the International Red Cross watch over and regulate our battles, so that our efforts are carried out while still protecting our civilian population. We declare now and always that we are subject to the Geneva Accord, forming the EZLN as the fighting arm of our liberation struggle. We have the Mexican people on our side, we have the beloved tri-colored flag, highly respected by our insurgent fighters. We use black and red in our uniform as a symbol of our working people on strike. Our flag carries the following letters, "EZLN," Zapatista National Liberation Army, and we always carry our flag into combat.

Beforehand, we reject any effort to disgrace our just cause by accusing us of being drug traffickers, drug guerrillas, thieves or other names that might by used by our enemies. Our struggle follows the Constitution, which is held high by its call for justice and equality.

Therefore, according to this declaration of war, we give our military forces, the EZLN, the following orders:

**First:** Advance to the capital of the country, overcoming the Mexican Federal Army, protecting in our advance the civilian population and permitting the people in the liberated area the right to freely and democratically elect their own administrative authorities.

**Second:** Respect the lives of our prisoners and turn over all wounded to the International Red Cross.

**Third:** Initiate summary judgments against all soldiers of the Mexican Federal Army and the political police who have received training or have been paid by foreigners, accused of being traitors to our country, and against all those who have repressed and treated badly the civilian population, and robbed, or stolen from, or attempted crimes against the good of the people.

**Fourth:** Form new troops with all those Mexicans who show their interest in joining our struggle, including those who, being enemy soldiers, turn themselves in without having fought against us, and promise to take orders from the General Command of the EZLN.

**Fifth:** We ask for the unconditional surrender of the enemy's headquarters before we begin any combat to avoid any loss of lives.

**Sixth:** Suspend the robbery of our natural resources in the areas controlled by the EZLN.

To the People of Mexico:

We, the men and women, full and free, are conscious that the war that we have declared is our last resort, but also a just one. The dictators have been waging an undeclared genocidal war against our people for many years. Therefore we ask for your participation, your decision to support this plan that struggles for work, land, housing, food, health care, education, independence, freedom, democracy, justice and peace. We declare that we will not stop fighting until the basic demands of our people have been met by forming a government of our country that is free and democratic.

JOIN THE INSURGENT FORCES OF THE ZAPATISTA NATIONAL LIBERATION ARMY!

General Command of the EZLN
December 31, 1993


## EDITORIAL

Mexicans: workers, campesinos, students, honest professionals, Chicanos, and progressives of other countries: We have begun the struggle that is necessary to meet the demands that never have been met by the Mexican State: work, land, shelter, food, health care, education, independence, freedom, democracy, justice and peace.

For hundreds of years we have been asking for and believing in promises that were never kept. We were always told to be patient and to wait for better times. They told us to be prudent, that the future would be different. But we see now that this isn't true. Everything is the same or worse now than when our grandparents and parents lived. Our people are still dying from hunger and curable diseases, and live with ignorance, illiteracy and lack of culture. And we realize that if we don't fight, our children can expect the same. And it is not fair.

Necessity brought us together, and we said "Enough!" We no longer have the time or the will to wait for others to solve our problems. We have organized ourselves and we have decided to demand what is ours, taking up arms in the same way that the finest children of the Mexican people have done throughout our history.

We have entered into combat against the Federal Army and other repressive forces: there are millions of us Mexicans willing to live for our country or die for freedom in this war. This war is necessary for all the poor, exploited and miserable people of Mexico, and we will not stop until we achieve our goals.

We call on all of you to join our movement because the enemies we face, the rich and the State, are cruel and inhuman. They will put no limit on their bloody instinct to destroy us. It is necessary to struggle on all fronts and from there, with your sympathy, your solidarity, the dissemination that you give our cause, your adoption of the ideals that we are demanding, your incorporation of the Revolution by raising up your people wherever they may be found, these are very important factors in our final triumph.

*El Despertador Mexicano* is the newspaper of the EZLN. It strives to inform the people about the development of the just war that we have declared against our class enemies.

In this first issue we present our Declaration of War against the Federal Army, and we publish the orders to be followed by the leaders and officers of the EZLN in our advance through national territory. Also in this issue are the Revolutionary Laws that will be enacted in the liberated territories in order to guarantee their revolutionary control and strengthen the bases so we can begin the process of building a new Mexico.

TO LIVE FOR OUR COUNTRY OR DIE FOR FREEDOM.

# Revolutionary Laws

## Women's Revolutionary Law

In the just fight for the liberation of our people, the EZLN incorporates women into the revolutionary struggle, regardless of their race, creed, color or political affiliation, requiring only that they share the demands of the exploited people and that they commit to the laws and regulations of the revolution. In addition, taking into account the situation of the woman worker in Mexico, the revolution supports their just demands for equality and justice in the following Women's Revolutionary Law.

**First:** Women, regardless of their race, creed, color or political affiliation, have the right to participate in the revolutionary struggle in a way determined by their desire and capacity.

**Second:** Women have the right to work and receive a just salary.

**Third:** Women have the right to decide the number of children they will have and care for.

**Fourth:** Women have the right to participate in the affairs of the community and hold positions of authority if they are freely and democratically elected.

**Fifth:** Women and their children have the right to primary attention in matters of health and nutrition.

**Sixth:** Women have the right to education.

**Seventh:** Women have the right to choose their partner, and are not to be forced into marriage.

**Eighth:** Women shall not be beaten or physically mistreated by their family members or by strangers. Rape and attempted rape will be severely punished.

**Ninth:** Women will be able to occupy positions of leadership in the organization and hold military ranks in the revolutionary armed forces.

**Tenth:** Women will have all the rights and obligations elaborated in the Revolutionary Laws and regulations.

## Urban Reform Law

In the urban zones controlled by the EZLN, the following laws will be enacted in order to ensure dignified housing for all dispossessed families:

**First:** The inhabitants of the zone who own their own homes or apartments will stop paying all taxes.

**Second:** The inhabitants of the zone who pay rent, and have resided in the same dwelling for more than 15 years, will stop paying rent to the owner of the property until the revolutionary government triumphs and new legislation is enacted.

**Third:** The inhabitants of the zone who pay rent, and have resided in the same dwelling for fewer than 15 years, will pay only 10% of the salary earned by the head of the family as rent, and will not pay at all after having resided in the dwelling for 15 years.

**Fourth:** Urban lots that already have public services will be opened for immediate occupation in order that dwellings may be constructed on said lots—even if the dwellings are only of a provisional nature. The freely and democratically elected authorities will be notified of these occupations.

**Fifth:** Vacant public buildings and large mansions will be provisionally occupied by families, who will divide the buildings among themselves. In order to facilitate this, the civil authorities will appoint neighborhood committees that will decide on requests that are presented to them and will grant living space on the basis of need and available resources.

## Labor Law: Additions to the Present Law

The following laws will be added to the current Federal Labor Law in the zones controlled by the EZLN.

**First:** Foreign companies will pay their workers an hourly salary in national money equivalent to what would be payed in dollars outside the country.

**Second:** National companies will increase their workers' salaries monthly, by a percentage determined by a local Prices and Salaries Commission. Said Commission will be composed of representatives of the workers, settlers, land-owners, business people and the freely and democratically elected authorities. The reduction of current salaries will in no way be permitted.

**Third:** All workers in the countryside and the cities will receive free medical care in any public or private health center, hospital or clinic. The medical costs will be covered by the employers.

**Fourth:** Every worker will have a right to a certain amount of non-transferable stock in the company for which they work, the exact quantity to be determined by the number of years that the worker has worked for the company—this in addition to their current pensions. The monetary value of said stock will be used for the worker's retirement, by his wife or by his beneficiary.

## Industry and Commerce Law

**First:** The prices of basic products will be regulated by a local Prices and Salaries Commission. Said Commission will be composed of workers, settlers, land owners, merchants and the freely and democratically-elected authorities. Increases in the prices of basic products cannot, in any way, be more than increases in salaries.

**Second:** The hoarding of any product is prohibited. Hoarders will be detained and turned over to the military authorities, accused of sabotage and treason to the country.

**Third:** The commerce of a given region should be able to ensure the provision of tortillas and bread for all in time of war.

**Fourth:** The industries and businesses that the landowners consider unproductive, and attempt to close in order to carry away the machinery and raw materials, will be passed to the management of the workers, and the machinery will become the property of the nation.

## Social Security Law

**First:** Abandoned children will be fed and protected by the nearest neighbors under the authority of the EZLN, before being turned over to the civilian authorities, who will protect them until they reach 13 years of age.

**Second:** Elderly people without family will be protected and will receive priority in housing and the distribution of free food coupons.

**Third:** Those incapacitated by the war will receive attention and work priority under the direction of the EZLN.

**Fourth:** The pension of retirees will be equal to the minimum salary established by local Price and Salary Commissions.

## Justice Law

**First:** All prisoners in all prisons will be liberated, except those guilty of murder, rape and the leaders of drug-trafficking operations.

**Second:** All government officials, from the level of the municipal president up to the president of the republic, will be subject to audit, and will be judged for misappropriation of funds in cases where evidence of guilt is found.

# REVOLUTIONARY AGRARIAN LAW

The poor campesinos' movement in Mexico demands the return of the land to those who work it and, in the tradition of Emiliano Zapata and in opposition to the reforms to Article 27 of the Mexican Constitution, the EZLN again takes up the just struggle of rural Mexico for land and freedom. With the object of standardizing the new agrarian distribution enacted by the revolution throughout Mexican territory, the following Revolutionary Agrarian Law is issued:

**First:** This law is valid in all Mexican territory, and benefits all poor campesinos and Mexican agricultural laborers regardless of their political affiliation, religious creed, sex, race, or color.

**Second:** This law affects all agricultural properties and agro/livestock businesses inside of Mexican territory, whether they are national or foreign-owned.

**Third:** All poor-quality land in excess of 100 hectares and all good-quality land in excess of 50 hectares will be subject to the Revolutionary Agrarian Law. The landowners whose lands exceed the aforementioned limits will have the excess taken away from them, and they will be left with the minimum permitted by this law. They may remain as small landholders or join the cooperative campesinos' movement, campesino societies, or communal lands.

**Fourth:** Communally held land and the land of popular cooperatives will not be subject to agrarian reform, even though they exceed the limits mentioned in the third article of this law.

**Fifth:** The lands affected by this agrarian law will be distributed to the landless campesinos and the agricultural laborers who thus request it as collective property for the formation of cooperatives, campesino societies or agricultural production/livestock collectives. The affected lands should be worked collectively.

**Sixth:** The collectives of poor, landless campesinos and agricultural laborers—men, women, and children without land title, or who have land of poor quality—will have the right to be the first to request land.

**Seventh:** In order to better cultivate the land for the benefit of the poor campesinos and the agricultural laborers, the expropriation of large estates and agricultural/livestock monopolies will include the expropriation of means of production such as machinery, fertilizer, stores, financial resources, chemical products and technical expertise. All of these means should pass into the hands of the poor campesinos and agricultural laborers, with special attention given to groups organized in cooperatives, collectives and societies.

**Eighth:** The groups that benefit from this agrarian law should dedicate themselves to the collective production of necessary foodstuffs for the Mexican people: corn, beans, rice, vegetables and fruit, as well as to the raising of cattle, bees, pigs and horses, and to the production of animal-derived products (meat, milk, eggs, etc.).

**Ninth:** In time of war, a portion of the products of the lands affected by this law will be designated for the sustenance of orphans and widows of revolutionary combatants, and to the support of the revolutionary forces.

**Tenth:** The purpose of collective production is primarily to satisfy the people's needs, to instill in those who benefit from this law a consciousness of collective work and benefit, and to create production, defense and mutual-aid units in the Mexican countryside. When a region doesn't produce some product, it will trade justly and equally with another region where it is produced. Excess production can be exported to other countries if there is no national demand for the product.

**Eleventh:** Large agricultural businesses will be expropriated and passed to the hands of the Mexican people, and will be administered collectively by the workers of those businesses. The cultivation machinery, seeds, etc. that are sitting idle in factories and businesses will be distributed among rural collectives, with the objective of making the land fertile and ending the hunger of the people.

**Twelfth:** Individual hoarding of land and the means of production will not be permitted.

**Thirteenth:** Zones of virgin jungle and forest will be preserved. There will be reforestation campaigns in the principal zones.

**Fourteenth:** The riverheads, rivers, lakes and oceans are the collective property of the Mexican people, and they will be cared for by not polluting them and by punishing their misuse.

**Fifteenth:** In order to benefit the poor, landless campesinos and agricultural workers, in addition to the agrarian redistribution established by this law, commercial centers will be created to buy the campesinos' products at a fair price and to sell to them, at a fair price, goods that the campesino needs for a dignified life. Also, community health centers will be created with every benefit of modern medicine, with capable and conscientious doctors and nurses, and with free medical care for the people. Recreation centers will be created for the campesinos and their families so that they may rest in dignity without the need for bars or bordellos. Educational centers and free schools will be created where the campesinos and their families can receive an education, regardless of their age, sex, race or political affiliation, and where they can learn the techniques necessary for their development. Housing and road construction centers will be established with engineers, architects, and the necessary materials for the campesinos' dignified housing and the construction of good roads for transportation. Service centers will be created in order to guarantee potable water, drainage, electricity, radio and television, in addition to everything necessary for housework: stoves, refrigerators, lavatories, mills, etc.

**Sixteenth:** The campesinos who work collectively will not be taxed. Nor will the *ejidos,* cooperatives or communal lands be taxed. From the moment that this Revolutionary

Agrarian Law is implemented, all debts—whether they are from credit, taxes, or loans—that are owed by the poor campesinos or agricultural workers to the oppressive government, to foreigners or to capitalists, are forgiven.

## LAW OF RIGHTS AND OBLIGATIONS OF PEOPLES IN STRUGGLE

In its liberatory advance through Mexican territory, and in the struggle against the government and against the large national and foreign exploiters, the EZLN will implement, with the help of the people engaged in struggle, the following Law of Rights and Obligations of Peoples in Struggle:

**First:** The peoples in struggle against the oppressor government and the large national and foreign exploiters, without regard to their political affiliation, religious creed, race or color, will have the following rights:

**A:** To choose, freely and democratically, the authorities of whatever type they consider convenient, and to demand that they be respected.

**B:** To demand that the revolutionary armed forces not intervene in matters of civil order or the disposition of capital relating to agriculture, commerce, finances, and industry, as these are the exclusive domain of the civil authorities, elected freely and democratically.

**C:** To organize and exercise armed defense of their collective and private goods, as well as to organize and exercise the vigilance of public order and good government according to the popular will.

**D:** To demand that the revolutionary armed forces guarantee the safety of people, families and private and collective property of neighbors or transients, when these people are not enemies of the revolution.

**E:** The inhabitants of every population have the right to acquire and possess arms to defend their persons, families and property, according to the laws of disposition of capital of farms, commerce, finance and industry, against the armed attacks committed by the revolutionary forces or those of the government. By the same token, they are fully authorized to make use of those arms against whatever person or group of people assaults their homes, the honor of their families, or attempt to commit robberies or attacks of whatever form against their persons. This is valid only for those who are not enemies of the revolution.

**Second:** The civil authorities of whatever type, who are elected democratically, will have, in addition to the previous rights and the attributions that are signalled by the respective revolutionary laws, the following rights:

**A:** They will be able to imprison, disarm and turn in to the Commands anyone they find robbing, raiding or looting any home or committing any other violation, for which they will receive their deserved punishment, even if they are a member of the

57

revolutionary armed forces. The same procedures will be employed against those who commit any violation, even if they are not caught in the act, if their guilt is sufficiently demonstrated.

**B:** They will have the right that, for their conduct, revolutionary taxes be imposed as established by the War Tax Law.

**Third:** Peoples in struggle against the oppressor government and the great national and foreign exploiters, without regard to their political affiliation, religious creed, race or color, will have the following obligations:

**A:** To give their services in works of vigilance, according to majority will or the military necessities of revolutionary war.

**B:** To respond to calls for help made by the democratically elected authorities, the revolutionary armed forces or by any revolutionary military person in cases of urgency, to combat the enemy.

**C:** To lend their services as mail deliverers or guides to the revolutionary armed forces.

**D:** To lend their services to carry food to the revolutionary troops when they are combatting the enemy.

**E:** To lend their services to transport wounded, bury cadavers or other similar works tied to the cause and interests of the revolution.

**F:** To give food and lodging to the revolutionary forces that are guarding or passing through the respective populations, to the degree that they are able.

**G:** To pay taxes and contributions established by the War Tax Law and other Revolutionary Laws.

**H:** They should not help in any way the enemy, nor give them articles of primary necessity.

**I:** To dedicate themselves to legitimate work.

**Fourth:** The civil authorities, of whatever type elected democratically, will, in addition to the previous obligations, have the following obligations:

**A:** To regularly report to the civil population on the activities under their command and the origin and destination of all of the material resources and human posts in their administration.

**B:** To regularly inform the respective Command of the revolutionary armed forces of any events that occur in their area.

## Instructions to Leaders and Officials of the EZLN

The following orders are obligatory for all leaders and officials of troops under the control the Zapatista National Liberation Army.

58

**First:** You will operate according to the orders that you receive from the General Command or from the Commands of the Front Line.

**Second:** The leaders and officials who are in military operations in isolated zones or with difficulties in communicating with the Commands should carry out their military work, combatting the enemy constantly, according to their own initiative, taking care to advance the revolution in the places where they find themselves working.

**Third:** You will submit a War Dispatch whenever possible, or at least monthly, to the respective Commands.

**Fourth:** You will endeavor to preserve, as much as possible, good order among the troops, especially when you enter populaces, guaranteeing in full the lives and interests of the inhabitants who are not enemies of the revolution.

**Fifth:** To aid the troops in their material necessities to the degree possible, you should impose war contributions on the businesses or property-holders who find themselves in the zones where you are operating, but only if they have important capital according to the War Tax Law and the Revolutionary Laws that affect commercial, agricultural, financial and industrial capital.

**Sixth:** The material funds that are gathered by these means will be employed strictly for the material necessities of the troops. The leader or official who takes any of these funds for his personal benefit will be taken prisoner and judged according to the rules of the EZLN by a revolutionary military tribunal.

**Seventh:** For the feeding of the troops, pasture of the horses, and fuel and repair of the vehicles, you should direct yourselves to the democratically elected authorities of the place in question. This authority will gather what they can from among the civilian population, for the material necessities of the Zapatista military unit, and will hand them in to the leader or official of the highest rank in said military unit, and only to him.

**Eighth:** Only those officials with the rank of Major or higher will change authorities in those places that fall under the power of the revolution, according to the will of the people, and according to available and relevant sections of the Law of Revolutionary Government.

**Ninth:** The people, in general, will take possession of their goods according to what is established in the Revolutionary Laws. The leaders and officials of the EZLN will give to these people their moral and material support, with the goal of carrying out what is set out in these Revolutionary Laws, whenever the same people request this help.

**Tenth:** Absolutely no one will be able to have meetings or treaties with the oppressor government or with its representatives without the prior authorization of the General Command of the EZLN.

# WAR TAX LAW

In the zones controlled by the EZLN the following War Tax Law will be instituted and will be made to function with all of the moral, political and military force of our revolutionary organization.

**First:** The War Tax Law will apply from the moment that a military unit of the EZLN begins to operate in a specific territory.

**Second:** The War Tax Law affects all of the civilian, national or foreign populations residing in or passing through said territory.

**Third:** The War Tax Law is not obligatory for the civilian population that lives by its own resources, without exploiting any labor whatsoever and without obtaining any advantage from the people. For poor campesinos, day workers, workers, employees, the unemployed, participation in this law is voluntary and in no way will they be obligated morally or physically to subject themselves to this law.

**Fourth:** The War Tax Law is obligatory for those in the civilian population who live by exploitation, by force or through work or who obtain some advantage over the people in their activities. Those small, medium and large capitalists of the countryside and the city can be obligated to obey this law without exception, in addition to submitting themselves to the Revolutionary Laws affecting agricultural, commercial, financial and industrial capital.

**Fifth:** The following percentages of taxes will be established, according to the work of each person:

**A:** For small commercial businesses, small property holders, workshops and small industries, 7% of their monthly income. In no way will their means of production be affected by the collection of this tax.

**B:** For professional people, 10% of their monthly income. In no way will materials strictly necessary for the exercising of their profession be affected.

**C:** For medium-size property-holders, 15% of their monthly income. Their property will be affected according to the respective Revolutionary Laws of agricultural, commercial, financial and industrial capital.

**D:** For large capitalists, 20% of their monthly income. Their property will be affected according to the respective Revolutionary Laws of agricultural, commercial, financial and industrial capital.

**Sixth:** All of the goods seized from the armed forces of the enemy will be property of the EZLN.

**Seventh:** All of the goods recuperated by the revolution from the hands of the oppressor government will be the property of the revolutionary government according to the laws of the revolutionary government.

**Eighth:** All taxes and burdens imposed by the oppressor government will be ignored, such as those debts of money or goods that the exploited people of the country and the city find themselves obligated to pay by those governing or by capitalists.

**Ninth:** All of the war taxes recovered by the revolutionary armed forces or by the organized people will become the collective property of the respective populations, and will be administered according to the popular will by the democratically elected civil authorities, giving to the EZLN only what is necessary to contribute to the material necessities of the regular troops, and for the continuation of the liberatory movement according to the Law of Rights and Obligations of Peoples in Struggle.

**Tenth:** No civil or military authority, whether it be of the oppressor government or of the revolutionary forces, will take for personal or family benefit any part of these war taxes.

## Law of Rights and Obligations of the Revolutionary Armed Forces

The revolutionary armed forces of the EZLN, in their struggle against the oppressor government and the great national and foreign exploiters, and in its liberatory advance over the Mexican territory, commit themselves to the carrying out and enforcement of the following Law of Rights and Obligations of the Revolutionary Armed Forces:

**First:** The revolutionary troops of the EZLN in their combat against the oppressor will have the following rights:

A: The troops that pass through a village will have the right to receive from the people, through the democratically elected civil authorities, lodging, food and the means to accomplish their military missions, according to the means of the inhabitants.

B: The troops that, by orders of the respective commands, are garrisoned in a place, will have the right to receive lodging, food, and means according to what is established in section (A) of this article.

C: The leaders, officials or soldiers who observe that some authority does not fulfill what is established by the Revolutionary Laws, and lack popular approval, will have the right to denounce this authority to the revolutionary government.

**Second:** The revolutionary troops of the EZLN, in their combat against the oppressor, have the following obligations:

A: To make sure that those peoples who have not named, freely and democratically, their authorities, proceed immediately to free elections of the same, without the intervention of the armed forces, which under the responsibility of their military orders, will let the population work without any pressure whatsoever.

B: To respect the civil authorities elected freely and democratically.

C: To not intervene in civil matters, and to let the civil authorities work freely on these matters.

D: To respect legal commerce that obeys the respective Revolutionary Laws.

E: To respect the agricultural redistribution carried out by the revolutionary government.

F: To respect the rules, customs and agreements of the people and to submit themselves to them in cases of civil-military relations.

**G:** To charge no taxes to the population, in no way and under no pretext, for the use of its land and waters.

**H:** To not take over, for personal use, the lands of the people, or of the estates taken away from the oppressor.

**I:** To obey all of the laws and rules issued by the revolutionary government.

**J:** To not demand personal services or works of personal benefit from the civilian population.

**K:** To report those subordinates who commit any crime, imprison them, and remit them to a revolutionary military tribunal, so that they may receive their deserved punishment.

**L:** To respect civil justice.

**M:** The leaders and officials will be responsible before the respective Commands for the abuses or crimes of subordinates who are not remitted to revolutionary military tribunals.

**N:** To dedicate yourselves to making war against the enemy until they are definitively removed from the territory in question or are annihilated.

# TESTIMONIES OF THE FIRST DAY

*[The following are excerpted transcriptions that were published in* La Jornada. *They were recorded in San Cristóbal de las Casas just after the EZLN liberated the city on January 1, 1994, and the transcription was published in* La Jornada *on January 19. They begin with Subcommander Marcos answering questions after reading the Declaration of War from the balcony of the Municipal Presidential Palace.]*

[*La Jornada,* 1/19]

*Q: Have there been any losses?*

**Marcos:** No. Neither ours nor the enemy's. Only in Ocosingo. There were two dead and two wounded and four prisoners on their side.

*Q: The military zone is here, less than 12 kilometers away. They have not responded?*

**M:** You have to take into account that it is a difficult situation, because this is the command of the 31st Military Zone. And they attack the back and three fronts. It is not as though you say, OK, now I will come and finish with San Cristóbal.

*Q: Why are some of you masked and others are not, although you are all from the same movement?*

**M:** Those of us who are more handsome always have to protect ourselves... What is happening is that, in this case, the officers are those who are masked, for two reasons. One, the primary one, is that we have to watch out for protagonism, in other words, that people do not promote themselves too much.

The mask is so that there is no protagonism, if you understand me, that we sometimes have a lot of, those of us who get into this business of appearing a lot. So now, since it is not well known who is who, probably in a little while another will come out, or it could be the same one. It is about being anonymous, not because we fear for ourselves, but rather so that they cannot corrupt us; for that reason some wear ski masks, so that they will not appear often and say, "What about me over here?" We know that our leadership is collective and that we have to submit to them. Even though you happen to be listening to me here now because I am here, but in other places others, masked in the same way, are talking. This masked person today is called Marcos here and tomorrow will be called Pedro in Margaritas or Josué in Ocosingo or Alfredo in Altamirano or whatever he is called.

Finally, the one who speaks is a more collective heart, not a *caudillo*. That is what I want you to understand, not a *caudillo* in the old style, in that image. The only image that you will have is that those who make this happen are masked, then. And the time will come when the people will realize that it is enough to have dignity and put on a mask and say: Well then, I can do this too, and OK, I do not need to be of a particular physique. That is the truth, and for that reason, you should not believe what I said when I said I was very handsome. I am doing propaganda for myself.

*Q: And women are in this movement voluntarily?*

**M:** Did someone obligate you to come? They are Tzotziles, Tzeltales, Tojolabales— Indians.

*Q: What is the average age?*

**M:** A scandalous 22 years old. It has gone up. When we started it was 16 years. Then, four years ago, it was 20, and now the average age is between 22 and 23 years old. There are people much younger than that, but the average of the troops is that. Those who have masks are officials or people that...

*Q: Command?*

**M:** No, that is what will not check out. You are going to check out all that you see with what you read. You will check Tupamaros, Montoneros, the Sandinista Front (Frente Sandinista), 26th of July Movement (Movimiento 26 de Julio), URNG. Nothing will check out. "They are a mess." "They are going to win." This is an organization that has been preparing itself for over 10 years without a single assault, robbery or kidnapping. "Where did they get money for what they did?" "Who protected them for so long?" They are going to say that we were part of the government. Today had to come so that we could demonstrate that we are not.

*Q: How many people make up the Zapatista Army... Can you tell us?*

**M:** I will tell you that there are thousands, and that they are all moved to take these actions.

*Q: Will there be more?*

**M:** Of course. After this, here, when we leave here, from these positions, when we advance, we are certain that more will join us. Three or four hours ago we received information that an element of the Federal Army deserted and joined our ranks. They have offered to show us the location of the barracks... No, he will not show us tactics. We know more than he.

Q: *Who was the source?*

M: The deserter from the Army who joined our ranks.

Q: *What assurances does the press have to enter into the zones?*

M: In our zones, with us, you will not have problems; but I am sure that the Army will not let information pass through. Or that your editorial boards or your bosses will not let you publish it.

Q: *Can you provide the resources of the City Hall for our work, what you have here, like the phone lines, fax?*

M: Go in and look for them if you like. Oh, you're asking... I was already up there looking for a telephone because I had to talk to Human Rights, to the National Commission. No, man, they have stolen everything. There are computers and all of that, we do not do anything with that... Yes, there is communication. The only thing I can guarantee is where we move, and if you present your newspaper credentials, they will let you pass.

Q: *Are you only here, in the state of Chiapas?*

M: No.

\* \* \* \* \*

M: [...] We hope that the people understand that the causes that have moved us to do this are just, and that the path that we have chosen is just one, not the only one. Nor do we think that it is the best of all paths. We only think that this is one that needs to be taken and we invite all of the people to do the same, not to rise up in arms, but to struggle for a truly free and democratic government in Mexico that can fulfill the aspirations of each and every person. We do not want a dictatorship of another kind, nor anything out of this world, not international Communism and all that. We want justice where there is now not even minimum subsistence. This is in the whole state of Chiapas. And one can say: Well, soon I am going to rise up in arms. No, but do demonstrate your agreement, each person where you work, students, teachers, and all of that, make count what they have denied us until now, which is the right to have an opinion, to feel, to dissent. That is what we want. We resorted to this because, well, because they did not leave us any other way, really.

Q: *Do you think the conditions are right to do what you are doing?*

M: Yes, we think that the time is ripe at an international level. We think that at the international level there is a sensibility for the Mexican people to rise up against a dictatorship of such long standing, in this case of a party, as it was in Europe. And at the national level, there is much discontent, but what was needed was for someone to give a lesson in dignity, and this fell to the most ancient inhabitants of this country that is now called Mexico, but when they were here it did not have a name, that name. It fell to the lowest citizens of this country to raise their heads, with dignity. And this should be a lesson for all. We cannot let ourselves be treated this way, and we have to try to construct a better world, a world truly for everyone, and not only for a few, as the current regime does. This is what we want. We do not want to monopolize the vanguard or say that we are the light, the only alternative, or stingily claim the qualification of revolutionary for one or another current. We say, look at what happened. That is what we had to do.

We have dignity, patriotism and we are demonstrating it. You should do the same, within your ideology, within your means, within your beliefs, and make your human condition count.

*Q: It is speculated that you are a member of some political party.*

M: Well, they have asked this question often, if we are a member of the PRD or of the PAN or some faction within the PRI that is against [then-Presidential-candidate Luis Donaldo] Colosio.

But the truth, we tell you sincerely, is that the political parties do not come to Indigenous people in Chiapas. They do not come and the people are tired of butting their heads against the wall. For that reason, we grew here, precisely because the political parties do not have consensus.

* * * * *

*Q: Don't you think that people are afraid of you?*

M: I think that they did not have bigger problems than us... Well, more than fear. That yes, but that we would rape and mutilate and all of that, no. But aside from that, I hope that the fear has gone. You should understand than any mess that we could have made here we would have done at dawn, when you were sleeping; that is, you should recognize that. You realized what was going on when the morning was quite advanced, when we were already here. You drank a toast to the new year and went to sleep, and we fell on you, but like a slap. I think that the force is not against everyone, quite the opposite.

*Q: Why did you pick those four towns, did you have that already planned?*

M: We have everything planned.

*Q: In the state [of Chiapas]?*

M: Comitán, Tuxtla, Palenque, Arteaga, Tapachula...

*Q: Not just four towns?*

M: Well wait, and we'll be right behind you. Everything is planned down to the hut of Tres Marías and the Cuernavaca-Mexico highway. And from there we have planned how to enter. Some say that we should stay and eat some quesadillas in Tres Marías... The plan is to go on to all of the towns. We will go on to all of the towns. The thing is that we are the majority. That is the truth. But we will try to follow the bosses of San Cristóbal and not cause any problems to the civil population and try to convince the Army to come over from the side of injustice.

The immediate objective is that our agricultural laws begin to operate in the liberated zones, that the campesinos organize themselves, taking land, respecting small rural property and working in collectives, ignoring all of the debts with the government. Banrural (Banco de Crédito Rural), all of the taken assets, all of that, we don't know anything about in the rural zone because where we move those laws will start to operate, that is, the old Constitution before they reformed it. That is the immediate plan that we have, that is, to organize the rural life of this country according to the will of the majority of our *compañeros*. That is, that there be land, because there is land, and that it be distributed, because they just said that they were not going to give any more out.

So before it was running around in Agrarian Reform, which they would probably give you. Well now, even if you run around, they won't give it to you. That is what Hank González and Salinas de Gortari said when they said: Land reform is over.

*Q: Listen, what about the stores?*

**M:** I said a little while ago up there that businesses will be permitted to open. We will not do anything to private commerce, only to the government. But everything, the mini-buses, the gas stations, we are not prohibiting them from opening. We guarantee them that we will not attack any store because the law about that says...

*Q: Could tomorrow be a normal day?*

**M:** Yes, let's see if you can live with that. In any case you will have to live always with that threat over your head, until the problem of social justice for these people is resolved, they will come back any moment. You were always scared of the black legend that we would kill you, rape you and mutilate you, and you saw that we didn't.

\* \* \* \* \*

*[In the tape a man can be heard who, with difficulty, reads a document.]*

I am going to communicate some of the decisions that our Clandestine Revolutionary Indigenous Committee, leadership of our revolution, has decreed today:

First: that the stores and businesses that belong to the oppressor government be opened so that the people of San Cristóbal can take from them what they need. Only the stores and businesses that belong to the federal and state government, nothing against local commerce.

Second decree: directed at the command of the 31st Military Zone with headquarters in Rancho Nuevo, of the federal government, to invite the body of officers, classes and troops to abandon the ranks of the evil government and pass, with all of their instruments and all of their experience, to the side of the struggle of the people. In case the garrison of the 31st Military Zone does not accept the abandonment of the cause of the evil government and embrace the cause of the people, then I am ordered to ask for the unconditional surrender of those barracks at the date and time that it be communicated appropriately. I make public, therefore, the offer for the 31st Military Zone and the battalions and units of the Federal Army to abandon the federal government and join our cause in one single army, respecting their ranks and their chain of command. [applause]

It has already been agreed and tomorrow a commission is ready to certify that we did not harm anyone: It will be allowed to leave on the side of Tuxtla. After this time [six in the morning] when the delegation is formed and can see that nothing happened to them, you will be able to leave the city on the side I already mentioned, and you will be able to come here for a safe conduct so that they will let you pass. We are speaking with the National Human Rights Commission so that there can be a representative of theirs on the other side to guarantee the passage of tourists without being harmed by the federal troops. This is a negotiation that we are doing. What we can guarantee is that when this delegation is formed, we will let them out. What happens beyond our lines? Go at your own risk. That's clear. Here they are fewer, but some people have approached us to ask how they can help us. I have told them clearly that what we hope is that they will understand the justice of our demands.

You may not agree with the path that we have chosen, but you have to understand that the conditions that brought us to this are very cruel and very desperate. If you can understand that, it is a great help to us. If you realize that we have done everything possible to respect your lives, your goods, because the problem is not with you, and if you can also take it into account, because right now the press and the propaganda are saying very much that we are raping, stealing, robbing gasoline stations, looting businesses and many things that you have seen with your own eyes, we have not done here in San Cristóbal. If anyone would like to go further [applause]... Also, here a person is telling me to make public the guarantees that we give to all civilians regardless of their political affiliation, nationality, race, or creed, that they will not be touched by our forces.

Whenever we can, what I want to say to people that want to go further, if you can give some food or money, it would be welcome. You know that we do not steal. Whoever wants to help us in something more material, they can give us that, food and money. If you cannot or do not want to, it is enough [to] understand why we did this. Then, we will be satisfied.

We will continue towards the regular troops of the Zapatista National Liberation Army and the orders that our leadership gives us to go where they direct us. Now they are sending us to Rancho Nuevo. Well, it will be there. If it is on the other side, then to the other side we'll go. But it should be clear that we are inviting the federal troops to come over to our side. That is all, if you have any question, that is all I can say. Don't worry about your goods or your persons. They will be respected, as will your liberty. In case of problems, we are not going to take hostages or take anyone by force with us to protect us. In the case that we have to leave, or that we have to fight, that is the guarantee, that we will not take civilians or hostages... [vigorous applause].

We will fight until the fall of the capital of the Republic. My *compañeros* have said it very clearly in their declaration of war, that their fundamental demands imply the creation of a transitional government that calls for elections, clean, real elections, and for that they are calling for the House of Deputies and the House of Senators to disregard and unseat the illegitimate president, Carlos Salinas de Gortari, and from among them a coalition government of various parties and people of known prestige; a transitional government that would call for clean elections so that the will of the people could win. That is what the *compañeros* explain. I was ready to talk with anyone but the only thing they have sent is airplanes. That should be clear: We have not denied the dialogue to anyone. There has been no attempt, other than that of the National Human Rights Commission, which did approach us to ask for the free passage of foreigners. All of us are Mexicans. The movement is national, and among our troops that fight here are people who have visited various states of the Republic but mainly the troops that are here are Chiapanecos and mainly Indigenous. We are not requiring the reaching of an accord as a condition for leaving San Cristóbal. We may leave even though there is no accord, according to orders that may tell us to leave and attack another place. We would have to march to other places. In this case Tuxtla, since if the order is that we have to go there, we have nothing to do here. What I want you to understand is our situation here. We have not prohibited any commerce, not the gas stations, not the bus stations, not the mini-buses, not that, nor have we prohibited the radio stations. The only thing we have prohibited is leaving the city because we cannot guarantee that the federal troops will respect you. As for the rest, we have not done anything but get things a bit dirty. That we have done, but we will try to fix that as well, very soon. So we advise with this, then, to the small and medium businesses, that they will not be touched, only the business that is of the federal and state government.

* * * * *

*[Marcos is speaking again.]*

M: Let me finish.

*Q: Wait a minute.*

M: Of course, finish.

*Q:* Compañeros *of Chiapas, Indians, permit me a minute, if you were brought tortillas, water,* pozolito, *would you accept it?*

M: Yes, of course. That is what we are eating. That is the situation. What has to continue is our advance to Mexico City. We started this very day. Today the North American Free Trade Agreement begins, which is nothing more than a death sentence to the Indigenous ethnicities of Mexico, who are perfectly dispensable in the modernization program of Salinas de Gortari. Then the *compañeros* decided to rise up on that same day to respond to the decree of death that the Free Trade Agreement gives them, with the decree of life that is given by rising up in arms to demand liberty and democracy, which will take them to the solution to their problems. This is the reason that we have risen up today. Any other questions, because they are going to cut me off?

*Q: We don't want free trade. What is happening?*

M: What I know is nothing more than you know. There were displays of adherence and sympathy in four or five states of the Republic, among them Veracruz, Oaxaca, Puebla and another state in the North that I can't remember. Our organization will also speak on a national level. A column was lost as they entered and then they went in there, they left to look, but we are not going to enter any civilian house. We did not do it when you were sleeping [applause], and won't now that you are awake. I think we did well, because you did not awaken until very late. [applause]

# 2. THE FIRST DAYS

## EARLY REPORTS

*[These are excerpts from some of the first newspaper reports about the uprising. These reports include interviews with officers and militants in the EZLN, as well as some reports of battles that occurred in the first days of January. These and other reports are what gave the Mexican public its first impressions of the EZLN.]*

## REPORT ABOUT EVENTS OF JANUARY 1, 1994

[*Macrópolis*, 1/10]
Roberto Carbajal, San Cristóbal de las Casas

From the top of the municipal presidential balcony, Commander Marcos proclaims with a vigorous shout: "Don't forget this: This is an ethnic movement!"

He bellows to his troops, the troops of the Zapatista National Liberation Army. They listen, undaunted, mute, still shocked by the presence of war in their always-tranquil streets, about 400 people congregated in the flower garden in front of the palace.

They are hearing, from the tall and strong man dressed in a uniform that combines red and black, that on this first day of 1994, Mexico is at war. Commander Marcos shouts:

"We have made a declaration of war to the Federal Army and to the government of Carlos Salinas de Gortari as a final measure, but only so that we will no longer die of hunger in the face of the insatiable dictatorship of over 70 years!"

He also shouts, almost furious, "We demand the restoration of the legality and the stability of the nation."[...]

The rebel accepts questions. His face is covered with a black ski mask. [...]

*"When did this start, when did this start?"*

"Man! Five hundred years ago! Was it not 500 years ago that our struggle against slavery started? We have been fighting five centuries for our independence, against North American expansionism, for the promulgation of our Constitution and against the French Empire... Later against the Porfirista dictatorship which provoked poor men like us to rise up in arms. And that is how our heroes of history came about: Villa, Zapata..."

*"Do you consider yourself a hero of modern times?"*

"I am only a mestizo; a man of the people who struggles so that these terrible inequalities will no longer be suffered in our country. I am a combatant."

*"Why? Why today?"*

"This is our response to the implementation of the North American Free Trade Agreement, because this represents a death sentence for all of the Indigenous ethnicities in Mexico, which are disposable for the government of Carlos Salinas de Gortari. [...]

"We decided to take four cities today because there are no conditions to effect free and democratic elections. In the Declaration of War we called on the powers of the union to make use of the constitutional right to depose the illegitimate government of Carlos Salinas de Gortari and to install a transitional government made up of people and political parties... And that it be this government that calls elections in equality of circumstances and not like those we have had, which have been illegitimate and unequal.

"You have to laugh about the reforms and counter reforms which the PRI and the PAN have designed in complicity. They do not allow any opposition political parties and much less civic movements. There is a lack of freedom and democracy... We do not even ask that a government of us be installed, but rather that it be a transitional one, with people more equalized. [...]

"And we will continue to advance to other plazas. The battle is not over today. We have orders to go as far as we can. When we have taken new plazas we will direct ourselves to others and so on successively..." [...]

One question bothers Commander Marcos: "Army or guerrilla?"

"Army, sir! Army! It is a trained army. For 10 years we have done political work, in a very slow and careful way. This is not a classic guerrilla army that robs, kidnaps or does spectacular strikes to later get the masses. We do not strike and retreat, but rather strike and advance. And our soldiers are prepared politically, and conscious that this is an ethnic movement."

### Ocosingo

They are about 800. They are armed with knives, ancient pistols, and some with modern AK-47's, the famous *cuernos de chivo*. [...] They live in the natural fear of those who will soon enter into battle. But they deny it: "No sir, we are combatants. And we are here to fight. If we die, we die for a just cause!" says Major Benjamin.

All of the officials of the EZLN appear to have one characteristic: they all cover their faces with ski masks. Not the troops...

72

And those troops speak with the reporter in a halting Spanish:

"Yes, sir. We's here in arms cuz they never resolve our problems. Look, sir: We have no house and work, or education. They never do us justice, sir, and many solicitations have been forgotten by the Secretariat of Agricultural Reform."

*"But they speak of the presence of Guatemalan and Salvadoran elements in your ranks..."*

"No, sir!" Juan Luis protests energetically. [...] "We are entirely Mexican, all of us, tired of promises and tricks, sir, of repression and the torture of our leaders, who they also assassinate. We struggle to bring the benefectivity of the Indian, sir."

Major Benjamin insists: "I am a campesino, sir, but I went through primary and two years of secondary school. I am with this Army because, like my *compañeros,* I am tired of the misery... I am tired of the rich; the hacienda owners of Chiapas have *guardias blancas* who repress the Indians, and that the government does nothing to them because they are rich." [...]

Major Benjamin says that soon the movement will be understood and supported by the people. "Right now they are just starting to get the idea."

*"With what political group do you identify?"*

"We are not Maoists or Marxists, sir. We are a group of campesinos, workers and students for whom the government has left no other path than arms to resolve our ancestral problems." [...]

### In the Lacandona Jungle outside of Ocosingo

In the Lacandona Jungle, 15 kilometers away from the war zone, speaking with Captain Roberto, commander of the forces in Ocosingo:

"Our organization was born after the massacre of students [1968]. First it constituted itself as a guerrilla group, and up there we walked, only in the mountains, without the support of the communities. In the towns they didn't give us anything. But then we did political work in the cities, directing ourselves to the masses, and then we achieved the support of many *compañeros,* above all campesinos. It was then, around 1983, that we formed the Army."

*"An army?"*

"Yes, we have ranks and military organization, like the Federal Army, but we are different, we are an army of the people, not of the bourgeoisie."

*"But that army that you fight is also made up of soldiers of the people."*

"Maybe, but supported by the bourgeoisie, by the dictatorship."

*"In any case, a powerful army."*

"That may also be true, but you know, we are stronger because we have a cause to fight for. And we can accept that there will be many injured and many dead among us, which in fact there already are. We can accept that they will occasionally defeat us, but we will never set down our arms. We will continue the revolution until we impose ourselves, arms in hand. That is our objective."

*"And then?"*

"After winning this war, which, you notice, is a clean war, an open and formal war, we do not want anything more than a change in government because this is a war for socialism. We want to end capitalism and institute socialism as they have done in many other countries."

*"And why socialism? It has been proven that it also produces great inequalities."*

"Yes, effectively, but Mexico is not the same as other countries. Its inhabitants are different, and here socialism will be successful. [...]"

"Because here, it has been proven, there is no democracy. And many people do not agree with the government and its system. NAFTA, the expropriation of petroleum... And, above all, I repeat, the farce of the elections: when there is a change of president, no one asks us if we are in agreement or not with the candidate. When we see the news on television or we hear the radio it is because the candidate is already there, without us being asked, and we already know that he will be the winner, even if he loses at the ballot boxes. Now there is Colosio, for example. But...did they ask the campesinos if we agreed that he be the one?"

He speaks proudly of the liberation of four cities...and introduces Captain Julio Alberto, known as the "ideologue" of the EZLN. He designed the first laws and plans of action, and it was his voice that was transmitted on Chiapaneco radio.

Captain Julio Alberto, also masked, explains the first seven laws of the EZLN:

Urban Reform: "The owners of apartments or homes will only pay housing taxes; residents for over 15 years will stop paying rent until the revolutionary government triumphs... The urban lots, public buildings and the great mansions will be used to build housing."

Labor: "Foreign companies will pay their workers, by the hour, the equivalent of what they would pay outside of the countries, and the salaries will be increased monthly according to percentages determined by commissions made up of residents, workers, students and freely and democratically elected authorities... The workers, in the country and in the city, will receive a share of stocks in the enterprises in which they work."

Industry and Commerce: "The prices of the products will be controlled by a commission. The increases in prices will not be more than the increases in pay... It will be treason against the country to hoard products, and the businesses that are declared non-productive will be taken over by the nation, by which we mean the machinery, the raw materials and their workers."

Justice: "All of the prisoners will be freed, with the exception of killers, rapists and heads of drug trafficking... All of the officials, from the president of the town to the president of the country, will be subject to hearings, and if they are guilty of embezzling, they will be sentenced."

Rights and Obligations of Peoples in Struggle: "They will be able to choose, freely and democratically, their officials, to demand general guarantees of the armed forces. In any case, that does not relate to any enemy of the revolution... They will be able to acquire arms to defend themselves, their families, and their property... The freely and democratically elected authorities will be able to imprison anyone they catch stealing, raiding, or committing any other crime, even if they are members of the revolutionary armed forces... They will be obliged to work in the mails, to take food and give lodging to the troops; to pay war taxes and carry out works of vigilance of the majority of the population... For their part the authorities will inform the civil population of their activities, as well as the origin and destination of the material and human resources under their administration."

Rights and Obligations of the Armed Forces: "They will respect legal commerce, carry out free and democratic elections, and will not intervene in civil matters... They will respect the agrarian redistribution decided by the revolutionary government, and will not take over the land of the large landholders for personal use, nor will they demand that the civilian population carry out work for them personally."

War taxes: "The small-business people will pay 10% of their monthly income; 15% for the medium property holders, and 20% for the large capitalists."

# INTERVIEW WITH MAJOR MARIO

[*La Jornada*, 1/3]
Rodolfo Reyes Ocosingo, Chiapas

"We have taken up arms because we are tired of the misery, because the rich, the large landholders of Chiapas, have *guardias blancas* that persecute the Indigenous people and the government does nothing because it is run by the rich."

Sheltered in a black ski mask, the face of a man can be made out, hardly 24 years old, full of confidence. The face is that of Major Mario, the commanding officer of the unit of the Zapatista National Liberation Army that took over Ocosingo at dawn yesterday. He gave this reporter a brief interview.

*"The people are aiding you?"*

"Right now, they hardly understand what's happening."

Constantly fiddling with his AK-47, one of the EZLN's few assault rifles, the Major asserts that "combat is a science that has a beginning and an end."

Just before the Federal Army retook this city of 110,000 inhabitants, the major confided that, "Our forces are perfectly trained for a confrontation with the Federal Army. Our Army is large, because it is made up of the exploited masses."

*"What is the EZLN's political affiliation?"*

"Look, we're neither Maoists nor Marxists. We are a group of campesinos, workers, and students for whom the government has left no path except armed struggle.

"The Zapatistas aren't only in Chiapas. We are also in other areas: the Clandestine Committee of Revolutionary Struggle (Comité Clandestino de Lucha Revolucionaria). We have guerrilla cells in strategic locations."

Furthermore, he said that since yesterday the EZLN had begun a strategy of defense and counterattack, "with which we will take other communities." (Hours later, almost 800 rebels would take the villages of Oxhuc and Huixtán.)

"Our Army is large, and little by little it will grow as we make our way toward the country's capital to unseat the government of Carlos Salinas de Gortari: This is our objective, to expand while other rebels, mostly adolescents and women, await instructions."

A few hours later, more than 800 rebels, many of them young women dressed in their gray uniforms with red bandannas around the neck, had a date with destiny: Armed with knifes, 20-year-old pistols and a few AK-47's, they were surrounded by the Federal Army in the market of Ocosingo.

# THE FIRST PACKET OF COMMUNIQUES

*[These are the first communiqués released by the EZLN; they were submitted as a group to the press on January 13 with the following letter from Subcommander Marcos.]*

## INTRODUCTORY LETTER FROM SUBCOMMANDER MARCOS

January 13, 1994

To the national newspaper *La Jornada*:
To the national newspaper *El Financiero*:
To the local San Cristóbal newspaper, *El Tiempo*:

Dear Gentlemen:

The CCRI-CG of the EZLN has produced a series of documents and communiqués that may be of interest to the national and international press. My *compañeros* of the CCRI-CG of the EZLN have asked me to find a way for these documents [of January 6, 11, 12, and 13] to reach their destinations and be made known to the public. For this we turn to you, to ask if it is possible for you, through your means, to put these documents into the public domain. These documents contain our position on the events that occurred between January 7-13, 1994. I clarify this because, to reach you, the documents packet must travel for days, crossing mountains and valleys and by-passing tanks, military vehicles, thousands of men dressed in olive-green uniforms, and all of the war arsenal with which they try to intimidate us. They forget that war is not a matter of weapons or a large number of armed men, but of politics. Anyway, the fact is that these documents and this letter will take a few days to reach you, that is, if they reach you.

We are fine, and in these documents we reiterate our disposition to dialogue to find a just solution to this conflict. At the same time, we are somewhat immobile as a result of all the military paraphernalia with which the government is trying to cover up the injustice and corruption that our actions have exposed. The peace which some now ask for has been a constant battle for us. It seems that Mexico's powerful men are bothered by the fact that Indians now go to die in the cities and stain their streets, which up till now were only littered with wrappers from imported products. They would rather they continue to die in the mountains, far from good consciences and tourists. It will not be like this any longer. The well-being of a few cannot be based on the suffering of the masses. Now they will have to share our luck, for better or for worse. They have had previous opportunities to turn around and do something about the nation's historic injustice against its original inhabitants, but they saw them as nothing more than anthropological objects, touristic curiosities, or part of a "jurassic park" (is that how you spell it?) that fortunately would disappear with a North American Free Trade Agreement that did not include them, except as disposable elements. Because in Mexico, death in the mountains still doesn't count. Everyone is guilty, from the highest-level federal functionaries to the last of the corrupt "Indigenous" leaders, and including a governor who was not elected by Chiapanecos according to their will and right, municipal presidents more concerned with ornamental works and strengthening relations with powerful men than with governing for their people, and officials on all levels, who deny the people who inhabited these lands even before they did, health, education, land, housing, services, just employment, food, justice, and most importantly, respect and dignity. They have forgotten that human dignity is not only the right of those who have their basic living conditions resolved, but also those who have no material belongings to differentiate themselves from things and animals: dignity. But it is just to recognize that in the middle of this sea of indifference there have been and are voices that have spoken about the misery that these injustices bring. Among these voices was and is that of honest journalism, which still exists locally and nationally. Actually, why do I bore you? It seems that you already have enough problems trying to convince the Federal Army to let you do your jobs. In sum, what we want is peace with dignity and justice.

Their tanks, planes, helicopters, and thousands of soldiers don't frighten us. The same injustices that they force upon us—no roads or basic services—are now being turned against them. We don't need roads, because we have always gotten around on footpaths. Not even with all their federal soldiers would they be able to close off all the paths that our misery once used, and that now are used by our rebellion. We also are not affected by the lies presented by television and in the press. Do they forget the illiteracy rate in the state of Chiapas? How many houses have no electricity and thus no televisions in these lands? If the nation falls for these lies again, there will always be at least one of us who is prepared to awaken them again. The Clandestine Revolutionary Indigenous Committees are indestructible. Since their formation they have had a command register. If one or several fall, another or several others will take their places and their future relief will sign up. They will have to annihilate all of us, absolutely every last one of us, in order to deter us militarily. And they will always be left with the doubt that they missed one of us, and that person will begin the rebellion all over again.

I will not distract you any more.

I hope that "Subcommander Marcos's half identification" did not harm "innocents" (the odds are two to one that with this "half identification" they will wind up detaining

Juan Diablós, star of the soap opera "Savage Heart" of the channel, "but of course," of the stars [Televisa]). One question: Will all this serve to teach "the Mexicans" to say "Chiapas" instead of "Chapas" and "Tzeltales" instead of "Setsales"?

Health and an embrace, if there is still a place and a way,

Insurgent Subcommander Marcos

## Concerning the Red Cross and the Press

January 5, 1994
Press Department of the EZLN

Red Cross:

A Red Cross ambulance was attacked with firearms and bazookas. This act of aggression has been attributed to our Zapatista forces. Because of this, we declare that at no time have we attacked in any manner the vehicles or people carrying the Red Cross insignia. Furthermore, we do not possess arms capable of causing the damage suffered by the Red Cross ambulance and its crew. We declare that this attack cannot be attributed to our troops, and we reiterate our respect for the life, well-being and work of the Red Cross. The weapons used in this attack should be looked for in the arsenal of the Federal Army, and not that of the EZLN.

Press:

On January 3, 1994 a caravan of press vehicles was attacked with firearms at El Aguaje, near the command of the 31st Military Zone in Rancho Nuevo. A reporter from the national daily *La Jornada* was wounded in this attack. Some sectors of the press have blamed our Zapatista forces for this sly attack. In response, we declare that at no time since this conflict began have we held a military position in the area of the attack. Before January 4, 1994, none of our troops had traveled or taken positions along the section of the road running from the Center for Ecological and Scientific Investigation (Centro de Investigación Ecológica y Científica, CIEC), in the outskirts of San Cristóbal de las Casas, to the barracks at Rancho Nuevo. For this reason, it is impossible that the shots were fired by Zapatista forces. As in the case of the Red Cross, these charges are the Federal Army's attempt to blame us for their aggression against the press and the Red Cross.

The case of the *El Tiempo* and *Excélsior:*

But in the case of the reporters of the San Cristóbal de las Casas daily *El Tiempo*, and the national magazine *Excélsior,* it is true that the reporters were detained by our troops in the municipal headquarters of Huixtán while said position was attacked by enemy forces. At no time were these members of the press attacked or tortured, and their papers were taken only to confirm their identities. Through a grave and regrettable error of the unit's command, N$700 (New Pesos) were taken from the reporters. Our EZLN asks forgiveness for this grave error committed against these members of the press, and offers to repay as quickly as possible the amount taken.

Attentively,
From somewhere in the mountains of the Mexican Southeast,
CCRI-CG of the EZLN

# Responses to Government Lies

January 6, 1994

*"Here we are, the always dead—dying again, but this time to live."*

To the people of Mexico:
To the peoples and governments of the world:

Brothers and Sisters:

As of January 1 of this year, our Zapatista troops began a series of politico-military actions with the principal objective of letting the Mexican people and the world know the miserable conditions that millions of Mexicans, especially we, the Indigenous people, live and die in. With these actions, we also let people know our decision to fight for our elementary rights in the only way that the governmental authorities have left us: armed struggle.

The grave conditions of poverty of our fellow citizens have a common cause: the lack of freedom and democracy. We believe that an authentic respect for freedom and the democratic will of the people are the indispensable prerequisites for the improvement of the economic and social conditions of the dispossessed of our country. For this reason, just as we demand the improvement of the living conditions of the Mexican people, we demand freedom and political democracy. To accomplish this, we call for the resignation of the illegitimate government of Carlos Salinas de Gortari, and for the formation of a new, democratic transitional government that would guarantee fair elections on all levels of government. We reiterate the strength of our political and economic demands—demands around which we are trying to unite all of the Mexican people and all independent organizations so that, by means of all different forms of struggle, a national revolutionary movement can form. This movement would include all the different forms of social organization that strive, with honesty and patriotism, for the improvement of Mexico.

Since the beginning of our war for liberation we have not only been subject to attacks by repressive government bodies and the Federal Army, but we have also been slandered by the federal and state governments and by the mass news media. They are trying to deceive the Mexican people and disparage our struggle by saying that our struggle is led by foreigners, professionals in violence, dark and anti-patriotic interests who only seek personal gain. Because of these slanders and lies, we, the EZLN, believe ourselves obliged to explain the following:

**First:** Our EZLN does not have foreigners in its ranks or among its leadership, nor has it ever received any support or training from revolutionary forces of other countries or from foreign governments. The reports that Guatemalans are fighting in our ranks, and that they were trained in the neighboring country are stories invented by the federal government to discredit our cause. We have not had, nor do we have now, any connection with the Salvadoran FMLN, nor with the Guatemalan URNG, nor with any other Latin American, European, African, Asiatic, or Oceanic armed movement. The military tactics that we employ were not learned from the Central American insurgency, but rather from Mexican military history: from Hidalgo, Morelos, Guerrero, Mina, from the resistance to the Yankee invasion in 1846-47, from the popular response to the French intervention, from the heroic exploits of Villa and Zapata, and from Indigenous resistance struggles throughout our country's history.

**Second:** The EZLN doesn't have any relations with Catholic religious authorities or with any other creed. We haven't received orientation, direction or support from any ecclesiastic structure, not from the diocese of the state of Chiapas, nor from the papal nuncio, nor from the Vatican, nor from anybody. The majority of the troops in our ranks are Catholics, but there are other creeds and religions.

**Third:** The commanders and troop elements of the EZLN are mostly Indians from Chiapas. This is so because the Indigenous people represent the poorest and most humiliated sector of Mexico, but also, as can be seen, the most dignified. We are thousands of armed Indigenous people, and behind us there are tens of thousands of our families. Therefore, there are tens of thousands of Indigenous people in struggle. The government says it is not an Indigenous uprising, but we believe that if thousands of Indigenous people rise up in arms, then yes, it is an Indigenous uprising. There are also in our movement Mexicans of other social origins and from other states of our country. They agree with us and have joined us because they do not agree with the exploitation that we suffer. Just as these non-Indigenous Mexicans have joined us, others will also join us—because our struggle is national, and is not limited only to the state of Chiapas. Currently, the political leadership of our struggle is totally Indigenous: 100% of the members of the Clandestine Revolutionary Indigenous Committees in the combat zones are ethnic Tzotzil, Tzeltal, Chol, Tojolobal and others. It's true that not all the Indigenous people of Chiapas are with us yet, because there are many people who still believe the government's lies and deceptions. But there are already thousands of us, and they must take us into account. The use of masks to hide our faces is in keeping with elemental security measures, and as a vaccine against *caudillismo.*

**Fourth:** Our people have a variety of weapons and equipment, and it should be understood that their total number and quality were not shown publicly to the mass media nor to the civilian populations in the municipal seats that we took over on the first and second of this month. These weapons and equipment were gathered little by little, and accumulated in silence over the last 10 years. The "sophisticated" means of communication that we possess can be bought in any imported-goods store in the country. To get weapons and equipment we never resorted to robbery, extortion, or kidnapping/hijacking; we always relied on what we were given by the humble and honest people throughout Mexico. It is because we never resorted to banditry that the forces of repression didn't detect us throughout 10 years of careful and serious preparation.

**Fifth:** Some have asked why we decided to begin now, since we have been preparing for some time. The answer is that before this we were trying other peaceful and legal means, but without result. During the last 10 years over 150,000 of our Indigenous brothers have died from curable illnesses. The social and economic plans of the municipal, state and federal governments don't offer any real solutions to our problems, and are limited to giving us handouts when there are elections; but the handouts are temporary, and then death comes again to our houses. Because of this we say that we have had enough—that we have had enough of dying a useless death, and that it is better to fight for change. If we die now it will no longer be in shame but with dignity, like our ancestors. Another 150,000 are prepared to die if necessary to wake our people up from the deceptive dream that binds them.

**Sixth:** The conditions of "reconciliation" that the federal government is trying to impose on us are unacceptable to our organization. We won't lay down our arms until they meet the demands that we set out at the beginning of our struggle. On the other hand, we propose the following conditions for the initiation of dialogue:

A: Recognition of the EZLN as a belligerent force.

B: Cease-fire on both sides in the war territories.

C: Withdrawal of federal troops from all communities, with full respect for the human rights of the rural population. Withdrawal of federal troops to their respective barracks in various parts of the country.

D: An end to the indiscriminate bombing of rural populations.

E: Using the last three conditions as a base, the formation of a national intermediary commission.

Our troops are committed to respecting these conditions if the federal government does the same. Otherwise, our troops will continue to advance on the country's capital.

The EZLN reiterates that we will continue to adhere to the laws of war approved by the Geneva Conventions: to respect the civilian population, the Red Cross, the press, the wounded, and enemy troops who surrender to our troops without fighting our forces.

We're making a special call to the North American people and government. To the first, we call upon them to initiate actions in solidarity with our fellow citizens. We call upon the North American government to suspend all military and economic aid to the dictatorial government which doesn't respect human rights, because said aid will be used to massacre the Mexican people.

Mexicans:

The military result of the fighting up to January 5 has had the following results:

1: Casualties of the Zapatista forces: nine dead and 20 seriously wounded who are being attended in our field hospitals. An undetermined number of slightly wounded that were reintegrated into their combat posts, and 12 missing in action. We haven't included in this total our combatants who, wounded, were killed in cold blood, shot from behind by officers of the Federal Army. We have not determined yet the number of these *compañeros,* since our troops are still fighting in Ocosingo.

2: Casualties of the enemy forces (including police and federal soldiers): 27 dead, 40 wounded and 180 prisoners who surrendered to our troops and were then released in good condition. There are at least another unconfirmed 30 federal troops dead. These casualties, along with an undetermined number of wounded, occurred January 4, in the mountains south of San Cristóbal de las Casas, when bombs dropped by the Mexican Federal Army (Fuerzas Armadas Mexicanas, FAM) fell on the trucks of federal soldiers who were maneuvering in that zone.

3: Enemy war material destroyed or damaged: three attack helicopters of FAM (one in the capital Ocosingo and two in San Cristóbal de las Casas), three FAM rockets, 15 radio patrols, four state Judicial Police torture centers.

4: Liberated prisoners: 230 from attacks on four prisons (two in San Cristóbal de las Casas, one in Ocosingo, one in Margaritas).

5: War materials captured: approximately 207 weapons of different calibers, M-16, G-3, M-2, grenade launchers, rifles, and pistols, and an undetermined amount of ammunition of various calibers; 1,266 kilograms of dynamite; 10,000 TNT detonators; 20 transport vehicles. An undetermined amount of radio communications equipment used by the police, Army and Air Force.

To the national and international press:

We call the attention of the honest national and international press to the genocide being conducted by the federal military forces in the municipal seats of San Cristóbal de las Casas, Ocosingo, Altamirano, and Margaritas, as well as on the roads bordering those points. In these places civilians were killed indiscriminately and later presented as casualties of the EZLN. Some of the Zapatistas that the Federal Army claims to have killed are in perfect health. The behavior of the federal troops in these cities contrasts with that of our forces, who are always concerned, as civilians in these cities can testify, with protecting innocent lives. The majority of the destruction to public and private buildings that is attributed to our troops was caused by federal troops when they entered the four principal townships.

To the Federal Army:

The present conflict unmasks, once more, the nature of the Federal Army, and it shows its true essence: the indiscriminate repression, the violation of all human rights and the lack of ethics and military honor. The murders of women and children committed by the Army in the area of conflict show an army out of control. We are calling on officers and troops of the Army to refuse to carry out orders handed down to them by their superiors to exterminate civilians or summarily execute prisoners of war and wounded, and to maintain military honor and ethics. We reiterate our invitation to you to abandon the ranks of the oppressive government and to join the just cause of the people—a people that, as you yourselves have proven, only longs to live with justice or die with dignity. We have respected the lives of soldiers and police who have surrendered to our forces. You take pleasure in summarily executing Zapatistas who you find wounded, unable to fight, and those who surrender. If you begin to attack our families and don't respect the lives of prisoners and the wounded, then we will do the same.

To the Mexican people:

Finally, we call on workers, poor campesinos, teachers, students, progressive and honest intellectuals, housewives and professionals, and to all independent political and economic organizations to join our struggle and to struggle with all possible means until we achieve the justice and freedom that all Mexicans desperately want.

We will not hand over our arms! We want justice, not forgiveness or handouts!

From the Mountains of the Mexican Southeast,
CCRI-CG of the EZLN

## A LETTER TO RIGOBERTA MENCHÚ

[*La Jornada*, 1/6]

Highly Esteemed Rigoberta Menchú:

In light of the recent developments that spread through our aching country—expropriated for the personal benefit of a few families, protected by an anti-popular and illegitimate government, against whom the poor campesinos of Mexico have said ENOUGH!—we want to communicate the following to you.

We are admirers of your struggle for Indigenous peoples over so many years; for that very reason you have been received and protected in our country—due mainly to pressure from several sectors of our people in Chiapas and in other parts of the country, as well as from poor campesinos, intellectuals, and several popular organizations, pressure exercised against a State that opted to receive the [Guatemalan] refugees and take advantage of the opportunity to transmit to the world an image of humanism and political openness—while it does not apply these same qualities to its relations with our own poor and exploited people, who suffer from the same genocidal and exclusive politics towards Indigenous peoples that is found in several Latin American governments.

For decades we have shared the little that we have with our refugee brothers and sisters. No one knows better than us their poverty and their desire for a dignified life, denied them in their home country. Of course, we are not those who impede or force the return of all of these brothers and sisters to their homelands. It also should not surprise us that it may no longer be important to the Mexican State that they keep that image of protector of refugees, in their desire to carry their repressive politics to all of the fields of Chiapas and Mexico. Don't be surprised if they even withdraw support and start to repress, accusing the refugees of being allies of and participants in our struggle, an irresponsible story which has already circulated among the authorities, who are always ready to look for enemies. They will find, however, only a dignified response to hunger and oppression. But our struggle will not be the cause of the worsening situation, nor will it impede our refugee brothers and sisters from returning to their lands. Both of these will be results of the repressive nature of the Mexican government.

What no one can forget is that the history of Mexico already contains a popular revolution to unseat dictatorships that had nothing to do with the interests and desires of our people. It is precisely because of that revolution that we have our Constitution, with, among others, Article 39, in which the people have, at all times, the inalienable right to alter or modify the form of their government. For this same reason we call on the powers of the union to carry out their political work in a responsible way, responding to this petition of the people, whom they have an obligation to serve. As long as they do not fulfill the Constitution, and legislate the way in which Article 39 can be applied, we have no other way out than to let our weapons speak for us.

That is all for the moment. We hope that you see our struggle as nothing more than the desire of leaving 500 years of misery and oppression, a vision which we hope you take into account and defend in the various international forums. We repeat our respect for so many of our refugee brothers and sisters, as well as for the work that you carry out.

Attentively,
Zapatista National Liberation Army

## ON THE PFCRN, GOVERNMENT TERRORISM AND THE APPOINTMENT OF CAMACHO

January 11, 1994

*"Our voice began to sound centuries ago, and it will never again be silenced."*

To the Mexican people:
To the people and governments of the world:

Brothers and Sisters:

We have been informed that our communiqué dated January 6, 1994 has been distributed, to some extent, to the Mexican and international press. Much has happened between January 6 and today, January 11, so we wish to speak our words again so that others might hear.

**First:** One of the things that has happened is that Aguilar Talamantes, national presidential candidate from the Party of the Cardenista Front for National Reconstruction (Partido del Frente Cardenista de Reconstrucción Nacional, PFCRN), in a public declaration in San Cristóbal de las Casas offered his party as "the peaceful arm" of the Zapatista National Liberation Army. He himself, Aguilar Talamantes, offered to be "the EZLN candidate for President of the Republic." We, the members of the Clandestine Revolutionary Indigenous Committee-General Command of the EZLN, have analyzed these declarations, and thought it would be best to respond in our own words, and so we say the following:

The Zapatista National Liberation Army did not rise up in arms to support one or another of the candidates for president of the republic. The EZLN does not want one party or another to win. The EZLN wants there to be freedom, justice, and democracy, so that the people can elect whomever they think best suited, and that their will, whatever it is, be respected and understood by all Mexicans and all people. The Zapatista National Liberation Army asks that the government, of whatever party, be a legitimate government, the result of a truly free and democratic election, and that it meet the most pressing needs of the Mexican people, especially ours, the Indians'.

The Zapatista National Liberation Army respectfully rejects the proposals of the Party of the Cardenista Front of National Reconstruction to present itself as "the peaceful arm of the EZLN," and that of Mr. Aguilar Talamantes to be the candidate of the EZLN for president of the republic. We say also, once and for all, that we reject any proposals to take our voice and our words. Our voice began to sound centuries ago, and will never again be silenced.

On the other hand, we greet and receive well all honest, good-faith proposals and offers of mediation between the EZLN and the federal government.

**Second:** The federal government has responded to our calls for dialogue and a bilateral cease-fire by bombing rural communities in the townships of Ocosingo, Las Margaritas, and Altamirano.

The belief, in some sectors of the government, that a military solution to this conflict, with the complete extermination of our EZLN forces, is both possible and desirable, is gaining ground within the government. We reiterate our willingness to dialogue, with the conditions laid down in the January 6 communiqué.

But it appears that this willingness to dialogue has been misinterpreted by the government military authorities as a sign of the weakness of our forces. Nothing could be further from the truth: To proposals for dialogue we respond with a willingness to dialogue, to attacks and indiscriminate bombings we will respond with our rifles. If the government wishes to continue deceiving the public, claiming that our defeat and annihilation are near, that is the government's business. The government has already lied, and everybody pays the price of that deception. But we know that our struggle will never be over. It will continue with the last drop of our combatants' blood. If the federal government wishes to cover our demands for justice, freedom, and democracy with blood, we will not hesitate to pay the price.

If the federal government does not demonstrate a desire for dialogue that is more than empty rhetoric, we will order all our active and reserve forces to attack every city within their reach. We realize the costs will likely be high, but we continue proudly on this path.

**Third:** In the past days we have heard of terrorist attacks against civilian targets in various parts of the country. Said attacks are attributed to members of our EZLN. The CCRI-CG of the EZLN declares that Zapatista troops fight against the Federal Army and police and not against the parking structures of commercial centers. No civilian targets will suffer military attacks at the hands of Zapatista troops.

**Fourth:** On January 10, 1994, the federal government announced changes in the office of the Secretary of Government, as well as other areas. It was announced that ex-governor of Chiapas Patrocinio González Blanco Garrido will no longer serve as Attorney General (Procurador General). Manuel Camacho Solís was appointed to head a peace commission to resolve the conflict in Chiapas. The EZLN declares that it is not familiar with Camacho Solís, but if in this man there is the honest and truthful desire to find a just and political way out, we salute his appointment and reiterate our willingness to dialogue under the terms expressed in the January 6, 1994 communiqué.

**Fifth:** The Clandestine Revolutionary Indigenous Committee-General Command of the Zapatista National Liberation Army declares that the only valid documents published by the EZLN and recognized by all EZLN combatants will be those signed by *compañero* Insurgent Subcommander Marcos.

From the mountains of the Mexican Southeast,
CCRI-CG of the EZLN

## Conditions for the Cease-Fire

January 12, 1994

*"Hope lives in our heart."*

To the Mexican people:
To the people and governments of the world:

Brothers and Sisters:

Today, January 12, 1994, we learned that Mr. Carlos Salinas de Gortari, as supreme commander of the Federal Army, ordered federal troops to cease fire. The National Secretariat of Defense (La Secretaría de la Defensa Nacional, Sedena) added that they would continue with the aerial and land patrols, would not abandon the positions that they presently occupy, and that they would impede the movement of our combatants.

The Clandestine Revolutionary Indigenous Committee-General Command of the Zapatista National Liberation Army welcomes Mr. Salinas de Gortari's decision, and sees it as a first step towards initiating a dialogue between the belligerent parties.

The conditions set forth by this Clandestine Revolutionary Indigenous Committee-General Command of the EZLN in their January 6, 1994 communiqué as requirements for initiating dialogue have not been adequately met. Nevertheless, Carlos Salinas de Gortari's decision is a beginning.

With regard to the above, the Clandestine Revolutionary Indigenous Committee-General Command of the Zapatista National Liberation Army, the collective and highest of the insurgent Zapatista troops, orders:

**First:** All regular, irregular, and urban command units of the different branches and services of the Zapatista National Liberation Army are ordered to suspend all offensive operations against federal troops from the garrisons and positions that these troops presently occupy.

**Second:** All regular, irregular, and urban command units of the different branches and services of the Zapatista National Liberation Army are ordered to maintain the positions they currently occupy and respond decisively and firmly if attacked by land or air troops of the Federal Army.

**Third:** The order for an EZLN offensive cease-fire will be put into effect immediately upon receipt of this communiqué, and will be maintained as long as this Clandestine Revolutionary Indigenous Committee-General Command of the EZLN considers it prudent and necessary.

**Fourth:** We will under no circumstances hand over our arms or surrender our forces to the evil government. The objective of this cease-fire is to alleviate the civilian population's situation in the combat zone, and to open channels for dialogue with all progressive and democratic sectors in Mexico.

Our struggle is just and true. It is not in response to personal interests but to the desire for freedom of the entire Mexican population, and particularly of the Indigenous people. We want justice and will proceed forward because hope also lives in our hearts.

From the mountains of the Mexican Southeast,
CCRI-CG of the EZLN

# On Requirements for the Commission for Mediation

January 12, 1994

*"We want peace with justice, respect, and dignity. We will no longer live on our knees."*

To the Mexican People:
To the people and governments of the world:

Brothers and Sisters:

In the last few days there have been several pronouncements about who should make up the Commission for Mediation to reach a political solution to the present conflict in the Mexican Southeast. One supposed communiqué, published in the national paper *La Jornada*, and incorrectly attributed to the EZLN, proposed as intermediaries the Bishop of Chiapas, Samuel Ruiz García, the Indigenous Guatemalan woman and Nobel Peace Prize winner Rigoberta Menchú, and journalist Julio Scherer, director of the magazine *Proceso*. Other voices and proposals have been heard, but up to this moment we have not given our opinion. For this reason we think that it is time that we give our thoughts on the subject:

The members of the Commission for Negotiation must fulfill the following requirements to be accepted as such by the CCRI-CG of the EZLN:

**First:** They must be Mexicans by birth. We require this because we believe that problems among Mexicans should be solved by Mexicans without any foreign intervention, even if these foreigners are upright and honest men and women.

**Second:** They must not belong to any political party. We don't want our just struggle to be used by one party or another to obtain electoral benefits, nor do we want the heart that animates our cause to be misinterpreted.

**Third:** They must maintain a neutral public position in regard to the present conflict. They should not be in favor of the EZLN, or of the federal government, and they cannot be part of the organizing structures of either.

**Fourth:** They must be sensitive to the serious social problems afflicting our country, and especially the difficult conditions under which the Indigenous people of Mexico suffer.

**Fifth:** They must be publicly recognized for their honesty and patriotism.

**Sixth:** They must publicly promise to put all their efforts into finding a dignified political solution to the armed conflict.

**Seventh:** They should form the Commission for National Mediation to mediate between the government and the EZLN.

The Clandestine Revolutionary Indigenous Committee-General Command of the EZLN believes that Don Samuel Ruiz García, Bishop of the Diocese of San Cristóbal de las Casas, meets the abovementioned requirements, and we formally invite him to participate, as a patriotic Mexican and not as a religious authority, since this is not a religious problem, in the future Commission for National Mediation. The Clandestine Revolutionary Indigenous Committee-General Command of the EZLN asks Mexican society to propose its best men and women for the formation of this Commission, whose principal mission is to find a political solution to the conflict. If these men and women fulfill the previously mentioned requirements, the EZLN will welcome their membership in the Commission, and listen carefully and respectfully to their voices and hearts.

From the mountains of the Mexican Southeast,
CCRI-CG of the EZLN

# ON THE GOVERNMENT'S VIOLATION OF THE CEASE-FIRE

January 13, 1994

*"Lies come from the mouths of the powerful."*

To the Mexican people:
To the people and governments of the world:

Brothers and Sisters:

Today, January 13, 1994, at approximately 1:30 p.m., federal troops violated the cease-fire ordered by the federal executive, Carlos Salinas de Gortari, when they attacked a Zapatista unit at a site near the community of Carmen Pataté in the township of Ocosingo, Chiapas. Federal troops, transported in 10 Army vehicles, with support from artillery, helicopters, and airplanes, tried to penetrate our positions and were fought off by Zapatista gunfire. Federal troops began to detain civilians from nearby communities with the intention of exercising reprisals or of presenting them as Zapatista prisoners, as they have done before.

In its communiqué yesterday, the General Command of the EZLN ordered Zapatistas to cease fire in response to Mr. Carlos Salinas de Gortari's order for federal troops to cease fire. In our communiqué yesterday, we ordered our troops to take no offensive actions and to only respond if attacked by the evil government's troops. This case of aggression on the part of federal troops makes the government's supposed will to seek a political solution to the conflict seem doubtful. The Zapatista National Liberation Army reiterates its willingness to dialogue, but it is not ready to be deceived. Either President Carlos Salinas de Gortari is lying or the Federal Army is not prepared to follow the orders of the federal executive.

The Clandestine Revolutionary Indigenous Committee-General Command of the EZLN calls to the Mexican people and the people and governments of the world. It will not allow itself to be taken advantage of by government declarations which, as today's events demonstrate, are nothing but lies.

From the mountains of the Mexican Southeast,
CCRI-CG of the EZLN

# ON US AID TO THE MEXICAN GOVERNMENT

January 13, 1994

To Mr. Bill Clinton, President of the United States of North America:
To the North American Congress:
To the people of the United States of North America:

Gentlemen:

We direct this letter to you to tell you that the Mexican federal government is using the economic and military support that it receives from the United States of North America to massacre Chiapaneco Indians. We would like to know whether the US Congress and the citizens of the United States of North America approved this military and economic support to combat drug trafficking or to assassinate Indigenous people in the Mexican Southeast. Troops, planes, helicopters, radar, communications equipment, arms and military gear are presently being used not to chase drug traffickers and the leaders of large drug cartels, but to repress the just struggle of the Mexican people and the Chiapaneco Indians, and to assassinate innocent men, women, and children.

We do not receive any help from foreign governments, persons, or organizations. We have nothing to do with drug trafficking or national and international terrorism. We organized ourselves from our own desire and life because of our tremendous problems and grievances. We are tired of so many years of abuse, lies, and death. It is our right to struggle for a life with dignity. We have at all times obeyed international laws on war respecting the civilian population.

With the support that the US government and people give to the federal government, they are staining their hands with Indigenous blood. Our longing is that of all the peoples of the world: true freedom and democracy. And we are prepared to give our lives for this desire. Don't stain your hands with our blood by making yourselves accomplices of the Mexican government.

From the Mountains of the Mexican Southeast,
CCRI-CG of the EZLN

# ON THE CAPTURE, CONDEMNATION, AND SENTENCING OF DIVISION GENERAL ABSALÓN CASTELLANOS DOMÍNGUEZ

[*La Jornada*]
January 13, 1994

Brothers and Sisters:

The Clandestine Revolutionary Indigenous Committee-General Command of the Zapatista National Liberation Army decrees the following conclusions of popular judgment against prisoner of war Absalón Castellanos Domínguez, division general in the Mexican Federal Army, accused of various injurious offenses to the Chiapaneco Indigenous population:

**First:** Division General Absalón Castellanos Domínguez was accused of having forced the Chiapaneco Indigenous population to rise up in arms against injustice, closing off all legal and peaceful means to achieve its just demands during the period in which he held the office of State Executive in Chiapas.

**Conclusion:** Division General Absalón Castellanos Domínguez, in complicity with the federal government during his state mandate, was found guilty of having compelled the Chiapaneco Indigenous people to rise up in arms, and of closing off any possibility of a peaceful solution to their problems. Patrocinio González Blanco Garrido and Elmar Setzer Marseille are accomplices of Division General Absalón Castellanos Domínguez in this crime, in that they followed him in office as state executive and, with the complicity of the federal government, continued forcing our people along this path.

**Second:** Division General Absalón Castellanos Domínguez was accused of having repressed, kidnapped, jailed, tortured, raped, and assassinated members of the Chiapaneco Indigenous populations who fought legally and peacefully for their just rights, before, during, and after the period in which he occupied the office of State Executive in Chiapas.

**Conclusion:** Division General Absalón Castellanos Domínguez, in complicity with the federal government during his state mandate, was found guilty of having repressed, kidnapped, jailed, tortured, raped, and assassinated members of the Chiapaneco Indigenous populations who legally and peacefully fought for their just rights.

**Third:** Division General Absalón Castellanos Domínguez, in complicity with the federal government, was accused of having dispossessed Chiapaneco Indigenous campesinos of their land before, during, and after the period in which he occupied the office of state Executive in Chiapas.

**Conclusion:** Division General Absalón Castellanos Domínguez, in complicity with the federal government before, during, and after his state mandate, was found guilty of having dispossessed Indigenous Chiapaneco campesinos of their lands and, in this way, making himself into one of the most powerful landowners in the state of Chiapas.

**Fourth:** After having deliberated over and analyzed all of the accusations against Division General Absalón Castellanos Domínguez, and having demonstrated his guilt, the Zapatista Justice Tribunal issues the following verdict and sentence:

Division General Absalón Castellanos Domínguez was found guilty of the crimes of violating Indigenous human rights, robbery, theft of land, kidnapping, corruption, and assassination. Without finding any extenuating circumstances in the commission of these crimes, the Zapatista Justice Tribunal issues the following sentence:

Division General Absalón Castellanos Domínguez is condemned to permanent imprisonment, and to doing manual work in an Indigenous community in Chiapas to earn his bread and the other things necessary for his subsistence.

**Fifth:** As a message to the people of Mexico and to the peoples and governments of the world, the Zapatista Justice Tribunal of the EZLN commutes the permanent imprisonment sentence of Division General Absalón Castellanos Domínguez, leaving him physically free and, in place of this sentence, condemns him to live until his final days with the embarrassment and shame of having received the forgiveness and goodness of those who, for so much time, he humiliated, kidnapped, robbed, dispossessed and assassinated.

**Sixth:** The Zapatista Justice Tribunal submits this resolution to the Clandestine Revolutionary Indigenous Committee-General Command of the Zapatista National

Liberation Army, so that they may take the pertinent and necessary actions related to the resolutions of this Zapatista Justice Tribunal; to this end, we recommend that the CCRI-CG propose to the federal government an exchange of Division General Absalón Castellanos Domínguez for the entirety of Zapatista combatants and civilians unjustly imprisoned by federal troops for the duration of our just war. We also offer to exchange the military man for food and other means of sustenance to alleviate the grave situation of the civilian population in the territories under EZLN control.

Dictated January 13, 1994, Chiapas, Mexico

Attentively,
From the mountains of the Mexican Southeast,
Zapatista Justice Tribunal,
Clandestine Revolutionary Indigenous Committee-General Command of the
     Zapatista National Liberation Army

# 3. The Cease-Fire

## Interviews With Officers and Militants

### Interview with Major Mario

[*La Jornada*, 1/16]
January 15, 1994
Ricardo Alemán Alemán, reporter, and Elio Henríquez,
correspondent, somewhere in the Lacandona Jungle

From the opening of a wool ski mask, a pair of brilliant black eyes sink in harshly on the reporters: "Let it be clear that we are respecting the cease-fire! We're not going to attack the federal government. We're going to respect their commitment, but if they come to bother us, we're going to respond," he nearly shouted.

His parents have been "*PRIistas* forever." He is between 23 and 26 years old, of Tzeltal origin, speaks Spanish with difficulty, and has "almost 10 years of political and ideological preparation." Major Mario of the Zapatista National Liberation Army received the reporters of *La Jornada*, to whom he said: "Very soon the Clandestine Indigenous Committee will respond to the government" on their proposals for dialogue.

Surrounded by 11 well-armed men—almost kids—Major Mario denied that the EZLN "seeks power." He explained: "We haven't proposed socialism," but said the Indigenous people and campesinos of Mexico "only want the fulfillment of the 10 points we have stated. We want democracy and elections without fraud, independence, land for all the campesinos, work, and housing. We want to have health care, justice, education—but not the kind to keep us stupid; that they stop killing the Indians, that they treat us like humans, that we eat not only *pozol*, but meat, like people elsewhere. These are very simple points," he explains vehemently in his rough Spanish.

The amiable Major Mario becomes indignant when he's asked about the presidential elections of 1994, the presidential candidates, and the validity of the electoral process.

"These elections will be illegitimate. The people vote very infrequently and have to be *PRIistas*. We aren't voting because all the candidates are the same. My brothers and sisters voted for the PRI and nothing happened, for the PAN and nothing happened, for the PRD and nothing happened. There are no results. There's no trust in anything. Now my brothers and sisters don't trust anything," he said in an agitated voice, with watery eyes, his index finger nearing the trigger of his AK-47.

After an 18-hour day, four of us on foot through the Lacandona Jungle, this paper's reporters neared an EZLN camp where a very young man, barely 25, gave us a warm welcome despite the cold and humidity of the forest.

"Kindly allow me to see your identification," said the youth, barely 5 feet tall, from an unidentifiable crack in the forest. He said that he was Major Mario, and he asked his superiors for authorization to see us.

Knowledgeable in handling arms, "ours and the enemy's," accomplished with the AK-47 rifle that he never stopped fondling, Mario jumped in without any preamble, leaving the reporters speechless. "What do you want to know?"

The reporters began a long interrogation in the forest highlands—we didn't know how we got there and had trouble getting out.

"We're not going to stop the war until there's a response to these 10 points. But I'll tell you, the war won't end soon. We're not going to give up our arms because we prefer to die fighting with dignity than to die of cholera, of measles, repressed by the landlords who treat us like pigs. We don't want crumbs; we want freedom, the right to express ourselves, to govern—for them to not send us to our deaths. We want democracy and real peace, like in other countries."

A member of an army "mainly of youth, with plenty of men and women," Mario explained that the Zapatista National Liberation Army "yes, is related" to the guerrilla movement in Ocosingo that was neutralized by the Mexican government in 1974. "Yes, we're from them. The examples remain, but there's no one here who was there then. The examples remain."

*"What caused this armed uprising?"*

"First, I want to point out that we haven't attacked the Federal Army; we are respecting the cease-fire, and they also have to respect it, as they promised. We haven't attacked the enemy, but if they come to attack us or bother our towns, we will respond, too. These are the orders we have now."

*"Have you also held the cease-fire?"*

"We have been respecting it for two days."

*"There haven't been any confrontations for two days?"*

"There have been. But it's the Army that isn't fulfilling what they said, and have come to attack us; we are only responding."

*"And has there been some meeting with Camacho Solís?"*

"At the moment, no. That will be decided by Subcommander Marcos."

*"Marcos is your main leader?"*

"Of the commanders, yes, but our orders come from the Clandestine Indigenous Committee."

*"In Mexico and abroad, they have tried to show that most of you are not Indigenous people and that there are foreigners [in your ranks]."*

"This is a lie. They accuse us of being foreigners, but not even the government knows us. We all speak Indigenous dialects and we are legitimate Mexicans and Chiapanecos; we all love our tricolor flag and our Mexican anthem."

*"And what about their saying that the priests and the Church were the ones who brought on this insurrection?"*

"No, it's clear that it's the people. If the people rise up, this isn't based in the Church, but in their own misery. We aren't religious, but we aren't against it either. We respect beliefs. Every one of us is struggling because of our poverty—Catholics, Protestants."

*"Do you recognize the Church or the Bishop of San Cristóbal, Samuel Ruiz, as an effective mediator to establish dialogue?"*

"Not according to what my other brothers and sisters are deciding. I tell you, there's a bunch of us; we're plenty and we're all over Chiapas."

*"Are you in other states?"*

"You'll see when the news comes out."

*"Is your intention to take power, or what is it concretely?"*

"No. Concretely, according to the Declaration of War, there are 10 simple points. We want land for all our poor brothers and sisters, our campesino brothers and sisters, because they don't have any. Look where they live—the best lands are occupied by the planters. We want them to have good jobs, but not only the campesinos here, because campesinos are ignored not only here, but throughout the Mexican Republic. My brothers and sisters here don't speak Spanish, and look at where they still are. We want them to have good housing; look what their houses are like, and where is the government aid? And the government wants to help us only when there's a confrontation. We would have wanted them to do this much earlier. Now they want to humiliate us like dogs, but this pains us as humans. For being Indigenous, they have cornered us in the wilds; we have no services, no education—only to keep us stupid. No, there's nothing, and if it's legal, we know that it's really for the landowners. The campesino makes a little move and they kill him. So the government, when there was no fighting, came to kill us, repress us, dislodge us, give us nothing and send us a few little things to shut us up. We aren't just anything; we're human beings, and they don't consider us people. We need work and land, and our campesinos and workers need to eat well. We all want to struggle so that we won't eat only *pozol*, because we want to eat meat like they do elsewhere. We don't have any, so we're fighting. We want democracy, for the people to freely choose, that they not carry out frauds and snares in the upcoming elections through force or money. We don't want this, nor do our ignored brothers and sisters. And they still tell us we're foreigners."

*"And how long will there be an armed uprising?"*

"Until they fulfill all of these 10 points, until they do all of this: bread, education, housing, health care, independence—so no one comes to kill us. Now they're coming to command everyone, and it isn't their country. We were born here, our grandparents died here, and they don't consider it ours. We will stop the war when all of this is done. We're not going to stop it now; we're not going to put down our arms."

*"And how long will the cease-fire last?"*

"This depends on what our leaders decide."

*"If they fulfill the 10 points you are asking, will you remain armed in the wilderness?"*

"It depends where we are, but our plan is not that our people only eat well, but that they not be controlled. We want to have freedom, the right to express ourselves, to lead, to have democracy, independence. We want peace, but not like before, when they treated us like pigs. We want there to be real peace like in other countries, that they consider us humans. We're not going to stop for crumbs."

*"Why did you take the name of Zapata?"*

"Because Zapata was a campesino leader and revolutionary. He loved us and wanted to give land to all, but it was taken away again by the bourgeoisie."

*"How many casualties have there been?"*

"Well, we have to clear up something, and I want to tell the truth, the whole truth. We confronted the enemy this time, but the enemy killed civilians while dressed as Zapatistas, accusing us of killing them, and that isn't true. It was they who killed many campesinos."

*"Were you in Ocosingo on January 1?"*

"Yes."

*"You led the fighting there?"*

"Yes. We attacked them; we ambushed them. And if there are many dead now, they died for their dignity, because they no longer wanted to be poor, because they no longer wanted to be humiliated. This is why we rose up and we're never going to give up our weapons."

*"Do you consider the withdrawal from Ocosingo a defeat?"*

"No, we withdrew to demonstrate to the enemy that they're not fighting drug traffickers or people who come to kill unarmed campesinos, as they think."

*"How did you get arms, and how is it that the federal troops didn't discover them for 10 years?"*

"We don't have support from abroad or anywhere else. We depend on our own strength. The Guatemalans haven't supported us."

*"Is Subcommander Marcos Mexican?"*

"Of course. He eats *tunas* and *nogales* [indigenous fruits]. It's not true that he's a foreigner," said the Tzeltal, laughing along with his 11 men.

*"Where did you get the weapons?"*

"The ones we have here, we have. I don't know where our leaders got them, but we're armed," he assured us. [...]

*"What do you feel about the Mexican soldiers? Is there any hatred or resentment?"*

"Yes, hatred exists, but mainly for their leaders, not for the plain soldier who comes from the class of the poor. And this seems to oblige us to struggle among ourselves, the poor," he said in a melancholic tone.

*"Why didn't you start the war before January 1, when they were discussing NAFTA?"*

"The Clandestine Indigenous Committee decided this, but I'll tell you straight out that the NAFTA will bring us poverty and the benefits will only be for the bourgeoisie. They already had screwed us enough, they had already destroyed Article 27, which Zapata won in the revolutionary struggle. Salinas de Gortari and his lackeys and his groups came and destroyed it in a minute. We and our families had already been sold out, or like they say, our pants were already sold. What could we do? There is no other remedy. We tried everything legal, we asked the government through elections and organizations and there was no result." [...]

*"How many people are members of the Clandestine Committee?"*

"There's a lot. It's a collective body that has to discuss how things are going," he says while gesticulating as if to show us the size of their Army with his arms.

*"What's the ideology of this committee and the Zapatista Army? Do they want socialism?"*

"They [the leaders of the EZLN] still have not considered socialism. What we want are the 10 points." And he repeats vehemently that they want democracy, clean elections, "education that doesn't make us stupid."

*"It's been said that you might have connections to people operating in Peru [Communist Party of Peru-Sendero Luminoso]."*

"No, this is untrue—pure ideology invented to scare the people."

*"Has there been any machine gun fire in the last two days?"*

"Yes, planes and helicopters have come firing and bombing to frighten the people," which agrees with the version in *La Jornada*, which reported on [the government's] non-compliance with the government-proposed cease-fire.

*"Will this war go on for a long time?"*

"Yes, until all the things we poor people are asking for are fulfilled."

*"Are you prepared to hold out? For how long?"*

"Until this is done."

*"Can you defeat the Amy?"*

"Yes, because war is long and hard. We don't want deaths, but it's necessary because we've suffered so much. Many here have died of cholera. We asked the government for aid and there isn't any. We prefer to die confronting bullets instead of cholera."

*"Did you carry out the attacks in Mexico City and elsewhere?"*

"No, we certainly know who is our enemy. We don't attack civilians because they are not responsible for the war. We aren't terrorists; we have rules for battle and we follow the Geneva Conventions."

*"You propose clean elections. Do you think that this year's will be legitimate?"*

"No, they're illegitimate. The people don't vote, and those few who do must be *PRIistas.*"

*"Which candidate would you vote for?"*

"We aren't voting for any candidate because they're all the same. My brothers and sisters have voted for the PRI, the PAN and for the PRD and nothing happened—there's no results and there's no faith in anything."

*"And what do you think of Samuel Ruiz?"*

"Well, he has a different job."

*"But do you see him as a supporter of your struggle?"*

"No, he's not supporting us."

*"Does someone support you?"*

"Only our own people. We count on them for what we have—beans, rice."

*"Can you tell us, Major Mario, if you're all young?"*

"The majority of us are young."

*"And are there women in the Zapatista Army?"*

"Many."

*"They say the commander herself is a woman."*

"No, no!"

*"What degree of preparation do the members of the Zapatista Army have?"*

"We don't have any preparation. Many of these people don't know how to read or write. All the government gives us is a third grade education—nothing more."

*"But haven't they fought? Weren't they in other countries?"*

"No, we have learned like Villa and Zapata; we learned to fight."

*"Apart from Zapata and Villa, is there any other Mexican figure with whom you identify?"*

"Yes, with Hidalgo and Morelos, priests who rose up with the Indians."

*"Have you read Marx and Mao?"*

"Yes, I've read them, but we're not Maoists."

*"Are you going to obstruct this year's elections?"*

"No, we're not going to obstruct them. We're going to keep fighting for the 10 points that we've demanded."

*"And why did you take San Cristóbal?"*

"Because we're angered by what's happening, we're upset by what they're doing. This is why there are dead among our troops. But we're not crying about it. On the contrary, they died for their dignity, they died like a human being should—so they wouldn't go to their grave in vain, dying of cholera or measles, like many have died here."

*"How old were you when you were invited to participate in forming this Army?"*

"Around 11."

*"How many weapons can you handle?"*

"I can handle the weapons brought by the enemy."

*"Do you have any kind of heavy weaponry?"*

"Yes, we do"

*"Can you tell us what kind?"*

"No."

With our discussion almost finished, Major Mario sent a message to the people of Mexico: "Don't fear the war. It's ours. We're fighting for all the campesinos, for all the Mexican people, so they can be free and not like they are."

# ELISA, LAURA, LEONEL AND A MILITIA MEMBER

[*La Jornada*,1/18]
January 19, 1994
Gaspar Morquecho, correspondent, in the mountains of Chiapas.

"When I lived in my house, with my family, I didn't know anything. I didn't know how to read, I didn't go to school. But when I joined the Zapatista National Liberation Army, I learned how to read, I learned all of the Spanish I know, how to write, and I was trained for war," affirmed Captain Elisa, one of the 12 women who, along with 100 other insurgents and armed militia members, received the national and foreign press in a wooded area.

To get to this place, we passed through three positions of the EZLN, which sent communications to the chiefs ahead. As we arrived at a small town, they told us that we would have to wait an hour and a half, since "some" members of the EZLN were coming to meet us; they asked us to not take photographs and to not film the town.

At about 2:30 p.m. on Tuesday, a member of the militia indicated that we could continue, and that they were waiting for us "further on." Two vehicles were in the opening, and we walked some 500 meters to the place where they were kept.

We spoke with Laura. She is Tzeltal, 21 years old, and for over three years has been the captain of an assault troop of the EZLN. She carried an R-10. "I was born in my town, grew up in my community, and I was able to study until the fourth grade; I was very small when I learned about the EZLN; I worked the land with the women that we joined with to produce food. That was where the conversation began, and we understood the misery and why we can't live better; there they recruited me. Study advisors came and we understood and advanced."

Laura was married on the mountain. She says that she does not have children so she can remain in the struggle, and that she uses birth control. Couples come together without any ceremony, and they only have to inform their commander, "so that all of the *compañeros* know what is going on."

"I began, out of conscience, to fight in favor of the poor, since it is not right that they keep killing the children. I participated in the combat at Ocosingo. When the enemy came, I felt brave, I wanted to kill someone, to shout with anger and hit them so that they would be humiliated as they have humiliated us for so long."

She explained that in the EZLN men and women fight equally. "We are in revolt and we don't have problems with the men. They treat us like *compañeras* and there is mutual respect from everyone. We share all of the work."

Leonel is 21 years old. We asked him why he joined the EZLN and he said: "The people are looking for their own organization, where they belong. I worked in San Cristóbal de las Casas as a plumber, a brick-laying peon: I looked at the work, and the pay didn't add up; it wasn't enough to live on. One time I came to my town for my papers to join the Federal Army. My family told me: It would be better for you to go join the EZLN.

"I said yes, and I went to the mountain with a guide from the town who was organizing with the Zapatista Army. There they treated me well, better than in my family. They started to talk about how 'here we are fighting because of poverty.' When I was there I quickly understood what the problem was like and that we had to take up arms."

Elisa has been in the mountains with the EZLN for six years. She is short, like the majority of Tzeltal Indians, and three years ago she married another insurgent.

Elisa remembers her life from when she was small. "I saw how my family lived, in utter poverty, and we organized ourselves to make war, to live better. We struggle for the 10 points: land, work, housing, dignified bread and education, freedom, democracy, peace, justice, and freedom.

"We want a better life and that is why I joined the EZLN. That is why. Because if the campesinos do not organize themselves, it will be very difficult for them to get anything. I want to tell people, the poor people of Mexico, that they should join the struggle, that they should help us. We are struggling for poor people, so that they can live better, that they should unite together to make war to live better."

The group agrees to carry out some exercises at the request of the television reporters and photographers. They quickly line up in ranks and stop in front of the underbrush, at the edge of a river. They receive the order to form ranks of three deep, move to the flanks, to the front and present arms. We see order and discipline.

The correspondent for *Libération*, Jean François Royer, notes that their arms are "very diverse and of varied origin, some old and reconstructed." He observes, "AR-15s, old AK-47s and Steins, which means that they have workshops and do good armory work. Their uniforms are of rudimentary manufacture, but they are well made. There are some Warsaw-pact tank shells." Royer, who has covered the wars in Central America—

mainly in El Salvador—commented that "their weaponry is quite inferior to that of the FMLN before the large offensive of '89."

From the moment we arrived in the zone, we insisted that we be allowed to spend the night in some of the towns, hoping for the possibility of interviewing a high commander.

Finally, at 6:30 p.m., we are given authorization to sleep in a town. The other reporters and photographers went to bed. The insurgents took off their masks and, with a group of three armed soldiers, we arrived in the town.

Our host had a party in his house: It was the "seating of the God Child." In a small, wooden room with a tiled roof there was an altar with the images of Saint Martin de Porres, Christ, and John the Baptist. They were adorned with colored, plastic flags and palm leaves. There is a candle lighting the room. A small wooden crib with a blue bandanna contained the nude God Child. The next day He was seated, dressed and covered with the bandanna.

This is like a movie, commented Royer: to be seated at a table, in front of an altar, with an armed force behind you, in an Indigenous town, eating beans, tamales, drinking chicken broth and coffee.

Outside, a marimba can be heard. It was about 7:30 p.m.; some candles were still lit, and young couples danced happily. The rain, which lasted all night, did not interrupt the procession, and the party ended at two in the morning. In the morning, we were brought hot coffee, and we were able to speak with the militia members.

These are people who offer support from the communities: They work in production and, "If it is necessary, they call us up. We can also go into combat, since we have about 15 days of training." Many members of the militia participated in the taking of various towns. There they were armed with sticks, or with nothing at all.

The testimony of a Tzeltal Indian who is not an insurgent or a militia member was the following: "I support them. I work on production, I help in carrying foodstuffs, and I want to go on to be a militia member."

"The communities send food to the EZLN on the mountain," a group of militia members explained to us. "This is not obligatory, but our children, our brothers and sisters, our flesh and blood are up there."

## CAPTAIN IRMA

[*La Jornada*, 1/27]
January 26, 1994
Oscar Camacho Guzmán, on assignment,
at an unknown location in the Lacandona Jungle, Chiapas

For the Zapatista National Liberation Army, during the 26 days of the current conflict in Chiapas, "the government has only made promises" that they are willing to resolve problems with the EZLN. The EZLN "will not set down our arms" until [the government] meets the 10 basic points of their struggle.

Captain Irma, an officer in the EZLN, affirms this when she receives [the reporters from] *La Jornada* in the Lacandona Jungle, and warns that as long as the government does not meet the 10 basic demands, the alternative will be to "win or die."

Captain Irma denounces, with irritation, the fact that the Mexican Army continues to fly over the region.

With respect to this she categorically affirms that "The EZLN will not violate the cease-fire, but if they attack us, we will respond."

In reference to Absalón Castellanos Domínguez, she explains that he is still alive, and that after the trial that he was submitted to by the EZLN Tribunal for Military Justice, "he maintains himself by eating beans or whatever there is, like the rest of us, and he is working also, like the rest of us."

Of the changes in the presidential cabinet, as well as in the government of Chiapas, she affirms that these are not determining factors in the resolution of the problems of the EZLN. She maintains that these were changes made under the same schema of designation, and not of democratic election.

She notes, for example, that the new head of Chiapas, Javier López Moreno, "was not elected by the people. He was designated by them [the government]."

The interview, solicited the day before, was given in the evening of this Wednesday, a little more than 24 hours since the Commissioner for Peace and Reconciliation, Manuel Camacho Solís, announced the government's peace proposal.

It is already the fourth week of the conflict. Captain Irma explains what the perception is in the EZLN about what the government has done to resolve the crisis.

"There have been no changes made by the government that will serve to resolve the problems of Chiapas. Until now, they have only made promises. They have not offered anything else."

*"What about the political changes, the changes in the government of Chiapas and the change of Patrocinio González in the Secretariat of Government? Aren't these important actions?"*

"No, because they have not been changes made by the people. It has not been the people who have chosen."

*"That means that, for you, the new governor of Chiapas is not the product of a democratic process?"*

"For us, no," Captain Irma responds, without hesitation.

*"What do you think of what Manuel Camacho Solís has done to bring peace to the state?"*

"We haven't seen him do anything that will improve the situation of Chiapas.

"We have 10 points and we still have them; that will not change until we have achieved them. There has been nothing about that. There has been no response to these 10 points. The government has not recognized them and so we think that they will not be met, even though they promise many things."

*"Do you need more actions than promises?"*

"Promises are all that we have seen until now."

*"What would you need so that the government could demonstrate interest, so that the peace talks could advance? That they begin actions around these 10 points, that they put in place a health system in the state, an agrarian reform...?"*

"The truth is that the government will not do anything. This is not the first time that we have asked. So many years have passed with us watching people die and the government not doing anything."

A group of Zapatistas accompanies Captain Irma, while the overflight of airplanes does not stop.

"Here comes the plane," Captain Irma indicates to her *compañeros*, and all of them hide in the brush. For a few minutes all that can be heard is the motor of the airplane and the sounds of the jungle.

"That is another thing that the government does not fulfill. They do not obey the truce, and have been sending airplanes. This means that for them, this thing has not stopped; on the other hand, we haven't been doing anything, but the government does not fulfill its promises. What are the military planes doing here? Every day they fly over. That is not respecting the cease-fire."

She is asked about the exodus of some of the communities of the highlands, and she is told that campesinos and Indians have complained that the EZLN pressured them to join the armed struggle.

"We are not fighting against the people. On the contrary, what we want to do is defend them. What we are asking for is for the people of the whole country, not just Chiapas.

"Those who are really of the people have no reason to be afraid of us, because we are not fighting against them, but so that they can live well, not like now."

*"Does the demand for the 10 points remain firm?"*

"It will continue until they have been achieved. We can only speak with our weapons, and we are not going to let them go until we get what we have asked for."

*"How can the situation improve, according to the EZLN?"*

"I cannot respond to that. Others of us need to answer that question."

*"How is Absalón Castellanos? There is talk of a trade..."*

"He is fine. We have not tortured anyone, because they are human beings like us, flesh and bones. Nevertheless, it seems like the government does not see it like that, and some of our detained comrades have not been treated like that.

"When they release those whom they have detained, we will let him go, in spite of the shame he has for having mistreated so many people, so many peoples. Anyway, he will be released, but in exchange for those that I talked about, our *compañeros* who they are torturing. His punishment is to work the same as anyone.

"But if he is released, they also have to release our *compañeros* and those who are probably not members of the EZLN. Absalón is fine, while our *compañeros,* we don't know how they have them, torturing them for sure."

*"Don't you feel you lose support here in the zone every time that some person says that they're leaving because they are being pressured?"*

"No, because we are not obligating anyone. Those who participate do so because of their own will, and because they know that it is their people."

*"Is there the possibility that the EZLN could meet with Salinas de Gortari?"*

"I cannot respond to that. Only the commanders can respond to that question."

*"Do you think that we are close to peace in Chiapas?"*

"I don't know, but the situation will last until we achieve what we came for. We are sure, and we are ready to win or die, if that is necessary."

*"What will happen if the Army breaks the truce?"*

"If they look for us, they will find us. We are respecting the truce, and as long as it lasts there will be no attack from us, because we respect what we say. But the government has not respected it, and if they look for us, we will respond," concludes Captain Irma there, someplace in the Lacandona Jungle, where the EZLN lives, supplies itself, governs and waits.

# SECOND COMMUNIQUÉ PACKET

*[This is the second group of communiqués that the EZLN released to the press. They were submitted as a group to the press, like the first communiqué packet.]*

## ON GOVERNMENT VIOLATIONS OF THE CEASE-FIRE

**January 17, 1994**

To the Mexican people:
To the people and governments of the world:

We are sending this message to the national and international press to denounce violations of the cease-fire by government troops. On January 16, 1994 at 11:30 a.m. approximately 35 military soldier-transport vehicles carrying 400 soldiers assaulted the municipal seat of Oxchuc and unjustly detained 12 civilians, accusing them of belonging to our EZLN. The CCRI-CG of the EZLN denounces the Federal Army for taking legal authority that does not belong to them, and for continuing to harass the civilian population. The Federal Army's predominant attitude with regard to the peaceful population constitutes a flagrant violation of the cease-fire ordered by the president on January 12, 1994.

On the night of January 16, 1994 bomber planes from the Mexican Air Force bombarded barracks near the town of Monte Líbano in the township of Ocosingo. Again, this violation of the cease-fire affects the civilian population. Our troops continue to follow the CCRI-CG of the EZLN's order to cease all offensive attacks against the Federal Army. We continue to be disposed to use dialogue as a means to find a just solution to the conflict. However, it is our duty to protect the civilian population in the conflict zone. For this reason we warn you that if the violations of the cease-fire continue, we may reconsider our decision to cease offensive attacks. We ask that the truce be carefully monitored by members of the federal government, because repeated violations will destroy the dialogue process, which is only just beginning.

From the mountains of the Mexican Southeast,
CCRI-CG of the EZLN

# LETTER ACCEPTING CAMACHO SOLÍS AS COMMISSIONER FOR PEACE AND RECONCILIATION

January 18, 1994

To Mr. Manuel Camacho Solís, Commissioner for Peace and Reconciliation in Chiapas:

Mr. Camacho Solís:

The CCRI-CG of the EZLN again addresses you. We have heard on the radio, with attention and respect, your words in response to our January 13, 1994 letter. Your thoughts reflect some things that we should think about and analyze carefully in order to be able to give a true response. The complete response to what you have proposed will have to wait a while, as we still haven't received the written communication, and we only have what you said on the radio to go on. However, in general, we see great value in your response and we welcome the spirit that your words carry. The CCRI-CG of the EZLN declares:

**First:** The CCRI-CG of the EZLN officially recognizes Mr. Manuel Camacho Solís as Commissioner for Peace and Reconciliation in Chiapas.

**Second:** The CCRI-CG of the EZLN recognizes Mr. Manuel Camacho Solís as a trustworthy speaker, and all his words and thoughts will be received with respect and attention, analyzed seriously and with care, and will receive formal and honest response.

**Third:** The CCRI-CG of the EZLN, in agreement with their official recognition of Mr. Manuel Camacho Solís as Commissioner for Peace and Reconciliation in Chiapas, guarantees the free movement of the above within territories occupied by the EZLN, and gives assurance that the Zapatista troops will respect his person and belongings.

Respectfully,
From the mountains of the Mexican Southeast,
CCRI-CG of the EZLN

# WHAT ARE THEY GOING TO FORGIVE US FOR?

January 18, 1994

Gentlemen:

I must begin with some apologies ("a bad beginning," my grandmother used to say). Our Press and Communications Department omitted the weekly national magazine *Proceso* when they sent out the January 13 letter. I hope that the people at *Proceso* forgive us for this mistake and receive the present letter without any ill feelings or resentment.

I direct myself to you to ask for the distribution of the accompanying statements from the Clandestine Revolutionary Indigenous Committee-General Command of the EZLN. In them, we refer to repeated violations of the cease-fire by federal troops, the government's initiative to apply the Law of Amnesty to the present conflict, and to Camacho Solís's performance as the one commissioned to negotiate for peace and reconciliation in Chiapas.

I believe that the documents that we sent to you on January 13 should have arrived by now. I ignore the response they will provoke and what the government's response to our proposals will be, and therefore do not address them. Up to today, January 18, 1994, the only thing we have learned is that the "pardon" which the government offers to our forces has been made official. What do we have to ask forgiveness for? What are they going to "pardon" us for? For not dying of hunger? For not accepting our misery in silence? For not humbly accepting the huge historic burden of disdain and abandonment? For having risen up in arms when we found all other paths closed? For not heeding Chiapas's penal code, the most absurd and repressive in history? For having shown the country and the whole world that human dignity still exists and is in the hearts of the most impoverished inhabitants? For having made careful preparations before beginning our fight? For having brought guns to battle instead of bows and arrows? For having learned to fight before having done it? For being Mexicans, every one of us? For being mostly Indigenous? For calling the Mexican people to fight, through whatever means, for what rightfully belongs to them? For fighting for freedom, democracy, and justice? For not following the leaders of previous wars? For refusing to surrender? For refusing to sell ourselves? For not betraying one another?

Who should ask for forgiveness and who can grant it? Those who, for years and years, sat before a full table and satiated themselves while we sat with death, as such a daily factor in our lives that we stopped even fearing it? Those that filled our pockets and souls with declarations and promises? The dead, our dead, who mortally died "natural" deaths, that is, of measles, whooping cough, dengue, cholera, typhoid, mononucleosis, tetanus, bronchitis, malaria, and other gastrointestinal and pulmonary diseases? Our dead, who die so undemocratically of grief because nobody did anything to help them, because all the dead, our dead, would simply disappear without anyone paying the bill, without anyone finally saying, "ENOUGH!" Those who give feeling back to these dead, our dead, who refuse to ask them to die over again, but now instead ask them to live? Those that denied us the right to govern ourselves? Those who treat us as foreigners in our own land and ask us for papers and to obey a law whose existence we ignore? Those that torture, seize, and assassinate us for the great crime of wanting a piece of land, not a big piece, not a small one, just one on which we could grow something with which to fill our stomachs?

Who should ask forgiveness and who can grant it?

The president of the republic? The secretaries of state? The senators? The deputies? The governors? The municipal presidents? The police? The Federal Army? Powerful businessmen, bankers, industrialists, and landowners? Political parties? Intellectuals? Galio and Nexos? The media? Students? Teachers? Our neighbors? Workers? Campesinos? Indigenous people? Those who died useless deaths?

Who should ask forgiveness and who can grant it?

Well, that is all for now.

Best wishes and a warm embrace; hopefully with this cold both things are appreciated (I think), even if they come from a "professional in violence."

## ON MOVING TOWARD A DIALOGUE

**January 20, 1994**

To Don Samuel Ruiz García, National Commissioner for Mediation:
To Mr. Manuel Camacho Solís, Commissioner for Peace and
Reconciliation in Chiapas:

Gentlemen:

The CCRI-CG of the EZLN adresses itself to you to tell you the following:

**First:** We have learned through the press that there exists an initiative for a law of amnesty which President Salinas de Gortari has presented to congress for approval.

**Second:** As we stated in point number three of our letter to Mr. Manuel Camacho Solís, dated January 13, 1994, "all proposals for dialogue or other matters the government wishes to discuss with us should be directed to us through Samuel Ruiz García, bishop of the Diocese of San Cristóbal de las Casas, Chiapas. We will only consider as valid those communications which we receive through Bishop Samuel Ruiz." We have not received any written communication on the supposed law of amnesty which is being discussed. Therefore, we cannot make an official declaration on its contents.

**Third:** From the little we have been able to gather from the press about the "Law of Amnesty," we can only say that in general the initiative is premature, since the social and political causes that impelled our movement continue.

**Fourth:** We ask that the dialogue process move slowly and take all the necessary steps to find a just political solution to the conflict, just as Mr. Manuel Camacho Solís has declared publicly on several occasions.

**Fifth:** We remind you that the conditions set out for beginning a dialogue have not been fulfilled entirely. The Federal Army continues to violate the cease-fire and remains outside of its bases harassing our forces and the civilian population.

109

**Sixth:** We believe that the process that you have begun is following a just and respectful path. We welcome your participation and reiterate our disposition to listen to you and to maintain the possible and necessary channels of communication open for the good of our people and the entire country.

Respectfully,

From the mountains the Mexican Southeast

## ON THE IMPORTANCE OF DIVERSE VOICES

January 20, 1994

*"The land that gave us life and struggle is communal."*

To our Indigenous brothers and sisters of other organizations:
To the Mexican people:
To the people and governments of the world:

Brothers and sisters:

We are speaking to you, Indigenous brothers and sisters of the different independent and honest Indigenous organizations of Chiapas and of Mexico. We, the Indigenous peoples of the CCRI-CG of the EZLN, are speaking to you to tell you the following:

**First:** We, the Zapatistas, have always respected and will continue to respect the different honest and independent organizations. We haven't obligated them to enter our struggle; when they have entered, it's always freely and of their own accord.

**Second:** We look at your form of struggle with respect; we salute your independence and honesty, if they are true. We took up arms because they didn't leave us any other way. If you continue in your way, we are in agreement with it because we are struggling for the same things, and the land that gave us life and struggle is shared.

**Third:** Our form of armed struggle is just and true. If we had not raised our rifles the government would never have preoccupied itself with the Indigenous people in our lands, and we would have continued on in poverty, forgotten. Now the government is very preoccupied with the problems of Indigenous people and campesinos, and that is good. But it was necessary for the Zapatista rifle to speak so that Mexico could hear the voice of the poor Chiapanecos.

**Fourth:** We will continue to respect you and your forms of struggle. We invite you to, in accordance with your organization and form of struggle, to unite our heart with the same hope of freedom, democracy, and justice.

All organizations and just one struggle!

From the Mountains of the Mexican Southeast,
Clandestine Revolutionary Indigenous Committee-General Command of the
    Zapatista National Liberation Army
Mexico, January 1994

# ABOUT THE MAIN DEMANDS AND THE FORMS OF STRUGGLE

January 20, 1994

*"We want all who walk with the truth to unite in one step"*

To the People of Mexico:
To all people and political and civil, democratic, independent, honest
    organizations of Mexico:
To the people and governments the world:

Brothers and Sisters:

The dignified struggle of the combatants of the EZLN has received the sympathy of various people, organizations, and sectors of the Mexican civil and international societies. The honest and decided result of the action of these progressive forces is that they have, truly opened the possibilities for a peaceful, just, political solution to the conflict that covers our skies. Neither the will of the federal government nor the glorious military actions of our forces have been so decisive for this turn in the conflict as have public protests: in the streets, the mountains, and the media of the different organizations and honest, independent people who are part of what we call Mexican society.

We, the last among Mexican citizens and the first of the patriots, have understood from the beginning that our problems and those of the whole nation can only be solved through a national revolutionary movement around three basic demands: freedom, democracy, and justice.

Our form of struggle is not the only one. Perhaps for many it may not even be an adequate one. There are many other valuable forms of struggle. Our organization is not unique; for many it may not even be a desirable one. There are other honest, progressive, independent organizations of great value. The EZLN has never pretended that our way of struggle is the only legitimate one. In fact, it is the only one we have been left with. The EZLN welcomes the honest and consistent development of all forms of struggle that take us all along the path of freedom, democracy, and justice. The EZLN has never pretended to be the only true, honest, and revolutionary organization in Mexico or Chiapas.

In fact, we organized the way we did because it was the only way we were left with. The EZLN welcomes the honest and continuous development of all independent and progressive organizations that struggle for freedom, democracy, and justice for the whole country. There are and there will be other revolutionary organizations. There are and there will be other popular armies. We don't pretend to be the one, only, and true historic vanguard. We don't pretend to group all honest Mexicans under our Zapatista flag. We offer our flag, but there is a much bigger and powerful flag with which we can all be covered. The flag of the national revolutionary movement where all the most diverse tendencies can fit, the most different thoughts, the different ways of struggling; yet there will only be one longing and one goal: freedom, democracy, and justice.

The EZLN calls on Mexicans to fly that flag, not the EZLN flag, not the flag of armed struggle, but the flag that is the right of all thinking beings, reason of our people and understanding of our people: freedom, democracy, and justice. Under that great flag we'll fly our Zapatista flag. Under that great flag our rifles will march, too.

The struggle for freedom, democracy, and justice is not the task of the EZLN alone, it is the work of all Mexicans and all honest, independent, and progressive organizations. Each one in its own area, each one in its own way of struggle, each one with its own organization and its own ideas.

The steps everyone takes with the truth should unite in one single path: the one that will lead to freedom, democracy, and justice.

Our struggle doesn't end, nor does our cry end after the "ENOUGH" we uttered on January 1, 1994. It is still a long walk. There are different paths but one longing: Freedom! Democracy! Justice!

We will continue to struggle until we achieve the freedom that is our right, the democracy that is our reason, and the justice that is our life!

From the mountains of the Mexican Southeast,
CCRI-CG of the EZLN

## Conditions for Dialogue

**January 20, 1994**

To Mr. Samuel Ruiz García, National Commissioner for Mediation:
To Mr. Manuel Camacho Solís, Commissioner for Peace and Reconciliation:

Gentlemen:

We, the members of the Clandestine Revolutionary Indigenous Committee-General Command of the Zapatista National Liberation Army, are addressing you again to tell you the following:

**First:** We have yet to receive any written communication concerning the "Amnesty Law" that has been mentioned. And we go on, but are unable to express ourselves in regards to it. Whatever it may say, we want to tell you that the content of the "Amnesty Law" is not, nor will it be, an incentive to dispose us towards dialogue that will lead to a just, political solution to the actual conflict. That is to say, independent of said law, we will move forward with the process of dialogue, if it isn't a condition to subscribe to this law to initiate a dialogue. If it is not a condition to sit down to discuss a political way out to our struggle, then we will continue with the process of dialogue.

**Second:** Since the letter of Mr. Manuel Camacho Solís, dated January 18, 1994, we have not received any other written communication from the commissioner for peace and reconciliation in Chiapas. We remind you that only written communications sent to us through Mr. Samuel Ruiz García will be considered valid by us.

**Third:** The Clandestine Revolutionary Indigenous Committee-General Command of the EZLN read with care the letter from Mr. Manuel Camacho Solís, Commissioner for Peace and Reconciliation in Chiapas, dated January 18, 1994. Regarding this letter, we have one question: In what capacity does the federal government recognize us in order to negotiate with us? As a belligerent force? As a political force? We need to understand this in order to know what guarantees we have during the dialogue process ,and for the fulfillment of the accords that eventually come out of that dialogue. It is not clear exactly what recognition was given to us by Mr. Manuel Camacho Solís in his letter of January 18, 1994.

**Fourth:** The Clandestine Revolutionary Indigenous Committee-General Command of the EZLN declares that it is holding no hostages. It only holds the prisoner of war, Division General Absalón Castellanos Domínguez, whose release is underway, as we will communicate at the appropriate time. After freeing Division General Absalón Castellanos Domínguez, we will have no hostages or prisoners at all, neither military nor civilian. They have all been set free.

**Fifth:** The CCRI-CG of the EZLN has learned, through the communications media, that the Federal Army will retreat from the civilian zones that it currently occupies and return to its barracks.

**Sixth:** The CCRI-CG of the EZLN declares that, from January 17 to today, there have been no violations of the cease-fire on the part of the federal troops.

**Seventh:** The CCRI-CG of the EZLN declares that the previous conditions for the initiation of dialogue with the Commissioner of Peace and Reconciliation in Chiapas have yet to be complied with, and we therefore exhort Mr. Manuel Camacho Solís and Mr. Samuel Ruiz García, so that we can begin the work underway at the beginning of a real public dialogue with full guarantees for the respect of life, freedom, free transit and well-being of those who are named as delegates by the CCRI-CG to personally attend the dialogue meeting.

**Eighth:** Once respect for the lives, liberty, free transit and well-being of Zapatista delegates is guaranteed by Manuel Camacho Solís and Samuel Ruiz García, we propose that the first point of the dialogue be to establish, by mutual accord, the agenda of discussion and the times for initiating them.

**Ninth:** The agenda of discussion being proposed by the CCRI- CG of the EZLN is the following:

**A:** Economic demands. All of these refer to the grave material living conditions that we, the Indigenous people of Chiapas, endure. The actual situation, and approaches to immediate as well as long-term solutions.

**B:** Social demands. All of these refer to what we endure as Indigenous people of Chiapas: racism, marginalization, lack of respect, expulsions, attacks on our culture and traditions, etc. The actual situation and approaches to a definitive solution.

**C:** Political demands. All these refer to the lack of legal space for the real participation of us, the Indigenous people of Chiapas, and of all Mexicans in the national political life. Actual situation, and approaches to an immediate solution.

D: An end to the hostilities and violent confrontations. Guarantees to both parties in conflict.

We await your written response to this.

From the mountains of the Mexican Southeast,
Clandestine Revolutionary Indigenous Committee-General Command of the
    Zapatista National Liberation Army

## A Letter from Subcommander Marcos to the Press

January 20, 1994

To the national weekly, *Proceso*:
To the national newspaper, *La Jornada*:
To the national newspaper, *El Financiero*:
To the local newspaper of San Cristóbal de las Casas, Chiapas, *Tiempo*:

Gentlemen:

We were trying to move nearer to each other, looking for the possibilities of personal contact with Mr. Camacho Solís, but were forced to fall back by the pressure of the federal troops. They have also delayed our deliveries. Here I send you another series of communiqués: one directed at other Indigenous organizations in Chiapas, another directed at the people of Mexico, another about the trial of Division General Absalón Castellanos Domínguez that has just been sent to me by the Zapatista Justice Tribunal, and the final one directed at Mr. Samuel Ruiz García and Manuel Camacho Solís. I thank you in advance for recognizing them as being in the public domain.

Time is running out; the walls are closing in. It is more and more difficult to send you things so that you can know us as more than ski masks, wooden rifles, spears, and frightening *cuernos de chivo* [AK-47's]. Sheltered by the supposed "cease-fire," the federal troops continue weaving an apparatus of military intelligence and repression that allows them to deliver the spectacular blow which, in the end, obscures their clumsiness in combat and their abuses of the civilian population. With military actions that they call "commando," the Federal Army touches the tempting possibility of reaching the central command group and annihilating it. For years now, all of this has been within the predictable for us. In the event that they are successful, nothing will change fundamentally. The succession of command and the omnipresence of the Clandestine Revolutionary Indigenous Committees will stand up to any blow whatsoever, no matter how spectacular and overwhelming it may seem.

Well, finally, I have had the opportunity of a few hours in which to read some of the publications that someone was kind enough to send me (the arrival of newspapers or subscriptions to the southeastern mountains is as improbable as a vacant seat on the metro in the capital city during rush hour). I have realized here the anguish that is caused by the ski masks and the "obscure" intentions of the Zapatista "leadership." I have mistreated you, consciously, by using you as interlocutors. Nevertheless, I believe that this inopportune and delayed correspondence has served everyone. Now the horizon begins to darken and every line may be the last. Therefore, reiterating the mistreatment, I take advantage of this to touch on several points even though they remain sketchy. I thank you for reading them, even more for publishing them. Over here the predictions are grim, and these could be the last.

I have the honor of having as my superiors the best women and men of the Tzeltal, Tzotzil, Chol, Tojolobal, Mam, and Zoque ethnicities. I have lived with them for more than 10 years and I am proud to obey them and serve them with my arms and my life. They have taught me more than they now teach the country and the whole world. They are my commanders and I will follow them along whatever paths they choose. They are the collective and democratic leadership of the EZLN, their acceptance of dialogue is as true as is their struggling heart, and as real as is their mistrust at being tricked again.

The EZLN has neither the desire nor the capacity to stop midway its project and its path toward all Mexicans. But it does have the capacity and the desire to add its force to the national force that gives our country life on the path of justice, democracy, and freedom that we all want.

If we have to choose paths, we will always choose that of dignity. If we find a dignified peace, we will continue the path of dignified peace. If we find war dignified, we will draw our weapons to achieve it. If we find a dignified life, we will continue living it. If, on the other hand, dignity means death, then we will go, without doubting, to find it.

What the EZLN seeks for the Indigenous inhabitants of Chiapas is the same thing that should be sought by all honest organizations in the whole country for all Mexicans. What the EZLN seeks with arms, should be sought by all honest organizations with different forms of struggle.

We will not take the country hostage. We neither want nor are able to impose on Mexican civil society our ideas by the force of our arms, as the current government imposes its project on the country with the force of its arms. We will not impede the future electoral process.

When one military-political force (such as the Mexican federal government) asks another military-political force (such as the EZLN) to turn in its arms, that means, in political and military terms, that they seek an unconditional surrender. In exchange for that unconditional surrender, the government offers the usual: an audit of internal accounts, a packet of declarations, promises and more bureaucratic dependencies.

Concretely, the request to "put down arms" is the one that provokes the greatest suspicions. National and Latin American history teaches us that those who turn in their arms, trusting the forgetfulness of those who pursue them, end their days riddled with bullet holes in any place by any death squad of any political or governing faction. What reason do we have to think that it would not happen like this in our country?

We think that revolutionary change in Mexico will not be a product of action in just one direction. In other words, it will not be, in the strict sense, an armed revolution or a peaceful revolution. It will primordially be a revolution that is the result of struggle on various social fronts, with many methods, under many social forms, with varying degrees of commitment and participation. And the result will be, not one of a party, organization, or coalition of organizations with its triumphant specific social proposal, but a sort of democratic space for the resolution of confrontation between diverse political proposals. This democratic space of resolution will have three fundamental premises that are inseparable, already, historically: democracy in deciding the dominant social proposal, freedom to subscribe to one or another proposal, and the justice to which all proposals will have to adhere. The revolutionary change in Mexico will not follow a strict calendar. It could be the hurricane that explodes after it accumulates for a while, or a series of social battles that, step by step, will overcome the forces that oppose it. The revolutionary change in Mexico will not be under one leadership, with one homogenous membership and one leader to guide it, but with a plurality of dominant forces that change, but turn around one common point: the trio of democracy, freedom, and justice upon which the new Mexico will be built, or it won't be built.

Social peace will only happen if it is just and dignified for all. The dialogue process for peace comes from a fundamental determination, not from a political initiative of the federal government, not from a political-military strength (that for the majority continues to be a mystery) but from a firm action of what they call Mexican civil society. From the same Mexican civil society and not from the will of the government or from the strength of our weapons, will come the possibility of a real democratic change in Mexico.

### Epilogue: "About ski masks and other face masks"

Why all the scandal about the ski mask? Isn't the Mexican political culture a "culture of the coverings?" But, to end the growing agony of some who fear (or wish) that some "Kamarrada" or Boggie el Aceitoso is the one who, in the end, is behind the ski mask and the "pronounced nose" (as *La Jornada* calls it) of the "Sup" (as the *compañeros* call me) I propose the following: I am willing to take off the ski mask if Mexican society takes off the mask that the anxieties of foreign vocations have already been imposing for many years. What would happen? The predictable: Mexican civil society (excluding the Zapatistas, because they know it perfectly well in image, thought and, deed) would realize, not without disillusionment, that the "Sup Marcos" is not a foreigner and that he is not as handsome as was promoted by the "personal record in the Attorney General's Office (Procuradora General de la Republica, PGR). But not only that, by taking off its own mask, Mexican civil society will realize, with a stronger impact, that the image that it has sold itself is a forgery, and that reality is far more terrifying than it thought. Each of us will show our faces, but the big difference will be that the "Sup Marcos" has always known what his real face looked like, and civil society will just wake up from a long and tired sleep that "modernity" has imposed at the cost of everything and everyone. The "Sup Marcos" is ready to take off the ski mask. Is Mexican civil society ready to take off its mask? Don't miss the next episode of this story of masks and faces that reaffirm and deny themselves (if the airplanes, helicopters, and olive-drab green masks allow it).

That is all...but there is not much missing. Well, this may be the end of a very short epistolary exchange between a ski mask of a pronounced nose and some of the best of the honest Mexican press.

Health and no hug now because it could awaken jealousy and suspicion,
Subcommander Marcos

# On Misunderstandings about the EZLN and the Real First Uprising

January 26, 1994

To national newspaper *La Jornada*:
To the local newspaper from San Cristóbal de las Casas, Chiapas, *Tiempo*:
Mr. Álvaro Cepeda Neri
"Conjetura" column, national newspaper *La Jornada*, Mexico City

Mr. Cepeda Neri and family:

I confirm receiving your letter, published in *La Jornada*, dated January 24, 1994. We thank you for your thoughts. We are doing well here. Helicopters and airplanes come and go, they get close, they see us, we see them, they leave, they come back, and so on, day and night. The mountain protects us, the mountain has been our *compañera* for many years.

I would like to talk to you about some things that happened around this land and that, for sure, will not appear in the newspapers and magazines, because everyday happenings are of no interest to them. And there is, believe me, a daily heroism that makes sparkles that from time to time light the seeming mediocrity of our country's history. A few hours ago I met with some members of the CCRI. They discussed the way they will name the members of the delegation to the dialogue with the commissioner for peace and reconciliation in Chiapas. After that, they went over some newspapers that arrived (late, of course). The journalists' notes and comments provoked diverse reactions in all of us.

Javier, a slow-spoken Tzotzil, who looks for words that tell the truth, has read now what happened in the state of Tlalmanalco. Indignant, he comes to me and tells me "We have to invite those people to come here with us." I start to explain to him that we can't invite them, because they are a political party and we can't intervene in the thinking of other political organizations, because that place is too far away, because they will be stopped at the Army checkpoints, because the beans won't be enough for so many, because re-etcetera, etc. Javier waits patiently until I finish speaking. He now tells me, in a very serious tone: "I don't mean the PRD," and adds, "I mean the police officers who beat them." Squatting, he decrees, sentences, and orders: "Invite those police officers to come here. Tell them that if they are real men they should come here and fight against us. To see if it is the same to beat peaceful, innocent people as to fight us. Tell them to write so that we can teach them to respect the humble people."

Javier, still squatting in front of me, waits for me to start writing the letter to the cops of the state of Mexico. I wonder...in that moment the guard announces that some reporters are coming in and that they want to talk to someone. I excuse myself to Javier, I go to see who is going to go speak with the journalists. The letter of invitation to police officers is left pending.

Now there's Angel, a Tzeltal, whose pride is to have read the complete book by Womack on Zapata ("It took me three years. I struggled, but I finished it," he says every time someone questions this feat). He comes to me with a newspaper in his left hand (he has an

M-1 rifle in the right). "I can't understand a world this man says," he complains to me. "He uses hard words and he doesn't know where he's going. He seems to understand our strug-gle, and then he seems to not understand our struggle." I look at the newspaper and Angel points out the editorial by "X." I explain to Javier what that man is saying, that it is true that there is poverty in Chiapas, but that it is not possible for the Indigenous people to have orga-nized so well and to have risen up with a plan, that the Indigenous people always rise up without a plan, just like that, all of a sudden. That means that there are strange and foreign people taking advantage of the Indigenous poverty to give a bad image of Mexico and its president, that the EZLN is among the Indigenous but does not represent them. Angel starts to turn around and around. Furious, he can't speak clearly, he hurriedly mixes words in dialect and Spanish. "Why do they always think of us as little children?" He throws the question to my face. I almost dropped the half-uncooked rice some novice cook has pre-pared "specially for the Sup." He keeps going, more calmly after he gets his own rice. "Why is it that, for them, we can't think on our own and have clear thinking with a good plan and a good struggle?" I understand that the question is not for me. Angel understands well that the question is for the improbable man of the "deep article." We both, Angel and I, know that this and other questions will receive no answer. Is it, perhaps, that intelligence only reaches the head of the *ladino*? Is it that our grandfathers did not think well when they were alive?" Angel asks and asks. Nobody answers, nobody will...

Susana, a Tzotzil, is upset. A while ago they were making fun of her because, according to the rest of the CCRI, the first uprising of the EZLN, in March, 1993, was her fault. "I am angry," she tells me. I, while I find out what is going on, seek protection behind a rock. "The *compañeros* say that it is my fault that the Zapatistas rose up last year." I start to approach carefully. After a while I discover what is going on: In March of 1993 the *com-pañeros* debated about what would later be the "Revolutionary Laws." Susana was in charge of going around to dozens of communities to speak with groups of women and put togeth-er, from her thoughts, the "Women's Laws". When the CCRI got together to vote on the laws, each one of the commissions got up: Justice, Agrarian Reform, War Taxes, Rights and Obligations of Reople in Struggle, and Women. Susana had to read the proposals that she had gotten together from the thoughts of thousands of Indigenous women. She started to read and, as she read on, the assembly of the CCRI became more and more restless. You could hear murmurs and comments. In Chol, Tzotzil, Tojolobal, Mam, Zoque and Span-ish. The comments jumped from one side to the other. Susana, undisturbed, charged on against everyone and everything: "We don't want to be forced into marriage with someone we don't want. We want to have the children we want and can take care of. We want the right to hold rank in the community. We want the right to speak up and to be respected. We want the right to study and even be drivers." And she kept going like that until she was done. At the end there was a strong silence. The "Women's Laws" that Susana had just read meant a true revolution for the Indigenous communities. The women responsible were receiving the translation in their dialects of what Susana had said. The men looked at each other nervously, restless. All of a sudden all the translators ended almost at the same time. And, in a single movement, the *compañeras* responsible for the laws started to clap and talk among themselves. Needless to say, the "Women's Laws" were approved unanimously. A

Tzeltal responsible for the law commented: "The good thing is that my wife doesn't understand Spanish, because otherwise..." An insurgent official who was a woman and a high infantry rank, jumped on him: "You're fucked, because we are going to translate it into all the dialects." The *compañero* looked down. The women responsible were singing, the men were scratching their heads. I, cautiously, called a recess. This story that now, according to Susana, started when someone from the CCRI read a newspaper that points to the proof that the EZLN is not truly Indigenous being that Indigenous people could not have agreed to rise up on January 1. Someone, as a joke, said that this was not the first uprising, that the first was March, 1993. They joked with Susana and she left with a sharp "Fuck you" and something else in Tzotzil that nobody tried to translate. That was the truth: The first EZLN uprising was March, 1993 and was lead by the Zapatista women. There were no casualties, and they won. Things of this land.

At midnight Pedro, a Chol with a big mustache, comes closer to me with a candle in his right hand. He sits next to me. He looks at me with his round black eyes and says nothing. "We have to go to Mexico [City]," he says to me and to himself. I start to scratch my head, thinking of the orders that will be given to start the march, the routes we will follow, the casualties we will have, coming to the city lights again, the asphalt of the roads.

Pedro interrupts me: "Mexicans say Chiapas is different from other places, that here things are bad, but they are good elsewhere in Mexico." Now I look at him; he doesn't return the look, but hands me a newspaper. I look for my lamp and start to read the article that Pedro points out to me. It says that our struggle is destined to fail because it is not national and it is not rational, because our demands are local, Indigenous. "That person's thinking is poor," says Pedro, "even poorer than we are because we want not only justice, but also freedom and democracy. And this man thinks that he is not poor even when he can't truly elect a government. He feels sorry for us. Poor little things." The candle burns between us. Pedro understands, I understand, the night understands... "Mexicans don't understand. We have to go to Mexico [City]," says Pedro while he leaves, taking the candle in his right hand. The cold is hard in the morning. The guard screams: "Halt! Who goes?" "The country!" another voice responds, and something warm reaches us.

Well Mr. Cepeda Neri, I wanted to take advantage of this letter to tell you these and other things, but that is all for now. We hope that you and your family are in good health. Until next time, which is improbable.

Health and respect to you and those who are with you,

From the mountains of the Mexican Southeast,
Insurgent Subcommander Marcos

**P.S.:** Javier just reached me happily to ask if this is the letter to invite the police officers of the state of Mexico. I tell him that it is not, that it is for a journalist. "Ah," he says disappointed. But he adds sharply: "Tell them to not forget us, that our truth is for them as well." All right.

# An Invitation to Members of the Press to Attend the Dialogue

[*La Jornada*, 2/2]
Mexico, January 29, 1994

To the national and international press:

Gentlemen:

The Clandestine Revolutionary Indigenous Committee-General Command of the EZLN respectfully addresses itself to you to put forth the following:

**First:** As is publicly known, the beginning of the dialogue for peace between the EZLN and the federal government, whose time and place have yet to be decided, is imminent. There are already fundamental agreements between this CCRI-CG of the EZLN and the commissioner for peace and reconciliation in Chiapas. There remain a few details to be finalized and a few previous agreements to be fulfilled, but the basic elements are decided.

**Second:** We know that your work is to report to the Mexican people and to the world about what happens in this stage of the just war of our EZLN against oppression, injustice and lies.

**Third:** There exist some informational media that have fully declined to report with objectivity what has happened in our state. Various media have specifically preached against our cause and the cause of the Chiapaneco Indigenous people. We have never asked any news media to become "spokespeople" for the EZLN, but we consider objective reporting to be your duty, and the right of the whole society.

**Fourth:** On the part of the CCRI-CG of the EZLN there is an open-door policy for all news media that, in our opinion, carry out their jobs objectively, without taking part on one side or the other.

**Fifth:** Therefore the CCRI-CG of the EZLN declares that all print media, regardless of political or party affiliation or ideological orientation, can, as far as the EZLN is concerned, cover the event of the Dialogue for Peace and Reconciliation. As for the television media, the EZLN would only veto the attendance of the national private television networks of Televisa and Televisión Azteca. The first because they do not need to look for news since they invent it and make it up to their taste and convenience. The second because their reporters have demonstrated a lack of professionalism by offering money to our combatants so that they would make statements. The rest of the national and foreign television media will be approved without any problems with the EZLN.

**Sixth:** The approval by the EZLN of whatever print media will be done by way of the National Commissioner for Mediation, Mr. Samuel Ruiz García, at the time and place that he finds appropriate.

**Seventh:** The EZLN wants to make a special invitation to the following news media:

**A)** Newspapers: *La Jornada, El Financiero, Tiempo* (of San Cristóbal de las Casas), *The New York Times, The Washington Post, Los Angeles Times, Le Monde, Houston Chronicle.*

**B)** Magazines and news weeklies: *Proceso, Siempre, Mira.*

**C)** Television: July 6 Channel, Multivisión, Channel 11, CNN.

**D)** News Agencies: AP, UPI, AFP, Reuters, Prensa Latina.

**E)** Radio stations: Radio Educación WM (of San Cristóbal de las Casas), Xeva (of Tabasco), Radio Red, Grupo Acir.

**Eighth:** The EZLN declares that, if it is at all possible, the reporters specially mentioned above attend.

**Ninth:** The EZLN reserves the right to give interviews or statements to any of the news media that approach them.

Respectfully,
From the Mountains of the Mexican Southeast,
Clandestine Revolutionary Indigenous Committee-General Command of the
    Zapatista National Liberation Army

# 4. SOLIDARITY

## LETTERS FROM THE CCRI-CG
## TO VARIOUS ORGANIZATIONS

*[The following is a series of letters that the CCRI-CG wrote to various organizations express-*
*ing and asking for solidarity.]*

### A LETTER OF INTRODUCTION

February 2, 1994

To the national weekly *Proceso*:
To the national newspaper *El Financiero*:
To the national newspaper *La Jornada*:
To the local newspaper of San Cristóbal de las Casas, Chiapas, *Tiempo*:

Gentlemen:

Here I send you a series of letters sent from the CCRI-CG of the EZLN to various destinations. I hope that you have space, if not to publish them as soon as possible, to comment on them or see that they reach their destinations.

For now, that is all. We wait patiently for that plane which flies over us to run out
of gas and fall. Opinions are divided in terms of whether, when it falls, we will eat it
roasted or boiled. The more detail-oriented recommend a marinade. The sanitation service warns us of the risk of indigestion from excessive aluminum. Anyway, salt is the
only thing we have too much of. Would you like a taste in any case? (They say aluminum keeps well).

Indigestionally (which is not to say that now I do not send health, obviously),
From the mountains of the Mexican Southeast,
Insurgent Subcommander Marcos

P.S.: How is it going anonymous? Pretty, isn't it?

## To the Council of 500 Years of Indigenous Resistance

February 1, 1994

*Zapatistas: valor came from our dead elders*

To The Guerrero Council of 500 Years of Indigenous Resistance, A.C.
(Consejo Guerrense 500 Años de Resistencia Indígena, A.C.)
Chilpancingo, Guerrero, Mexico:

Brothers and Sisters:

We want to tell you that we received the letter that you sent January 24, 1994. We are very happy to know that our Indigenous brothers and sisters, Amuzgos, Náhuatls and Tlapanecos, understand our just struggle for dignity and freedom for the Indians and for all Mexicans.

Our heart is strengthened by your words, which came from so far away, which come from the entire history of our oppression, death and misery that the evil officials have dictated for our communities and our peoples. Our heart is made large by your message, which comes to us leaping over mountains, rivers, cities, countries, distrust, and discrimination.

In our name, in your name, in the name of all of the Indians of Mexico, in the name of all Indigenous and non-Indigenous Mexicans, in the name of all good people of good paths, we receive your words, brothers and sisters, brothers and sisters yesterday in exploitation and misery, bothers and sisters today and tomorrow in the dignified and true struggle.

Today we mark a month since the first time the Zapatista light brightened the night of our peoples.

In our heart there was so much pain, our death and misery were so much, and nothing would change, bothers and sisters, in this world in which our grandparents told us to keep living and struggling. Our pain and suffering was so much that it no longer fit in the hearts of some, and it started overflowing, and went filling other hearts with pain and suffering, and the hearts of the young men and women filled, valiant all of them, and the hearts of the children filled, down to the smallest of them, and the hearts of animals and plants filled, and the hearts of the stones filled and all of our world filled with suffering and pain, and the wind and the sun were pained and suffered, and the earth had pain and suffering. Everything was pain and suffering, everything was silence.

Then this pain united us and made us talk, and we recognized that in our words there was truth. We knew that it was not just pain and suffering inhabiting our tongue. We knew

124

that there was still hope in our breasts. We talked with each other. We looked within ourselves and we looked at our history. We saw our elder parents suffer and struggle. We saw our grandparents struggle. We saw our parents with fury in their hands. We saw that everything had not been taken away from us, that we had something more valiant, which made us live, which made our path go over plants and animals, which made the rock be under our feet, and we saw, brothers and sisters, that it was DIGNITY that was all that we had, and we saw that it was a great shame to have forgotten this, and we saw that DIGNITY was good for men to be once again men, and dignity returned to inhabit our heart, and we were new still, and the dead, our dead, saw that we were new still, and they called us again, to dignity, to struggle.

And then there was no longer only pain and suffering in our heart. Courage arrived, valor came to us from the mouths of our elders, already dead but living again in the dignity that they gave us. And we saw then that it is bad to die with suffering and pain. We saw that it is bad to die without struggling, and we saw that we have to win a dignified death so that all can live well one day. Then our hands looked for freedom and justice. Then our hands, empty of hope, filled with fire to ask and shout our anguish, our struggle. Then we rose up to walk again. Our step became firm again. Our hands and hearts were armed. "For all!" says our heart, not only for some, not for the few. "For all!" says our step. "For all!" shouts our spilt blood, coloring the streets of the cities where lies and plundering rule.

We left behind our lands. Our houses are far away. We all left everything. We took off skin to dress for war and death. To live, we die. Nothing for us, everything for everyone, what is ours and of our children. We leave everything.

Now they want to keep us alone, brothers and sisters. They want our death to be meaningless. They want our blood to be forgotten between the stones and the dung. They want our voice to be silenced. They want our step to be once again far away.

Do not abandon us, brothers and sisters. Take our blood as sustenance. Fill your hearts, and the hearts of all good men of these lands, Indigenous and non-Indigenous, men and women, elders and children. Do not leave us alone. Let it not all be in vain.

The voice of the blood that united us when the land and the sky were not the property of great masters calls us again. May our hearts join their steps. May the powerful tremble. May the heart of the small and the miserable be happy. May the dead always have life.

Do not abandon us. Do not let us die alone. Do not leave our struggle in the vacuum of the powerful.

Brothers and sisters, may our path be the same for all: freedom, democracy, justice.

Respectfully,
From the mountains of the Mexican Southeast,
CCRI-CG of the EZLN


# To the Non-Governmental Organizations

February 1, 1994

To all Non-Government Organizations in Mexico:

Gentlemen:

The CCRI-CG of the EZLN respectfully addresses all of you to make the following request:

As it is publicly known, the beginning of a dialogue for peace between the EZLN and Mr. Camacho Solís is imminent. The fact that this dialogue will take place within a zone of conflict implies risks of provocation which could hinder or obstruct it. With the objective of minimizing undesirable friction between the involved parties, it is necessary to form a "safety belt" or "belt of peace" around the area in which the dialogue is to take place which will, with its presence, prevent pressure, intimidation, or even aggression by one party of the conflict against the other.

We know that non-governmental organizations have remained neutral in the present conflict and have been concerned at all times with alleviating the conditions of the civilian population. They have also made efforts to attain the peace with dignity desired by our forces as well as by all honest Mexicans.

For these reasons, we would like to ask you to gather together to form this "belt of peace" which will prevent both federal and EZLN troops from interfering in the physical space of the negotiating table. It should be understood that this does not mean that you have to make any commitment to or even sympathize with the just causes of our struggle. We will continue to respect and welcome your neutrality and humanitarian efforts.

We hope for a prompt response.

Respectfully,
From the mountains of the Mexican Southeast,
CCRI-CG of the EZLN

## To the State Council of Indigenous and Campesino Organizations

February 2, 1994

To the Executive Coordinating Comision of the State Council of Indigenous and Campesino Organizations (Comisión Coordinadora Ejecutiva del Consejo Estatal de Organizaciones Indígenas y Campesinas, CCE del CEOIC):

Brothers and Sisters:

Great happiness came to our heart when we received your letter dated January 31, 1994. We want to answer you with the total attention and respect that you deserve, Indians like us, exploited like us, rebels like us.

Our heart thought that we were alone in the state of Chiapas. Our heart thought, in error, that our brothers and sisters in misery and struggle had sold their dignity to the dark and dividing forces of the evil government. Our death walked alone, without other Indians hearing its clamor for justice, freedom and democracy. Our word sings out again: WE ARE NOT ALONE, our blood and our race unites us over the bayonets and tanks of war.

We, the most humble of your brothers and sisters, greatly feel the honor of receiving your words of unity and support. We grow large with the honor that you give us with your support for our demands.

The struggle of the EZLN is not only for the Zapatistas, it is not only for the Chiapanecos, not only for the Indians. It is for all Mexicans, for all of those who have nothing, for the dispossessed, for the greatest in poverty, ignorance and death. With humility and gratitude, we receive your greeting with the thunder of our rifles. With honor and respect we thank you for your support so that the blood-bath of the supreme government towards our people could be stopped. Your honest and resolute participation makes it possible to open a just and true dialogue. Our voices join as brothers and sisters. The supreme government will have to recognize the right of our people to govern and to govern ourselves, because there is within us reason and justice for equality and peace in our Indian lands. We do not need the police and the armies of the evil government for there to be justice in our homes. We can govern with reason and prudence, as our ancestors did.

Brothers and sisters, we want to tell you that it would be a great honor and happiness for us if you would send us the resolutions you agreed upon on January 22, 23 and 24 in the Second Meeting of Indigenous and Campesino Organizations that was carried out in San Cristóbal de las Casas, Chiapas, Mexico. We will analyze them with attention and respect, and if death does not come to us first, we will send you our comments.

Brothers and Sisters of the CEOIC, with the same frankness with which you tell us of your concern about the lack of respect for the human rights of the campesinos who do not sympathize with our just cause in the zones under control of the EZLN, in truth we say: This Clandestine Revolutionary Indigenous Committee-General Command of the EZLN has taken with all seriousness your denunciation. Members of the CCRI-CG of the EZLN traveled to the places you mentioned and sanctioned those Zapatistas who were VERBALLY harassing the inhabitants who were not part of our struggle. Neither physical nor verbal threats to obligate anyone to join our struggle will be permitted among our troops or sympathizers. Our laws of war are very clear with respect to this, and we now act to remedy what has been done wrong and to prevent the problem from becoming worse. But, brothers and sisters, it is with justice that we speak to you in the same frankness: There are great lies that are being spun against us by the Federal Army and the evil government. Some of the authorities and heads of ARIC-Union of Unions are complicit in these lies, as they sell themselves to the supreme government and its armed forces, and offer dispensations and money to inhabitants who come to Ocosingo trying to meet their needs and are used to make declarations dictated by the evil government. There are testimonies of people unknown to us, but with dignity and shame, who, crying, told us that they had to lie out of hunger and under threats, which obligated them to learn by heart what they had to tell to the reporters and the bishops. That was the only way to get food for their great necessity. Some, not all, of the authorities of the ARIC-Union of Unions and its heads have sold out and are accomplices. Why? Are they not poor Indians, too? The answer, brothers and sisters, is that these people fear the Zapatista justice, as it is known by all that a large part of the assistance from the federal government designed to alleviate our conditions has remained in their hands. They have fear, these men, that this great robbery will be discovered: their complicity with the state and municipal authorities against their brothers and sisters of race and blood. Brothers and sisters, distance yourselves from these traitors and do not listen to their words. They come from a politics of "two faces" to trick everyone and obtain personal benefits.

We offer you, Mexico, and the world our best efforts to keep the already-difficult situation from getting worse for the civilian populations of the territory in conflict. Please, do not lend yourselves to the campaign of lies whose only end is to give local legal justification to a massive military campaign against our positions in the towns of Las Margaritas, Altamirano and Ocosingo. Do not stain your hands with our blood supporting the lies of the evil government and their treacherous accomplices. We are ready to permit a commission of yours (in which traitors are not included) to enter our territory and verify personally what our troops do among the civilian population which, as we all know, is mainly Zapatista, and what we do with those who are not Zapatistas but sell themselves in exchange for a dispensation. The great military offensive of the Federal Army against the Zapatista positions will fill the Lacandona Jungle with Indigenous blood. The leaders and corrupt advisors of the ARIC-Union of Unions will have the dubious honor of telling their grandchildren that they sold the blood of their brothers and sisters in exchange for a few coins. They will live with shame. We will die with dignity.

Our struggle is real. If we commit errors and excesses we are ready to correct them, of that you can be assured, brothers and sisters.

As you mention at the end of your letter, the dialogue with the Commissioner for Peace and Reconciliation, Manuel Camacho Solís, is about to start. We will make every effort to arrive at a PEACE WITH DIGNITY and, whatever the end of the dialogue is, we will continue forward, struggling for what you note is the motto of your organization: "For dignity, peace, and the development of our peoples."

Respectfully and fraternally,
From the mountains of the Mexican Southeast,
CCRI-CG of the EZLN

## WE ARE INVINCIBLE. WE CANNOT, WE DO NOT DESERVE TO LOSE

[*La Jornada* 2/7]
February 2, 1994

To Mr. Gaspar Morquecho Escamilla, *Tiempo* newspaper,
San Cristóbal de las Casas:

Sir:

I have just recently received your undated letter. At the same time, I am reading a newspaper in which you and other noble people are accused of being "spokespeople for the EZLN" or "Zapatistas." Problems. If you would like to know where these denunciations and threats come from, look in the directories of the ranchers' associations and you will find much cloth to cut. Well, passing on to another subject, and since this is about memories, I hope that you have finally been sent the mix of drunken crudeness with which you tried to interview us that beautiful first day of January. Perhaps all of you do not remember it well, but that time the one who was interviewed was you, because you would ask a question and then would answer it yourself. I do not know whether you would have been able to take anything coherent for the newspaper out of that monologue of questions and answers about the surprise and fear that took over the ancient capital of the state of Chiapas on the first day of the year. We were many, that day, who burned our bridges that early morning on the first of the year and assumed that onerous path of the ski mask wrapped around our faces. There were many of us who took that step of no return, knowing full well that the end that awaited us was probably death and improbably to see triumph. Taking power? No, something far more difficult: a new world. Nothing is left for us, we have left everything behind. And we have no regrets. Our path continues to be firm, in spite the fact that they are now seeking thousands of grotesque green masks in order to annihilate us. However, Mr. Morquecho, it turns out that we have long known, and not without pain, that we had to become strong with the death of those who fell by our sides, dying from bullets, and yes, with honor, but always dying. We had to shield our ears, Mr. Morquecho, in order to endure seeing *compañeros* of many years in the mountains, their bodies sewn with bullets and torn by grenades, mortars, and rockets, their bodies with hands tied and the mercy blows to their heads, to be able to see and touch their blood, our blood, Mr. Morquecho, flowing brown in the streets of Ocosingo, of Las Margaritas, on the earth of Rancho Nuevo, in the mountains of San Cristóbal, and in the plantations of Altamirano. And understand us, Mr. Morquecho, that in the middle of that blood, of those shots, of those grenades, of those tanks, of those machine-gunning helicopters and those planes throwing their explosive darts, understand the simple truth: We are invincible... We cannot lose... We do not deserve to lose.

But as we say here, our work is this: to fight and to die so that others can live better lives, much better than the ones that were ours to die. It is our work, yes, but not yours. So therefore please be careful. The fascist beast is bitter and directs its attacks at the most defenseless.

Of the accusations being made against you and the entire team of noble and honest people who deliver (because the technical conditions of producing a newspaper must make it a real birth) that standard of impartiality and truth that carries the name of *Tiempo*, I want to say several things:

The authentic heroism of *Tiempo* does not come from putting out a newspaper with Fred Flintstone's equipment. It comes from, in a cultural environment so closed and absurd as San Cristóbal's, giving voice to those who have nothing (now we have arms). It comes from defying, in four pages, the powerful men of commerce and land who have their goods in the city. It comes from not submitting to blackmail and intimidation to obligate them to publish a lie, or to neglect to publish a truth. It comes from, in the middle of that asphyxiating cultural atmosphere that sews up its own mediocre self-reflection, seeking fresh and lively air, actually democratic, in order to clean the streets and the minds of Jovel. It comes from when the Indians came down from the mountain (note: before the first of January) to the city, not to sell, not to buy, but rather to ask that someone listen, but finding only closed ears and doors; one door was always open, had been open for some time by a group of non-Indians who put up a sign that said the same thing: *Tiempo*. After passing that door, those Indians that today enrage the world with their audacity of refusing to die without dignity, found someone who would listen, which was already plenty, and they found someone who would put those Indian voices in ink on paper and with the heading *Tiempo*, which was before and is even more so now, heroic. It turns out, Mr. Morquecho, that heroism and valor are not to be found only behind a rifle and a ski mask, but they are also in front of a typewriter when the zeal of truth animates the hands that type.

I find out now that they accuse all of you of being "Zapatistas." If stating the truth and seeking justice is being a "Zapatista," then we are millions. They should bring more soldiers.

But, when the police and inquisitors come to intimidate you, tell them the truth, Mr. Morquecho. Tell them that you simply raised your voice to warn everyone that if changes were not made in the unjust relations of daily oppression, the Indians were going to rise up. Tell them that you simply recommended seeking other paths to follow, legal and peaceful, for those who surround the cities of all of Chiapas (and Mexico, don't believe Salinas who says the problem is local) with desperation. Tell them that you, with other honest professionals (a true rarity), doctors, reporters, and lawyers, searched for support wherever it was in order to force economic, educational, and cultural projects that would relieve the death that was being sewn in the Indigenous communities. Tell them the truth, Mr. Morquecho. Tell them you always searched for a peaceful and just, dignified and true way. Tell them the truth, Mr. Morquecho. But, please Mr. Morquecho, don't tell them that which you and I know happened to you, don't tell them what your heart murmurs to your ear in the anxiety and commotion of day and night, don't tell them that which wants to leave your lips when you talk and hands when you write, don't tell them the thought that keeps on growing, first in the breast, and keeps on rising gradually to the head as soon as the year passes and advances its pace through mountains and ravines, don't tell them what you now want to shout: "I am not a Zapatista! But after this first of January... I would like to be one!"

Greet, if it is possible for you, that man named Amado Avendaño. Tell him that I haven't forgotten his cold blood when, that happy morning (when less for us) of the first day of our triumphal entrance "into the First World," I notified you that it wouldn't be advisable for you to approach to talk with me and you told me: "I am doing my job." Taking advantage of the trip, greet Concepción Villafuerte [editor of *El Tiempo*], whose integrity and courage to write we greet with joy when the improbable link arrives and brings the newspaper. Greet all those of that periodical which not only deserves better machinery but also the regards of all the honest journalists of the world. Greet those professionals of Chiltak who sacrifice the desire for money and commodity to work with and for those who have nothing. Tell all of them (from *Tiempo* and from Chiltak) that if those who rule today had half the moral stature that you have, neither rifles nor ski masks, or blood in the mountains south of San Cristóbal, or in Rancho Nuevo or in Ocosingo or in Las Margaritas or in Altamirano would have been necessary. And perhaps, instead of writing to you now beneath the harassment of planes and helicopters, with the cold numbing my hands but hopefully not my heart, we would be speaking, you and I, with no more of a barrier than a couple of beers between us. The world already would not be the world but something better, and better for all. Certainly, if the truth were to come out (God wouldn't want it to, but it might), I don't drink alcoholic beverages, so it would actually be: "with no more of a barrier than a beer (yours, without offending) and a soda (mine) between us."

Health and a great affectionate hug. And, please, learn to put the date on your letters, although history passes so rapidly that, I think, it would be better to include the time.

From the mountains of the Mexican Southeast,
Insurgent Subcommander Marcos

Ten p.m., it's cold and the noise of the airplane that flies above, menacing, until it almost seems to coo.

# INTERVIEW WITH THE CCRI-CG

*[This is the first interview with the CCRI-CG that was granted to the press.]*

*[La Jornada, 2/4 & 2/5]*
**February 3 and 4, 1994**
**Blanche Petrich and Elio Henríquez,**
**Lacandona Jungle, Chiapas**

Javier starts: "I am going to explain a bit to you. How we, as *compañeros*, have been commissioned to be members of the CCRI. How we came to be the CCRI, since we had been organizing ourselves for a long time. The fundamental base of our organization is all of the situation that has come about for our people, who have struggled peacefully for so many years in the face of the government. We have struggled in the way that many peoples have struggled over matters of land, of housing, for all that is needed. But instead of solving the problems, the government has responded with repression, beatings, assassination, evictions, and imprisonment of our leaders.

"So, we decided that there is no way other than to organize and rise up like this in armed struggle. So we began to organize ourselves like that, secretly, in a revolutionary organization. But, as it advanced, each people has elected its representatives, its leaders. By making the decision in that way, the people themselves proposed who will lead these organizations. The people themselves have named us. So first, someone from each people has been named responsible. In that way we advanced town by town, and so there was time, then, to name delegates. In that way we came to be the CCRI.

"Why are they the 'Clandestine Revolutionary Indigenous Committee?' Well, 'Committee' because we are in collectives, [organized] collectively. 'Clandestine' because we know that the government is not in our interest; if we rise up like that, in armed struggle, they will not like it. For that reason we have been organizing clandestinely. 'Revolutionary' because we are conscious, and there is no other way left open to us than to rise up in arms, to struggle, to see if that way works for us and if they will respond to our needs.

"'Revolutionary' because we want a change. We don't want to continue in this situation of so many kinds of injustice. For that reason we want there to be a new society, with another, new life, for that we struggle for there to be a revolution."

Another voice, that of Isaac, the youngest:

"I want to add a little bit about the CCRI. It has already been said that it was elected democratically. If the people say that a *compañero* who is a member of the CCRI is not doing anything, that we are not respecting the people or are not doing what the people say, then the people say that they want to remove us. Why not? How could someone be there, occupying a space without doing anything? We should try to do what the people have told us to do. A plan is made of what the people want to see.

"In that way, if some member of the CCRI does not do their work, if they do not respect the people, well *compa*, it is not your place to be there. Then, well, excuse us but we will have to put another in your place. [We do] what the people say, then. That is how the Committee is constituted: in a democratic way."

*"How did you decide collectively to rise up in arms? How did you launch the offensive of January? Why don't you speak to us a little bit about these elections, about how they were?"*

"Oh, that has been going on for months now, since we had to ask the opinion of the people and because it was the people's decision. Since, why would one small group decide to jump into war? And what if the people don't support them? What if the people haven't spoken yet? Then you can't struggle in that way.

"It was the people themselves who said 'Let's begin already. We do not want to put up with any more because we are already dying of hunger.' The leaders, the CCRI, the Zapatista Army, and the General Command, if the people say so, well then, we're going to start. Respecting and obeying what the people ask. The people in general. That is how the struggle began."

*"How did you carry out your assemblies?"*

"They are done in each region; in each zone we ask the opinion of the people. Then that opinion is collected from different communities where there are Zapatistas. And Zapatistas are everywhere in the state of Chiapas. They are asked their opinion, to say what they want: if we should start the war or not."

*"Will the people also be asked whether they want to negotiate?"*

"They will also be informed. If the people say, 'no, negotiate already, we don't want war any more, we are already tired,' then we have to analyze, we have to reflect deeply on what we will win with that, whether the demands will really be met like that, whether we will get the result we want. Any other way would be to fail in the struggle that we have been working on for years. It is a shame to leave it all, what we have organized and constructed over years. That is why we want to reflect on every step that we make.

"And we want to reflect on every proposal that the government, or Camacho in person, makes to us. We cannot go to take actions we are not sure of."

Moisés: "Camacho thinks that we are going to negotiate everything without consulting. But we have to consult the people about everything. They have elected us to carry out the work of the revolution. But, in other towns, the people feel like they don't really understand. Why? Because we are advancing in one part of our state. But we hope that we will start taking this struggle to the state and national levels. Why? Because the situation that we're living in is not just about one state or just of some people. We know and have met brothers and sisters—many other peoples—who are suffering in many other states, just as we are suffering where we live. That is why are advancing. We have hope that the revolution will triumph some day."

Isaac: "We cannot dialogue or negotiate by ourselves. First we have to ask the people. At the state level, where there are *compañeros*, we have to consult about whether we are going to negotiate or not over there. If the people say so, we are doing what the people say. Why? Because we are fulfilling our commitment to the people. Because the people have lived with this for so many years: a life that is so hard, with every kind of injustice. Because of this, it isn't easy to enter the dialogue so quickly. If the people go to dialogue, well fine. If not, 'sallright. No. That's why it is not easy.

*"What do you think of the proposal for dialogue that Manuel Camacho, Commissioner for Peace, has made to you?"*

"As we are still advancing in war, we have not yet decided whether we will go to a negotiation with Camacho. We know that we are invited to negotiate, but we still have barely begun the war and we don't yet know what reality we could bring to a negotiation. As long as there are no solutions to our problems—to the necessities—as long as the people are not given what they need, then it is not easy to go to a negotiation unless we have expectation that they will come, that they will meet our demands.

"We don't just want a hand-out, to rise up quickly and then negotiate quickly. We know that so many suffer, and that there are so many kinds of injustice that we know they have laid on us as Indigenous peoples, campesino peoples, working peoples.

"We feel that Camacho has been changing his tone, as if it were easy to manage to calm or negotiate the war. But we are conscious that it will go further. There is no way other than to demand the fulfillment of the peoples' demands."

*"Mr. Camacho has sent you the message, in one of his communiqués, that all of Mexican society is demanding you follow the path of peace. What do you think of this petition?"*

"Yes, we know that there are many people, that we have to come to a negotiation. But we are still waiting to see. We're waiting to see how it advances and how things are carried out. If things are carried out, if we have reached our objective, some day we will go to dialogue, to see whether our demands are met. That is what we are waiting for. Because the same government that asks us to negotiate, to dialogue, but... but we are still thinking. Because we are conscious that what we are asking of the government cannot be accomplished quickly.

"Years and years have passed like this. Because we have been negotiating where we live, since 1974 I think, for land, housing, the construction of roads, rural clinics. But it has not resulted in anything. The only response we have gotten is deceit, false promises, and lies."

*"Did you, those of you present here, participate in the struggle for land in campesino organizations before taking up arms?"*

"Yes we did, yes. But even that way we didn't accomplish anything."

*"What organizations do you come from?"*

"Well, some independent organizations. We have struggled that way, but we haven't achieved anything. Many of us have struggled that way, but the only thing we have gotten is imprisonment, murder and repression. Those are the reasons that we are participating in armed struggle.

"Because the government tells us that we aren't right, that that isn't the solution to our problems—the needs of our people—rising up in arms like this. But we have certain needs. If we had been able to find a solution peacefully, not militarily, well, good.

"You could say that we don't have patience, that we aren't right. But we have struggled in a peaceful way, a legal way, to ask for our needs to be met. But the state and national officials have not listened to us. That is why we had no other way left. To rise up in arms to see if they would listen to us. But when we rose up with our arms on the first day, we had a good objective. Not to threaten or fuck up or kill the civilian population. We have to respect the population. We have to respect them. Why? Because we know well who is the enemy and who is the friend of the people. Because even though many people say: 'Ah, they've already sent them to kill us; they are already killing us...' No, it's not about that, it's not true. We respect the lives of the civilian population."

*"One of your protests in the Declaration of the Lacandona Jungle is for land: land to work and to live on. Don't you have your parcels?"*

"I am going to answer that question. In these parts, it is a miracle that the people are alive, because families of seven to 12 people have survived on a piece of land of about one hectare, one-half of a hectare of infertile, uncultivatable land. That is how our people have survived. And that is why we feel an urgency to have land in our hands, as campesinos. We need that land. And yes, we understand that it is not just one village, one town, one township that is lacking that land. All Indigenous peoples need land. That is why, for 30 or 40 years, we have been struggling for a piece of land that they have not given us. We know that there are people who are not campesinos who own thousands of hectares of land where cattle are fed. This means that it is better to have hundreds of cattle than hundreds of campesinos. That means that we are worth less than animals. For those reasons the people have always demanded the land, but the government has never understood, never listened."

*"But how will you achieve it? You are at war. Can the government, in a negotiation such as the one Camacho wants, resolve your problem of land?"*

"That is why we distrust this dialogue proposed by Mr. Camacho. Because we see that it will not solve our problem, because our demands are really very large. What has not been resolved in 20, 30 years cannot be solved in 20, 30 days. Because the proposal of Camacho is just to calm us down, or that we as Indians are just playing, that is what they want us to understand. How can Mr. Camacho think that our struggle does not have transcendence, that it does not have long-term process?"

*"What do you think is needed for campesinos to have their land? To return Article 27 to the way it was before? Another agrarian reform? Another revolution? A revolution like Emiliano Zapata's?"*

"We would have to make use of new laws made by the people themselves, and we have to make new laws to divide up the land, maybe different from how Zapata said: to give one piece of land to each campesino. We now understand this differently. We see that if the land is divided in pieces, it may run out. We need another form of working, of organizing ourselves. But ownership of the land should pass into the people's hands. That is why we have to make use of some revolutionary laws that the people themselves have made."

*"And what about theIndigenous reality?"*

"We think that we have to have our Indigenous people. There are many ways. But it can be a simple way. As Indians, we believe and feel that we have the capacity to direct our own destiny. There is no need for them to hold our hand. As mature people, as conscious people, we can direct our own destiny. We can govern our own destiny, we can govern our own people. We believe that our people are capable of governing themselves because our people are aware.

"That is why we don't need a government that only wants to manipulate us, to have us under its feet."

*"Would it be a government of each ethnicity? What kind of self-government do you propose?*

"It could be like that: that each ethnic group have its own government. We have not decided exactly yet, but it could be like that. Each Indigenous people, each ethnicity, could have its own government. But they would govern with autonomy, and that there is no need to be crushing or manipulating anyone. As Indians, we need our own autonomy, we need that identity, that dignity. Dignity to live and respect."

## 2

The authority of ceremonial rule is present in this Clandestine Revolutionary Indigenous Committee. Holed-up in the depth of the jungle, far away from their birthplaces, they guide the political content of the Zapatista struggle.

They come with their arms crossed across their chests. But they say: "We are people of peace, of much patience. Otherwise, we would have risen up long ago."

Before the four electric-blue ski masks and two red bandannas of the six commanders of the CCRI stands Subcommander Marcos, high military commander of the EZLN. Before them, as they exchange their sticks for carbines or rifles, a guerrilla column presents arms in formation. But they, according to the tradition of millenarian democracy that has managed to survive, never make a step without popular consultations.

To get to the CCRI-General Command of the Zapatista National Liberation Army required a long exchange of courtesies and letters traded secretly. The dates are changed and the moment is delayed, according to the come-and-go of the latent war that Chiapas lives in.

Moving into the depths of Zapatista territory in the jungle required a complex security operation, designed by Subcommander Marcos. Most of the travel was done at night. Or, if there was still daylight, with an order that sounded more like a friendly invitation: "Now you are going to sleep a little bit; close your eyes."

Many of the troops open up silently, or with a whispered order: "Who lives?" asks one shadow. "The country," responds the other.

And we also have to exchange passwords that sound like Mayan poetry: "There is among us one face and one thought. Our word walks with truth. In life and death we keep walking. There is no pain in death, there is hope in life. Choose."

There is a watch posted and a rest at midnight, in the heart of a nameless village. It is a Catholic hermitage, with its poor cross, its Bible and its saints, its roof with garlands of paper and china and its sedge rugs (made of the flower of the pine that is used for ceremonies in Chiapas and Guatemala).

Two well-armed guerrillas—a young man and a young woman—guard the door while an Indigenous official comes to check our press credentials. The courtesy is extreme. So are the security measures. Watches, recorders, backpacks and all of the work equipment of the excellent photographer Antonio Turok, of a group of independent Mexican television and they are already in the hands of a column of militias who will walk two nights to take us to the meeting site.

We travel by horse, and during long stretches we are blindfolded, feeling the abrupt descents and rises of the horses, crossing rivers and farms, through dense vegetation. It rains, clears up, and rains again. By daylight they offer us lodging in humble huts, rest and coffee.

The site of the meeting, beneath enormous trees, is guarded by a column of, mostly, young people, all of their faces covered with gray or black ski masks. Their armament is varied: M-16s, R-15s, AKs, carbines, shotguns and rifles.

The guerrilla column, with a discipline similar to devotion, presents arms and gives honors when the six Indigenous commanders ceremoniously approach the small clearing chosen for the first interview that they have given.

Ramona, the only woman, and the only monolingual (Tzotzil) of the group, represents all of the Indigenous women in her zone in the General Command. She has no children, having chosen long ago between maternity and the old carbine that she now embraces. She is small, with much-covered military boots beneath her traditional skirt. She is one of the oldest leaders of the guerrilla group.

At the beginning, the intellectuals who analyzed the first pronouncements of the Zapatista guerrillas concluded that it was not of purely Indigenous origin, due to the prominence of political democracy on its agenda.

The CCRI speaks about the vision of Indigenous insurgents of politics and democracy in this second part of the interview:

Moisés: "Yes, Mr. Salinas and Mr. Camacho have spoken to us about there being democracy, that there should be justice. But we don't understand what kind of democracy they are talking about, because, with each election that happens, there is only the imposition of the government. They don't take us into account."

Javier: "Salinas says that now there is already a candidate for president who might occupy the presidency of the republic, who is Colosio. And for us, as campesinos, as Indians, that is where the distrust starts. Because no campesino and no Indian has said that this candidate Colosio should be president. And who has elected him? A group of people who occupy the great powers: the legislators, the senators. They are the ones who have elected this person, but when Colosio goes out to campaign, he says that he is elected by the people. Not a single campesino, not a single Indian, no Indigenous campesina woman has said that that person should stay.

"That is why we are clear that the democracy that Salinas speaks of is a joke for us. He treats us like dolls, like puppets that support them, so that they can get into power. That is what we feel. And Salinas still says: Colosio cannot be changed. He is a candidate of force. But when have we campesinos elected anyone? When did Salinas come to ask us if he could name Colosio as our candidate?

"We have not elected him. Even if Salinas says a thousand times, a hundred times that there is democracy, there is absolutely no democracy in our country."

*"And why does the PRI always win so many votes in Chiapas? They win 90%...many, sometimes even more...?"*

"We are conscious of the fact that it is not like that. That it is pure fraud. Even when we don't vote, they count it as if we did, grabbing our hands, putting our cross as if we had voted that way.

"The officials and the candidates know that it is easy for the politicians to use us Indians as a step towards their rising to power; and then, when they are in power, in their cabinet, they go and forget.

"When we go to ask for a solution, the only response we have been given is repression, torture, disappearance, murder of our leaders. That is the solution that we have received, that is why we are not going to forget anything. We have to advance in our struggle until we change things.

"One of the things is that the candidates of the PRI are the only ones who have reached the government and the presidency. Why have the people supported them? Well, there are several reasons: One, the government takes advantage of the ignorance of the Indigenous campesino by illiteracy, because it knows that Indigenous campesinos don't know how to think, don't know a single letter, don't have opinions, and believe everything that they are told. That is why the government, when it is campaigning, brings a gun and a cookie, and fools the campesino, the people. And from not knowing, from ignorance that has not been cured, from the lack of education, from the lack of many things, the campesinos accept it, even though they are given garbage. Why? From the lack of experience, from the lack of consciousness, from lack of education, from the lack of many things.

"That is why the government has always won its elections. But, on the other hand, just because they win the voting, it does not mean that the people have voted, although maybe, out of their ignorance and illiteracy. No. Of course, the majority of the people have not voted, but, shamefully, those are PRI frauds: piles and boxes full of papers that a person gives their vote on. They fill out those pieces of paper so that, a little bit later, the candidate says that the people have already voted, and that they supported the PRI candidate; but it isn't true. That is what we don't want any more of.

"That is why we, as we already said, govern the people according to what they want, whether they see us, whether they recognize our work.

"That is why we are no longer taking up arms to ask for candy, like before, or for them to give us money, to give us a sombrero to cover our eyes. What we are going to ask for is freedom, justice and democracy. That is what we have come to ask for. We are not asking for candy or a piece of bread or a t-shirt that the government should give us, as has always been done before."

*"How will you end* caciquismo *in Chiapas? What do you propose?"*

"In order to end *caciquismo* in the towns it is necessary for the people to become conscious, for the people to speak, to demonstrate. If the people are going to always be there, quiet all of their life, then the *caciques* are going to be happy in power, because they will have political power, economic power, power at all levels. If the people start to become conscious and to demand their rights, they will have to say 'I won't allow the *caciques* to keep dominating me.'

"But while the people let themselves be manipulated by the *caciques*, those caciques are also clearly supported by the State. It will be difficult for the people to get out of this domination. But, shamefully, there are now many poor people—but really poor like us—who are supporting the *caciques*, the government, and are saying that the Zapatistas are evil, assassins, killers. They don't understand that we are also fighting for them to have a better life. They don't understand that. That bothers us and makes us sad as well, that people who are so poor could not understand that the struggle has a just cause. This is because they are manipulated by the *caciques*."

*"How many commanders are there in the CCRI? How is it organized?"*

"We are a fuck of a lot of people. Those of us that came here are just a few, we were just delegated."

*"Are there hundreds?"*

"All over, yes, we could say that there are a hundred in the committee because there are committees all over, so we are many."

*"How long ago did you come together?"*

"The Committee only started a few months ago; not years, since we saw that the time had come to start to struggle stronger, so we had to organize more, structure things more."

*"And Subcommander Marcos follows you? You are the highest authority?"*

"The highest authority is the Clandestine Committee."

*"And Marcos is beneath that?"*

"Well, Marcos is a subcommander. Marcos speaks good Spanish. We still make a fuck of a lot of mistakes. That is why we need him to do many things for us."

*"Who commands the military?"*

"In military matters, over all, Subcommander Marcos... We are more in the political and organizational questions."

*"Why have men, women and children participated in a revolutionary organization?"*

All eyes turn to Ramona, the small commander. "Well..." and she lets fly a cascade of words in her Mayan language. Quickly, the order is issued to find a *compañera* soldier of the same ethnicity to translate:

"Because women are also living in a more difficult situation; because women are the most exploited and strongly oppressed, still. Why? Because women, for so many years, for 500 years, have not had the right to speak, to participate in an assembly.

"They do not have the right to have an education, to speak to the public, or to hold any position in their town. No. Women are totally oppressed and exploited.

"We get up at three in the morning to prepare the corn, and from there we have no rest until everyone else is sleeping. If there is not enough food, we give our tortilla to the children, to the husband.

"We demand that we be truly respected as Indians. We also have rights. All discrimination against our rights should end, so that we can participate as a people, as a state, as a country, because they have not let us, and many of our officials have left us like that, like a stepping stone.

"And my message is that the exploited *compañeras* feel like they are not taken into account, they feel that they are very exploited, that they should decide to rise up in arms, as Zapatistas."

# 5. Broadening the Struggle

## Interview with Subcommander Marcos

[*La Jornada*, 2/8]
by the correspondents of *La Jornada*, February 4 to 7
Blanche Petrich and Elio Henríquez, Lacandona Jungle, Chiapas

Subcommander Marcos is the military strategist as well as spokesperson and interpreter of the Zapatistas. Wearing his mask, he is all eyes and voice.

"Now that the dialogue is about to begin, the Zapatista Army needs Mexican civil society as never before. We are depending on the rest of the country."

He also says that the Chiapaneco insurgency is "complete and at home," and that the early-January military offensive was so successful that now the EZLN has more people, more ammunition and more weapons.

Paradoxically, he speaks of the decision made by the leaders of Clandestine Revolutionary Indigenous Committee to go to the negotiating table as a risk-filled choice; they are risking a political trap. "If the government succeeds in isolating us, as the *compañeros* put it, what happened to the Chiapases in the Grijalva [during the conquest] will happen again: They will be trapped by the river and the *compañeros* will throw themselves into the river rather than surrender and give up their arms."

Finally, he says, the door to dialogue was opened "when the federal government realized that the total annihilation of our forces was improbable at best, or impossible at worst."

Sarcastic and a poet of sorts, with a rifle-cartridge belt crossed over his black poncho, the military leader of the EZLN will participate in the dialogue only if the superior command orders him to do so. But he does not forget what he calls his ghosts: Chinameca and the image of Venustiano Carranza standing behind President Carlos Salinas when he announced the amnesty.

141

We had arrived from one side of the mountain, and he, after a short wait, appeared from the other side in the company of a convoy of guerrillas wearing ski masks like those of the chief. The dew of the fog sometimes fills the ski mask with pearls. He constantly adjusts the mouth hole so that his voice may be heard.

The upcoming dialogue is what most concerns him:

"We have just received the ultimatum from Camacho. It's been answered by the *compañeros*; there are some concrete questions that must be resolved, such as whether or not they will carry weapons, whether the International Red Cross will participate in order to guarantee neutrality, and so on. And of course, the Red Cross allows no weapons other than those given by God. They're the only weapons we can bring.

"It's unclear whether the negotiations will also incorporate national political issues. Even though these discussions may not be binding, the *compañeros* say these issues must be on the table. And the notion of a political force in a formative stage is being contested. That really pissed off the *compañeros*. It's as if the Indians are no longer children but adults in a formative stage.

"As it stands, this dialogue is a monologue. Right now the *compañeros* are saying that they will have to dialogue. They want dialogue, but they want a dialogue with civil society. Right now, thanks to the military siege, there aren't too many options."

*"The peace emissary, Manuel Camacho, speaks of a dialogue in the forest."*

"No, we are thinking that the dialogue must take place in the city."

*"Return to San Cristóbal?"*

"No, not in San Cristóbal; there are problems there. It must be somewhere where the government is forced to respond with civility. We don't want it in the jungle because if Camacho comes in and something happens to him (meaning they do something to him) they will say it was our fault. We can't guarantee security here. Not Camacho's, not Don Samuel's."

*"In Mexico City?"*

"Yes, if they want to annihilate us by asphyxiation, they can take us there. The smog will accomplish what Godínez's rockets could not do."

Our encounter with that unknown face, almost like that of an old friend, began at noon and lasted until almost eight that night, when he dismissed us with the phrase "this dude is moving on to another window display." There was military analysis, political discussion, personal confessions, complaints about the press ("there is very little honest press"), and many anecdotes about the seizure of San Cristóbal de las Casas on the first of January, which launched the EZLN's "Enough is enough."

Informally, he characterizes the Zapatistas' armed struggle as anti-dogmatic:

"We see armed struggle as part of a broader complex that could become decisive, depending on how the process moves along. This approach has worked. Proof of its effectiveness can be found in the changes that have taken place since the first of January. The federal government's sudden attention to Indian questions comes only after the first of January. The cult of social-liberalism and everything it implies has been suddenly set aside;

nobody speaks about that now. And, all of a sudden, the success of the Mexican economy is being questioned; the genial myth of the poverty in Mexico has reemerged and is leading even the most reactionary sectors to beat their chests in public. Now they say, `Yes, poor little Indians, I'll never do it again, let me help you.' We have a clear sense of the uprising's impact, and we think that non-militarized organizations at the national level also understand that these changes are a product of the armed uprising of desperation."

He explains why his CCRI commanders decided to go to the negotiating table even though they were conscious of the dangers of a political trap: "They thought that it wouldn't be a bad thing for civil society to hear the Committee. Specifically, that it wouldn't be a bad thing for them to see that, despite what Godínez might say, they're not Cuban drug traffickers, Boogie El Aceitoso or the unemployed mercenaries left over from the Central American wars. They want people to see that they are human beings, moreover that they're Indians, that they are the leaders, and that their words are their own."

As a strategist, his inspiration with regard to the regular Army is "Pancho Villa in matters of the regular Army; Emiliano Zapata in regard to the transformation of the campesinos into revolutionaries and the revolutionary into campesinos." The rest, he says as the column conducts some drills "we got out of a Mexican Army manual that fell into our hands, from a little manual put out by the Pentagon, and from a French general whose name I don't remember."

But he is more serious about his vision of guerrilla warfare:

"We don't understand armed struggled in the classic sense of the previous guerrillas. That is, we do not see armed struggle as a single path, as one single almighty truth around which everything else spins. Instead, from the start, we have seen armed struggle as one in series of processes or forms of struggle that are themselves subject to change; sometimes one is more important and at times another is more important."

He hesitates before taking on the defendant's seat that's been set up for the interview: "So, are you setting me up for the firing squad or what?" But he sits. And the interview begins.

"The spark of the offensive didn't catch fire; it did not become an insurrection, people didn't set up barricades, the city didn't rise up in arms...."

"We weren't expecting that kind of result. We weren't expecting the Mexican people to say: 'Oh, look, the Zapatistas have taken up arms, let's join in,' and that then they would grab kitchen knives and go after the first policeman they found. We believed that the people would respond as they did, that they would say, 'Something is wrong in this country, something has to change.' Because if there's one thing you can't challenge the Zapatista Army *compañeros* on is the question of an alternative path. Nobody can say, 'No, you should have tried elections.'

"For example, how can it be that the State of Chiapas had the highest percentage of votes in favor of PRI and that it has the highest percentage of guerrillas? That contrast points to electoral fraud of gigantic proportions.

"As far as legal avenues for acquiring land, there was the reform of Article 27, which required subsisting with the farm owners as neighbors. Really there was no other way.

143

On the other hand, there was another danger: that people would say, 'No, they are drug traffickers. No, they are agents of Soviet social imperialism,' well, that one doesn't exist any more; Or people would say, 'they're agents of Chinese social imperialism,' but that one is moving in another direction (I don't know where). Or, they'd say we were CIA agents, or whatever else. The danger was that people would not really recognize or see the problems and issues that drive this movement. And that failure of understanding would give the government the opening to use the fashionable pretext of narco-terrorism or narco-guerrilla as an opportunity for repression."

*"And why this moment, the entrance of the NAFTA, the fact that it's an electoral year?"*

"It's like the myth of the ski-mask. We wear it because it's very cold in the mountains. Suddenly people like it, and the ski-masks become a symbol.

"We had not planned to attack on the first of January. One year ago, towards the end of January, the Clandestine Committee said, 'We are going to take arms.' And they gave me the order, 'Hey you, take charge of this, we're giving you a time limit to work with, choose when.'

"We tried several dates. We had to take many things into consideration. For example, we had to be certain that we would not create the impression that we were a narco-guerrilla group. It had to take place in the cities, and not in the country. If it had been in the country, they would have been able to dismiss it, to say, 'It doesn't matter, it stays in the jungle.' That's what they did when they found us in the barracks of the Corralchén sierra. They said 'No, they are luggers, they're marijuana planters; no, they're Guatemalans' and other things of that sort. We could not speak out at that time because we were thinking and waiting to see what would happen.

"The civilian population presented another problem. If we attacked the cities, what would happen to the civilians? For the guerrilla, the civilian population is even more important than the cause. A guerrilla is willing to die for the cause, but he is also willing to die rather than hurt a civilian. No way; it's something that hurts more than being caught by the Army.

"From then on the *compañeros* put aside the political aspects and began to take into account the logistical challenges of the uprising. So, for example, one of the factors we had to weigh was when can we get more reserves of foodstuffs. We assumed from the beginning that it was going to be a long war, that we might be under siege, surrounded and pressed against the mountains. Given this need, the uprising had to take place after the harvest, when we could gather money.

"National politics weren't central to the question of timing. That wasn't important for the *compañeros*. The despair was so acute that we didn't want to take it anymore, so international or national conditions didn't matter."

*"And now that there is a proposal to negotiate, what about the weapons? You've spent 10 years preparing for war ..."*

"There is a risk that the government might be able to politically isolate us on a national level, to present us as desperate extremists, intransigents, all those descriptions that are currently floating around. There is a risk that civil society might say: 'Yes, long that are currently floating around. There is a risk that civil society might say: 'Yes, long live peace, death to the extremists,' and leave us alone.

"The military option reemerges in that scenario. And believe me, the *compañeros* won't waver; if they have to die they will. But this time there would be carnage; we will not leave them alone, and we are not moving anywhere else."

*"Do you feel trapped?"*

"Yes. Definitely. They're telling us we either come to an agreement here or we don't come to one at all. A hardening, as it's called. There has been a strange change in Camacho, and the Committee is puzzled by his change of tone. I don't know whether the absurd idea of a 'political force in formation' belongs to *monsieur* Córdoba, but if there is a juridical aberration, this is it.

"The *compañeros* say, 'No. What's all this about a political force under formation? This situation is about a military force under annihilation.' In the end it's the same old thing, and the *compañeros'* assessment is quite harsh. They say, 'We're still considered little children, but now they will not refer to us as children; now they will call us adults in formation, but they'll continue to treat us like children.'"

*"And even under these conditions, you will sit down to negotiate?"*

"We believe that in this situation we owe an answer to civil society, not to the government or to Camacho. What we want is to sit and talk with civil society.

"We know that Camacho will say yes or no depending on the instructions he's received from above. But we have a debt to the nation, perhaps, to the country, but not to their Mexico. We have to respond in case the dynamic of 'exterminate them, forgive them' emerges in an accelerated way.

"The negotiations are not a product of our military success, nor of Córdoba's astute understanding that we must negotiate, and his advice to Salinas to do so. The negotiations are the result of something that's occurring in society; they're telling us, 'you cannot do that, you have to find another way.'"

*"In Camacho's last statement, the problem of negotiating with the Zapatista Army is narrowed or reduced to the dimension of Chiapas or the Indigenous communities. But according to you, your claims have a national dimension. How should the national, the Mexican, and not just the Chiapaneco questions, be approached in a negotiation with the State? And up to what point can the State provide you with proposals or answers to the things you are asking for?"*

"Well, the *compañeros* are very clear on this: It's a lie to think that our problems are going to be solved at the state level in Chiapas. I am speaking about a group of very political people. They may not speak Spanish very well, but they are nevertheless very clear, and they have authority over people who will follow them no matter what. That's why thousands arrived in the cities—because they follow them. And they say: We have a series of problems, and if we believe that these are going to be resolved by changing [local officials like] Setzer or Patrocinio, we are kidding ourselves and we are kidding our people.

"We know that things will only change if there is also change higher-up. The *compañeros* say, 'They are changing the leaves of the trees, but the roots are damaged.' We proposal, and we have said repeatedly that we will not impose it on anyone. We will not say, 'Well, we believe that Mexican society should be this way, and those who disagree will be shot, as long as we can get away with it and have to use brute force to enforce our views.'

"Then, we say, 'Let's make a deal, let's make a democratic space, and the one who convinces the people, that's the one who wins. If we win, then we win; if some else wins, then...' But that space doesn't exist, and that space needs to be a national space. It's absurd for anyone to still insist that this can be resolved at the state or regional level. Too many things would have to change for that to be possible."

*"It is not possible that the nation doesn't want to listen to this national political proposition?"*

"It's invalid for Camacho to say that he isn't going to negotiate national politics with an armed group. The *compañeros* think that the government would rather wash its hands than arrive at an agreement, and if they arrive at an agreement, the government will not fulfill it. The *compañeros* say that they want to isolate us, that the government wants to bring us to our knees. This is a false dilemma. It isn't about peace with democracy. For us, it's about peace with dignity, or war with dignity, but we still believe we have a debt with civil society."

*"What about Camacho's refusal to allow the electoral question to enter into the negotiations..."*

"They don't want to touch themes around which there's already consensus. They're going to say, 'Well, the poor Indians are very poor, very poor indeed, and therefore we will help them.' And their first request will be to ask us to surrender our weapons. That maneuver is very obvious, but it seems that society doesn't want to see it. In the last communiqué the *compañeros* addressed civil society directly, and asked why it doesn't act. Aren't they aware of what's going on? How can it be that there is a pact of civility...and a few hours later the government pops up with this line of 'Don't get into that mess,' and nobody says anything. It's as if there hadn't been a first of January, as if nothing had happened."

*"Do you think the State has the capacity, as it stands now, to democratize itself?"*

"No, not if they aren't forced to do it. If there's to be some political reform that will truly advance democratization, it will only result from the pressure of civil society. We have made it very clear that political space isn't going to come out of our offices."

# 2

Subcommander Marcos takes pleasure in being an enigma. "Marcos, I don't know who he is...a ski mask with a pronounced nose. He could be anyone."

We figure he's around 40. Light brown eyes, not green. [During the first several weeks of the conflict, the Mexican media reported widely that Maros had green eyes, contributing to the overall impression that he and other Zapatistas were not really Mexican.] Cold blooded and good-humored. The way he tells it, one day he had to choose a path. "I imagine everyone has to chose at some point. We either kept living a comfortable life, materially comfortable, or we had to be consistent with a certain type of ideals. We had to choose and be consistent and so...here we are." He feels he chose well.

As a *ladino*, one day he turned up in the Chiapaneco jungle. In this interview, he tells what happened after his arrival:

"The military issue began when we got there. There was nothing there when I arrived. We arrived, and we set to work. At the national level, the country was following a process similar to the one the state of Chiapas is experiencing now: Political avenues are closed. Mexico, already divided in two, is split once more, because there are really three Mexicos: the Mexico of the powerful, the Mexico that aspires to be part of the powerful, and the Mexico that nobody takes into account. In Chiapas it's the Indigenous people no one takes into account, but they have other names in other places. That's where we are coming from: something had to be done."

*"Generationally speaking, are you a product of '68?"*

"Aren't I 25 years old? That's how the PGR identifies me. As Krauze says, the political avenues can't possibly have been exhausted because, if he is 25 years old now, he was six in '68. But seriously, yes, I'm definitely post-'68, but not the core of '68. Because as I discovered later—word about some things doesn't filter to the mountains—it became very fashionable to assume that everyone here had participated in the events of '68. But no, I didn't. I was a little kid. But I do come from everything that followed, especially the electoral frauds, the most scandalous one in 1988, but others as well."

*"It must not have been easy..."*

"For a *ladino*, the Lacandona jungle is the worst thing that can happen to you, worse than a program like *24 Horas*. We came in through a teaching-learning process. The *compañeros* taught me what they know about the mountains, and I taught them what I knew. And that's how I began to move up through the ranks: sub-lieutenant, lieutenant, first captain, second captain, subcommander. At that point they gave me a "press" exam and they flunked me, so I've remained a subcommander."

*"It's clear that we reporters haven't made a very good impression on you..."*

"The first day they asked me why I was subcommander. I told them that to be a commander I still had to learn how to have patience with reporters. I've never learned that. But hold on a minute: there are good ones and there are bad ones. It's just that around here Juan de la Fregada has slipped in. Not too long ago, one came in and offered the *compañeros* milk and jackets in exchange for an interview. That really offends the *compañeros*. We have jackets and more milk than we need."

*"OK, so you arrived in the jungle and then what? How did the guerrillas get their start?"*

"Of course we were thinking about armed struggle. But not as the only strategy, not as the only way to bring all this together, but rather as part of something broader that had to be prepared, integrated. And I think we succeeded because we followed the correct path. No, we didn't go around robbing banks, killing police, kidnapping. Instead, we devoted ourselves to learning without anyone teaching us because, well...imagine someone coming from Mexico and saying: 'I'm going to make guerrilla warfare, help me.' No way. We'd be crying out in the desert. And until January 3 we were still alone."

*"Are there a lot of ladinos in the EZLN?"*

"A great big three of us."

*"Let's do some free association. How about love?"*

"I don't know what generation you're from, but we were taught something called love of the country. That's how we grew up. When we say love of country, we are saying a lot of things, and that's what we put above all else.

"Here's an anecdote: When they were voting on the war, because the other scandalous thing here is that this war was voted for democratically—it was not the Committee's decision, but rather the Committees went around and asked each man, and each woman and each child if it was time to start the war or not. They drew up documents and collected signatures. Those documents are floating around somewhere, or they've burned them already; I don't know where those hundreds of community documents ended up. Anyway, in one of those documents, a particular group of Indigenous people supporting the war stated their reasons very clearly: "What we don't agree with is the selling of our country to foreign interests. However you want to see it, people are going to die of hunger, but what is happening is that people who are not Mexican run this country."

"Of course, according to some intellectuals, this type of consciousness of country or nation is not possible in an Indigenous person, but they don't know these Indigenous people."

*"Indigenous?"*

"Right now the Indigenous people are the prime example of what a dignified and honest Mexican should be, not only in Chiapas but in the whole country. They are, right now, the vanguard of this country. I'm not suggesting any political implications by using that term, what I'm saying is that they're the human vanguard. Everything they have given and are willing to give, knowing that they won't reap anything because no one's going to offer these people ambassadorial posts; they're illiterate. There's no way that the government will tell them, 'No, look, if you calm down I'll give you an embassy in such and such place.'

"They can't give them anything, nothing more than lead, in any case. And, however you want to see it, they're doing what they're doing, and they're doing it with such dignity and such a sense of democracy, even given the absurd military requirements of a war. This is the lesson the country has to learn if it wants to continue being a country."

*"Death?"*

"For us it is life, in that absurd logic of daily death that has become so normal in these situations. It's living, you see, it's happiness. One month after the war began, an anniversary party was organized to remember the *compañeros* who had died. Everyone was saying, 'We see their death with happiness, because it is life for others.' That is very critical language, but at the same time it is so rich."

was saying, 'We see their death with happiness, because it is life for others.' That is very critical language, but at the same time it is so rich."

*"Victory?"*

"Victory...so far away sometimes! We think it'll be up to others to harvest the fruits of victory. For us victory means sacrifice right now. It'll be others who will really receive that 'V'."

This subcommander is definitely a *chocarrero*. An attentive reader of Monsiváis, Aguilar Camín, Krauze. Cautious of the image he projects.

"Look at what I'm carrying, and they say that the leaders are better armed than the combatants," and he takes a .22 carbine from its holster. A little old, but well kept. The cartridges, red like EverReady batteries in the cartridge belt, are his ammunition. Any one of his escorts is better armed than he is. For example, Major Pedro, who is responsible for the armory of the EZLN. And Major Ana María, commander of the operation for taking the municipal palace of San Cristóbal. And Lieutenant Romeo, who is responsible for our security during our incursion into Zapatista territory.

Only he doesn't mention the other large pistol he wears on his belt, this one really menacing. Another detail: he smokes a pipe.

His passion is military strategy, of which he boasts:

"What a shame, you all don't ask anything about the war. Go ahead, ask me. The taking of San Cristóbal is a poem in itself...."

And he is, of course, a reader of *La Jornada*. He sends messages: to the cartoonist Magú, "an insult to his mother." To the photographer Pedro Valtierra, of Cuartoscuro, in response to his petition for an exclusive photograph in *El Correo Ilustrado*, he says "I'll give him a date real soon."

And he's calculating too, "How much do you think I could get for my ski mask? Three thousand, seven thousand dollars?"

Quick with answers:

*"The stamp of Liberation Theology appears on the whole story of the Zapatista guerrilla. Even Bishop Samuel Ruiz has been accused of the insurrection..."*

"To link the Church to us is a ploy, just like what happened with the foreigners, and with that phrase 'professionals in violence.' It'll soon go out of style. It's the prominent role of the Church that bothers many sectors, not Don Samuel's participation. There was no support, not even consent, nor approval from anyone in the Church. On the contrary, some who realized that something was being organized, kept insisting that it was crazy, that it was absurd."

*"Don't you think that some of the present Zapatistas became conscious of the need for rebellion through the teachings of Liberation Theology?"*

"No, I don't think so. Because the work of the Church or of the Diocese (in this case of San Cristóbal), of Don Samuel, which covers all of the rain forest and all the townships of the highlands, went in the other direction. It was the opposite. So the *compañeros* had to find an option for life, a way to participate politically, to search for means of autonomous subsistence. The church placed great emphasis on self sufficiency, on community health projects, and so on. In reality, the whole project of the Church with the *compañeros* was what they called a project of life, while ours was a project of death.

"What happened is that the Church-led projects failed, and the *compañeros* realized that even this strategy didn't offer them many options. If they organize into cooperatives, they get harassed, and the cooperatives are broken. If they organize themselves to ask for land, they are rejected. If they organize to take over the land, they are killed. They don't have good health; they're dying. That's the source of the "boom," the source of thousands of Zapatistas.

"Don't believe the Pentagon figures that place Zapatista numbers at 1,500. There are many thousands of *compañeros* who are products of that arbitrary, unjust, and authoritarian policy that is carried to its maximum irrationality. An irrationality so extreme, that for you, we don't even exist.

"Let me clarify. Our death didn't exist. Ours...I speak for the *compañeros*. The neo-positivists are right when they say that things exist only when they are named. Until someone names it, Chiapaneco death doesn't exist. But now it exists."

*"They named it by dying..."*

"Yes. They named it by dying in that way, because no matter what, we were dying. It wasn't until you turned around to see, the press that is, that you named it."

*"Don Samuel says that you have come to the conclusion, an incorrect one in his opinion, that all doors are closed. He believes some doors still remain open."*

"Yes, we know that he believes there are possibilities of social democratization, in political participation. He believes that there were other forms of economic organization that could overcome the limitations created by the reform of Article 27. But the *compañeros* have lots of experience with all that: They really tried all avenues. They have the final say in this, and they say 'Enough is enough.' They said it first, and no one heard them. Then, they told me, 'We aren't going to wait any longer. Join us or stay behind. We think the time is now.' And I say to them, 'No, but look, the correlation of international forces, the national situation, the political reform, NAFTA, political options ... There won't be consensus.'

"And they said, 'No, no matter what, death is ours and now we are going to decide how to take it. So, you figure out how. Hopefully, it will work out. If not, well, that's that. But choose.' And they told me to choose, 'You go with us or you stay,' and I chose."

*"There is much speculation about whether you are a well-armed group or not—if you are financed from the outside or not. What armaments do you have? Where do they come from?"*

"There are three principal sources of provisions. A small part came from stockpiling a little bit at a time. Another important source is the Mexican police and Army, in part from their anti-narcotic campaign. When they capture the drug traffickers and take away their weapons, only a small part of those weapons are turned into the authorities—the rest go on the black market.

"We bought AK-47's, M-16's and other weapons from them. They thought they were selling guns to other groups of drug traffickers, who eventually would be arrested again and whose weapons could be sold again. Great business, no? And the third source are the *guardias blancas* of the ranchers, who are trained by Public Safety Officers and the Army. They have good weapons: At the end of last year they got Uzi machine guns. And there is a fourth source of provisions, which are the weapons that the campesinos all over Mexico have, like hunting rifles and other rudimentary arms. We don't have the quantity of weapons that we would like to have, nor the munitions. There is no foreign support."

*"And the bulk of the fighters, where do they come from?"*

"From the mountains and the jungle. The EZLN went from one stage to the next in a very orderly way. For our campesino *compañeros*, the EZLN was born as a self-defense group. That is, the ranchers' *guardias blancas* are a very powerful armed group; they take away the *compañeros'* land and mistreat them, and they limit the social and political development of the Indigenous peoples.

"The *compañeros* soon saw that the problem was not the self-defense of one community, or of the protection of one set of common lands. They realized it was necessary to establish alliances with other communities, and they began to form military and para-military contingents, still working with the idea of self-defense. There was a standstill until the supreme government had the brilliant idea of reforming Article 27. That was a powerful catalyst in the communities. Those reforms canceled all legal possibilities of their holding land. And that possibility is what had kept them functioning as para-military self-defense groups.

"Then came the electoral fraud of 1988. The *compañeros* saw that voting didn't matter either because there was no respect for obvious, basic things. These were the two detonators, but in my view it was the reform of Article 27 that most radicalized the *compañeros*. That reform closed the door on the Indigenous people's strategies for surviving legally and peacefully. That's why they rose up in arms, so that they would be heard. They were tired of paying such a high price in blood.

"Here, when someone gets sick and the family takes him to the doctor and the doctor writes a prescription, the family calculates which is cheaper—to buy the medicine or to buy the coffin. Just like that, in the coldest manner you can imagine."

*"And the idea of the armed struggle, more precisely, the one to form this unique guerrilla group, how did it get started?"*

"We arrived with campesinos; we didn't arrive as *ladinos* to go into the jungle in order to organize ourselves later. Earlier, while we were looking for different avenues, we found some Indigenous campesino sectors here in the Southeast, and we talked with them, and we began working with them; we interrelated. And then they started organizing themselves and doing directed work. They're the ones who said, okay, we have to get involved here, with a guerrilla group that is mostly Indigenous.

"The Indigenous peoples taught us to walk around here, they taught us how to live in the mountains, to hunt, and there we began to learn about weapons. That's how the EZLN got started, but the first phase was pure survival: We had to learn how to survive in the mountains, to get the mountains to accept us. From the beginning, it was always the Indigenous political leaders who talked with the communities, because these communities would not accept a *ladino*."

"*Did you plan to take power through armed means?*"

"No. We don't think like the Maoists. We don't think that the campesino army from the mountains can fence in the cities. That's not how we think; if there are no workers, nothing is possible politically or militarily."

"*Are you a national force?*"

"In the sense that our fundamental, core demands are national in focus and have their sympathizers, yes..."

"*In regard to the workers, are there any possibilities of alliance, of getting the workers of the urban areas interested in your cause?*"

"Well, the EZLN would have to incorporate the demands of the worker's movement among its own demands; not in the style of Fidel Schwarzenegger, of course. What I want you to understand is that when one speaks of death and misery in Chiapas, when one speaks of desperation, one is speaking of a shocking reality. That's why the *compañeros* say "Enough is enough." There's no question about consensus over armed struggle—we either die in struggle, or we die anyway. And they've clearly stated, it's better to die with dignity."

"*Does that mean that the EZLN cannot come to have some points of agreement or collaboration with other popular movements?*"

"It would have to be a more open space, under a much larger flag. It would not be within the EZLN; that common point of agreement would have to be something bigger and wider. That's why we talk about a national revolutionary movement. This point of correspondence would be around a point larger than the EZLN. If someone raises that flag, we would go there..."

"*In regard to the 10 points laid out in your declaration, do you have concrete proposals to resolve them?*"

"Yes. The *compañeros* that are going to go to the dialogue have clearly defined what we want."

"*Does that imply creating regional authorities in the zones where you are located?*"

"Autonomy, the *compañeros* say, like that of the Basque or the Catalans, which is a relative autonomy, because they have very, very little confidence in governments of the state. For example, in the case of the *compañeros*, it's not so much the Federal Army that they hate the most, it's the Security Forces, the state police, and the judiciary. If they see us, they'll eat us alive. So then they say that it is necessary to negotiate a statute of autonomy in which our government, our administrative structure, is recognized by the government and with which we can live without outside interference."

"*To what extent do you think the United States could intervene?*"

*"Oh, against you, of course."*

"We think that a generalized military intervention against us is unlikely. There could be intervention, but it would be against the PRI. It's not the Zapatistas who are worried about [the US] Congress's meeting. It leaves us unmoved; the mountain is birth, and it will also be death. It's the federal government that's worried. We think it's premature to talk about US intervention."

*"You say that the detonator of this war was the lack of land. Now, what do you want? Agrarian reform, Article 27, what?"*

"We're thinking that issues of agrarian reform should be reconsidered, but an important step would be to annul the Salinas reforms of Article 27. I'm talking about people who have poor land or those that have no land. What the *compañeros* say is that land is life, that if you don't have land you are living dead, and so why live? It's better to fight and die fighting.

"Annulling the Salinas reforms won't be enough, but it would be a start. It would be a way to open a wider discussion in which the countryside can taken into account alongside the governmental commitment to NAFTA. It's NAFTA that really directed those reforms of Article 27.

*"And what about the democratization?"*

"Respect of political demands. The Lacandona Jungle Declaration maintains that there cannot be a democratic transformation that's overseen by an illegitimate, or, if you don't like that term, undemocratic, government. It's absurd when eight political parties say, 'Yes, democracy now,' and one party comes and says 'Don't make trouble.' We ask ourselves, 'How can that document be guaranteed? What hope is there?' That's why we insist that this party has to leave so that another can come in and say, 'Now, let's fight without weapons and see who wins.'"

Night falls and the cold sweeps in. The subcommander orders a military parade and the column presents arms to the journalists because, the leader tells them, "They're good people." They sing their hymns for us, "The Insurgent" and The EZLN Anthem—It's sung to the tune of "Carabina 30-30."

*Let's go, let's go, let's go forward*
*to push our struggle onward*
*for our country demands and needs*
*all the effort of the Zapatistas.*

On his way back from the camp he starts telling jokes and anecdotes. Like this one from January 1:

In the Headquarters of the Municipal Police of San Cristóbal de las Casas, at dawn, the phone rang:

"Is this Police Headquarters? Listen, we want to warn you that a lot of armed people are coming here, through Centenario Avenue."

"It's all right. We have already been informed. Don't worry. Everything is under control."

Marcos is the one who answered. He coordinated the occupation of the police precincts. Of course, he burst out laughing.

Little by little, the *compañeras* from the kitchen climb the hill, carrying large pots of stew and coffee. They give the military salute, "*Compañero* militiaman".

When everything is ready, the *compañera* Major Ana María, stands at attention.

"Subcommander, we are ready to serve." And Marcos gives the order, "Eat."

But he doesn't eat himself. There's the problem of the ski-mask, and the journalists are still here.

# 3

The inspiration came from Pancho Villa in the sierra of Corralchén, with one or another modification. They built a Hollywood-style film set. They used stones to make four streets complete with street signs. Facades of houses and of a make-believe municipal building were built with bamboo and adobe. A small bus was constructed out of wood and labeled "82nd Regiment," and a real motorcycle was carried all the way out there on someone's back just to give the scene a realistic touch. It was on that "set" that the January 1994 offensive was rehearsed. When the Army attacked this camp half a year earlier, in May 1993, the Army generals concluded, "This is the plan of attack against Ocosingo." But actually, there was much more to it than that.

"If you look closely," Subcommander Marcos tells us in hindsight, "the facades of the municipal buildings of San Cristóbal, Margaritas, Ocosingo and several others are identical." That is how the EZLN trained to take those towns. [...]

During the 12 days of combat not everything happened according to the EZLN strategist's plans. In the case of Ocosingo, no combat had been planned. The Army surrounded the town from two sides and the civilian population was caught in the middle. In that situation, Marcos tells us, "Our troops did what they had to do, die for the people."

Despite his pleasure in the fact that his own stroke of genius worked, and that they were able to simultaneously seize five municipal authorities, he admits realistically:

"Right now we can't defeat the Federal Army, nor can the Federal Army defeat us. The crux of a war is not military confrontation but rather the politics put into play in that confrontation."

While the *ladino* subcommander speaks, a glance from the Indigenous Commanders (from one of the Clandestine Revolutionary Committees of the Zapatista National Liberation Army) present during the interview, shows their agreement:

"We accept that we've suffered deaths. We'll never lie about the number of casualties. To die like this is an honor for us. Right now we're already living on borrowed time."

Between weapons and negotiations, between war and peace, deep in their territory, the Zapatistas know one thing for certain, "It's definitely not yet time to lay down our weapons."

When asked about the influence of the Central American wars of the '80s on the experience in Chiapas, he points out that the Zapatistas learned to distrust the purely

When asked about the influence of the Central American wars of the '80s on the experience in Chiapas, he points out that the Zapatistas learned to distrust the purely electoral option from the Sandinistas. They learned to distrust disarmament from the Farabundistas. And from the Guatemalans, their closest neighbor... Well, that's perhaps the only question left unanswered.

Other than that, the influence stems purely from "Villa and Zapata. We also learned what not to do from the mistakes of the Mexican guerrillas of the '70s."

Now, during this defensive waiting period in their own territory, the Zapatistas have started to mine the roads to block the advance of the Army's armored vehicles. Subcommander Marcos wants this known, especially as a warning to those journalists who imprudently cross the check points of the EZLN, "It's already happened. Some madman didn't obey the order to stop and continued on. We were sweating bullets trying to deactivate the mines."

### May 1993: Corralchén

In May of 1993 the Mexican Army discovered a guerrilla enclave in a town called Corralchén, in the township of Ocosingo. At the time, it was said the camp contained insurgent propaganda, leftover ammunition, and a model of a town that revealed possible attacks against the municipal authority of Ocosingo. But the official version fell short; there was much more.

*"General Miguel Angel Godínez, Commander of the Southeastern zone, says that what you did the first few days of January was an act of propaganda and that it was a complete failure."*

"It was an act of propaganda, and it was a total success. We have to give credit where it's due. It was a military wonder, and nobody seems to want to admit that. Now everybody says that those who speak about military matters are rash warmongers who haven't realized that the military course of action is not inappropriate for Mexico. In my view that's the reason people from the press and the intellectuals have criticized the military aspect of this affair. We were going to start at zero hours on the 31st of December with the New Year's fireworks. We figured people would be on vacation so there wouldn't be any civilian population. The majority of people would be at home and wouldn't be on the streets in case of a shoot-out. The officers of the Federal Army would also be on vacation, or maybe Godínez should explain the whereabouts of his officers' corps. I know where each and every one of them were. The entire country was relaxing.

"I am going to tell you once and for all how we did it, because, if I don't, they're going to say I copied the '89 offensive in El Salvador. We did what a gentleman by the name of Francisco Villa did when he attacked Ciudad Juárez, Chihuahua. If you remember, he feigned the attack on Chihuahua and then hit Juárez.

"We simulated an attack on Ocosingo, and if you check the press, three days before the whole country knew that a guerrilla group was in San Miguel (near Ocosingo), and everybody pretended not to know.

155

"That's when the enemy thought we'd hit Ocosingo, and we started to move a battalion and a half towards San Cristóbal. When they realized what was happening, they really got scared since they'd expected the attack to be at Ocosingo."

*"What really happened last May in the mountain range of Corralchén, when the Army attacked you? Was it a battle you were expecting or did it happen by chance?"*

"No, it was an accident. We thought that either someone had betrayed us or that the column of soldiers had simply stumbled on our headquarters accidentally. What's certain is that not a single Zapatista remained on that sierra by that very same evening. In other words, we got out immediately, and avoided entrapment. The encounters that followed were among their own troops; we had already retreated into the jungle.

"The Army filled the sierra with soldiers, and they began advancing until they clashed and killed each other. We counted 12 dead soldiers and six wounded, just like that, from mortar fire. In strategic matters, communication failures make things very difficult. We suspect that those in command are unwilling to say, 'We made a mistake and hit our own people.' Instead they're claiming the casualties were guerrillas. So Godínez sent more and more soldiers, and they completed the circle.

"That's when we were finally able to relax, because the CCRI said, 'If they touch any of the towns, we start, otherwise we don't.'

"But we were already waiting. The Army made a mistake by retreating because they were already there. We were on the verge of activating the offensive that was planned for the end of the year. All of a sudden, Bishop Juan Jesús Posadas was murdered in Guadalajara. Then the problem reached the national press and stopped the offensive. Otherwise it would have started, and you would have been interviewing me in May."

*"You say that the published information has hardly touched upon the military aspect. Do you think there is a deliberate effort to diminish the military importance and thus diminish this phenomenon?"*

"Yes, It seems clear to me that there is consensus among the government, all of you [the press], and civil society that the world has to be shown that military alternatives are not a viable option."

*"Why?"*

"I don't know why. The January offensive demonstrated that it's possible to carry out sizable military operations if a series of conditions are present, and that military knowledge need not be drawn from traditional guerrilla or Central American guerrilla tactics. Rather, it can be drawn from our own country's history. I don't think anyone wants to deal with that."

*"Would you say it's because somebody might follow the example?"*

"Yes, the example of trying it, or of planning it out well and then one day carrying it out, not the example of taking up arms all of a sudden and attacking the municipal building. They say, these are definitely desperate, hungry, illiterate natives, but they came up with a military plan. They carried it out well and ended it well."

*"Despite the military successes of the EZLN, there seems to be a certain fatalism when you talk about your outlook, as if you've accepted that there's not much of a future from a strictly military standpoint."*

"Like we said from the beginning, we are living on borrowed time. I have to be sincere with the people and tell them: This might be the last time that I write to you, and that's the truth. It's not cancer or AIDS, it's just that they want to kill us. Either the feds shoot and kill us or the journalists will kill us because of their recklessness."

*"How do you expect to do anything against a well-equipped army that has logistical support?"*

"Well, what's decisive in a war isn't military confrontation, but the politics at play in that confrontation. We know that this war isn't going to define itself in military terms, not even if we had the superior weapons. What matters are the politics that move one or the other party. We don't think there has been a military defeat on either side. We know that we cannot defeat the Federal Army, but we also know that the Federal Army cannot defeat us militarily.

"We didn't go to war on January 1 to kill or to be killed. We went to war to make ourselves heard. In that sense, the reasoning behind the Committee's "Enough is enough" declaration is quite clear. It was neither suicidal nor adventurous. We had few casualties and our military capability is not only intact, it grew. We came down from the mountain with several thousand people, and when we fell back we had even more people.

"We don't lie about our casualties; it isn't necessary. We're not going to hide the fact that we die. For the *compañeros*, death under these circumstances is an honor; it's dignified. If the Army says they've killed so many guerrillas, well, we say it's not true. Who knows who they killed? We're not making unfounded claims when we say that the Army kills civilians and then says they're Zapatistas. We have more people, more ammunition and arms; where's the suicide?"

*"There's a lot of photographic evidence showing that many Zapatista combatants were sent to war with wooden rifles. Isn't that suicide?"*

"No. When the combatant doesn't have a weapon, s/he still has to learn to move as if s/he has one; carrying something in their hands and learning how to move with it is part of their training. And the tale that we sent the little Indians out with wooden rifles and followed them up with foreigners carrying ultra-modern weapons is a lie."

## Ocosingo, a Mousetrap

*"What happened in Rancho Nuevo and Ocosingo? What were those operations like?"*

"The attack on Rancho Nuevo took place because an army hungry for weapons and ammunition has to go where there are weapons and ammunition. Then, on the second, we faked another attack on Rancho Nuevo. I don't know who was in command at Rancho Nuevo, or if anyone was in charge at all, but whoever was there did a good job; they organized a good defense. We pretended to attack from the right in order to attack

157

from both sides, but they defended themselves on both sides as well. So, when we sent a patrol to fight, the clash took place. There were casualties on both sides, and we did what any well trained, fed, and disciplined army does: We ran. They had dismantled our attack. We were still learning. We are still learning.

"According to our plans, each municipal seat had to be cleared without gunfire, but we were thinking of Rancho Nuevo. Rancho Nuevo was secure because we had just attacked in order to allow for an orderly withdrawal, a political one, as we say, from Ocosingo, Chanal, Margaritas, Oxchuc, and Huistán.

"But the Army sent troops through Palenque, something we were unprepared for because of tactical mistakes. As we were regrouping, the Army came in and clashed with our reinforcements. And this time what happened to us at Rancho Nuevo, happened to the Army. We dismantled and dispersed them, even though Godínez won't admit it. We place enemy casualties at the same numbers acknowledged by the Army, but according to our intelligence services, on January 15 there were 180 corpses of federal soldiers in the seventh military region of Tuxtla Gutiérrez. But what we haven't confirmed, we don't announce as fact. The plan was to withdraw the troops that took Ocosingo, and they were a big force. They began withdrawing in stages, but then we had a problem with the civilians. The *compañeros* in San Cristóbal realized that civilians had mixed in with our troops, out of sympathy, curiosity or what have you. And then they got caught in that mousetrap of the market. Our troops were in position, but we couldn't leave the civilians there.

"In order to remove the civilians, our sharpshooters had to start firing and caused Army casualties. The Army then fixed our positions and started to attack us with mortar fire. The wounded we have in our field hospital were wounded by shrapnel from rockets and mortars, not by bullets.

"Our combatants were shooting from a fixed position, which is suicidal for any sharpshooter, because to protect themselves they really should keep changing positions. A fighter has to protect the civilians, so they stayed put in order to allow the civilians to get out. They maintained their positions for a long time, until they surrendered them. We lost, at worst, 40 *compañeros*."

*"That's a lot."*

"It's serious because they're *compañeros*. Even if there had only been four it would have been serious. But there are only nine confirmed casualties, we don't know if the others were taken prisoner, or if they disappeared. Some days later some *compañeros* started to appear in small groups in other places. Those soldiers know the mountains very well.

"So, Ocosingo was not a planned combat, but the troops did what they had to do—they died for the people. That is where a guerrilla cannot choose. If s/he has to die for a civilian, s/he will do it. Not everyone understands that."

*"Were the five casualties in the market Zapatistas?"*

"That we don't know. *Compañeros* have told us of a wounded fighter who was captured; a soldier tied his hands behind his back, and then another arrived and sprayed him with bullets. Another *compañero* saw them taking four prisoners (again with their hands tied behind their backs), but those were civilians. According to our "ears"—we have them everywhere—the exhumation at the public ministry was done at night, and left until the next day. The Army arrived at night and dressed the corpses up as guerrillas. I couldn't say with any certainty that they were all Zapatistas."

*"This week negotiations begin. Has the time come for you to turn over your weapons?"*

"Definitely not. I've spoken with the *compañeros* of the Committee, as well as with the troops. But since it's the Committee that's in charge here, we have to do what they say. And they say that we cannot turn over our weapons because, up until now, the government has only given us promises that things are going to change. And that's what we've always gotten from the government during elections anyway, even without an armed movement. During elections, there are always promises and proclamations. The *compañeros* say that the surrender of arms has to be part of a later process, after negotiations, when we see that the agreements are being fulfilled."

*"Does keeping your weapons serve as a warranty for the agreements?"*

"We think so. In this case there has to be a double guarantee. First, that the government will do what it promises, and then a guarantee of survival. Because there's something that the media hasn't paid attention to, and that is the existence of *guardias blancas,* which are a type of death squad. They are one of our main suppliers of weapons, by the way, since you are so worried about our weapons.

"When Patrocinio González was in office, the Union for the Defense of Ocosingo (La Unión para la Defensa de Ocosingo) was organized to serve the landowners who had 400 armed men. When we went to take their weapons, we found everything from rifles to M-16's and R-15's. Even if the Army agrees to the peace proposals, how can we turn over our weapons when there are other military forces functioning in the area? The *guardias blancas* are the ones in charge here, particularly in the Lacandona Jungle. The ranchers' *guardias blancas* are the third force that needs to be dismantled."

*"With so many people moving around, how did you keep such a big operation secret?"*

"Because the people are on our side. When the EZLN and the Clandestine Committee speak of controlled territory, they are referring to everything but the city area and the roads in Chiapas. The rural areas are under Zapatista control. Otherwise, how could we mobilize thousands of people from the forest, and move them to a city that is only 12 kilometers away from the largest military base in the Southeast, the one in Rancho Nuevo? How could we camp for days ahead of time in the surrounding areas? There had to be complicity, support not only in those specific areas, but all along the entry and exit routes. That's what allowed us to withdraw without casualties."

*"Are you saying that a lot of people covered up the operation with their silence?"*

"With silence and support, because you have to move the people, feed them, hide them. But most people helped us with silence. The majority may not be Zapatista, but they would say, 'this is aimed at those who are bothering us, so it's OK; I'm not going to report it to those who bother me. On the contrary, I hope they get through and I wish them well.' That's what they told us."

*"And how is the EZLN doing now? Are they in these territories? In camps, in villages? Where?"*

"I'm glad you asked me that because they say we are vandalizing the ranches and it's not true. We are waiting for an attack, waiting in trenches all along the entry points. We can't afford the luxury of stealing cattle or pigs. Right now, in military terms, we are in a defensive situation within our own terrain. But this is what we've been planning and anticipating for a long time now, so it presents no problems for us.

"The attack on January 1 was the big headache because everything that's a defensive advantage is a disadvantage in an attack. Take, for instance, the dispersal of our forces. Right now we have troops in several places, armed, located, and with knowledge of the area. But for an offensive, you have to gather all those troops and take them somewhere outside their terrain to fight. That was the great difficulty we faced in January. How to orchestrate such a mobilization and concentration of troops without being detected by the enemy.

"Initially I had thought about doing it on December 28, but later I thought: Anyone who talks and says we are mobilizing people won't be trusted because it's Holy Innocents Day. That's why we cancelled those plans and moved it to December 31."

*"If everything was so well planned, why did you stop the advance? Because of the government's cease-fire?"*

"Look, I'm going to tell you what happened. We started, they gave us a run, we got into place, we fought well, we withdrew, and then we were putting mines in a road we knew the tanks would be using as their point of entry. And all of a sudden the *compañeros* tell me to cease fire. Chin. Hold on. Wait, something's happened. But a cease-fire wasn't supposed to happen until we'd been fighting for months.

"I went to the Committee and told them that I'd heard the news about the cease-fire. Something has to be going on. This is not about us. Let's also have a cease-fire so we can see what's going on. We were running. We were not facing enemy bullets with our brave chests. But we started to catch on that something was happening that we didn't know about. And then we discovered what it was. We have to acknowledge, with honor, that the civil society provoked that cease-fire. And the press, what little this country has of an honest press, well, the press played a starring role."

# 4

These days political activity in Zapatista territories is very intense. Already, the Clandestine Revolutionary Indigenous Committees of each zone have selected two delegates to participate in the dialogue, and they are in the process of consulting with their communities to define the mandate those leaders will bring to the negotiations. The communities will define what they can accept and what they cannot accept.

Fifteen Zapatistas, representing committees and fighting groups, will sit face to face with Manuel Camacho Solís.

On the other hand, the leadership of the Zapatista National Liberation Army is preparing for a broader and more substantial dialogue.

On one side, with the political parties.

According to Subcommander Marcos, perhaps someday, maybe soon, all presidential candidates will be invited by the CCRI-CG to visit their territories, "to sit down with us, so that we can see what they tell us about our problems."

For them, the Zapatistas have a message: "There is a larger movement, one that goes beyond the armed struggle, a movement in which everyone has something to do to make this country more just."

*"The electoral board has changed considerably because of what has unfolded since January first. You aren't a political party, but what's your position regarding the August elections? Are you planning to participate in the electoral field?"*

"From the mountains that would be difficult. If the president doesn't resign, there have to be reforms that will ensure that the federal government is no longer the body that oversees and sanctions the electoral process. We can see that the current system favors only one party. Another body must sanction the process. It should be a binding principle that the secretary of government shouldn't participate. The electoral college should say, 'This one won, that one lost.' And the electoral college shouldn't have ties with the federal government.

"But things don't work that way. The federal government, along with its main leader, have already chosen one candidate. "Don't make trouble," they said. There aren't going to be democratic elections unless there is a change in the electoral law.

"If there was a reform in the electoral process that would prevent the government from sanctioning the elections, it would be like decapitating the ruling party. And that's what's happening."

*"It doesn't matter to you if it's Colosio or another candidate who runs for the PRI?"*

"Yes, to tell the truth, it doesn't matter. We aren't concerned about who wins the elections. The *compañeros'* view is that if there is really democracy in Mexico, anyone elected has to respond to what the people demand; if not, he will be ousted. That's the nature of the *compañeros'* democracy. For example, they are elected democratically. If they don't do their job, their base discharges them. They say the country should work like this. If the PRI wins, it must win properly, in such a way that if it doesn't deliver what it promised, we have to remove it and another party has to replace it.

"And when this "holy" character, Aguilar Talamantes, appears and says that he could be the political arm of the EZLN, the *compañeros* do not approve. They have to say no to him; they have to say no to everyone. Fight, win, but there must be something that says that whoever wins has to do what was promised, otherwise, no. Because if we support a party and it's going to be the same old thing ... What we need is a space in which to make that candidate or that president accountable.

"In this they are quite clear and quite radical. Now they say, 'No, you don't need to support this or that party.' If Colosio is going to win, he has to win properly, and to win properly means that he has to deliver what he promised. The same thing if Cárdenas [PRD] or Diego Fernández de Cevallos [PAN] wins.

"They are planning to invite the candidates to speak with them or to listen to what they have to say. If they don't want to come, then they plan to send them a letter and tell them. In the end, what the *compañeros* discuss with the government will be decided by the next president, and that future president, for good or for bad, will be one of the nine—or I don't know how many now—current presidential candidates."

*"Are the Zapatistas willing to constitute themselves as a political force?"*

"That would have to be considered by the *compañeros,* because there is a lot of distrust regarding the whole idea of a political party. They have to consider what sort of guarantees it gives them, what type of recognition it would bring them. But then they say, OK, we didn't rise to take power. If a political party wants to take power, then what will happen to us as leaders?"

*"You were saying that the reforms of Article 27 were a trigger. And what about Patrocinio González's government?"*

"Yes. Patrocinio was completely absurd. But more than Patrocinio himself, what was absurd was what he supported: the Ocosingo Defense Union (la Unión para la Defensa de Ocosingo), the Altamirano Ranchers' Associations (las Asociaciones Ganaderas de Altamirano), of Margaritas, very reactionary associations. They are the most reactionary of all the bourgeoisie, very aggressive, despotic, racist. Compared with other governors that either attacked or didn't do anything about the bourgeoisie, Patrocinio praised it. Yes, he had a lot to with the process of radicalization."

*"What's your message? Do you sense that you are being heard?"*

"The message is that there is a larger movement, one that goes beyond the armed movement, and that everyone has to do something. That everyone has to work to transform this country into a just country, into a country that offers justice for all, not simply for one group. Some people understand this. I think that the ones who least understand the message are the political parties. They should be more aggressive, not in the sense that they should take up arms, but they should push further and work to secure and open more political spaces for participation. It seems that their declaration supporting peace owes more to the fact that at some point they felt obliged to say something about Chiapas. Moving from 'wipe them out,' like Fidel Schwarzenegger, to 'No, violence, no. Relax, peace, peace, peace.'

"In order to convince civil society that armed struggle is not the way out, there has to be a truly democratic space. But what is being done to open that democratic space, aside from making statements and writing articles in the newspapers? I think that if all the political parties—here I am speaking across the spectrum; I am not referring to any one of them in particular—that are a part of that civic pact, the one that Salinas annulled by saying 'Don't dream,' if they don't begin to do something different, no democratic space is going to be built.

"They can negotiate peace in Chiapas in February, and in June the country will rise again. If the system is not revolutionized before the elections, with or without the Zapatistas, whether they kill us or not, the country is going to rise up. And then it will not only be Indigenous people or the guerrilla group, but there are going to be many forms of struggle, and the political parties will see themselves overthrown as they were here."

*"Do you see them bypassed here?"*

"Well, the fact that the *compañeros* have said that there is no electoral option makes that clear."

*"What happens if, after all of this, the state returns to normal, to the way it was before? Would you strike again?"*

"That type of decision depends on a collective process. Those decisions do not depend on Marcos deciding to attack tomorrow, or the fact that he was angered by Payan's January 2 editorial. I can't decide that. I have to consult with the Committee, and, whether it is convenient or not, the Committee has its own complex process of consultation with the communities. Decisions of such magnitude are not up to a single individual."

### On the Road to Chinameca?

*"Are you going to participate in the negotiations?"*

"I don't know. The Committee still has to decide. If it decides that I should participate, I'll have to do it. I'm telling you, the *compañeros* in the Committee and the rest of us are still carrying the remains of the Chinameca ghost and the haunting image of Carranza standing behind Salinas de Gortari as he announced the Amnesty Law. We do not rule out that kind of a coup; it has been considered. There is supposed to be a succession in military commands, and there's people to relieve the *compañeros* in the Committee. As of today, February 2, there's no specific decision on who will participate. But the petitions to be presented at the dialogue have already been agreed on. They reiterate The Declaration of the Lacandona Jungle and the EZLN communiqués. There are no changes in this regard. It's not that we said that Salinas must resign, and that now we are retracting that. There is no change. In any case, some demands that were quite general before are much more concrete now. Why do you ask the question? Do you want to see me there?"

*"In other processes, the military issue prompted the dialogue. Do we need more bullets in Mexico to convince all parties that there must be dialogue?"*

"We have thought about it, but, the way things are right now, we can't take that sort of initiative. We can't say that we're going to end the game, because we haven't even begun to talk. That's the situation now. I'm not saying that's what's going to take place if the dialogue doesn't work."

*"Then you are going to talk with weapons in hand?"*

"Definitely. The *compañeros* have been very clear in that regard. The first item in the negotiation can't be the surrender of arms. The first item of negotiation is the conditions we live in."

*"Could it turn out to be a dialogue between deaf people?"*

"It's clear to us that the government is preparing the political atmosphere to support a large-scale military operation. The dialogue process, or, as Mr. Camacho calls them, the Conference for Peace and Reconciliation, rests on an ultimatum: We negotiate or..."

*"How many delegates are going to the dialogue, all of the CCRI?"*

"No, the Clandestine Committee is made up of dozens of *compañeros*. Each Committee controls a territory, and each Committee is nominating two delegates. They're telling those two delegates: You can say yes to this, to this you must say no, and this, don't even touch it. And this is what you are going to ask for. When you say, 'yes, I accept this,' it means that it's valid, and when you say that you don't accept it, it means that no one is going to accept it."

*"How many people will attend?"*

"We estimate around 15, counting regular combat forces and committees, because we think that representatives of the combat forces, which are the active ones, also have to go—their voice has to be heard too. But we don't know. We just got the letter. We're just now sending it to Camacho. We'll have to see how he replies."

*"And how will the presence of the press be handled, will you limit it or...?"*

"We said that everyone will be admitted, only Televisa will be barred for obvious reasons. We want the struggle to be known. We're not going to charge anybody a fee; on the contrary, they're doing us a favor dealing with this as they used to deal with our grandparents."

*"And how do things stand one month after the beginning of the conflict?"*

"We have passed very rapidly to a phase for which we were not prepared: dialogue. We were prepared for a long process of war, of attrition, of military clashes, of political disputes over the towns and villages, of ideological struggle. And afterwards, if the government co-opted these, there would be a dialogue, but only after all that."

*"You had no idea it would go this fast?"*

"Actually, no. That's why I say that when we were preparing the defense, the mines and explosives, and the cease-fire occurred, we discovered that something had happened, and I think it was the press that provoked all that."

*"In some places you have the support of the people, but in many other places, not. There is either fear and ignorance or straight out rejection..."*

"Those things are part of a strategy, an old strategy that's been around at least since Vietnam: What the Federal Army is doing is offering provisions and money to people who arrive in Ocosingo and Altamirano in exchange for them denouncing the Zapatistas and saying that we expelled them from their communities, that we robbed them, that we beat them up. Everything that's coming out right now in the press—the Committees have been examining the cases—it turns out that it's people who said "I'm going out to buy salt," and suddenly they show up making statements. According to what one of those returning told us, Army personnel told him, 'Say that they're bothering you and we'll give you your provisions.' In this strategy, the Federal Army goes from being the aggressor against the civilian population to being the savior of the civilian population, positioning itself against us, the transgressors of the law, that is to say, the Zapatista National Liberation Army.

"But that has to be seen as part and parcel of what is being done at the national level with this strategy of a monologue disguised as a dialogue or a developing dialogue. Just as we are a 'developing political force,' the government's monologue is a developing dialogue."

*"You mean to say that, the way things are, no great results can be expected from this negotiation?"*

"Political results, yes."

*"From what you say, it's clear that you are not going to give up your arms. But, what good are weapons if you're politically bound not to use them, as you are now?"*

"Well, right now arms can't be used offensively for political purposes, but materially they can be used as a defensive measure. We are in our own territory. To get us out they have to come and get us. That's the reason the government has to think twice about trying to finish us off once and for all."

*"It would seem that part of the government's strategy, specifically their acting in great haste to quell the war, complicates your use of military action. Is that true?"*

"No, I have to disagree. The military conflict is a latent one; it's not taking place right now, but it's there and can erupt at any moment, and that's why we can't give up our arms. They are our defense. January 1 was our way of making ourselves heard. Now the arms are our way of surviving, of making sure that they don't annihilate us. Or that if they have to annihilate us, it will be at a very high cost to the country. We don't give arms a value they don't have. We don't worship arms, but we understand what they represent at one political moment or another. In our view, at this moment, arms are our guarantee of survival, a guarantee we are ready to defend with dignity."

*"What lessons do you take from the experience of Central American struggles and revolutions? What conclusions do you draw?"*

"Well, what we've learned from the Central American revolution is to greatly distrust the surrender of arms, as in the case of El Salvador, or having confidence only in electoral processes, as in the case of the Sandinistas. But our military training comes from Villa, principally, from Zapata. It also comes by way of negative example from what was done by the guerrillas of the 1970s. They started with a local military movement and expected that the base would increase slowly, either illuminated by this guerrilla force or by approaching sectors that were never going to support them. We think that those were errors of interpretation and judgement made by the guerrillas of the '70s, errors we have understood well. Up until now, we can't be faulted on military grounds. Of course we haven't faced the military power of the Federal Army in its entirety, but in questions of tactics or strategy there is no connection with foreigners.

"There is an intellectual who edits a magazine who says that the proof of Central American influence in the EZLN lies in, one, the fact that we withdrew our wounded and our dead (something he says we copied from the FMLN), and, two, the attack on the cities, (which he says we took from the FSLN). We took both things from Francisco Villa. He had trains to evacuate his wounded; what we did was hijack trucks to take away our wounded and our dead to our towns and villages and field hospitals."

The time came to say good-bye.

Perhaps we reporters were left with many questions on the tips of our tongues or in our knapsacks. On the way back, during the nighttime journey and in the comfortable darkness of blindfolded eyes, many of these questions came to the surface, but there was no way, it was too late. Subcommander Marcos, the figure who captured the imagination of many Mexicans on January 1, had stayed behind. The militia members who accompanied us out of the Zapatista territory walked in silence, absorbed in thought. We went along thinking of one question, the only one that the Sup had asked us:

"And all of you, what are you going to do?"

# 6. BUILDING TIES

## SOLIDARITY LETTERS

*[These letters were written in response to letters received by the EZLN as they were preparing for the dialogue. Several groups offered their solidarity, as well as sending pleas for peace. These responses continue the EZLN's efforts to reach beyond the mountains of the Mexican Southeast.]*

### A LETTER OF INTRODUCTION

February 8, 1994

To the national weekly *Proceso*:
To the national newspaper *La Jornada*:
To the national newspaper *El Financiero*:
To the local newspaper of San Cristóbal de las Casas, Chiapas, *Tiempo*:

Gentlemen:

Here I give you another series of letters that the CCRI-CG of the EZLN sends to various recipients. I hope that you have time to make sure they arrive to their addressees.

I understand your desperation (and that of your editorial chiefs for the high expenses in hotels, restaurants and gas stations) over the delay in the initiation of the dialogue. It is not our fault (or the Commissioner's), or putting on airs to make ourselves wanted. It is not over disagreements in the agenda or anything like that. It is because we still lack details on the security of our delegates, details that we must take care of in order to avoid ugly "surprises." In short: serenity and patience, lots of patience.

As a consolation I will tell you that the dialogue will not be in the jungle. Among other things because there [in the jungle] those who can communicate through satellite would have the advantage, since telephone or fax, forget it. And, if time is on the side of

169

the small ones, we prefer democracy and the equality of opportunity for the communications media, and that the news should not be only for the powerful.

Good health and patience,
From the mountains of the Mexican Southeast,
Insurgent Subcommander Marcos

# A Thank-You to the
# University Student Council of UNAM

February 6, 1994

To the University Student Council (Consejo Estudiantil Universitario, CEU), National Autonomous University of Mexico, (Universidad Nacional Autónoma de México, UNAM), Mexico City:

*Compañeros* and *Compañeras:*

We received your letter of January 29, 1994 signed by Angel Gómez C. We thank you for the thoughts you send us.

The majority of us are Indigenous, illiterate and discriminated against. We had no opportunity to finish even elementary school. We would have wanted not only to finish elementary school and junior high, but to have reached college.

We gladly receive your greetings and support, men and women who struggle in other lands and through different ways to achieve the same freedoms, democracy, and justice that we all long for. We know that in other times the brave voice of Mexican students has made the evil government tremble, and that if your voice were to be united with ours and with that of all of the dispossessed, nothing would remain standing of this gigantic lie that they make us swallow every day, every night, in death and life, always. That is why we want to address you, men and women students of Mexico, to respectfully ask you something:

If it were possible for you to organize, and once things calm down a bit, for you to come to our mountains to visit us and chat with us and to help us with what you know of technology and writing and all that comes in books that never come our way. We do not want you to come to politicize us or to pull us into one or another political current. In this I think that you would be more likely to learn from us what a truly democratic and participatory organization is. But you can help us cut the coffee, prepare the corn field, and in the community work of our villages. You can help us learn to read and write, to improve our health and nutrition, to use techniques that get more from the land. You can come to teach us and to learn. You can come even for only a few days so you get to know this part of Mexico that already existed before January 1 and in spite of it...

If you were to accept our invitation then you would need to send some delegates, so that through an intermediary we come to agree on the details, because we need to organize everything very well so spies of the evil government will not come in. It does not matter if you cannot come, brother and sister students, but continue struggling in your land so there will be justice for the Mexican people.

That is all, men and women students of Mexico. We await your written response.

Respectfully,
From the mountains of the Mexican Southeast,
CCRI-CG of the EZLN

P.S.: Sup's section: "The recurrent postscript"

P.S. to the P.S. of the CEU that said: To Sup Marcos: "Do not worry, we will take the Zócalo for you." I have told the CCRI-CG that Mexico City is on the other side of the world and there aren't enough fighters, and furthermore, as I-don't-remember-who said, guerrillas that take *zócalos* sooner or later become hamburgeoisie [a play on words combining hamburger and bourgeoisie]. By the way, and taking advantage of the trip, bring two hamburgers without onions or ketchup. Thanks.

P.S. to the previous P.S.: Since we are on postscripts, which of all the CEU's is the one that writes us? When I was a good-looking 25-year-old (Hey! Tell the computer at the Attorney General's office [Procuraduría General de la Republica, PGR] to calculate that) there were at least three CEU's. Did they finally unite?

P.S. to the P.S. of the P.S.: In case that you, oof!, took the Zócalo, do not be uncool and set a piece apart to sell handicrafts because I could suddenly become an unemployed "professional in violence," and it always is better to be a sub-employed "professional in violence" because of that NAFTA stuff, you know.

P.S. to the nth power: These postscripts really are a letter disguised as postscripts (because of the PGR and etceteras with their dark, well-built glasses) and, but of course, do not require a response, or return address, or addressee (there are indisputable advantages to letters disguised as postscripts).

Nostalgic P.S.: When I was young (Hey? PGR? Here is some more information.) there was a lightly wooded field located more or less between the Central Library, the College of Philosophy and Literature, the Humanities Tower, Insurgents Avenue and the internal drive of the University Campus (Ciudad Universitaria, CU). We used to call that space, for reasons known to those initiated, the "valley of passions." It was assiduously visited by various elements of the fauna populating the CU from 7 p.m. onwards (the time at which good consciences drink chocolate and the bad ones get like water boiling [hot and bothered]) from the areas of humanities, sciences, and others (are there others?). At that time, a Cuban (Hello? Ambassador Jones? Take note of more proof of pro-Castroism.) who lectured in front of a piano the color of his skin, and went by the name of Snowball, would repeat:

You cannot have conscience and heart...

P.S. of *finale fortissimo*: Did you notice the exquisitely cultured and delicate tone of these postscripts? Are they not worthy of our entering the First World? Doesn't it make you realize that such transgressors prepare themselves to be competitive in NAFTA?

P.S. of happy end: All right, all right, I'm going... But it's because that airplane has me fed up, and the guard, for a change, fell asleep, and someone is tired of repeating "Who's there?" and I tell myself that it is the country...and you?

## TO THE CIVIC FRONT OF MAPASTEPEC

February 8, 1994

To The Civic Front of Mapastepec (Frente Cívico Mapastepec), Mapastepec, Chiapas:

Brothers and Sisters:

We want to tell you our word. We received your letter dated February 6, 1994.

The great majority of the presidents of Chiapaneco townships are the result of electoral fraud, of the trampling of popular will. All the municipal presidents in Chiapas should resign or be deposed. In their place, municipal councils should be democratically elected by those who are governed. Collective government is better than the government of one person, but it must be democratic. If the state government substitutes a president imposed by a municipal council equally imposed, then the anti-democratic council must also fall. This must be so until the just will of the majority is respected.

The EZLN supports, without conditions, the just demands of the people of Mapastepec who struggle for an authentic democracy, and the demands of all the popular forces which, now and in the future, struggle against the arbitrariness of imposed municipal presidents. The demand for municipal democracy is already part of the list of Zapatista demands.

Out with the imposed municipal presidents!
Long live the democratic municipal councils!

Respectfully,
From the mountains of the Mexican Southeast,
CCRI-CG of the EZLN

## TO THE MUNICIPAL PRESIDENT OF J. SIXTO VERDUZCO, MICHOACÁN

February 8, 1994

To Citizen Mario Robledo, Municipal President
Township of J. Sixto Verduzco, Michoacán, Mexico:

Brother:

We received your letter dated February 5, 1994. We are very happy to receive your greeting from Michoacán. But our happiness is even greater knowing that there are, in some municipal presidencies of this country, brave and honorable people, people who walk with truth and prudence. These people exist and it is good that they are in government if their villages order them there. Because what comes from respect for the will of others is a good path for all.

We, little men and women, have taken the task of being big, to live this way even if we are dying. We saw that in order to be big, we must look at all those suffering in this land and go walk with them. And we saw that we couldn't. And we saw that we couldn't

172

stop being brothers and sisters in peace and justice. And we saw that it is the evil government that separates our steps. We saw that it is for good and truthful men to struggle for the government to change. We saw that they wouldn't change willingly. And we saw them take up arms. And all this we saw and so we did it.

But we also saw that it is not only the mouth of fire that attains freedom. We saw that other mouths need to open and scream so that the powerful tremble. We saw that the struggles are many, and many are the colors and languages of those that struggle. And we saw that we were not alone. And we saw that we will not die alone.

Good health Michoacán brothers!

That the struggle does not end! Let hope not die!

Respectfully,
From the mountains in the Mexican Southeast,
CCRI-CG of the EZLN

# TO THE SUPREME COUNCIL OF INDIAN PEOPLES

**February 8, 1994**

To the Supreme Council of Indian Peoples (Consejo Supremo de Pueblos Indios):
To the National Coordinator of Indian Peoples (Coordinadora Nacional de Pueblos Indios, CNPI), Tenochtitlán, Mexico City:

Brothers and Sisters:

We want to speak our words to you. We received your letter dated February 5. Our heads bow from the honor of receiving the truthful words that you send us. Our arms are down in order to listen to the words of our Indigenous and Mexican brothers from the whole country. The wisdom of your thoughts is great in reminding the whole world that Mexico belongs to Mexicans. Our essence is the community, mutual aid, justice, freedom, and dignity.

We, as Indian people, Mayan and Mexican, unite our forces and our thoughts with the great word of truth hoisted by the National Coordinator of Indian Peoples. Let us not allow our dignity to be offered in the great market of the powerful! If we lose our dignity we lose everything. Let the struggle be happiness for all our brothers and sisters. Let our hands and steps come together in the path of truth and justice.

Long live the Mexican eagle and the Zapata of its coat of arms, brothers and sisters of the CNPI!

Long live the unity of those who struggle for justice!

Freedom! Justice! Democracy!

Respectfully,
From the mountains of the Mexican Southeast,
CCRI-CG of the EZLN

# To the National Plan de Ayala Coordinating Committee

February 8, 1994

To the National Plan de Ayala Coordinating Committee (Coordinadora Nacional Plan de Ayala, CNPA):

Brothers and Sisters:

We received your letter dated February 5, 1994 and we wanted to share with you some things and thoughts of ours.

We salute the independent and true struggle of the National Plan de Ayala Coordinating Committee. We thank you for the unconditional support of our just struggle declared in your brave and determined pronouncement. The Indigenous peoples, the poor campesinos, and agricultural laborers, united, will completely change the agrarian system of exploitation and scorn that exists in our country. From the unity of our strength will surge a new Mexican countryside, more just and equitable, where the severe gaze of General Emiliano Zapata will watch, so that oppression will not be repeated under another name.

Campesino brothers of the CNPA, it will be a great honor for us to be able to talk with you and listen to your words of truth and justice. With humility and attention we will stand before you who have struggled so long for land and liberty. We, small people of the land, will listen to the word of your great independent organization.

Good health brothers and sisters of the CNPA!

Long live Emiliano Zapata and the organizations that honor his name!

Down with the Salinista reforms to Article 27 of the Constitution!

Respectfully,
From the mountains of the Mexican Southeast,
CCRI-CG of the EZLN

# To the Regional Liberation Association for Human, Economic, Social, and Political Rights

February 8, 1994

To the Regional Liberation Association for Human, Economic, Social and Political Rights (Asociación Regional Liberación en Pro de los Derechos Humanos, Económicos, Sociales y Políticos AC, ARELIDH):

C. Lucrecia Ortega Sanchez, Administrative Director:

The Clandestine Revolutionary Indigenous Committee-General Command of the Zapatista National Liberation Army respectfully addresses you to thank you for your letter dated February 7, 1994, in which you tell us of your agreement to form the peace belt around the dialogue table between our EZLN and the federal government.

We know that your organization has remained neutral in the present conflict and that it has always been concerned with providing help to alleviate the grave conditions of the civilian population, as well as to strengthen efforts toward peace. We salute this with respect, since honesty goes, invariably, with neutrality and the enthusiasm for peace with justice. We thank you, in advance, for extending the invitation that you accepted to other NGO's [non-governmental organizations], since so far you are the only ones who have answered and accepted.

We are asking Mr. Samuel Ruiz García, bishop of San Cristóbal de las Casas and the National Commissioner of Mediation, that when the date and location of the dialogue are determined, he promptly contact you so you will know in advance.

Respectfully,
From the mountains of the Mexican Southeast,
CCRI-CG of the EZLN

## To the Children of
## Beatriz Hernández Elementary School

**February 8, 1994**

To the Solidarity Committee of the Boarding School of Elementary Education No. 4, "Beatriz Hernández" (Comité de Solidaridad del Internado de Educación Primaria Num. 4, "Beatriz Hernández"):

Boys and Girls:

We received your letter dated January 19, 1994 and the poem *Plegaria de Paz* [Prayer of Peace] that came with the letter. We are happy that boys and girls living so far away from our mountains and misery are concerned that peace come to our land in Chiapas. We thank you very much for your short letter.

We want you, and the noble people who are your teachers, to know that we did not pick up guns because of a taste for killing and dying, that we do not seek war because we do not want peace. We were living without peace; our children are boys and girls like yourselves, but infinitely more poor. For our boys and girls there are no schools or medicine, there are no clothes or food, there is no dignified roof where we can keep our poverty. For our boys and girls there is only work, ignorance and death. The land we have is worthless. In order to get anything for our children we go out to find pay in the land of others, the powerful, and they pay us poorly for our work. Our children must work from a very young age in order to get some food, clothes, and medicine. The toys of our children are the machete, the ax, and the hoe. Playing and suffering, they go out in search of firewood, to cut the forest, and sow, as soon as they can barely walk. They

175

eat the same as we eat: corn, beans and chilies. They cannot go to school and learn Spanish because the work kills the whole day and sickness kills the night. That is how our boys and girls have lived and died for 501 years. We, their fathers, their mothers, their brothers and sisters, no longer wanted to be guilty of doing nothing. We sought peaceful solutions to attain justice and we found taunts, we found prison, we found blows, and we found death. We always found pain and sorrow. So we had to take the path of war, because what we asked for with our voices was never listened to. And, boys and girls of Jalisco, we do not ask for handouts and charity. We ask for justice: a fair salary, a piece of good land, a dignified house, a school of truths, medicine that cures, bread on our tables, respect for our culture, freedom to say what we think and freedom to open our mouths so that the words will unite us with others in peace and without death. That is what we have always asked for, boys and girls, and they did not listen to what our voices clamored for. And then we took up arms in our hands, then we made the tools of work into tools of struggle, and then they waged war on us, the war that killed us without you knowing about it, boys and girls of Jalisco. We turned it against them, the big, the powerful, those who have it all and deserve nothing.

That is why, boys and girls of Jalisco, we started our war. That is why the peace that we want is not the same one that we had before, because it was not peace, it was death and scorn, it was sorrow and pain, it was shame. That is why we tell you, with respect and affection, boys and girls of Jalisco, to raise the flag of peace with dignity and write poems of *Plegaria a una Vida Digna* [Prayer for a Dignified Life] and seek, above all, the justice that is for everybody equally or for no one.

Good Health boys and girls of Jalisco.
From the mountains of the Mexican Southeast,
CCRI-CG of the EZLN

## ON ADDRESSING COMMUNICATIONS TO THE PRESS

February 11, 1994

To *El Sur, 21st Century Journalism* newspaper:
Attention Jesús García, Claudia Martínez Sánchez, Pablo Gómez Santiago:

Gentlemen:

I received your letter dated February 9, 1994. Ooof! If you report with half the aggressiveness of the letter you sent me, when this country really becomes free and just you will win the National Prize for Journalism. I accept that you are calling me to task (in reality it is a scolding, but this morning I woke up feeling diplomatic). I would like it if, in the middle of your full indignation, you could find the space to listen to me.

We are at war. We took up arms against the supreme government. They are looking for us to kill us, not just to interview us. We confess that we do not know of *El Sur, 21st*

*Century Journalism*, but you confess that it is something difficult to reproach us for, sur-rounded as we are, without food and under constant threat from armed aircraft. Fine, we have mutually confessed. A lot of honest journalists have come to the jungle, some not so honest, and others who are not even journalists but present themselves as such. We must mistrust all whom we do not directly know because, I repeat, the government wants to take our picture...dead. I know that for the "professionals in violence" death is a natural consequence, but there is a big difference between knowing this and helping the enemy. I am not trying to move you, I only want you to understand the conditions in which we found and find ourselves. We have very little room for maneuvering and, paradoxically, we need now more than ever to contact the media that tells the truth. The entrance and exit of journalists through our lines is a strong blow to our security system, and there exists the risk that in the entrance or exit, the workers of the communications media will suffer from an attack and our forces will be blamed. I do not consider myself to have been interviewed enough. In fact, the interview published by *La Jornada* is the only one I have given in my life, and I think that there are a lot of gaps that the journalists of that publication left open and that could have been filled with questions which were not asked. So I am not behaving as a debutante who "chooses" whom and that not to address with his honorable word. I am simply taking into consideration that wherever I make myself present, I place all who are present, and those who arrive, at extra risk. We are behaving like what we are, people persecuted by the government, not by journalists.

Anyway, if you had begun with the support that the San Cristóbal newspaper *Tiempo* gives you, you would have saved yourselves the just indignation that fills the three pages of fax that I received. For me, the word of *Tiempo* is enough to accept the honesty of someone, so I am sending a letter to the National Commissioner of Mediation, Bishop Samuel Ruiz García, to give you a pass to cross our lines and take the pictures that you want and conduct the interviews that you can (remember, please, that we are at war). I solemnly promise that as soon as it is possible, I will have the honor of receiving you personally and replying to your questions, if they can be answered.

Until that improbable day arrives, I send you this writing. All right, there it goes, without any prior anesthesia, the writing titled...

### Reasons and Non-Reasons Why We Say Yes to Some Media

When the bombs were falling on the mountains south of San Cristóbal de las Casas, when our combatants resisted the attacks of the federal troops in Ocosingo, when our troops regrouped after the attack on the Rancho Nuevo barracks, when we were fortify-ing ourselves in Altamirano and Las Margaritas, when the air smelled of powder and blood, the CCRI-CG of the EZLN called me and told me, more or less: 'We must speak our words so that others will hear. If we don't do it now, others will take our voice and lies will come from our mouth without our wanting them to. Look for ways to give our truth to others who want to listen to it.' That is how the CCRI-CG put me in charge of seeking communication media that could publish what was really happening and what we were thinking. As I have said before, newspapers do not come to the mountains. What does come are the airwaves of radio stations (most of them government-run). As a result, we had to decide whom to address based on the previous experiences that we had. We had to consider a number of things: First, the publication of our communiqués would bring a logical question to the media that would receive them: Were these communiqués authentic? In other words, were they really from those who took up arms, or forged? Afterwards, suppose they answered "yes" (no one could say with certainty that they were authentic), the key question would come: 'Should we publish them?' To assume the authenticity of the communiqués is already a risk for the editorial committees of these media, but the responsibility of publishing them implies many other things, so many that maybe only they can tell that story of the decision to open up to a movement that no one, beside ourselves, knew well. A movement whose origin was an enigma in the best of cases, and a provocation in the worst. The EZLN had risen against the supreme government, it had taken seven municipal seats, was fighting with the Federal Army, and was formed, at the very least, by some Indigenous people. This was a fact. But who was behind the EZLN? What did they really want? Why through those means (the armed ones)? Who financed them? In short, what was really going on? There must have been a thousand more questions. Those media will some day tell the story (an important one, surely). We thought about all of this and asked ourselves: Who will take all these risks? The answer we gave ourselves was, more or less, this one: It will be those media whose zeal to know the truth of what is happening is bigger than their fear of the risks in finding it. Well, the answer was correct (I think), but it did not solve anything. The most important thing was missing: to decide on the recipient of those initial letters and communiqués. I will briefly narrate how and why the addressees that have appeared until now began appearing. It is clear that these must now be expanded.

*Tiempo*: The decision to address this paper was unanimous in the CCRI-CG of the EZLN and, you can say, by acclamation. You must remember that our *compañeros* do not take up arms just like that, in search of adventure. They have traveled a long road of political, legal, economic, and peaceable struggles. They know various local and state prisons and torture centers. They also know who listened to them yesterday and who shut their doors and ears. I have explained in a letter to a journalist of that publication what *Tiempo* means to the Indigenous people of Chiapas, so I will not repeat myself. However, deciding to put *Tiempo* among other addressees was not easy. We were sure of the honesty and impartiality of these people, but there was the problem of war, and in a war it is easy to confuse the lines that divide one force from the other. I am not referring to the front line only, but also the political and ideological lines that separate and confront both sides. What do I mean? Simply, that by publishing our communiqué, *Tiempo* could be accused, gratuitously for sure, of being a "spokesperson" of the "transgressors of the law." For a large newspaper this could mean problems, but for a small newspaper this could mean its certain disappearance. In any case the *compañeros* say: "Send it to *Tiempo*, if they don't publish it, at least they deserve to know what's going on." That is part of the story about the selection of *Tiempo*. What is missing, of course, is the part about how the noble people of *Tiempo* decided to risk everything, to the point of gambling their existence as a newspaper, and publish what we sent them. Whatever that story may have been, we can do no less than salute the braveness of that newspaper which, among all, was the one that had the most to lose, if not everything. That is why the CCRI-CG of the EZLN has always insisted that I send a copy of everything that we send out to *Tiempo*.

After deciding on a local news medium to address, the problem of deciding on a national news medium arose. Television was eliminated for obvious reasons. For us the radio presented the problem of getting the material to them without additional risks. Then there was the problem of the national print media. You must remember that we did not know what was being said in the press about what was going on; we were fighting in the mountains and the cities. So, as I said earlier, we had to decide based on the record that we had.

*La Jornada*: Then we evaluated what *La Jornada* had previously done. Its editorial policy was, as we say today, plural. In other words, different political and economic currents had space there. In that newspaper a wide spectrum of interpretations of the national and international reality could be, and still can be, appreciated. That is to say, that newspaper presents, with quality, a very representative ideological mosaic of so-called Mexican society. I think this is demonstrated in the gradual transition from the harsh condemnation of the EZLN (remember the January 2, 1994 editorial) to the critical analysis of what was happening. *Mutatis mutando* [all things being equal], I think that is what happened with the so-called civil society: From condemning us, it went to making an effort to understand us. There is in *La Jornada* what used to be called the Left, Center, and Right, as well as the multiple subdivisions that history makes and destroys. There is healthy polemic of a high standard. In short, I think it is a good newspaper. It is difficult to write it off as Leftist or Rightist or Centrist (although the Mexican Anti-Communist Front (Frente Anti-Comunista Mexicano) places it among the former). I think that this myriad of editorial currents is an important part of the success of this newspaper (and editorial success of a newspaper during my times as a journalist meant the ability to put out the next issue). It was not the existence of this ideological mosaic that made us decide to include *La Jornada* among the addressees, however. What was decisive was the bravery and honesty of its journalists. We have seen brilliant journalistic pages (fieldwork, they used to call it) in articles and interviews in this newspaper. For some strange reason, these journalists (and many others, I agree, but now I am talking about *La Jornada*) are not satisfied with the official bulletins. They are irksome (for those covered) to exhaustion in their zeal to know what is happening. Furthermore, when something important (as they understand it) happens, they are not satisfied to send a single journalist, but rather form a true assault unit that begins to reveal diverse sides of the event that they are covering. They have what, in my times, they used to call total journalism, as if it was a movie with various cameras with different focuses and angles of the same event. What is hypnotic in the movies, in the press moves to reflection and analysis. Fighting still with fire and lead, we thought that, maybe, they would want to know the face behind the ski mask. I am not saying that others would not want to (including the federal government), but now I am talking about this news medium. With things this way, what makes us add the name of *La Jornada* to the addressees is, above all, its journalistic team. There are other reasons less determinant, such as the eventual or regular sections of "La Doble Jornada," "La Jornada Laboral," "Perfil," and last but not least, "Histerietas" [sections in *La Jornada*].

*El Financiero*: Somebody asked me why we choose a newspaper that specializess in economic issues as our interlocutor. To say that *El Financiero* is a finance newspaper is to miss the truth in the best of cases, and in the worst it means that you haven't read it. *El Financiero* has, it is our understanding, a serious and responsible team of columnists performing their journalistic tasks. Its analysis is objective, and above all, very critical. The ideological plurality of the articles that make up *El Financiero* is also a richness that is difficult to find in other national newspapers. I mean it is a balanced plurality. Its editorial policy is not satisfied with splashing a critical pen among those aligned with the powerful. It opens real spaces for incisive analysis of both sides. (I doubt that there are only two sides, but the literary figure helps, I think.) Its journalistic team has the instinct to dissect reality, which is what finally distinguishes a journalist from an observer. *El Financiero* seems to tell us and show us that a social event is a reflection of ("a reflection of?" I think I should say: "conditions and is conditioned by") several economic, political and cultural aspects. Like reading a history book, but of present and everyday history which, by the way, is the most difficult history to read. When I was young and beautiful, intellectuals tended to group around a publication, dig up positions, entrench themselves, and throw truths to the ignorant world of the mortals. In those times they called them the elites of the intelligentsia and there were as many as there were magazines and ideological currents in fashion. Publications to be read by those who published them. Lucha calls them "an editorial masturbation." If you, innocent earthling, wanted to brush up against these ivory towers, you had to follow a rough process. If any editorial medium seems to distance itself from this elite journalism that pours off, selects and eliminates, it is *El Financiero*. This national newspaper did not react with the immediate condemnation of a movement that nobody understood, it did not jump into intense intellectual study that affected, and affects, other media. It waited, which in the art of war is the most difficult virtue to learn; it investigated; it reported and, on a firmer base, it began to weave that interdisciplinary analysis that its readers can now appreciate. We did not know this until, some time later, an issue got to our hands. We congratulated ourselves for a good choice, although, it is only fair to acknowledge, we had nothing to lose. If for *La Jornada* it was the journalistic team that made us decide, in *El Financiero* it was the editorial team (not withstanding Mr. Pazos).

*Proceso*: For this weekly, it is worth repeating the apology for its late inclusion among the addressees. The reason for this I have explained elsewhere. I would like to recall an anecdote, of the many that run loose in our minds and chats, of January 1, 1994: At dusk, a majority of the civilian population, who had been curious and scandalized by what they saw, with us in the municipal palace at San Cristóbal de las Casas, had gone into their houses and hotels, scared by the insistent rumors that the Federal Army would try to assault our positions in darkness. However, one or two drunks for whom the New Year's party had gone on for 24 hours, showed up. Keeping their balance with difficulty, they would address us, asking what religious procession we were from because they saw many 'Indians' in the central park. After we would tell them what was happening, they would invite us to a useless sip from an empty bottle and they would leave, staggering and discussing whether the procession was for the Virgin of Guadalupe or for the Fiesta of Santa Lucía. People in their right mind, or at least so they appeared, would also approach us. And then it happened: Spontaneous war strategists and military advisors surged, telling us how to run when the federal troops attacked us and avoid many losses, because with respect to our defeat there was unanimity among them.

One of them, later in the night and when our troops were getting ready to move to new positions before the assault on Rancho Nuevo, came up to me and, with a tone more paternalistic than doctoral, told me: "Marcos, you made a strategic mistake by initiating the war on a Saturday." I adjusted my ski mask that, along with my eyelids, was beginning to droop over my eyes, and ventured, timidly, "Why?"

"Look," says my impromptu advisor of military strategy, "The mistake is that on Saturdays *Proceso* closes its edition and therefore the analysis and truthful reports about your struggle will not come out until next week." I continue fixing my ski mask, to give myself some time more than because it was out of place. My military advisor from San Cristóbal adds, relentless: "You should have attacked on Friday." I try, timidly, to argue in my defense about the New Year's Eve dinner, the fireworks, the celebrations, the etceteras that I don't remember now, but I must have been saying something, because the character I had in front did not let me continue and interrupted me, saying, "And now who knows if you will last until next week." There was no pity in his tone. It was a lugubrious death sentence. He left, giving me an understanding pat for my strategic blunder of attacking on a Saturday. I have not read the *Proceso* of that week previous to January 1, but if there is something on which the strategist was right that night, it is in that in *Proceso* truthful analysis and reports do appear. I can add little to the virtues that everyone points out in the journalistic work of this weekly magazine recognized worldwide. It suffices to call attention to the depth that is always present in the articles of *Proceso,* the diverse focuses on a problem, whether it be national or international.

Others: I agree with you that there are other media, of equal or greater value than those above mentioned. We will look into increasing the number of addressees or, simply address the press in general. I believe that, finally, this will be the wisest, since there are truly many and good news media that do this: inform.

*El Sur* (Oaxaca): I repeat that we did not know about it. I counter-repeat that we do not have the advantages of the Federal Army to give interviews or press conferences, I arch-repeat that we are surrounded and at war. But I propose a deal: Until a personal interview becomes possible, we could advance something by mail. I know that an interview through letters is not ideal for a reporter, but we could send something. Furthermore, I commit myself to finding interviews with other officials of the EZLN, and this without any requisite other than coming to Chiapas and picking up, at the office of the National Commissioner of Mediation, the accreditation as war journalists that the EZLN provides.

As you must know, the dialogue has not started. Maybe we are waiting for you.

Well, journalists of *El Sur* of Oaxaca, I believe I must have bored you enough. However it may be, the great advantage of this long letter is that no medium will dare to publish it. All right.

Good health and a sincere embrace without rancor...agreed?

From the mountains of the Mexican Southeast,

Insurgent Subcommander Marcos

**P.S.:** Could you send us an issue of your newspaper? We solemnly promise to pay for it in the improbable case that one day we have money. (Would you accept letters instead of cash?)

Another **P.S.:** That airplane simply won't fall, and the water in the pot evaporated while waiting. Why don't you bring some Oaxaca cheese when you come? They say it is very tasty. We will provide the tortillas and the hunger. You're welcome.

cc: *Tiempo*, San Cristóbal, Chiapas.
cc: *La Jornada*, Mexico City
cc: *El Financiero*, Mexico City
cc: *Proceso*, Mexico City

# 7. Before the Dialogue

## Communiqués Concerning Conditions For The Dialogue

*[The following are several communiqués concerning the dialogue that were released as preparations were being made and delegates were still being chosen.]*

## A Letter of Introduction

February 16, 1994

To the national weekly *Proceso*:
To the national newspaper *La Jornada:*
To the national newspaper *El Financiero:*
To the local newspaper of San Cristóbal de las Casas, Chiapas, *Tiempo:*
To the national and international press:

Gentlemen:

Well, here I send you the communiqué of the CCRI-CG of the EZLN that defines, in general, the position that it will take to the discussion with the Commissioner for Peace on February 21.

We are intent on seeing that the delegates arrive on time at the points where they will be picked up.

I am not sure if the noble city of San Cristóbal will welcome them, but, after all, that is the risk we have to take.

While the CCRI-CG of the EZLN decides whether or not to send me to the dialogue, I am very worried about what clothes to wear (if I do go). I looked with skepticism through the giant wardrobe that I carry in my bag, and I worry anxiously whether winter clothes are still in fashion or if I need to take something coquettish for the spring. In the end, I decided on a coffee-colored shirt (the only one), a pair of black trousers (the only ones), a bright red bandanna (the only one), a pair of dirty boots (the only ones), and a ski-mask in a discreet shade of black (the only one). Whatever happens, whether I go or not, the CCRI-CG has ordered me to written silence, therefore I will keep my powerful communiqué machine (a pen) until the end of this.

I wish you health and good luck in the journalistic cannibalism. (Note: leave something for the smallest ones. Take the political initiative and inaugurate the Pronasol of communication, a press-pool, that is.)

"The Merchant's Postscript" Section

P.S.: How much would a dirty, smelly ski mask cost in dollars? How much more for the Attorney General (Procurador General de la Republica, PGR)?

P.S. to the P.S.: How much can you get if some brand of bottled soda appears on the dialogue table?

P.S. For a high interest rate: How about a *streap tease* (is that how you spell it?) of ski masks? *How much for this show?* In other words, how much dough for that?

P.S. On the decrease of the Stock Market: How much for one minute of speaking nonsense? How much for a half minute of truths? (Remember that truths are more in demand than lies, and therefore, fewer are sold.)

P.S. Macho but sought after in the Stock Market: How much for the half personal information from the waist down?

P.S. Of *crack* in the Market: How much for an exclusive, a *close up*, of the big nose?

P.S. Devalued by "external" pressures: And the "communiqué machine," how much for it to continue? How much for it to stop?

P.S. It has no monetary value: And for our dead, what is their pain worth? How much light do they fill their pockets with? How much more blood so that their silence will not be useless? Who wants the exclusive on their pain? Nobody? Well...

P.S. Which pulls out of the stock exchange: Goodbye... I thank those of you who tell the truth. My deepest condolences to those who follow the path of lies. All right.

El sup in ostracization
(*I merengues*)

# AN INVITATION TO THE POLITICAL PARTIES TO ATTEND THE DIALOGUE

February 13, 1994

To the Mexican and international press:

To the registered political parties:

To the candidates for the presidency of the Mexican Republic: Attention: PAN, PRI, PRD, PFCRN, PT, PARM, PVEM, PPS

Gentlemen:

We speak to you through this medium, we the Clandestine Revolutionary Indigenous Committee-General Command of the Zapatista National Liberation Army, to say to you the following:

**First:** As everyone knows, in a few days the negotiations for peace and reconciliation in Chiapas will begin between the federal government and the EZLN, with Bishop Samuel Ruiz acting as intermediary.

**Second:** Opening dialogue is an important part of the peace process, if we set out from the start in the direction of a peace with dignity, justice, freedom, and democracy. However, we think that the accords that we will be able to reach with the federal government's representative may be poorly implemented in the future electoral process and in the coming change in electoral powers.

**Third:** Because of this, we invite all of you to send delegations from the national leadership of your political parties in order to keep yourselves informed of the advances of the dialogue for peace, and so you can give us your opinion about the way in which the accords can be implemented, if agreement is possible. We understand that the presidential candidate of one of your parties' will be the next federal executive of our country, and this next President of the Republic will also be responsible for the implementation of the above-mentioned accords.

**Fourth:** We hope that our invitation to participate in the dialogue will be accepted by the leadership of your parties and the campaign teams of the individual aspirants for the country's highest office. It will be a great honor for us to speak with delegates you may be able to send.

Respectfully,
CCRI-CG of the EZLN

# To The Conac-LN

February 14, 1994

To the organizations that make up the National Coordinating Committee of Civic Action for National Liberation (Coodinación Nacional de Acción Cívica para la Liberación Nacional, Conac-LN):

Brothers and Sisters:

We received your letter of February 9, 1994. It is a great honor, and our ranks are inclined to recognize the words of our General Emiliano Zapata coming from the mouths of workers, students, teachers, and intellectuals, honest men and women that make up the Conac-LN.

Following the words of Zapata, we call on the Mexican people who might be aided by the just cause that inspires the song of our rifles. We respectfully salute the return of this call to unity that comes from other parts of our country.

Brothers and Sisters:

For years and years, we have harvested our own death in the countrysides of Chiapas. Our children were dying at the hands of an unknown force. Our men and women were walking in a long night of ignorance that darkened our paths. Our people went without truth or knowledge. They wandered—without a destination—merely living and dying.

The oldest of our peoples' elders spoke to us words that came from very far away, from before our lives began, from when our voice was silent. And there is truth in the words of the oldest of our elders. And we learned from their words that our peoples' long night of pain comes from the powerful, that a house for the powerful was built on top of the bones and dust of our ancestors and our children. We learned that we weren't allowed to enter this house, and that the light that illuminated it fed on our darkness, and that the abundance of their table fills itself with the emptiness of our stomachs. Their luxuries were born of our misery, and that the strength of its roofs and walls were raised upon the fragility of our bodies. The health that filled its spaces came from our death. The wisdom that lived there was nourished of our ignorance. The peace that it sheltered was war for our peoples. Foreign vocations sent them far from our land and our history.

But the truth that is passed along in the words of the oldest of our elders was not only of pain and death. The words of the oldest of our elders also brought hope for our history. And in their words the image of one like us appeared: Emiliano Zapata. And in that image we saw the place where our paths should lead to be true. And it returned our history of struggle to our blood, and our hands filled with the cries of our people, and dignity returned, once again, to our mouths, and our eyes saw a new world.

And then we made ourselves soldiers, war covered our soil, and we struck out on our paths, newly armed with bullets and fire. Our fear was buried with our dead, and we saw to take our new voice to the land of the powerful, and we carried our truth to plant it in the middle of the land where falsehood rules. We arrived in the city carrying our dead to show them to the eyes of the blind compatriots, the good and the bad, the knowledgeable and the ignorant, the powerful and the meek, and the rulers and the subjects. Our cries of war opened the deaf ears of the supreme government and its accomplices. For years and years before our voice of dignified peace could not descend from the mountains; the rulers raised strong, high walls to hide our death and misery. Our force must break down those walls in order to enter, once again, our history, which they have stolen along with the dignity and reason of our people.

In that first blow at the deaf walls of those who have everything, our blood ran generously to wash away the injustice that we are living. In order to live, we die. Our dead return to travel the paths of truth. With mud and blood we pay for our hope.

But the words of the oldest of our elders didn't stop there. They spoke the truth, saying that our paths cannot be travelled alone, that our history of pain and hardship is repeated and multiplied in the flesh and blood of brothers and sisters of other lands and skies.

"Raise your voice to the ears of the other dispossessed, raise your struggle to other struggles. There is another roof of injustice over he who hides our pain," said the oldest of our elders. We saw in these words that if our struggle was alone, once again it would be useless. So we directed the flow of our blood and the paths of our dead to find the path of others who walk with truth. We are nothing if we go alone, we are everything if we walk together with others who are dignified.

Brothers and sisters, our thoughts have reached our hands and our lips. And we begin to move forward that your paths should come towards us, brothers and sisters of the National Coordinating Committee of Civic Action for National Liberation, our heart is open to your word and truth. We have little to offer you, since we continue to feel the huge poverty of our lands and our very small place in Mexican history. But together with your path, and that of all good people of this world, we will grow and find, in the end, the place our dignity and our history deserve.

Good health, brothers and sisters of the Conac-LN.

Liberty! Justice! Democracy!

Respectfully,
From the mountains of the Mexican Southeast,
CCRI-CG of the EZLN

## An Invitation to the PDM and the UNO to Attend the Dialogue

February 15, 1994

To the registered political parties:
The Mexican Democratic Party (Partido Demócrata Mexicano, PDM), the National
    Opposition Union (Unión Nacional Opositora, UNO):
To their candidates for the presidency of the Mexican Republic:

Gentlemen:

We speak to you through this medium, we the Clandestine Revolutionary Indigenous Committee of the Zapatista National Liberation Army, to say to you the following:

**First:** Due to a regrettable error caused by haste and a lack of attention, the names of your political organizations were omitted from the list of addresses of our invitation to send delegations to the negotiations for peace and reconciliation in Chiapas. We deeply regret this error and sincerely hope that you will forgive us and honor us with the presence of your delegates at such an important event.

**Second:** The opening of the dialogue is an important part of the peace process; if we set out from the start, in the direction of a peace with dignity, justice, liberty, and democracy. However, we think that the accords that can be reached with the federal government's representative may be limited in their implementation by the future electoral process and the change in federal powers that is drawing near.

**Third:** Because of this, we invite you to send delegations from the national leadership of your political parties in order to keep yourselves informed of the advances of the dialogue for peace, and so you can give us your opinion about the way in which accords can be implemented if agreement is possible. We understand that one of your parties' presidential

189

candidates will be the next federal executive of our country, and this next president of the Republic will also be responsible for the implementation of the above-mentioned accords.

**Fourth:** We hope that our invitation to participate in the dialogue will be accepted by the leadership of your parties and the campaign teams of the individual aspirants for the country's highest office. It will be a great honor for us to speak with delegates you may be able to send.

Respectfully,
From the mountain of the Mexican Southeast,
CCRI-CG of the EZLN

## REGARDING THE LIBERATION OF ABSALÓN CASTELLANOS DOMÍNGUEZ

February 15, 1994

To the Mexican and international press:
To Mr. Samuel Ruiz García, National Commissioner of Mediation:
To Mr. Manuel Camacho Solís, Commissioner for Peace and Reconciliation:

Gentlemen:

We, the Clandestine Revolutionary Indigenous Committee of the EZLN, address you once again to say the following:

**First:** In order to expedite the prompt beginning of dialogue for the dignified peace that we all, as Mexicans, want, and as a sign of the sincere willingness of our EZLN, we announce that on Wednesday, February 16, 1994, Division General Absalón Castellanos Domínguez will be freed.

**Second:** Division General Absalón Castellanos Domínguez will be handed over to the Commissioner for Peace, Manuel Camacho Solís, and the Commissioner of Mediation, Samuel Ruiz García, in the community of Guadalupe Tepeyac in the township of Las Margaritas, Chiapas. Division General Absalón Castellanos Domínguez's state of health should be examined at the moment of his release by a doctor of the International Red Cross.

**Third:** In order to decrease tension in the war zone during the dialogue for peace with dignity, the CCRI-CG of the EZLN announces also its decision to suspend the collection of war taxes in the territories under the control of its troops for the day of February 17, 1994.

Respectfully,
From the mountains of Southeast Mexico
CCRI-CG of the EZLN

190

# FROM THE GUADALUPE TEPEYAC COMMUNITY

*[The following is from a manuscript entitled "Popular Love in the Chiapaneca Jungle"*
*(Amor popular de la selva Chiapaneca), read after handing over Absalón Castellanos. The*
*Guadalupe Tepeyac Community is at a hospital built with federal funds, but poorly staffed*
*and stocked.]*

February 16, 1994

To Manuel Camacho Solís, peace envoy, we present the following:

In the following we are addressing you with the aim to show you the reality of the zone of the jungle of Chiapas. As a health concern, we would like for the clinic to begin functioning on a normal basis, that it be stocked with medical supplies as soon as possible, and that it be staffed with doctors specializing in different areas.

Moreover, we still have not received all of the materials because Mr. Salinas de Gortari has provided us with an incomplete clinic, according to its director, Wilfrido Mendoza. He declared to inhabitants of the various communities that the operating room was incomplete, and for this reason no type of surgery is performed. There are also no personnel to take x-rays.

While it was being built, no one received service, and they were taken to the city of Comitán or to Tuxtla Gutierrez. Also, most of the personnel have no training in curable diseases. Our zone needs doctors who are experts in different curable diseases, since the marginalization, misery and poverty of our communities prevents us from going to the city to seek care. This is why we are asking that the clinic be made functional as soon as possible.

As far as education goes, we have had no support for many years. Teachers have been divided into two sectors, those who are democratic, and those who are called *charro*. We want for there to be only one class of teachers and that they be permanent at the place they work instead of working as they have been, no more than a week or three days per month. We also need teaching and construction materials for the development and training of our children as future professionals. We need scholarships for those who want to continue at secondary or preparatory schools and universities.

Another point is the holding of land. The campesinos do not have fertile land, farm machinery or all the innumerable things needed for production, since it is the *latifundistas* who get the best land, as well as the machinery, fertilizers, credit and loans.

The government has paid the most attention to them, while the poor people all over Mexico, who deserve it the most, do not have their support. Nevertheless, they are asking us for the ecological reserve and the mountains, as well as reforestation of the same zone. How can the government not figure out where to exploit wood and other natural resources that are exploited? Those that clearly have no land to survive on, what hope do they have to cultivate anything, if they have nothing?

Another important point is housing. The Mexican government has ignored the question of housing just like all the other issues. They say that they have helped some people, but that is not true, since the campesinos themselves constructed their houses out of materials from the region with unqualified labor. Nevertheless, they use construction costs to continue taking advantage of the people. Another thing is that when we want to make things with local materials, we campesinos are forbidden from using wood that we know will last, because that same government has implemented laws that forbid this from happening.

As with the situation of using materials of the region, what can be said of the situation with electricity, potable water, and decent housing, which is what our people really need, because the majority of the income of our rich country, which has so many natural resources, comes from us.

We also need bread and food. We don't even have the basic things, not even meat, eggs, fish, etc., to complement the daily, healthy diet that the health officials sent by the government talk about so often. All of this because of what was mentioned before: the bad land, lack of machinery and technical advice that would allow us good production. As a consequence of all of this, our children do not receive good education, much less what they need for good health.

**Democracy.** The Mexican government speaks about democracy, but only for a select group of people who support it, the oligarchy, the monopoly, be they Mexicans or foreigners. It is this group of people who decide who will rule, they choose between the senators and deputies who will govern and look after their interests without taking into account the population or the Mexican people.

The senators never come to propose who will govern. No, we don't elect them, we don't even know them. They are elected because they are known, and they publish in other countries that Mexico's government is legitimate so that they can get loans and help, but only for them.

We know that the lawyer Salinas de Gortari is illegitimate because he got his position by cheating, fraud, violations and threats. We believe that democracy is what we put forth in our programs of struggle that the people elect their government freely and democratically, which should have the interests that the people need. For this to happen, it is necessary that we be honest about all of the rights that belong to the Mexican people.

**Work.** How is it possible that after all of these years we're still working with primitive tools like the machete, hatchet, hoe, etc, in these the poorest areas of all Mexico, when we have all kinds of large industries that can manufacture the best machinery for the Mexican countryside and can produce a good agricultural development like the big businesses do?

This shows that the government has no interest in the campesinos, the laborers or the working class who produce so that the government can live. The laborer's salaries are very low, and not even enough to survive on, because there is so much deducted for loans and the taxes that are applied are very high.

**Freedom.** The Mexican government talks about freedom. Mexicans don't know what freedom the government is talking about, because when we have to travel to the capital city, we face the immigration and have to show our identification, explain where we're from and where we're coming from. We think that it is not true that we have freedom, because we're not even free to go from one place to another without the judicial police chasing us like dogs. We don't have freedom of expression either, because when campesinos, teachers, laborers or students express their feelings, the government immediately orders them killed, tortured, detained or threatened and they are accused of being agitators.

They do not worry about removing the bad functionaries because they are all from the same class and and the same family. For this reason we say there is no democracy or freedom in Mexico. It is remarkable because the governments have been practicing it for many years. With a capitalist system we lack the means, such as television, radio or the press, by which to spread our ideas. It is not in the government's interest to have everyone else have thoughts that could be used to defend our rights as exploited workers.

**Independence.** As one can see clearly, we are not independent because the Mexican government is directed and managed by foreign governments that are interested in our natural resources. But also because foreign businesses can get cheap labor here in Mexico.

Changes put in place are foreigners' plans and ideas that will once again lead us into slavery. NAFTA will not benefit us campesinos of Mexico, because we lack the machinery we need to be competitive. The Mexican government lets itself get easily carried away by foreign governments. This is why we say that the government doesn't (...interruption in tape...) of misery, inequality and injustice. The Army mistreats the people, threatens them, burns their houses, and many other things, treats them like animals, not human beings. For example, right now the Federal Army is bombing, using machine guns, and using other methods to repress the civilian population. The people want the same peace that the Mexican oligarchy has. If the people don't achieve the things we have mentioned, we will keep struggling.

We have another point. We would like to ask you directly to stop coming in helicopters to chase us in the roads where we are working. We wonder what kind of peace it is that they are proposing if we can't even work in our corn fields, coffee fields, or other places where we work. They follow us and fire on us, which is why we believe that this kind of peace proposed by the government is not necessarily peace.

We want for the federal troops that are still on the sidewalks of the municipal buildings and other streets where we walk, to pull out so that the civilian population can move around freely. Right now they are detaining anyone who passes by areas where there are troops. Because of them, humanitarian aid meant for our Indigenous people, such as from the House of the Images (*Casa de las Imágenes*) and other humanitarian aid organizations cannot get through.

We want for the EZLN to be respected and recognized with respect to the different issues it raises. All of this, Mr. Camacho, we want to be known to you.

# Communiqués Before the Dialogue

## On the Opening of the Dialogue

February 16, 1994

*"Those who fight with honor, speak with honor."*

To the people of Mexico:
To the peoples and governments of the world:
To the national and international press:

Brothers and Sisters:

The Clandestine Revolutionary Indigenous Committee-General Command of the EZLN is honored to address all of you, to speak its words, what is in its heart and in its mind:

On Monday, February 21, 1994, a dialogue will begin between the federal government and the EZLN, with the purpose of finding a just and dignified political outcome appropriate to the present conflict. Honoring its promise, the CCRI-CG of the EZLN has freed General Absalón Castellanos Domínguez and has now named the delegates that will represent it in the debate with the national intermediary commissioner, Mr. Samuel Ruiz García and the commissioner for peace and reconciliation in Chiapas, Mr. Manuel Camacho Solís. In spite of the risks to their lives, our delegates will be present at the determined location and will represent with honor and truth the minds and hearts of the men who walk in truth.

The word of truth that comes from the depths of our past, from our pain, from our dead that still live among us, will fight with dignity on the lips of our chief. The mouths of our rifles will be silent so that our truth can be spoken with the words of every person. Those who fight with honor, speak with honor, there will be no lies in our hearts, being true men.

Our voice will carry the voice of the majority, those who have nothing, those condemned to silence and ignorance, ripped from their lands and their history by the sovereignty of the powerful, of all good men and women who walk in a world filled with pain and rage, of the children and the elderly who died from solitude and abandonment, of the humiliated women and the small men. The dead, our dead, will speak through our voice, so alone and so forgotten, so dead and yet so alive in our voice and in our steps.

We will not ask for forgiveness or implore, we will not beg for alms nor gather up crumbs that fall from the abundant tables of the powerful. We will go to demand that which is everyone's right and reason: freedom, justice, democracy; everything for everybody, nothing for us.

For all the Indigenous people, for all the campesinos, for all the workers, for all the students and teachers, for all the children, for all the elderly, for the women, for all the men, everything for everybody: freedom, justice, democracy.

For us, the smallest beings on the earth, faceless, with no history, armed with truth and fire, we have come out of the night and out of the mountains, true men and women, the dead of yesterday, today and always...for us nothing. For everyone, everything.

If the lies return to the mouths of the powerful, our voice of fire will speak again, for everything for everyone.

Receive our blood, brothers and sisters, so that all this death is not in vain, so that truth can return to our lands. Everything for everyone.

Freedom! Justice! Democracy!

Respectfully
From the mountains of the Mexican Southeast,
CCRI-CG del EZLN

## ABOUT THE EVICTIONS OF INDIGENOUS PEOPLE

February 17, 1994
San Cristóbal de las Casas, Chiapas.

To those evicted from San Juan Chamula:
To all Indigenous persons evicted from their lands and from their history:

Brothers and Sisters:

We received your letter of February 15, 1994. It is a great honor to receive word from you. We would like you to receive our humble word that speaks the truth.

For several days The Clandestine Revolutionary Indigenous Committee-General Command of the Zapatista National Liberation Army met in order to make a list of their demands for the supreme government to carry out. Since that time, the *compañeros* of the CCRI-CG of the EZLN realized that great injustice is alive in the hearts of the *caciques* and that the truth is that all men and women deserve the freedom of and respect for their thoughts and beliefs.

For this reason, the demand for the unconditional return of *all* evicted persons to their rightful lands and the punishment of those who oppress their own race and bleed their own brothers and sisters appears high on our list of demands, and on the world path of truth and justice that will have to come from our death.

Your voice, brothers and sisters, *and the voice of all of the evicted,* will be heard in our voice. Men and women all have the right to freedom, to justice and to democracy. When we achieve this, the world will be a world, and not this long chain of injustices that bind and oppress our history.

Good health to our evicted brothers and sisters!
Your demand for justice and respect is our demand!

Respectfully,
From the mountains of the Mexican Southeasr,
CCRI-CG of the EZLN

# INTERVIEW WITH MARCOS
# BEFORE THE DIALOGUE

[*Proceso*, 2/21]
Vincente Leñero reporting.
By reporters from *Proceso*, *El Financiero* and *The New York Times*

*"Did Patrocinio make a fool of himself? Did he misinform the President?"*

"The first military action was in May '93, when the Army accidentally discovered a camp where the January attack was being planned. Then the Army proceeded, as an army should proceed: It discovers an enemy, begins to deploy and cut off, and tries to destroy the guerrillas. But suddenly, a few days later, it pulls out. This was not a military decision, but a political decision. In military terms, they thought that our group could be exterminated. But actually exterminating it, and sending troops, would mean that the national government had to acknowledge the existence of the guerrillas. And we believe, after careful thought, that on the eve of NAFTA withdrawal was not a mistake by the Federal Army. I'm sure that it was a top-level political decision. It could only have been made by the president of the Republic."

The one speaking is Subcommander Marcos.

It's three or four in the morning on Thursday, February 17. It's cold and everyone's tired. It's drizzling outside.

The room, large but simple, is part of a campesino building on a hill, who knows where: in the tangle of "the mountains of the Mexican Southeast," as the Zapatista Army's communiqués are signed. A lightbulb hanging from the rafters is the only light, but it's enough. The shelves leaning against a wall are stacked with books and notebooks, falling apart from use. Over a dozen combatants with ski masks, and Indian men and women without uniforms, are gathered on the floor drowsily, fighting off sleep to hear Marcos' words. Some are already asleep, with checkered blankets covering them, even their heads. All are toward the back, against the walls.

"The Zapatista movement is a wake-up call. When everything in the world was saying no to armed struggle, because the option of communism had disappeared, we thought that people here would also say no to change, and particularly to armed struggle. It was logical, there was tremendous ideological bombardment. But the opposite happened in the communities. That was when more people joined us, when more people joined the Zapatista Army militia, when more towns declared: 'We are being left with no other choice.' When everything internationally was saying no to armed struggle, Indigenous campesinos in Chiapas were saying yes, yes, yes."

Sitting on a low board turned into a backless bench by vertical legs, Marcos responds to the questions posed by the three reporters he agreed to see in his second public meeting with journalists: representatives from *The New York Times*, *El Financiero* and *Proceso*. The Subcommander only authorized one camera, from *Proceso*, to take pictures of him from any angle:

"If you could just wait a minute so the *compañeros* in the background can put on their ski masks." And he explains: "They have relatives in the communities here who could be endangered if they were identified."

The conversation about the EZ, as Camacho abbreviates it, about the peace talks expected to begin on Monday, about the situation in Chiapas, about the August elections, about the country's future...had become lengthy, covering some subjects that had already been reiterated in communiqués from the Clandestine Committee, as well as by the Subcommander himself in his interview with *La Jornada* and *Multivisión*.

Marcos insisted on the subjects he was interested in—to clarify points, give details of events and narrow down concepts. Suddenly, the questions become quicker, a virtual barrage aimed at finding out a little more about Marcos' personality.

*"Come on, subcommander, tell us once and for all, who is Marcos?"*

As in the withdrawal from Rancho Nuevo, he defends himself and counterattacks with silence, evasive anecdotes and a quiet chuckle, as if to himself. But a few things do slip out.

Of course Marcos isn't named Marcos. He refuses to tell his real name, hiding behind a quiet laugh, but admits that it is a pseudonym, or rather, a symbol.

*"For Saint Mark, the first evangelist who..."*

"Heaven help me, no," he says, turning to Oscar Hinojosa. "Contrary to what Carlos Ramírez says, that they took pictures of me at a religious service, I want to say that the last religious service I attended was when I took my First Communion. I was eight years old. I didn't study for the priesthood, or for Pope, or for Papal Nuncio," and he laughs.

*"You mean to say you're not religious in the sense of..."*

"Hold it. I'm not a catechist, or a parishioner, or anything. Put it like that, because before you know it they'll be saying I'm Joel Padrón."

The name Marcos was actually taken from a *compañero* named Marcos who died years ago, in this struggle of his group. He was a dear friend who had earnestly studied the guerrilla [tactics] of Arturo Gámiz, founder of the September 23 League (Liga 23 de Septiembre), while Marcos studied the guerrilla [tactics] of Pancho Villa. They used to talk a lot, exchange ideas, discuss issues. But then he died... And Subcommander Marcos' already soft voice becomes softer. He looks up as he lifts the slippery edge of his ski mask over his nose.

*"A symbolic name then, like the ski masks?"*

"Because of Marcos' work, no one can know who Marcos is. That is, if Marcos becomes identified and disappears, it will bring problems to the Army."

*"I don't understand."*

"If Marcos disappears with his ski mask, anyone of us can put on a ski mask and become Marcos."

He only uses it in front of strangers, of course. Many had used the masks before to shield themselves from the cold and the elements. And, since "it was cold as hell" the day they attacked San Cristóbal, many put them on. Then the press arrived and a reporter from Televisa asked him "What's your name, Commander Tiger, Commander Lion or Commander Dog?" He saw that this was useful and kept using it.

Marcos just has one ski mask. "Why would I want two?" he says, laughing, when asked how may he has. They are made of wool, knit in Chiapas of course, and purchased in the markets of San Cristóbal and Ocosingo. But there aren't any around these days. He laughs again, showing some premature smile wrinkles. "At my age of 63?" he jests.

*"How old are you, really?"*

"Blanche Petrich says 39, but that's only a feminine hallucination. What does the Attorney General of the Republic (PGR) say, 25?"

*"Hiding one's face is unusual in guerrilla movements. Fidel Castro, El Che, and Tomás Borge didn't hide their faces."*

*"Superbarrio,"* notes [*New York Times* correspondent] Tim Golden, joking.

*"It gives the impression of something clandestine, to hide crimes."*

"I don't even have traffic tickets."

*"Or to be here today with the ski mask and tomorrow somewhere else and no one would recognize you, Marcos."*

"No, rather, it's," and he becomes serious as he presses his nose with both hands together, in a typical gesture., "rather, it is respect for the true protagonists, or the corruption that could occur, and that message that anyone can be Marcos. Anyone, not only in the EZLN, but in this country."

*"It is also associated with terrorism, and you aren't terrorists, I suppose."*

"Definitely not."

*"Or with Shining Path. They were the only ones who used ski masks."*

"Also because of the cold, I imagine. It must be cold in the Andes."

Marcos drops the cunning tone and pats the reporter on the back. The low position of the bench forces him to frequently straighten his back with his hands on his thighs, while he glances towards the floor. He entwines the fingers from both hands.

*"And so, what about during the talks, will you take off your ski mask?"*

"At some point I'll have to take it off. I mean, specifically: We won't take them off during the talks. We were going to talk to the commissioner without the masks, and then put them on in front of the press, or the police," he adds jokingly. "But as the lesser acknowledgement came of 'emerging political force' we decided: If you don't acknowledge us, you won't see us. Not even at the level of Camacho."

*"How would you evaluate Camacho's role to date?"*

"There have been changes in Camacho. Sometimes he has a certain attitude, and later it's as if something is pressuring him, and it's not exactly our armed forces. I think it's from the federal level, the government..."

*"The president?"*

"Specifically, yes. Some of the power groups. He makes a proposal and later has to take his word back. Not of his own free will, but because someone is pressuring him. Clearly he's under a lot of pressure."

*"Just a minute. A matter of order."* The reporters are all speaking at the same time and the conversation is bouncing from one subject to another. *"We must get back to the Marcos of the ski mask. The one who's from Mexico City?"*

"No, I'm from a province."

*"From Nuevo León?"* Golden asks.

"It's no fair if you're going to go through all 32 states until you get it."

*"From the North?" Golden insists.*

"No."

Marcos says he was a professional journalist, not a student. He studied in the university, graduated and got a master's degree, though, he says, "he can't say" which profession, or if he went to the UNAM. But, he emphatically denies, with a long "Noooo," almost of repulsion, Oscar Hinojosa's question of whether he is an anthropologist.

He does open up, though, when telling of his experience in 1983 when a group of 12 young people, organized as a political group, decided to go to Chiapas to do precisely that, politicize.

"We felt invincible. We felt that just with our conviction we could defeat any army. That's when we started talking to the communities, and where they taught us a huge lesson. The democratic organization of Indigenous social life is very honest, very clear. It is very difficult to act like a fool or become corrupt. In addition, we saw many people die, many children. They died in our hands as we were carrying out the health campaigns that the government didn't do, and we had to do ourselves. Not out of charity, but rather because they were our people. Vaccination campaigns, record keeping. For quite a while our fighting forces were doing that. And people died on us. There were children of four or five who played at being Zapatistas and said: 'When I grow up I'm going to give vaccinations.' But a few days later we would learn that they had died of diarrhea, fever... Before the war, and even more so now, the girls played that when they grew up, instead of getting married, they would go to the mountains to make their lives, to learn Spanish, which is almost an impossible dream for an Indigenous woman. From that to learning how to handle a weapon is a big step. So, when they decided to set a deadline to begin the war they gave that argument: 'What's the problem, if death is ours? The only difference is that now we'll chose how we're going to die. Come with us, or stay behind,' they would tell us. And we couldn't answer: 'No, wait another five years to see if the administration that takes office in 1995 changes things.' We had no right to, because every year that passed we had seen more and more people die. So, with that logic of death, we decided to struggle. The *compañeros* taught us the mountains, they taught us to walk, to carry loads. The only way to be accepted is if you can carry the same load they do, if you walk the path as they do, when you get fucked the same as they do. Then, they will accept you."

*"And that committed you forever, Marcos? Did you at one point plan on coming and then going back?"*

"I placed all my bets on the mountains. The government should know that, once and for all. If they're going to offer a governorship or something, no way."

Marcos isn't married and doesn't have a *compañera*.

"Nor am I homosexual."

He can't say if he's an atheist or religious.

"The *compañeros* have prohibited me from using those words. Because if you say you're religious, they'll say the movement is religious. If you say you're Catholic, they'll say it's Catholic. Or the same if you say you're Muslim. Whatever you say."

*"But the faith of the Indians must be contagious."*

"There are two kinds of faith. The kind that is in books, and the kind that is in the mountains. When *compañeros* go to the mountains they learn stories that come from far away and they hear them when on guard duty, or at campfires. Stories of ghosts, of magical worlds, that cross over from one ethnic group to another. Stories of the great fear created by the mountains. It's sad to be in the mountains, isn't it? Well yes, it is. There are stories that dance in the mountains... I don't know if I'm making myself understood or if I understand your questions."

The subject of magic leads to the subject of death.
Marcos already said that he was ready for death.

"Yes, I'm living on borrowed time, because we thought that the world would come down on us on January 1. When January 2 came around, and we were still alive, everything from then on has been extra. That's why now I'm writing like crazy, everything that I hadn't written. So if Petrita writes a letter to Subcommander Marcos, I send back everything that I ever meant to say and didn't say. I'll send Petrita six, seven, or eight pages. I've got nothing to lose. So if they are going to criticize my literary style, it doesn't bother me. I also don't give a damn if people like or don't like the letters."

In his literary days, Marcos wrote literature and published something under his own name, "but I won't do it again." He says it is a style of literature to give to women, not to be published.

*"Poetry, you're a poet."*

*"I read an interview with [Mexican writer] Heberto Padilla that said: 'Well that Marcos should be given a governorship, or publish a book to calm him down. You can see he's a poet. All guerrillas are poets.'"*

As a youth, Marcos read Neruda, León Felipe, Antonio Machado, Vallejo. He read Ernesto Cardenal and Borges later, as well as the Mexicans Efraín Huerta, Rosario Castillo, Sabines, Montes de Oca. He says he only likes Paz's poetic essays.

Although he is an avid reader of Carlos Monsiváis and remembers the first time he read *Días de Guardar*, he won't confess whether the joking style of his messages from the mountains were influenced by Monsi, or perhaps by Ibargüengoitia? He just laughs.

He doesn't write the messages on computer or electric typewriter, as one might guess when reading an original [communiqué] with Marcos' signature at the bottom. He writes them by hand, or dictates them, and then someone types them and prints them on pages that he has previously signed. He used to have a portable Olivetti, to write operative orders, but that was the first thing he dropped when they fled Rancho Nuevo.

*"Ask Godínez if he has it. I don't think so."*

He also gradually rid himself of the many books he read.

"I used to carry books around in the mountains, and was scolded for it: why was I carrying them around? It really was suicide. When you first come, you want to bring your whole library, right? But the load of ammunition, food and everything else is divided equally, and on top of that you're carrying books. You end up getting rid of them, because no one is about to say: 'Well, since you're carrying so many books, I'll give you less ammunition.' No, you carry the same amount... And I got rid of them gradually in the different camps."

He says he had a lot. A good reader. Monsiváis; Poniatowska's *La Noche de Tlatelolco*. Everything from Cortázar, Fuentes, Vargas Llosa "when he was still palatable" and García Márquez, "who's another story, that is, special."

"When we arrived in the mountains we were very lonely, and then some officer would say, like in García Márquez's book, 'Marcos has no one to write him,' because I was moping around."

Of course he has many political books, which he doesn't go into details about, except for his favorites of *Los Agachados* and *Los Supermachos*, by [Mexican political cartoonist] Rius.

"In the provinces, politics either came with Rius, or didn't come at all. I learned English," he laughs because the question comes from Tim Golden, "reading Playboy and Penthouse. I speak English like Inspector Calzontzin: *'Esta table es green.'* *'The pen-*

*cil is okey.'* Actually I read it because I had to translate the manuals from the US Pentagon. I don't speak Russian. I don't speak Chinese. Now that's enough."

This man who jokes and laughs frequently like a simple, unassuming, mischievous teenager, switches from frivolity to, at other times in the conversation, radicalism and visions of political utopia, which at times seems idyllic, disingenuous. This is the Subcommander Marcos who has turned national politics upside down since the beginning of the year.

He doesn't budge from the uncomfortable wooden stool. The opening of his mask seems like a slice of a tangerine with a sparking glance.

Behind him an increasing number of members of the Army are sleeping. From sitting against the wall, they have slid down to the floor. They pull blankets over themselves, prepare for sleep. The weapons are leaning against the wall, like brooms or work tools. You could say he seems happy to speak with strangers from the city, because even though Marcos now has plenty of people to write him letters, he is trapped, and far from what we call civilization.

He gets nostalgic recalling the dozen *compañeros* who arrived in Chiapas in '83. "The 12 quickly became 10; two died; five are elsewhere," he says briefly, but one might believe that they are still involved in radical activities in some other place, or maybe they gave up all together; and three are left. He and two others who must hold important Zapatista positions in key areas of Chiapas, but to whom Marcos does not refer, perhaps for strategic reasons.

He becomes emotional when speaking of fear. Fear that the operations will fail or that the combatants will not survive the attacks, as happened in the takeovers in the townships of Oxchuc and Ixtán. And he was in charge of the operation.

*"But what about personal fear, Marcos. The kind that settles in one's stomach?"*

"Oh, yeah, when they're shooting at you and you feel everything go weak. I loose my appetite. Others, like that *compa* over there," he turns to point out one of the ones still awake in the room, "get hungrier than usual. But then you center yourself on the mechanism of response, and you don't notice or feel fear. Until later, when you remember: 'Goddamnit! How could I do that shit, going out by myself with no one on the flanks to protect me!' Fear makes you go weak all over, that's the truth."

He becomes rational in speaking of the mythical stature that Subcommander Marcos has taken on.

*"Does it bother you?"*

"It doesn't affect me."

*"You see it as prudent."*

"I don't see it. It doesn't benefit me and we don't know if it is good for the organization. I really don't know, you see, what's happening. I only find out when a journalist gets mad because I don't give an interview. And I say: 'So since when am I so famous that they scold me because I'm being exclusive, and the bright lights and I don't know what else.' As they say up there, that's all ideology, right? We don't have *caudillismo*."

*"No?"*

"It doesn't affect us inside."

*"It doesn't cause envy, jealously among your combatants?"*

"The moral authority of Marcos," the Subcommander becomes emphatic and shakes two fingers up and down, "didn't start on January 1. That was earned before, among the troops. If out there they say stuff like, 'oh he writes so nicely,' or whatever, people here don't give a damn. No matter what, they keep respecting Marcos for what happened before, not because of what's going on now."

The day begins to dawn. As the door is opened briefly, we no longer see the dark face of night that covered the blind travelers who followed impossible trails to come to this guerrilla stronghold.

We can see the drizzle, and a gust of air enters the room. One can make out green branches hanging from the eaves, and the light of a slow dawn.

Marcos doesn't seem to be cold. You can tell he's wearing several layers, and the thick, black, wool, poncho that's called a *chuj* in Chiapas. And on top of that, like an X tying in his soul, the two crossed ammunition belts; some are huge red shotgun shells, who knows what the others are.

He scratches his mask, low by his chin, in what looks like a nervous tick, or itch.

*"Does your beard itch, Marcos?"*

Marcos looks at Tim Golden as if saying "sly bastard" and jokes: "I don't have a beard, I have no facial hair."

He's lying of course. From a meter away, you can sometimes make out through the mouth of the mask, the revealing hair of a beard coming up to his lower lip. It's a gray beard, and seems to be quite thick.

Also through the opening for the face, on the upper edge of the weaving, you can see a lock of black, not brown, hair that sneaks out near his temples.

"Don't help the PGR out," Marcos protests, when Tim insists on the beard.

It's almost his last smile of the talk, because the mysteries of a character who reminds Castillo Peraza of the lasting myth of Robin Hood, and who others consider an unattainable gallant, something like Kevin Costner, or a Rambo playing the part of a leftist villain, or just the current faddish idol... From strictly personal mysteries, this talk always comes back to the serious problems that generated, and continue to generate the Zapatista uprising.

"From the beginning we said that we didn't want power. We said: 'Salinas de Gortari has to get out, and there must be a provisional government.' What I pointed out is that we weren't going to impose our will on 'civil society,'" he uses the term even though he dislikes it, "through the force of weapons. We were not going to take it hostage. The government yes, but not civil society."

*"The main point for you,"* Golden asks, *"would be the composition of the Federal Electoral Institute, the Electoral Tribunal, the electoral authorities?"*

"There's another option. That Salinas resign and create a transitional government, and that the latter be organized according to existing electoral laws. What we are saying is that the arbitrator must really be impartial. So there are two alternatives: Reform the Electoral Law to give someone impartiality, or have the federal government resign and create a transitional government, and have that one certify [the elections]."

*"And if that doesn't happen?"*

"We'll continue the struggle. Maybe fighting, maybe not."

*"What is your critical analysis of the candidates, Marcos? Of Colosio, Cuauhtémoc, and Fernández de Cevallos?"*

Marcos lowers his gaze and thinks about it, longer than usual. In general, he has responded quickly, as if hitting the ball back in handball. Now he thinks about it and looks forward, as if saying he was sorry:

"That's precisely one of the things I can't talk about yet. The Committee doesn't allow me to. The Committee has told me that in referring to political parties I must be very cautious. The members of the Committee are very proud of their independence, at least up until now. And if we start giving opinions about one or the other, it will look like the EZLN supports a party, or said something to make another party mad. The Committee believes that until we have a clear idea of what one says to the other, what one offers to the other, we shouldn't say anything. Basically, they won't allow me to comment."

*"What are those guns that look like AK Stopers?"* asks Tim, an expert. *"Are they rifles or..."*

"They are AK rifles, donated by the PGR and the Federal Army."

*"And what the* compañeros *had before, were they Uzis or Mac-10's?"*

"Mac-10's, we just adapted them."

*"How did you get them?"*

"In the United States. I think we just bought two. At the time they cost around $200. But we couldn't get much there, because US laws are very strict."

*"But Mexican police go to Arizona to buy their weapons..."*

"We bought them from Mexicans, it was easier. What we never found was an arms trafficker. If we'd found one, now we'd be talking in Cerro del Ajusco."

And Marcos laughs. Openly now, loudly, amazed at his own exaggeration. Perhaps he dreams of it, but he doesn't even believe it himself.

The subject of weapons relates to war. And the subject of war settles on the bad omens of pessimists who fear the failure of the talks that are only just about to begin. It seems that they will.

*"Who has benefited from the truce?"*

"The government has taken advantage of this impasse to finish placing its troops, complete its intelligence gathering, and define where we are, to be able to attack us without touching the civilian population. All of this time has been used by the government to do all that."

*"Do you consider the possibility, or the risk involved, if they launch an extermination offensive?"* asks Hinojosa, very formal as usual.

"Definitely. Any middle-rank officer says eight days. And they said that four days ago. So I have four more days," he raises his eyebrows. "The Federal Army already has us surrounded to be able to attack and exterminate us. I don't think the situation will change. All that's missing is for the tanks to roll in, unless something happens to change that impulse. Perhaps it could be the presence of the *guardias blancas*. The ranchers who are taking up arms; or rather, that have to rearm, because we had disarmed them. They can now rearm and start to attack."

Marcos seems prepared to repel them. With his crossed ammunition belts, and the shotgun he put aside somewhere, and a pistol on his right belt, he seems to be on the alert. As they say, he has his boots on. And they're quite muddy too, from trudging the paths who knows where in the mythical Lacandona Jungle.

*"You seem pessimistic about the dialogue, Marcos."*

"We're not overly concerned about the agenda, because in the end it will also result from the negotiation process. We want to talk as much as possible. So they know what it is that we want, and we know what they want, and so that each side can pull for itself on a common point. But finally, I say, what is the government going to commit to if it signs the agreement, to what, with whom, if we don't exist?"

*"The commissioner doesn't exist as a legal figure either. Then, who will guarantee the agreements that arise from dialogue?"*

"If the federal government is really willing, it would have to give the commissioner legal standing. Or create a commission just to take responsibility for that."

*"Would you propose that during the dialogue?"*

"We would say: 'So, what about these agreements we're going to sign? Do you really want to reach an agreement, or did you just close us in here to do what you're going to do anyway? If you are really willing, what structure will carry this out? Because this commissioner doesn't really exist.'"

*"The disarmament of the Zapatista Army seems very far off."*

"As the *compañeros* say, we've waited 500 years. We can wait another 500."

*"What will the press see and not see during the negotiations?"*

"It's an operative matter," says Marcos. "For example, if we are going to set forth, as the *compañeros* of the Committee are going to set forth, autonomy statutes, we will need legal advice. What reforms are needed to the Constitution, what laws should be considered to formulate the specific proposal. All that. In this push and pull of whether to reform the Constitution, or how to do it, the press won't be involved. But what should be public, open, is when we declare: We said this, the commissioner said that, and the intermediary said that,

205

and we agreed on this and didn't agree on that; and we fought about this, and we cussed each other out about that, whatever happened. We will tell it all clearly."

*"At the end of a meeting, will there be a reading of the minutes?"*

"We are proposing to the commissioner to hold a press conference every day. But apparently you journalists have driven him crazy, and he isn't very willing."

*"Have you spoken personally to Camacho?"*

"Not personally. By letter. Letters that are more serious than the other ones, of course."

And he laughs through the hole of the mask, which is too small to show the breadth of his smiling mouth.

*"What does the commissioner say, that it can't be done logistically?"*

"He says we have to see. We were proposing a daily press conference, but he thought it should be after a subject was exhausted."

Marcos doesn't seem tired from talking so much and thinking about what he's saying. He has stayed still, not shifting his rear like the three journalists who can no longer find a way to be comfortable on the hard seat, and he gives the impression that he could keep talking throughout the day that is beginning, through nightfall. His eyelids are a bit heavy, that's true, because he has shared this overnighter, but he's still going strong: He seems strong, although even through the mask, his face has sharp features.

*"What's most important for you in the negotiations?"* Golden asks.

"Administrative and political autonomy of Indigenous regions."

*"Explain that to us."*

"The *compañeros* say that in the communities where the majority is Indigenous, they already have their specific form of government, that underlies the official one. And they say 'What the government should do is recognize that ours is the one that works, and they should respect it and not interfere with us.'"

*"At the community level?"*

"In entire regions. What the *compañeros* are saying is where there are Tzotziles, Tzeltales, Choles, Tojolabales, the way they have of organizing *ejidos* works. For example, they elect their representatives and replace them whenever they need to. Then that is the way it should be. And if someone commits a crime, they try to resolve it there, in the community, not send it elsewhere. But the government sends in judicial police, and that bothers them. They say, 'Why do they want to take them to jail, if we've already punished them? If I've already fined them, why do you intervene? You're interfering with my chain of command.'"

*"So that means, in this case, not acknowledging police authority."*

"Yes, that's what not acknowledging means. That the state police should not get involved."

*"Not in anything?"*

"Only if called upon. When the community itself says: 'Okay, this is too big for us, and we can't deal with it. Take him.'"

*"This kind of change would require constitutional reform."*

"The Fourth Article of the Constitution would be reformed to acknowledge the existence of regions populated by several ethnic groups that have their own structure... What the *compañeros* are really proposing in the end is a collective government at all levels. The need for a state governor to govern in conjunction with a group of Indigenous governors, for each ethnic group."

*"Is this a proposal that will be made?"*

"Yes, it will be made."

*"To have parallel elections for a state governor and governors for the Tzotzil, Tzeltal, Chol, Tojolobal...?"*

"Yes, The state governor will be the governor, but in everything relating to Indigenous matters he will have to come to an agreement with the co-governor or whatever that post is called. And in the entire state, everyone needs to come to an agreement."

*"I understand that democracy in Indigenous communities is very different from democracy as we know it."*

"The community makes an agreement and everyone must uphold that. Anyone who doesn't fulfill the agreement is removed. It's not like they say, Marcos is going to win or Felipe is going to win. They say, this is what the community has agreed on. Who will carry it out? Let's say this guy, and if he doesn't, we'll get rid of him. Every so often they meet and evaluate: Has this agreement been upheld? The agreements don't change. They see whether they have been upheld or not. This is the kind of democracy that was adopted by the EZLN. The Zapatista Army was not born democratic, it was born as a political-military organization. But as it grew, the organizational methods of the communities began to permeate and dominate our movement, to the degree that the leadership of the EZLN had to become democratic in the Indigenous manner. They say: There are fundamental agreements that cannot be negotiated, there is no margin. Aside from those fundamental agreements, you can do other things. One of our fundamental agreements was to begin the war, at the latest at zero hour on January 1. You have to fulfill that. You can start on January 1, 1994 or on December 31, 1993, but you have to start."

*"Was that same system used to select the Zapatista delegates to the dialogue?"*

*"Will you go, Marcos?"*

Marcos doubts that he will take part in the talks and confides to the reporters, confidentially during the interview, what Camacho later made public: that the sessions will begin this Monday in San Cristóbal de las Casas. He then responds to the unanswered question.

"To elect the delegates the Committees, and there are several Clandestine Revolutionary Indigenous Committees, meet and say: 'This is what is going to be demanded, and you can say this. You have to ask me about that, this other one is a definite no.' One of the things that is a flat no is turning over our weapons to begin the dialogue. So, then they say, who should we send? Who are we going to negotiate with? The government. Then they start choosing those who can express themselves and argue best, the ones who more or less speak Spanish. Those are the ones being sent. But they've already told them how to do it. They don't want little chicks, either, each Committee is sending its roosters."

Golden is distracted for a moment watching Marcos' hands which are in front of him, fingers entwined.

*"Do you bite your fingernails, Marcos?"*

"No, I cut them that way."

*"How many Indigenous delegates will go to the talks?"*

"Fifteen."

*"Where is the ghost of Chinameca that you have alluded to in the past, Subcommander?"* asks Hinojosa.

"Throughout the dialogue process. Whenever the government decides that it is possible to give a blow like that. No one doubts that it should think it out carefully, and will. When it comes and says, 'OK, I can now do it and come out with a good hand,' it will. That is: Exterminate whoever is there, because the government knows that we send our leadership, not a commissioner. The government sends a commissioner, but we send the leaders of our movement. It could be done at any time they can get away with it, and they can handle the protests that arise. Whether it happens in San Cristóbal or the jungle, or anywhere, it will be done."

The disorderly questions continue, as the reporters are tired but anxious not to run out of time to ask all the questions they planned out a long time before heading for the mountains.

*"I hope you don't scold us like you did the ones from* La Jornada, *for not asking the questions they should have."*

The subcommander shakes his head. He laughs and hides the lock of hair that has come out of the mask. He has delicate hands, like those of a pianist: long, thin fingers that end bluntly, whether he bites his nails or not.

*"And human rights people don't raise hell with you?"*

"Of course. Although there have been violations on the part of our *compañeros*. Especially verbal harassment in some areas. That's what the Human Rights Council denounced, and it was true. Our Committee investigated that. And it was true. Some people were threatening people to get them to join the Zapatista Army. Because if they didn't, when the soldiers came, they would kill everyone. So our Committee found out and arrested four guilty *compañeros*. What isn't true are the accusations of breaking and entering and everything else they are piling on us."

208

Suddenly, the subject jumps to Liberation Theology.

*"You have implied, whether intentionally or tacitly, the possible influence of Liberation Theology on the Zapatista Army."*

"There are no religious people, or people from the religious structure, or religious hierarchy, in the leadership or ideological orientation of the Zapatista Army. That is the truth. The thing is, that in this state, particularly, there has been a great deal of social work on the part of the Church. And the *compañeros* know that very well: That work went diametrically against armed struggle, even though it was popular in El Salvador, Nicaragua, and other places. It was said that it's okay there, but it isn't possible in Mexico. Here we must have peaceful change, with open democratic demonstrations. All of the efforts of the Church here were in that direction."

*"In some way the Church made the communities aware of their situation."*

"No. As soon as we arrived there was a conflict. We said: Armed struggle is necessary and we must prepare for it. They said: 'No. Our efforts should be directed toward economic and health projects that solve the needs of the Indigenous people.'"

*"And did that create conflict?"*

"Yes, but we let reality take over. The *compañeros* did the projects, made the efforts, but the state kept strangling them and the number of deaths grew and grew. When we arrived, we found that people were very clear about their living conditions. They weren't thinking that they were living well or that they were poor because God wanted it that way. Politically, the Church provides a path for open political participation. We come and say, 'We have to prepare ourselves in a different way.' But we tried not to enter into conflict, but rather wait and let time show that we were right. And in the meantime, we needed to prepare ourselves, and learn, because no one was giving us military advice or weapons or anything. We had to learn everything from how to get ready, how to stand at alert, to salute and everything."

*"Don Samuel has been accused of creating a breeding ground that favored armed struggle in the Church."*

"We who were there know that the efforts of the diocese were going in exactly the opposite direction. If there wasn't a direct conflict, it's because we avoided it. We also think that reality educates. And that the Mexican State was on our side in the sense that it was going to show that that kind of struggle was not sufficient, and that another kind was needed."

*"The mediating role of Don Samuel."*

"The situation is that the real leadership of the Zapatista Army is Indigenous, and that isn't just propaganda. And they acknowledge Don Samuel as someone who is not an enemy, and they also know that he isn't one of us. When they ask, 'Who should be the one in the middle to be able to talk,' the answer was 'Don Samuel. He's always been in the middle.' "

*"In all this process how do you evaluate the role played by Don Samuel?"* insists Tim Golden. *"The fact that he launched such a strong call, so soon, made it possible that the real*

*causes of the uprising be known. Didn't he play an important role in changing the perspective of Mexican society towards you?"*

"The truth is, I'll tell you what I think. What made society change the way it looks at us was the press. Not even television; the written press, photographers and all that. Because it's not that Don Samuel doesn't see the causes. It's when journalists themselves say: 'You see? They really are Indigenous people, they aren't foreigners, and we've seen that this is the way they live,' and all that. So it really was the written news media that began to awaken that change, or critical distrust, that reality was totally different from what the government was saying. That was it. It wasn't the government, or our weapons; nor was it Don Samuel or Camacho. It was the press, that looks and looks and starts to bring out more and more information, and makes people say: 'Wait a minute, look, something is happening.'"

*"You do have a beard Marcos."*

"What happens is that the press itself, in its dialectic movements, turns against itself. First its Marcos, Marcos, Marcos. And now, goddamn Marcos, goddamn Marcos, because all we hear is Marcos. And the truth is that Marcos didn't say anything. The whole mess was made up by the press, and now they're complaining that why is Marcos the protagonist? I feel like I'm being interrogated in San Cristóbal."

The day has definitely dawned. Its eight. Time to finish.

*"And what about the country, Marcos? What do you think about the country's future?"*

"I'll give you an example. There is a guerrilla law about the speed of a guerrilla column. It says that the speed of the guerrilla column is as fast as the slowest man. In this case, the country is the same. What should its economic pace be? As fast as its poorest state. So it's impossible for part of the country to enter the First World while the other part, our part, is exterminated."

*"There can't be two Mexicos?"*

"In this case there are three, because we're in the basement. Bring us to Guatemala to enter the tour."

The subcommander of the Zapatista Army rises for the first and only time throughout the interview. Now he does look tired like the rest. His knees seem tired, or legs cramped. He shivers, but more from lack of sleep than from the cold, which is already giving way, even outside.

One of the masked people stretched in a corner. Others stand up, at attention. Oscar Hinojosa checks his tape recorder, while Tim Golden gives Marcos photocopies of clippings from the US press. He also receives a cassette with the music of Federico Bonasso and the rock group El Juguete Rabioso, and the great non-fiction book about the dirty war in Argentina by Miguel Bonasso. Marcos looks at the cover and reads the title: *Recuerdos de la Muerte [Memories of Death]*. And asks, smiling, "Are you trying to scare me?"

The three reporters leave the simple room and begin their difficult return to today.

# 8. The Dialogue

## Report By Subcommander Marcos On the First Day

February 21, 1994

The Clandestine Revolutionary Indigenous Committee-General Command of the Zapatista National Liberation Army speaks through my mouth for the purpose of informing the people of Mexico, the peoples and governments of the world, and the national and international press about what occurred today at the table of the peace conference.

Today, the representatives of the EZLN explained to the commissioner in what capacity they are here, how they were named by the various regions, by the towns, by the communities, by location.

The *compañeros* explained clearly to the commissioner that they are not here to ask for forgiveness, that they do not regret having fought for their rights, but that they see that this may be a good moment for the true men who make up our Army to speak in words that come from their hearts, rather than with gunfire.

We listened attentively to the commissioner's position. He explained to us in what capacity he comes to these talks and what his position is: to listen, to patiently and with dedication learn the lessons that the *compañeros* brought with them from their communities throughout the state.

Both parties agreed to be mutually respectful when addressing each other, and we expressed our willingness to hear the federal government's word, because we believe that the commissioner is willing to hear the Zapatista Army's word. In this way, we made all the necessary preparations for beginning the discussion of our list of demands tomorrow.

We spent practically the whole day today deciding on the agenda for the talks that have begun this day, and which we hope will proceed in the same spirit that has been present today.

**February 22, 1994**

Good evening. This is going to take a while, so change your cassettes; censors, get your scissors ready, because the Clandestine Revolutionary Indigenous Committee-General Command of the Zapatista National Liberation Army would like to say a few things, taking advantage of the fact that the major media are here, before speaking on what is happening at the dialogue table.

First, we have learned that there is a person claiming to be a member of our Army who is in the United States of North America, passing himself off as a spokesperson for and combatant in our Army. This is untrue. We don't have combatants in other countries doing this kind of work.

The second thing is that our Army's ban on the already-named newspeople of a certain TV network is still in force. Just remember: Just say no to piracy. We can't do anything about it—we don't have any satellites to jam the signal with—but at least let it be clear that it doesn't meet with our approval.

We would like to address Mexico and the peoples of the world again, now that you, the national and international press, are here.

The Zapatista National Liberation Army speaks through my mouth.

When we came down from the mountains carrying our packs, our dead, and our history, we came to the city to look for our country. The country that had forgotten us in the most remote corner of the land: the loneliest, the dirtiest, the worst.

We came to ask this country, our country: Why did it leave us there for all these years and years? Why did it leave us there with so much death? And we want to ask it again, through you: Why is it necessary to kill and die, to get you, and through you, the world, to listen to Ramona here say such terrible things as that Indigenous women want to live, want to study, want hospitals, medicine, schools, food, respect, justice, dignity?

Why is it necessary to kill and die so Ramona can come and get attention for what she says? Why should Laura, Ana María, Irma, Elisa, Silvia, and so many other Indigenous women have had to pick up the gun, become soldiers instead of becoming doctors, lawyers, engineers, teachers?

Why was it necessary for those who have died to die? Why is it necessary to kill and die? What is happening in this country? And we are asking everyone, the governors and the governed: What is happening in this country that makes it necessary to kill and die in order to say a few small, true words without seeing them lost in the void?

We came to the city armed with the truth and with fire, to speak through violence on the first of this year. Today we return to the city to speak again, but not with fire; our weapons of fire and of death have fallen silent, and the road has been opened for the word to rule again in a place it should never have left: our soil.

We came to the city and we found this flag, our flag. That is what we found. We didn't find money, we didn't find riches, we didn't find anyone to hear us again. We found an empty city, and we found this flag, and we saw that our country lives under this flag: not the country forgotten in books and museums, but our living nation, the one and only, the one that suffers, the one that hopes.

This is the Mexican flag, our flag. Beneath this flag lives a part of the country whose existence was ignored and dismissed by the powerful; deaths and more deaths have piled one on top of the other, without other Mexicans turning to see, without you turning to see.

Why do we have to sleep with our boots on and our hearts on a string, taking care of this flag? Why do we go marching through jungles, over mountains, through valleys and canyons, down roads and highways, carrying and taking care of this flag? Why do we carry it with us as our only hope of democracy, freedom, and justice? Why do our arms accompany and watch over this flag day and night? Why?

And we would like to ask you if there is another way to live under this flag, another way to live with dignity and justice under this flag. You have told us that there is, you have spoken to us with truthfulness, you speak to our hearts saying: Give peace a chance.

We have gotten your message and we have come here in an honest and truthful spirit. We do not bring two hearts: There are no dark forces behind us, nor do we come here seeking anything other than to talk and listen, unarmed.

When we sit down at the negotiating table with the mediator, Bishop Samuel Ruiz, and the Peace Commissioner, Mr. Manuel Camacho Solís, we take our weapons off, we put them aside, and we go in and we speak man to man, without pressure tactics and without threats.

If we go armed now, or when we are not at the table, this is for our personal protection, to defend ourselves if we are attacked by someone who feels offended and threatened by our words of truth and justice.

You told us to give peace a chance, and we come here in the spirit of truth and honesty. If there is another road to the same place, the place where this flag will fly in democracy, freedom, and justice, show us that road. We will not toy with our people's blood. If it is possible to raise this flag, our flag, YOUR flag, with dignity, and without the death that makes the soil it stands on fertile, if this can be done, then let it be done. But if it isn't, if they close the door to us again? And if the world does not manage to climb the walls of arrogance and incomprehension? And if the peace is not a true and dignified peace, then who, we ask, who will deny us the sacred right to live and die as true and dignified men and women? Who will stop us from dressing in the garb of war and death and journeying through history again? Who?

It is up to you: the governors and the governed, all the peoples of the world. Answer; we'll listen. We ask you to make a place in your hearts for our thoughts: Don't leave us alone.

With you we're everything. Without you, we go back to being that dirty and forgotten corner of our country.

We, the Zapatista National Liberation Army, have come here with the same hopes that we came here with on January 1: not the will to power, but the hope for a peace with justice, dignity, democracy, and freedom.

That is why we became soldiers: so that one day soldiers will not be needed. We chose this suicidal path of a profession whose purpose is to disappear: soldiers who are soldiers so that one day no one will have to be a soldier.

And it was for the sake of this flag that we became soldiers. But if our people, if you, tell us that this can be done without blood and death, we came to listen to you and to learn from you.

Our country is not just an idea in books. The country that we all want has to be reborn. This flag must fly again over our broken bodies, over our dead, and over our hope.

Whatever happens, we know that we all have contributed something to this long, painful, historic beginning. Love and pain not only rhyme ["*amor y dolor*" in Spanish], they go together and they travel together. That is why we are soldiers who want to stop being soldiers, because the dead of yesterday and of tomorrow, the living of today and of always—all those we call the people and the country, those who have nothing, the eternal losers in the face of tomorrow, we who have no name, we who have no face— can grow the powerful tree of love, a wind that cleans and that heals; not small and self-ish love, grand love, the love that makes better and makes great.

To grow among us the tree of love, the tree of duty, to put our whole life in this undertaking, body and soul, vigor and hope. You have told us that it is possible to achieve this without war, that it is possible that peace will open the door to hope for our people. We hear you all, governments and the governed.

We are willing to see if the door will open again, and if it is real, we will go through it. That is the frame of mind we came here in: with willingness and the desire to finally speak, and we have told the government what our demands are: democracy, freedom, and justice.

We see in them a willingness to listen and a willingness to look for a way. And that is what we are looking for now.

We want to say to the people of Mexico, and to the peoples and governments of the world, to you, the representatives of the national and international press, that the talks are going well. We have found ears to hear us and a real willingness to look for solutions.

I would like to talk about the concern that exists about our faces and weapons. We do not understand why you are so concerned with what our faces look like, when before the first you didn't even know they existed. On the first, this country didn't know that Ramona or Felipe or David or Eduardo or Ana María or any of the others existed.

But, if you want to know what the face behind the ski mask is like, it's very simple: Look in the mirror. We would like to say to you—those of you who have told the truth, not those who have followed the path of lies—that when death stopped the day it did, it was thanks to you and to the people behind you.

We ask you—as brothers and sisters—those of you who are speaking the truth, to go on speaking it, and, if possible, that those of you who are speaking lies not say them so loudly.

We want you to support this dialogue, we want you to report clearly what we say. What we are saying is the truth. It is not good to look for double dealing where there is none, because that can bring more trouble elsewhere.

I have already explained that we carry weapons not so much out of distrust of the government, but rather because of other forces, whose interests have been affected by our movement. But we think, on this second day of the talks, and now that our demands have been presented and have been weighed by the Commissioner, that we are making progress in finding the road to a solution, and thereby in arriving at concrete solutions, if in fact they are possible.

What the Committee has asked me to say clearly, and in so many words, is that it is truly willing to look for another road, if there is one. And to hear all of your opinions and to accept your support in this search for the peace with dignity that we hope for.

In my silence, the Zapatista National Liberation Army falls silent. Through my mouth, Marcos speaks again.

We would like to take this opportunity because we have been criticized a lot for talking to one person and then the other, or for talking to some people and not others. And we sincerely want to say to you that we do want to talk with everyone, and we will, but please give us a break; we just got here and we're struggling with the translation of the proposals, because we have four languages represented on the Clandestine Committee at the moment.

Any initiative we take or demand we raise, or any answer from the commissioner, takes a long time because we have to translate it. But we promise you, whom we owe so much to, to tell you with our ski masks off whatever you want to know about us.

That will be all, thank you very much.

# REPORT BY SUBCOMMANDER MARCOS ON THE THIRD DAY

February 23, 1994

The Clandestine Revolutionary Indigenous Committee-General Command speaks through my mouth to inform the people of Mexico, the peoples and governments of the world and the national and international press, about what has happened [today] at table of the peace talks in our state.

The Zapatista National Liberation Army has presented the list of demands for which it rose up in arms on January 1, 1994, with the Declaration from the Lacandona Jungle.

The Commissioner for Peace and Reconciliation in Chiapas, Mr. Manuel Camacho Solís, received and heard patiently and attentively our demands and the explanation [of the demands] given him by the *compañero* delegates from the Clandestine Committee.

He later presented a document in answer to our demands, or at least those that can be resolved here at the table in San Cristóbal, because both parties are clear in our own minds that we have demands that go far beyond anything that can be settled at the San Cristóbal table, and that must be discussed at the national level.

The Clandestine Revolutionary Indigenous Committee has analyzed part of the commissioner's answer, and I say part because, please remember, our Committee is multi-ethnic, which means that we have to translate everything into the languages of the various groups it is composed of as we go along.

We can say that although there are still problems of wording, up until now our demands have received satisfactory answers in regard to the following issues: health care, education, accurate and timely information, housing, respect for the culture, the rights, the traditions, and the dignity of Indigenous peoples in Mexico. The rest of the points on our list of demands are still being studied and translated for the *compañeros* on the Committee. But we have arrived at substantive agreements with the commissioner on the above points.

The Committee has asked me—has ordered me—to explain to you its position on the dialogue and on the peace.

When on January 1, 1994, war came to Ocosingo, Altamirano, Las Margaritas, Chanal, Oxchuc, Huixtán, and San Cristóbal de las Casas, the voice that came to declare war in these townships came from many places.

What they want you to understand, what the Zapatista Army is asking you to understand, is that just as the war was a democratic decision, so will the peace necessarily have to come out of the same democratic process. They want me to explain to you that their power to make decisions is set out for them by the democratic decision-making structure of the Zapatista National Liberation Army.

This means that neither they nor I can take any personal initiatives with regards to any agreement worked out at the table of the Dialogue for Peace. And when I say this I mean that the negotiators have to comply with the conditions laid out for them by the *compañeros* so they can come to the talks: They have to obtain a satisfactory response, and they absolutely cannot make any decisions on their own.

They have to go back to their regions, they have to go back to their communities and explain to the *compañeros* the proposal for the resolution of the issues that caused our action on January 1, 1994. And the communities are going to answer yes or no; the final yes or no at this dialogue table will be a majority decision.

They want you, and the country, to understand that if the war was decided upon in this democratic fashion, the peace—if it comes at all—cannot help but follow the same road, if it is to be a real peace.

So the *compañeros* are asking me to explain this to you. The *compañeros* who have been named as delegates have been named by four groups of Clandestine Revolutionary Indigenous Committees, which mainly control four ethnic groups.

They are the ones who command, and they in their turn have to ask the various regions their opinions, and the regions have to ask the communities theirs, and in the communities, the men, women and children meet and decide, on the basis of the information they have, how to proceed.

Then comes the reverse process: The communities send their representatives to the regional meeting, the regional group tells that ethnic group's Clandestine Committee, and the Committee tell its delegate what the answer is. It's a somewhat complicated process, but one we consider logical—one the Zapatista National Liberation Army finds logical—and in any case, it's the one that makes us invincible.

As long as we respect the agreement and reason of our people, there will be nothing that can destroy us; if we betray them, or follow a different path, begin to make decisions without consulting them, we will have no authority over them in any case. This is what we want to explain to you, so you can get more rolls of film, or cassettes, or ask for an advance to pay for your hotel room, because this is going to take a while. It won't be as fast as you might think.

But the Committee has also asked me to make it clear that we have received serious responses to our demands, some of which, as I said, have already been approved by our delegates and now must be approved by the communities, and others which we need to review and discuss with the team of legal advisors the National Commission for Mediation has provided for us.

This is what we wanted to say to you today. Tomorrow we will continue talking to the media, because we have received many requests for interviews. So, we're fitting them into the schedule of the talks, so they can interview us.[...]

What we are asking is that you respect the pace of the talks. The *compañeros* don't understand your—or other people's—hurry to see results; and I don't mean you in particular, I mean the hurry another world may be in. They are in a process of reflection, of understanding what they are being presented with, because for them something very important is at stake: Whether they live as dignified human beings or whether they go back to the same old story.

So they are taking things calmly. I don't know how long it will take because I'm their subordinate and I do what they tell me. Right now we're on the fourth part, and the rest might take many or a few days, or maybe it will be resolved in a matter of hours. But they are asking everyone to respect the pace of the peace process, just as the timing of their decision to go to war was respected.

Thanks, again. There will be no more questions.

## PRESS CONFERENCE WITH SUBCOMMANDER MARCOS ON THE THIRD DAY

[*La Jornada*, 2/24]
February 23, 1994
Ricardo Alemán Alemán, correspondent,
San Cristóbal de las Casas

The problem of democracy in Mexico is a problem "that goes beyond the negotiations in San Cristóbal," said Subcommander Marcos, explaining that "it is up to civil society, the media, and the political parties to make proposals regarding that subject, since they are the ones who are in a position to change this country's course." [...]

"That," he emphasized, "is the new country we are talking about, the one we wish to speak to, and which we are willing and able to follow down whatever path it chooses. If that path is the peaceful and legal path, then that is the path we will take."

"Civil society," he added, "has shown its maturity. It didn't say 'I want the Zapatistas to win,' or, 'I want the Federal Army to win.' It said, 'Talk, don't fight!' And

I think it has sufficient moral authority throughout the country to organize an election on the scale of the one that will be held next August, but some changes will have to be made in the election law."

Concretely, Marcos said, "Democracy is an issue that must be dealt with at a higher level than San Cristóbal, and the changes we are asking for to Article 27 of the Constitution are also an issue that has to be dealt with at a higher level. Regarding state issues, it is very likely that our demands for liberty, democracy, and justice will be resolved satisfactorily.

"But understand that we cannot say to the nation: We have already negotiated democracy at the San Cristóbal table," he said—almost shouted—to the journalists. "Because then the country is going to say to us: 'Who appointed you our spokesperson?' For that, there has to be a larger movement. And for there to be democracy in Mexico, there has to be a larger discussion: a nationwide discussion."

A journalist from the US spoke of the United States' role in conflicts such as those in Nicaragua, Guatemala, and El Salvador, and asked about the possibility of our northern neighbor attempting to intervene in the same way. "The government and people of the US need to be clear that there is nothing in our movement that affects their interests. Our platform is: Things change or we starve to death," Marcos said.

The people and government of the United States "are going to realize that we have nothing against them, and if the people of the United States intervene, it will be to send help. We don't want power, we don't want to invade or take the White House, or to exterminate the white race or the gringos. What we want is to be allowed to live in peace."

"It is more dangerous for them to pursue a policy of economic extermination of Indigenous people, which is what is happening, than to have changes occur that will raise everyone's living standard," he said.

And about NAFTA, he stated: "It is a problem for us, because there is no section on Indigenous peoples. The treaty comes into effect, and supposedly it is the skilled labor in the companies that are going to compete. And we don't know how to read and write. What possibility do we have of competing in the world market? Doing what?"

The subject of democracy came up repeatedly, as did the EZLN's insistence on calling for the resignation of President Salinas. "We did not do this as a pressure tactic. We don't even know how to speak Spanish. But the root cause of all our problems of health care, education, housing, nutrition and justice is that there is no freedom and democracy."

And, in a didactic tone, the subcommander stated: "So we say that there has to be a change in the democratic system that will guarantee that there are no privileges, and that whatever political option wins, wins an honest victory. And if the federal government cannot guarantee a free and democratic election, then we say that there will have to be another federal government, a transitional government. Alternatively, there will have to be a modification to the election law that establishes that the federal government will no longer be the party that sanctions the elections." [...]

Commander Ramona also spoke, and said, "Women are the ones who have been the most exploited, the most oppressed, throughout history." On this subject, Marcos stated, "The longest sections in our list of demands is the one on Indigenous women."

# REPORT BY SUBCOMMANDER MARCOS ON THE FOURTH DAY

February 24, 1994

The preceding was our salute to the flag, because today is Flag Day; it was the Zapatista Army's salute to the Mexican flag.

The Clandestine Revolutionary Indigenous Committee-General Command of the Zapatista National Liberation Army speaks through my mouth for the purpose of informing the people of Mexico, the peoples and governments of the world, and the national and international press about what occurred today at the talks with the National Commissioner of Mediation, Bishop Samuel Ruiz García, and the National Commissioner for Peace and Reconciliation in Chiapas, Mr. Manuel Camacho Solís.

We have resolved 50% of our list of demands and we have received answers to the following points on the list of demands, presented by the Clandestine Revolutionary Indigenous Committee-General Command of the EZLN:

The demand for providing electricity to Indigenous communities and the redistribution of federal spending in the state; another regarding the impact of NAFTA on Indigenous communities; others regarding health care, accurate information—as we said yesterday; housing, education—in particular the construction of schools, the provision of teaching material, and an official, binding policy of appointing bilingual teachers in Indigenous communities; the demand for the penalization of the discrimination and contempt Indigenous people suffer; demands regarding the issues of nutrition, of financial assistance to the victims of the war and to those who have been widowed or orphaned by the conflict; the demands of Indigenous women regarding the course to be followed so that Indigenous people may live in peace.

The other demand, so that the non-governmental human rights organizations can increase in number and be strengthened, is the need for the formation, at the appropriate moment, of a National Commission for a Peace with Justice and Dignity, that would have the responsibility of overseeing compliance with the agreements arrived at at this table.

And the last point we have agreed on is that humanitarian aid to the war zone is to be channeled through authentic representatives of the Indigenous communities.

These are the agreements we have arrived at up until now. I repeat, 50% of the list of demands presented by the Committee has been answered satisfactorily by the commissioner.

I have another message from the Committee, regarding the direction of the consultations to be held with our bases and with our leadership in the Indigenous communities, on the agreements we arrive at here. The Clandestine Revolutionary Indigenous Committee of the Zapatista National Liberation Army has decided that when there are more specific and finished results coming out of these talks, it will send the respective documents to all the non-governmental organizations, to the national and international press, and to civil society at large. These documents will be of three kinds: documents regarding our demand list, the federal government's answers, and the agreements arrived at.

221

This, the *compañeros* say, is for the purpose of hearing the views and the consensus of everyone who has expressed an opinion on this conflict, on the road to peace with dignity. This decision of the Committee, to broaden the consultation on the signing of the peace, is to be carried out as soon as we arrive at a more finished agreement.

# PRESS CONFERENCE WITH SUBCOMMANDER MARCOS ON THE FOURTH DAY

[*La Jornada*, 2/25]
February 24, 1994
Ricardo Alemán Alemán, correspondent,
San Cristóbal de las Casas, Chiapas

If things don't change in Mexico, "January 1 in Chiapas will repeat itself over and over again, in different years, and not just in the Mexican Southeast, but in various regions," Subcommander Marcos said during a press conference with reporters from national and international radio stations, during which he stated, "Everyone will surely benefit from our call for democracy, liberty, and justice, because those are the three lines along which a people is free, true, and powerful." In the same gathering, the military chief of the Zapatista National Liberation Army criticized the political parties who, at the invitation of the rebels, attended the talks as observers. "All we want is for them be on the alert, to not leave us alone, because if there is a different road for our demands and it is the road of peace, we are willing to go down it."

"But the people who came did nothing but start talking, competing, seeing who... as if this were the House of Deputies. We waited to see when they would stop talking, but they were no longer talking to us, they were talking to each other. They started to debate, and we waited to see how long it would take for them to get tired. When we saw that they would *never* get tired, we said 'We have to go, our beans are getting cold,' and we left."

In an ironic tone, Subcommander Marcos said "We only ask two things of you: Don't leave us alone, and if you ever come to power, we hope you will listen half as much as you talk. It is clear to us that the political parties are only approaching us for the photo opportunity...if they have something else in mind, well, I'm not into that, or maybe they're trying to lead our movement," he clarified amidst laughter.

Immediately afterwards, the rebel chief said that the EZLN "understands the political situation we are in, in which someone might try to use the movement in favor of one party or the other. That is why we are so insistent that we are not a party and do not subscribe to the positions of any of the parties. We say to them, 'Take each other on in the electoral arena; just be sure that whoever wins, wins an honest victory.' If that doesn't happen, then it will be January 1 all over again."

The press conference began with a message from the general command of the EZLN to the peoples and governments of the world: "How can we accept the interests of other countries if what we are asking for is the right to elect those who govern us, and for that choice to be respected by the government and the governed? What harm can we do to the interests of other countries if we ask for freedom of thought and for the right to speak according to our ideas, without harming others?

"What harm can we cause the interests of other countries or peoples if what we are asking for is justice, hospitals, and schools where we can learn to read and write, the housing, fit for human habitation, that we lack? We are asking for food for our children, who are dying of hunger, respect for our dignity, our traditions and our culture. We are asking for what any European, North American, or Latin American people would take for granted, and here in the Southeast of Mexico, it isn't even the least we can expect."

## PRESS CONFERENCE WITH SUBCOMMANDER MARCOS ON THE SIXTH DAY

[*La Jornada* 2/27]
February 26, 1994
Julio Moguel, Ricardo Alemán and Victor Ballinas,
San Cristóbal de las Casas, Chiapas

*Q: In the beginning of January you declared to the press that the Salinista reforms to Article 27 of the Constitution had been a determining factor in the Zapatista decision to make war. How does this particular point look at the negotiation table? Does the demand to reform Article 27 and its regulatory law stand outside of your list of demands because it deals with a national issue? In any case, how do you link the particular agrarian demands of the EZLN, in the region or in the state, with federal legal limits on the possibilities of the changes you propose?*

M: We think that we have the moral high ground to deal on a national level, as much with the issue of land as that of the Indians. That is how we have thought of it since the beginning, and that is how we consider things now. This is what we hope for: That, together with other forces, we can roll back the Salinista counter-reform of agrarian lands, returning the original spirit of the legislation, or completely remodeling Article 27 at a constitutional congress.

The concrete demand in our list says "Return to the spirit of Article 27 approved in Querétaro in 1917," where the thinking is that which was put forth by Zapata, which is land and liberty, and not large, neglected landed estates. I am summarizing for you what that point says. Starting from here, we have a minimal and a maximal demand. The minimum is, I repeat, the nullification of the agrarian reforms of 1991 and 1992; the maximum is that we carry out a wide-ranging discussion with the campesino organizations, with those who have studied this matter, with the whole society, to reform Article 27 according to the new conditions. But for this, both the minimum and the maximum, we need a larger movement, capable of implementing what we believe to be a broad consensus among the campesinos and the majority of inhabitants of the Mexican countryside.

At the concrete level of negotiations, here at the table in San Cristóbal, this point appears to be one of the most difficult. Most likely, the commissioner will look for some small part of Article 27 from which to take the solutions to the concrete problems of the state (because we have to say, for sure, that we have already won this: That we discuss this and resolve at the state level and not just in the Zapatista townships). But our list of demands clearly puts forth federal reform, not just an amendment that resolves what is secondary.

What I want you to understand is that dialogue is one thing and negotiation is another. Because some media are saying that 50% of the demands have already been granted. The truth is that until now the government has not resolved even 1% of our list of demands; it has answered 50% of them, but it has not carried out anything. The only thing that has been won is that we are seated here, discussing an agenda. That has to be clear. There is, for example, the problem of peace and disarmament. The *compañeros* have said that they will not hand in their arms in exchange for a pile of papers.

*Q: Will the reform of Article Four of the Constitution, and the discussion and democratic approval of its regulatory law, complement your demands for agricultural lands? What do your proposals for legislative change on the Indigenous question mean?*

**M:** I am going to tell you what we hope for. We have asked the government to issue a broad call to discuss and approve Article Four in the Congress, as well as its regulatory law. Our proposal remains defined at a general level, but we say that said reform must consider at the least some aspects. One of them is that the traditional authorities of Indigenous communities can exist and exercise their functions with a level of legality. For example, in the communities of the jungle and the highlands the authority is the assembly, but legally it is not. There is the case of judicial questions. When they decide to punish a crime, the problem is solved inside the community. But then society or the State imposes or overimposes on the person in question a new punishment, based on its codes and laws. We say that if the community has already punished, there is no reason for another punishment. And that should be established by law.

Another important point: There are regions of Chiapas in which there is hegemony of a particular ethnicity. There exists there a society and an underground government that the government puts itself on top of. I am going to give you the example of how the PRI nominates candidates to the municipal presidency in the highlands. The community gathers together and decides among them who is the candidate for the PRI, and that one will be the president. Then the party registers that person, as is the case of San Juan Chamula. There the *caciques* make an agreement and therefore the PRI does not care who is the candidate. They just register them, knowing that with the vote for *cacique* goes the vote for governor, for senator, for deputy, and for president of the Republic. With this I return to what I said before: This causes a situation in which the government that exists below, which is the one that functions, is not recognized. It causes, at the same time, corruption. That which is underground must emerge.

Another case is that of justice. If you kill someone in an Indigenous community, it is almost certain that the community will apply the punishment of making you work for the widow. That is your sentence. The justice of the mestizos puts you in jail, which leaves two widows. That is something they cannot understand. If you go and do dam-

224

age to the pig or the house of another, mestizo justice puts you in jail. The justice of the communities sets you to repairing the damage: You even have the right to eat the pig, since you have already paid for it. There is, then, a logic that is very logical, which is in conflict with the penal code.

There can be many other aspects, but they are not put on the table at San Cristóbal. The government must commit to convening at a very broad level to carry out the necessary constitutional reforms, and then the proposals of the Mayas will come in, and of the Yaquis, of the Tarahumaras, as well as the people who have studied the problem.

With respect to democracy, we also have put forth demands that cross from the local to the national level. We want civil society to be that which has the most weight, for example, in the approval of the elections. Right now, the federal government and the PRI have a majority of people in the organs that regulate and decide the electoral processes. One small part corresponds to the parties. We say that a third factor in power and decisions, that of people of honor and prestige in civil society, is what should have the most weight. They should hold the veto power, not the government or the political party. That is how we understand things.

At the municipal level, we put forth the democratic naming of councils. This is the form of government that we are proposing, which is what operates in the communities. And we demand that the authorities can be removed at the very moment that the communities decide and agree on it. This could be through a referendum, or other similar mechanisms. And they want to transmit that experience at every level: When the president of the Republic is no good, he should be automatically removed. That simple. They understand that if we can make agreements between Tzeltales, Tzotziles, Choles, and Tojolabales, who all speak different languages, it would have to be easier to have a whole country agree, if they all speak the same Spanish. That is more or less the idea lthat we aspire to.

*Q: Returning to Article 27: One of the questions that led to the Salinista reform was the elimination of patrimonial land in the* ejidos, *and also in the communities, since these have the possibility of passing over to the* ejidos. *What do you think about this particular point in the negotiations?*

M: At the table in San Cristóbal we have defended and won on that point—that the . plot be kept as family patrimony. And that, until now, in what is called the Indigenous side, to carry out the formulation of the regulatory law of the Fourth Article of the Constitution. For us, in addition, the plot should be free of any tax burden. But the government does not appear to want to apply this formulation of Article 27 since, as we said before, it implies the reform of this article. The most serious problems of the negotiations are here, and, of course, also the question of democracy.

*Q: The CCRI of the EZLN sent a communiqué to the Council of Indigenous and Campesino Organizations of Chiapas (Consejo de Organizaciones Indígenas y Campesinas de Chiapas) in which they strongly criticize the ARIC Union of Unions, particularly some of its leaders and advisors. What importance do you give to this conflict? Are you still critical?*

M: We differentiate ARIC from its advisors. It was the latter that lent themselves to the counterinsurgency campaign. They used local radio to make calls for accusation, encouraged the people to turn in their favorite Zapatista. It was at that point that we decided to put forth a position. And even if it seemed to you to be very radical, in reality it was a middle position—if we measure it in relation to the feeling that there was. We said: This is happening, they are going to pile on top of us and smash us. But nevertheless, we are going to die with dignity and they with shame.

The conflict was not caused precisely because of the problem or the discussion about the peaceful way or the armed way. What really bothered the *compañeros* was when the advisors of the ARIC started to have a very close connection with the government. They began to lend themselves to political campaigns, to a presidential candidate; that is what pissed them off.

But the thing has been diluted. There started to be agreements in the streams. Just now a letter came to us from the authorities of the ARIC, that they want to speak with us, but now the advisors are no longer on the letter, only the authorities signed it.

*Q: Recently the authorities of the Sedesol and other functionaries presented a book in Mexico City about the National Program of Solidarity (Programa Nacional de Solidaridad, Pronasol). One of the participants in the conference indicated that the armed conflict in the state of Chiapas did not put that program in doubt. They said, moreover, that rather than being eliminated or modified substantially, the program would have to be amplified and improved. What is your opinion on this question?*

M: Pronasol is poorly-given charity; the only thing that it brought about was corruption. It did not resolve a single problem. All of the help filtered down like in a funnel, and it stayed with the leaders, as well as in the command structure of the federal, state, and municipal governments. Nothing came to us. Look at how ridiculous this is. During the government of Patrocinio González, the only health-related construction that was finished was the hospital at Guadalupe Tepeyac, which has 40 beds to serve almost 25,000 people.

Among the constructions accomplished by Solidaridad are the Cereso Number Five, the jail in San Cristóbal, the barracks in Rancho Nuevo, the other jail in Yajalón, the one in Tila. Jails and barracks are what were built by Solidaridad. They also painted schools white and put "Pronasol" on them. But the government says that they did send the money, just that it never came. The truth is that they never bothered to find out whether it was arriving. And everyone knows that when Salinas came to inaugurate the Guadalupe Tepeyac hospital, when the party left, behind them went a truck that carried away part of the things of the hospital. They left a shell. A hospital that does not have water.

We saw that since Pronasol began, it was set up to revert in 1988. It was clear that the Solidarity committees were set up to be a structure directed toward buying the vote. Procampo is not very different: The functionaries come to the communities and they say: Sign here and we will give you the money in July, that is, days before the elections. The Solidarity committees have been converted into pro-vote committees, in the sense of a strategy of electoral counterinsurgency.

*Q: The process of the formation of the EZLN—was it for you at the same time a process of reforms or economic and social changes in the communities? Did the transformation in the relationship between men and women have any effect?*

M: Yes. In general, the *compañeros* used to struggle separately on the *ejidos*. One *ejido* did not mess with another except to fight or to rob women. When the EZLN began and regional structures formed, then several *ejidos* began to come into contact, first to defend themselves against the *guardias blancas* or other judicial police, and later to help themselves in questions of health and other necessities. Before that, for organizational, paramilitary, political, study, or economic organizational questions, such as when several towns got together to get a boat, in order to make a hanging bridge, or to plot their territorial limits.

Then there is a relationship between one stream and another, the "zone" that we talked about. That is also something that is brought by the EZLN, consisting in the development of an effective unit, not just of representatives, but of communities. But that does not mean that the impulse has come from outside, but rather from the Zapatistas right there, who, from within, went promoting the organization, which gives us territorial cohesion.

The change in the behavior of women has been very strong, considering, of course, the great differences that exist between women in the jungle and in the highlands. In the process of struggle, women first learn Spanish. They leave their houses. Traditionally, when a woman leaves her house in the communities, it is because she is going with a man; if she goes with a group of men she is thought of as a common person. But this changes. We say that first they learn Spanish; then to add and subtract. One day they come with arms and they know how to handle them, and they teach you. Then there is a star, then two. Further on, you realize that she participates in a troop of nothing but men, and then you see that they obey her. That motivates other women, who ask, "But who washed your clothes? Who cooks for you?" And they respond: "Sometimes me, sometimes the *compañero*." The EZLN is composed of 33% women.

## INTERVIEW WITH MAJOR ANA MARÍA

*[This text was transcribed from an interview with Major Ana María of the EZLN, taped inside of the Cathedral at San Cristóbal during the dialogue. It is previously unpublished.]*

**February 28, 1994**

*Q: ...With Major Ana María of the Zapatista movement, today is February 28...*

AM: Yes, well, the thing is that we are interested in getting information about our struggle published at a national and international level. We want the whole world to understand what we are. Until now, the Mexican government has not wanted to recognize us a real force. They think that we are a little group, as they have called it, of "transgressors of the law" or "delinquents." But we know that we are not. We are a people that is organized and wants to be heard, wants its demands to be met. This is something that has not been done for many years. We have been struggling as human beings, as Mexicans. So far, the government thinks that we are a group of foreigners, that we are from other countries, and they think that it is only a small group tricking the people, pulling the people into an armed struggle like this. That is what the government thinks. But we say: But who is it then, if we are all the people who are here? Right now, for example, the Committee is here. They are those who command, those who give orders. Well, not those who give orders but those who lead us, the leadership. It is the people, the campesinos, the Indigenous people who are here.

There are some *ladinos* who are here. They are those who are helping the ones who understand. For example, Subcommander Marcos is a *ladino*. But they are not foreigners. We know where he is from. We are not being fooled by anyone. It is us, the campesinos and the Indigenoud people who think that this needs to be done, what we did in January. It was already necessary, because we could not find any other way out of this situation. We had spent years struggling peacefully, we held marches, we had meetings, we went to the municipal palaces and the Government Palace, and we went to Mexico [City] to the National Palace of Mexico to shout, to ask, to agitate in front of the government. They never paid attention to us. They always gave us papers full of promises. Then, what good is a piece of paper, filled with promises, to us? And we would look at that paper when we went back to our towns. We would read the papers and the promises and nothing ever came. Or, with that Pronasol they sent some things, they ordered a clinic built, but they left it half-built. They left buildings with no medicine, no doctors. What good is a building, a house like that, to us? Or, for example, we asked for schools. The only thing they did, that work of Solidaridad, was that they sent paint and they painted the school, and they painted "Solidaridad" on the wall. But they did nothing else. They didn't send teachers, they didn't send materials, which are necessary, teaching materials necessary for the studies. None of that came. They were nothing but promises.

So then we got together, the campesinos and the Indigenous people...

*Q: When did you begin to get together?*

**AM:** About 10 years ago. We started slowly, to get together, to talk and to understand: Why is the situation like this? Why does the government not resolve our problems? And when we wanted to do something, when we go and we take farms, for example, because the land is there, where we live. It is like our mother that takes care of us and feeds us. Without the land, we can't live, we would die. But since they never give us lands, they never have, we started to organize legally, without arms or anything, peacefully, and they went and took a farm, an abandoned farm. Since not all of the farmers live there, some leave them. We are told that that land belongs to so-and-so, and we don't even know them. But we see, there is the land, and we work on it. If the owner is not there, we work on it. We went in there, the campesinos went in there, to work the land. They built their houses there and took the land. It's been called an invasion; we invaded the land. And then they sent the Public Security, since that is what the government does, send its Public Security forces, to burn the houses that had been built, to evict the people with canes and beat the people. They took our leaders. They put them in jail. They dragged them with horses to torture them. That is how they responded.

*Q: Then all of this has been happening for the last 10 years?*

**AM:** Yes, over the last 10 years all of this has been happening. And so we took up arms. We cannot do this peacefully. The government has its Army. It is not true that the Army has military autonomy. That it's job is to defend the Mexican people, defend the nation; this is not true. They are in favor of a few. It is not just. It is not just that the Army massacres its own people, its own race, the same people as they are. So we said, "No, to defend ourselves we have to take up arms, as well." If not, how? They will continue killing us like that. They kill us with hunger. And if we struggle to survive, we look for land that is not being used, they order us killed by the Public Security, who are the ones that come the most often. So this people said, "We have to unite. Unite and get arms and fight, too... If the government does not pay attention to us peacefully, then we will make them pay attention to us with force."

*Q: I heard that there is something written called the Women's Law. How did you put this together?...*

**AM:** Right now we could not bring anything. We do not have it here. But if you have patience to wait for the next one, because we know that this time the dialogue will not be completed because there are many things that the government will not approve of that are on that paper now. As they have always done, they give you a ton of paper, which is what they have done until now. The government has committed itself to meeting 50% of the demands that we have. But they are leaving off the most difficult ones, like the last one, which is about democracy and justice and land, for example. So there are still some points left there. And more than that, about democracy, because they tell us that we cannot, that this problem cannot be fixed at a state level. It has to be looked at at a national level. So that is where we are up to now.

And we think that if they do not accept our demands, as we ask them to, the dialogue will not be completed this time. We will have to go, consult with the people, ask the people if they agree with what the government commits to, and come back again, to say "yes" or "no."

*Q: Are you also part of a group of women?*

**AM:** Yes. I am part of the Zapatista National Liberation Army. Within the EZLN there are insurgents, and I am an insurgent, a military person. Then there are a group of militias, which are our *compañeros* who live in their towns. But when it is necessary for them to prepare with their arms, then they prepare with their weapons and they go and fight when they are needed...

*Q: Women?*

**AM:** No, I was speaking in general. Then I will speak to you of the women, how the Women's Law came about. So that is the make-up of the Zapatista Army. Then there are other people as well. They are what we call bases, bases that support the combatants, give us food. So with all of that, we form the Zapatista National Liberation Army.

About the Women's Law, well there are many women within the Zapatista Army; there are insurgents, who dedicate ourselves to military life, we prepare ourselves with weapons...

*Q: But do any of you have families? For example, do you have children?*

AM: No, I don't.

*Q: But you are married. I can see the ring.*

AM: [laughs] Yes.

*Q: You're young?*

AM: Of course.

*Q: How old are you?*

AM: I am 25 years old. When I was very young, I joined the Zapatista Army. I saw almost the whole process of this organization, of how it moved forward. I was one of the first women who was part of the ranks of the Army. We were a few *compañeros*, men and women, and we began to work, and then we began to go out to the towns, to the communities, and explain our struggle. And also to see what they thought, what they felt needed to be done. We saw that the life that we were living there was too unjust...

So, then in our work, since I was a woman, an Indigenous woman, a campesino. Even though I have light skin, but it is a family thing... But just for that we do not stop being campesinos, or Indians. They saw that I was a woman, and they saw that women can also do things. That women can organize themselves, and that they can do things other than what they do in their houses and their homes. Women have the capability of doing other kinds of work as well. And then women started to enter into the Army. Women started to get together and organize themselves, and they started to join the ranks of the Army. And then other women did not join, but organized themselves into women's groups, women alone. They organized themselves. They formed ranches of pigs. They did collective projects such as baking and sewing, and that is how they started to organize themselves as women's groups. And also many, many women started entering our organization. For example, for each family, for each man that entered into the struggle, and said, "Yes, I agree with the struggle and I want to struggle," many people came to look for us alone. And we would accept them, help them, because that it what we were there for. They would join with all of their family, and within the families were women: women, children, old people, everyone. We integrated them all into the Army. And that is another way that women entered the struggle. And some went to be insurgents, others stayed in their towns as civilians doing political work, organized in women's groups. Then, when we were many people, a very large organization, we said, "We now have the necessary force to fight. Now we will make the government know what we are, to see if this way, with arms, they will pay attention to us."

*Q: Where do the arms come from?*

AM: That I do not know. Only our command knows that. But I can tell you that these arms were obtained by the people with their own efforts. They took their little money...

*Q: You saved your money to buy them? This was your own....*

AM: Yes, their own effort. Where they got them? That I don't know.

*Q: There are rumors that you bought them from the federal forces that took arms from the druff traggiffers [mispronounced in Spanish]...*

AM: Drug traffickers [laughs]. Yes you can see the corruption...

*Q: Yes that, and they thought that you would sell them again to the drug traffickers. But instead of this you kept them. I don't know if this is a rumor, or whether it has been written, but this is what they told me. Taking advantage of corruption...*

AM: Yes. That is how we went gathering arms, but it was with the sacrifice of the people. Little by little, it took many, many years, that sacrifice. And now they tell us: "Hand over your guns." And we say, "No. No, because it is ours, it is something that belongs to us." How can they say that? It would be a humiliation to hand in what is ours, what was gotten through so much sacrifice. So now we say, "No, we will not hand in our arms until we see our demands being met, and all of what we need, which is what we ask for. All of our principal demands, and also the demand of the Mexican people for democracy." So now we say, "No, we cannot hand in our arms."

So, that is how the people started to get together. That is also how the women got organized. So now there are women who represent the women as well. And not just women, but we represent all of our people as well, women, children, everyone.

*Q: There are many rumors. I heard that there was, in the group of women, in one of the manifestations, the women said that they would be in charge. "We will pick our partners, we won't stand for the abuse any more."*

AM: This is part of the Women's Law, something that I was going to tell you about. The Women's Law was born when we had already started to think: "There are now many of us, and we are armed. We have enough weapons, and now we are going to vote to see if people are agreed that now is the time." We asked all of the people, but the people were demanding, "It is time to fight, we need to fight, because we can't stand this situation any longer." And they were demanding this of us. And so what we did was find out the opinion of everyone. And everyone said that they agreed and that they thought it was important to make our laws. And so we decided that we should make our laws. Let's put on paper what we want to demand of the government. A general law was made, but there was no women's law. And so we protested, and said that there has to be a women's law when we make our demands. We also want the government to recognize us as women. The right to have equality, equality of men and women. And that they respect and recognize what we are. And so there was a law where we ask that they give us the right to freely choose our husbands, without being obligated to, because within Indigenous life we are obligated to get married even when we don't want to. Another is to have children, the number of children you want to have, but not to have to have so many children that your hormones run out. We have to choose, to decide. That is the petition that we made.

*Q: This interests me, and this explains a lot. In other underdeveloped countries as well, and in traditional cultures, it is also true that women don't have any rights. Their fathers can order them, and can even choose who [they marry]... Was this the same for you, before?*

**AM:** In Indigenmous campesino life... A young man comes who wants to get married, wants to ask permission to marry someone. He comes, but he asks the father, he doesn't ask the opinion of the young woman. And then what happens is that the father accepts, many of them accept without asking the opinion of the young woman, whether she likes him or doesn't like him. And so they sell her.

*Q: They sell her?*

**AM:** Yes, that is, in exchange for the young woman marrying the young man he has to pay some money... Women do not like this. Many times they do not even know the man, what he's like. They cannot live with him because there is no time spent as partners, nothing like that. They ask for you, the father gives you, and when the time comes to get married, you get married. Many women go crying, because they don't want to. That is why this came out in the law, that they give us, that we should have the right to choose, that they can not sell us like the land. That they can not obligate us to get married, to have many children. This is very difficult, very difficult for women. We think that women suffer more than men. Of course, they suffer the same exploitation, and the children as well, the same exploitation, the same misery, the same injustice. But in addition to that, women are also dominated. This is by the same ideology that we have, that all of us have. Of course, we do not place all of the blame on men. It is from the same ideology, the same condition that we live in in our country. There is mistreatment of women.

In addition to this, suffering this injustice, suffering this misery, they suffer to see their children die of hunger, of curable diseases. And this is why this law was born. And another thing is that in the Women's Law we demand that there be respect for women. We demand respect. Many times, they don't respect us. They think that women are something worthless. So this is also why this law came out, demanding respect, demanding that we be respected. And it demands punishment for men that rape, that grab by force. This has happened many times, and more among Indigenous women, campesin women. They see her all fucked up, and all of that, that she'll let them, and they grab her. Here in San Cristóbal, for example, many women have been raped. They just grab them. Servants and all of the women that work in the houses of the ladies, they grab them and rape them. Many times these rapes are not publicly known, they are not published, they are not told of, they do not accuse them of all that happens.

And another of the demands in the law is that women do have the capacity, if they are taught to do other kinds of work, not just grind the corn, make the tortillas and the food, take care of the children, sweep the house, go get firewood when the husband is not home. This is the work of Indigenous women in the home. But it is not taken into account that if women are given studies, education, they can do others kinds of work. We realized this when we started to enter this struggle. That if we are going to do many of the thing that men are doing, we can study, we can be leaders. I am the leader of a unit. And that we can be representative of something big. For example, Ramona, a *compañera* who represents several women and who is a leader of a group of women. But before, this did not exist. Because people always thought that women couldn't do anything.

*Q: For how many years have women been in positions of power? You said that you have been struggling for over 10 years. Can you calculate for me how many years women have been leaders?*

AM: Yes, since we started to enter into this struggle. Since we started to form part of the struggle. Yes, we had opportunity to participate...

*Q: There are Indigenous people in the [Federal] Army. There may be a point at which people say, "Enough, that is enough..."*

AM: We know that not all of the [Federal] Army is so stupid as to do all of that massacre, like they did in Ocosingo, for example. We know that many of the soldiers do not like to do that, because they are Indigenous people, too, of the same campesinos. We know that there is a lot of discontent in the Army. They are not happy that they are ordered to kill, because they are killing their own race.

*Q: Have there been any soldiers that left the Army?*

AM: Yes.

*Q: Did you know them? Did you speak with them?*

AM: No, others told us about them. There were some...

*Q: Rumors...*

AM: No, they are not rumors. They are real. Because we have people who tell us what is happening with that. These are real things. Several soldiers who deserted got to one town and said that they were not in agreement with what was being done. They send the new troops in front and they send them with 30 bullets! According to that report, they send them with 30 bullets. In other words, they send them like meat, so that they confront us and they are killed first so that these officials can defend themselves. We know this and we know that not all of the Army is ready to kill their own people. There are people who do have hearts. For this reason, at the beginning, when we began the war, we asked them to surrender. We also know that many people [in the Army] are Indigenous people, were campesinos. We asked for their surrender so we would not fight against them....

*Q: How do you feel, as a woman, learning how to handle a rifle and then feeling the capability of killing... Do you understand my question? You do not appear to me to be a violent person. Well, you speak very quietly....*

AM: Yes, taking up a gun, that is something very, very important. I am proud to being able to do that. Of course, we do not like to kill. We kill, not out of taste, but out of need. They have obligated us to take up guns and kill to get what they have never given to us. But I, as a woman, feel good. I don't feel like a delinquent. I don't feel like a transgressor of the law, as the government has been calling us. I don't feel like that because I know I am representing a people. A people who struggle, a people who are doing something just and something necessary. Even if we do not kill, if there is no war, it is as if there is, because day by day our people are dying. Our children are dying of hunger and of curable diseases. We cannot do anything else, because we have absolutely nothing. There are no hospitals, there are no schools, there is no food, there is nothing. Our children are dying, our people are dying. Because of this our struggle is just, it is just that we have taken up arms. And for women, it is just that women take up arms to defend themselves. That is what we have arms for, to defend ourselves. We are not delinquents. We don't like to kill. [...]

We have been attacked. The Mexican Army complains that we attacked them in Rancho Nuevo. But what happened during the past years when they came, when they attacked us in other places, when they evicted us? They don't take this into account, what they have done to us. We have been attacked. They don't say what they did when we were not even armed. When we weren't even prepared. They attacked us. But we know the history of our Mexico, our country, and we grab onto these roots. We have roots. It is the same people who have killed throughout history, that do this now. It is the same Army, the same governments of always. Even though they change, they act in the same way...

*Q: I think that if I were threatened, I would be able to kill someone, too. I don't think I would like to do it. I would rather avoid any problems.*

**AM:** That is what we are trying to do now. That is why we have sat down to dialogue. We do what the people ask. The people have asked that we try this way, and we are going to try it. We are going to try it, because we don't like to kill and we don't like to make war. Because of that, we have sat down to dialogue, to see what we can get out of it. But if things are not resolved this way, we will have to continue what we have set out for ourselves.

# COMMUNIQUÉS ISSUED DURING THE DIALOGUE

## LETTER FROM THE CCRI–CG TO THE NGO's

February 20, 1994

To all non-governmental organizations (NGO's) in Mexico:

Brothers and Sisters:

The Clandestine Revolutionary Indigenous Committee of the Zapatista National Liberation Army addresses all of you respectfully so that our words, which speak the truth, will reach you.

As everyone knows, the EZLN is willing to enter into true and fair talks. These talks are taking place in a zone of armed conflict, and this implies the possibility of provocations that could hinder them. It is also possible that the delegates on either side might suffer attacks on their lives or freedom. In order to reduce the risk of this happening, it was necessary to go to honest and true people and ask them to create a "security belt" or "peace belt" around the site of the talks.

We know that the non-governmental organizations, as they are known, have become a fundamental part of the movement for a dignified peace for we who have nothing and for we who found ourselves forced to take up arms to assert ourselves as human beings. The NGO's have maintained neutrality; their efforts to protect the human rights of all, including when members of our EZLN forces have committed human rights violations, are plain for all to see. Furthermore, they have concerned themselves at all times with the alleviation of the grave conditions the civilian population finds itself in.

If we have entrusted our lives and our freedom, during our trips to and from the site of the talks and the time we are there, to the NGO's, it is because we have seen in them the future to which we aspire. A future in which civil society, with the strength that true justice gives it, will make not only war, but armies as well, unnecessary, and a future in which governments, whatever their political orientation, will have over them the severe and constant vigilance of a free and democratic civil society.

If we have arrived alive and well at the site of the talks, we owe it to the protection and vigilance of all those good people who, without receiving anything in return, gave us their time, their efforts and their work, and, risking their own lives and freedom, protected us, the smallest of all Mexicans.

For all of the above reasons, we would like to respectfully request that you accept the EZLN's salute to your work. However this process turns out, our country's history will remember, more than our voices and the voices of our guns, the bravery of the women and men, namely you, who, without asking for anything in return, and [receiving] only the satisfaction of having done your duty, gave everything.

Good health, brother and sister NGO members.

Respectfully yours,
From the mountains of the Mexican Southeast,
CCRI-CG of the EZLN

## Letter from Marcos to the PRD

February 25, 1994

To Mr. Mario Saucedo, Mr. Samuel del Villar, and Mr. Alejandro Encinas, representatives of the National Executive Committee (Comité Ejecutivo Nacional, CEN) of the PRD:

Dear Gentlemen:

I have just received your rightly indignant letter. Imagine my pleasure at being able, for the first time in quite a while, to answer immediately, without waiting for a letter to arrive and for my answer to get back.

I understand your dismay. Look, you (or some of you) were here when we were paid a visit by the representatives of political parties. You heard how at least two of those parties started a political oratory contest, to the great delight of their fellow party members and to our surprise, since, in our naivete, we thought they'd come to listen to us, not to make such long speeches at us.

When we managed to break the spell of these gentlemen's words, we left, saying "Don't leave us alone. And we hope that some day you will learn to listen." Everyone who was there knows which political party representatives grabbed the "platform" of the cathedral. I am expressly forbidden by the CCRI-CG of the EZLN to speak in favor of or against ANY political party, so when I brought up the incident in an interview, I spoke of "the political parties."

You know who did this, and you also know that it wasn't you, so why get upset? I accept the justifiable anger in your letter, but please understand that I cannot disobey my superiors, so I cannot publicly say which political parties talked senselessly. Nevertheless, I think I can say who didn't: You didn't.

Good health, and no more postscripts, because they may bring replies, and we are mildly exhausted, *c'est a dire*, totally.

Respectfully yours,
From the mountains of the Mexican Southeast,
Insurgent Subcommander Marcos

## DEMANDING THE RESIGNATION OF SALINAS

February 26, 1994

To the people of Mexico:
To the peoples and governments of the world:
To the national and international press:

Brothers and Sisters:

The CCRI-CG of the EZLN addresses you respectfully to speak its word, what is in its heart and in its thought.

When the EZLN was just a shadow creeping through the mist and the darkness of the mountains, when words justice, freedom, and democracy were just that: words. Barely a dream that the elders of our communities, true guardians of the word of the dead, had passed on to us at the exact moment when the day gave way to the night, when hate and death were beginning to grow in our breasts, when there was nothing but desperation. When the days repeated themselves, with no way out, with no tomorrow, when everything was as unjust as it was, the real men spoke, the men with no faces, the men who walk at night, the men who are the mountain, and this is what they said:

"It's the reason and will of good men and women to look for and find the best way to govern and be governed. What's good for the majority is good for all. But, the voices of the minority must not be silenced. They should continue in their place, waiting for hearts and minds to come together in the will of the majority and the desires of the minority. In this way the peoples of the true men and women grew toward the inside and they became large. And there is no force from the outside that can break them or take their path in another direction."

It was always our way that the will of the majority would be one with the heart and mind of the men and women in command. The path of the commanders must follow that majority will. If the leaders' walk strayed from what was right for the people, the heart of the commander should give way to another, who would obey. That is how our movement was born in the mountains, those in command obey if they are true, those who obey command for the communal heart of true men and women."

Another word came from far away so this government would have a name, and that word named this path we walked even before words traveled the world: "democracy."

Those who walk in the night spoke: "And we see that this way of governing we are referring to is no longer a road for the majority; we see that it is the few who rule, and they govern without obeying, they rule by giving orders. And the few pass around the power to govern, without listening to the majority; they rule by giving orders, without obeying the will of the majority. The few rule unjustly. The word from far away calls it undemocratic, not by the people. We see that this injustice committed by those who rule by giving orders is what is bringing us our pain and is feeding the pain of our dead. And we see that those who rule by giving orders must go away so that truth and right will return to our soil. And we see that things need to change, and we see that that word which comes from far away to name this way of governing, 'democracy,' is good for the many and for the few."

The faceless men went on:

"The world is another world, the will and purposes of true men no longer rule, we are few and forgotten, we are small, our word is fading away, silence has inhabited our homes for a long time. It is time to speak to our hearts and to the hearts of others, our dead must come out of the night and the earth, let them dress in the garb of war so their voice may be heard. Afterwards, let their word fall silent and let them return again to the night and to the earth, let them speak to other men and women who walk in other lands, let their word convey the truth, let it not be lost in lies.

"Let them look for the men and women who govern by obeying, those whose strength lies in the word and not in fire. When they find them let them speak to them and turn over to them the staff of command. Let the faceless ones, those who are of the mountain go back again to the earth and the night. If reason returns to this land then let the fury of fire fall silent, let those who are of the mountain, those who have no face, those who walk at night, finally rest together with the earth."

Thus spoke the men with no faces, they had no fire in their hands and their word was clear and without duplicity. Before the day overcame the night they left and on the earth their one word remained:

"Enough is Enough!"

The men and women of the EZLN, those who have no faces, those who walk at night, those who are of the mountain, sought words others would understand, and they say:

First: We demand the calling of truly free and democratic elections, where the political organizations competing for power will have equal rights and obligations, and with authentic freedom to choose one alternative or the other, and respect for the majority will. Democracy is a fundamental right of all Indigenous and non-Indigenous peoples; without democracy there can be no freedom, justice, or dignity, and without dignity there is nothing.

**Second:** So that truly democratic and free elections may be held, it is necessary that the heads of the federal and state executives, who came into power through fraudulent elections, resign. Their legitimacy does not derive from respect for the majority will, but from their acts of usurpation. Consequently, the formation of a transitional government is necessary so that all political currents may be equal and respected; the freely and democratically elected federal and state legislative powers must assume their true function of making just laws, and seeing that these laws are carried out.

**Third:** Another way to guarantee free and democratic elections is to legitimize, in federal and state law, the existence and work of citizens and groups of citizens unaffiliated with any party, to keep watch on the electoral process, sanction its legitimacy and results, and guarantee, as the real supreme authority, the legitimacy of the entire electoral process.

This is the word of the EZLN. With democracy, freedom and justice are possible. In deceit, nothing flourishes; in truth, everything is possible.

Freedom! Justice! Democracy!

Respectfully,
From the mountains of the Mexican Southeast,
CCRI-CG of the EZLN.

## DEMANDS SUBMITTED DURING THE DIALOGUE

March 1, 1994

To the Mexican people:
To the people and governments of the world:
To the national and international press:

Brothers and Sisters:

The Clandestine Revolutionary Indigenous Committee-General Command of the EZLN addresses itself to you with respect and honor to make known to you the list of demands presented at the dialogue table during the days of peace and reconciliation in Chiapas.

*"We do not ask for charity or gifts. We ask for the right to live in dignity, with equality and justice like our ancient parents and grandparents."*

To the People of Mexico:

The Indigenous people of the state of Chiapas, who have risen up in arms as the Zapatista National Liberation Army against misery and the evil government, present the causes of their struggle and their principal demands:

The reasons and causes of our armed movement are that the government has failed to find solutions to the following problems:

**First:** The hunger, misery and marginalization from which we have always suffered.

238

**Second:** The complete lack of land on which to work in order to survive.

**Third:** Repression, displacement, imprisonment, torture and murder as the government's response to the just demands of our people.

**Fourth:** The unbearable injustices and violations of our human rights as impoverished Indigenous people and campesinos.

**Fifth:** The brutal exploitation we suffer in selling our products, in our workday, and in the buying of merchandise of basic necessity.

**Sixth:** The lack of indispensable services for the majority of the Indigenous population.

**Seventh:** The government's lies, deceit, promises and intrusion that have lasted over 60 years. The lack of liberty and democracy to decide our destinies.

**Eighth:** Constitutional laws have not been followed by those who govern this country; instead they make us, the Indigenous people and campesinos, pay for even the smallest mistake. They lay upon us the weight of a law that we did not make, and those who did are the first ones to violate it.

The EZLN came to dialogue with the word of truth. The EZLN came to speak its word on the conditions that gave rise to its just war and to ask all of the Mexican people for a resolution to these political, economic and social conditions that led us to take up arms in defense of our rights and our existence.

Therefore, we demand...

**First:** We demand that free and democratic elections be convened with equal rights and obligations for all political organizations that struggle for power, with true freedom to choose one proposal or another, and respect for the will of the majority. Democracy is a fundamental right of all Indigenous and non-Indigenous people. Without democracy there can be no freedom, justice or dignity. And without dignity there is nothing.

**Second:** To ensure that there are truly free and democratic elections, it is necessary for the head of the federal executive and occupants of state executive offices who reached their positions of power through electoral fraud, to resign. Their legitimacy does not come from the respect for the will of the majority, but rather from its usurpation. Consequently, the formation of a transitional government is necessary so that there may be equality and respect for all political currents. The federal and state legislative powers, elected freely and democratically, should assume their true function of passing fair laws for all and ensuring their enforcement.

Another way to guarantee the realization of free and truly democratic elections is to legitimize, in the nation's great laws and at a local level, the legitimacy of the existence and work of citizens and citizens' groups who, without party militancy, will oversee the entire electoral process, sanction its legality and results, and guarantee, as the maximum authority, the legitimacy of the entire electoral process.

**Third:** The recognition of the Zapatista National Liberation Army as a belligerent force, and of its troops as authentic combatants and the application of all international treaties regulating armed conflicts.

239

**Fourth:** A new pact between Mexican Federation members to do away with centralism and allow regions, Indigenous communities, and townships to govern themselves with political, economic and cultural autonomy.

**Fifth:** General elections for the whole state of Chiapas and the legal recognition of all the political forces in the state.

**Sixth:** As a producer of electricity and petroleum, the state of Chiapas pays tribute to the nation and receives nothing in return. Our communities have no electric energy and the economic bleeding, a product of oil exports and internal sale, brings no benefits to the Chiapaneco people. Therefore, it is of the utmost importance that all Chiapaneco communities receive electric energy and that a percentage of the income earned from the commercialization of Chiapaneco petroleum be applied to industrial, agricultural, commercial and social infrastructure projects for the benefit of all Chiapanecos.

**Seventh:** The revision of the North American Free Trade Agreement signed with Canada and the United States, since its present form it does not take into account the Indigenous population, and it sentences them to death because it does not include any labor qualifications whatsoever.

**Eighth:** Article 27 of the Magna Carta [a reference to the Mexican Constitution] should respect the original spirit of Emiliano Zapata: Land is for the Indigenous people and campesinos who work it, not for *latifundistas*. We want the large tracts of land that are in the hands of ranchers, national and foreign wealthy land-owners, and other people who occupy a lot of land and are not campesinos, to be passed over to the hands of the people who have absolutely no land, as it is set out in our Revolutionary Agrarian Law. The redistribution of lands should include agricultural machinery, fertilizers, insecticides, credits, technical assistance, improved seeds, cattle, and fair prices for our products such as coffee, corn and beans. The land that is redistributed should be of good quality, and it must be accessible by roads, public transport, and have adequate irrigation systems. Campesinos who already have land also have the right to receive the support mentioned above to facilitate their work and improve production. New *ejidos* and communities should be formed. The Salinista reform to Article 27 of the Constitution should be annulled and the right to the land should be put back into our Magna Carta.

**Ninth:** We want hospitals to be built in all of the municipal seats, and that they have specialized doctors and sufficient medicine to attend to all patients, and rural clinics in the *ejidos* and communities, with training and fair salaries for health representatives. Already-existing hospitals in the area should be rehabilitated as soon as possible and have complete surgical services. Clinics should be built in large communities, which have sufficient doctors and medicine to more closely attend to the needs of the people.

**Tenth:** That Indigenous people be guaranteed the right to true information about what happens on local, regional, state, national and international levels, through an Indigenous radio station that is directed and managed by Indians.

**Eleventh:** We demand that housing be built in all rural communities in Mexico and be provided with all necessary services, such as: light, potable water, roads, sewage systems, telephones, public transportation, etc. And also that they have the advantages of the city, such as televisions, stoves, refrigerators, washing machines, etc. The communities should have recreational centers for the healthy diversion of residents: sports and culture that dignify the human condition of Indians.

**Twelfth:** We want an end to illiteracy in Indigenous communities. For this we need better elementary and secondary schools in our communities, which have free teaching materials and teachers with university degrees who are at the service of the people and not just there to defend the interests of the wealthy. In municipal seats there should be free elementary, secondary, and preparatory schools. The government should provide uniforms, shoes, food and all study materials for free. Centrally located communities that are far away from the municipal seat of the respective townships should have boarding secondary schools. Education should be completely free, from preschool through university, and it should be available to all Mexicans regardless of race, creed, age, sex or political affiliation.

**Thirteenth:** That the languages of all of the ethnicities be official and that their teaching in primary, secondary and preparatory schools and at the university level be mandatory.

**Fourteenth:** That our rights and dignity as Indigenous peoples be respected and that our culture and tradition be recognized.

**Fifteenth:** We do not want to be subject to the discrimination and scorn which we, the Indians, have always suffered.

**Sixteenth:** As the Indigenous people that we are, we demand that we be allowed to govern ourselves autonomously, because we no longer want to be subject to the will of national and foreign powers.

**Seventeenth:** That justice be administered by the Indigenous communities themselves according to their customs and traditions, without intervention from illegitimate and corrupt governments.

**Eighteenth:** We want to always have dignified jobs with fair salaries for all workers, both in the countryside and in the cities of the Mexican Republic, so that our brothers and sisters are not forced to resort to bad things such as drug trafficking, delinquency and prostitution in order to survive. The Federal Labor Law should be applied to rural and urban workers with bonuses, loans, vacations, and the true right to strike.

**Nineteenth:** We demand fair prices for our products of the fields. For this we need to have free access to a market to buy and sell without being subject to the *coyotes* who exploit us.

**Twentieth:** That the plundering of the riches of our Mexico and above all Chiapas, one of the Republic's richest states, but one in which hunger and misery grow every day, cease.

**Twenty-first:** We want all debts, whether they be credits or loans and taxes with high interest rates, to be cancelled, as these cannot be paid back due to the poverty of the Mexican people.

**Twenty-second:** We want an end to hunger and malnutrition, because they alone have caused the death of thousands of our brothers and sisters both in the countryside and in the city. In every rural community there should be cooperative stores supported economically by the federal, state and municipal governments, and the prices in these stores should be fair. Moreover, there should also be transport vehicles, owned by the cooperatives, for the transport of merchandise. Moreover, the government should send free food for all children under 14 years old.

**Twenty-third:** We ask for the immediate and unconditional release of all political prisoners and unjustly imprisoned poor people in all the jails of Mexico and Chiapas.

**Twenty-fourth:** We ask that the Federal Army and Judicial and Public-Safety Police no longer enter rural zones, as they will only intimidate, evict, rob, repress and bomb campesinos who are organizing to defend their rights. Because of this, our people are tired of the presence of soldiers and Public-Safety and Judicial forces, because they are so abusive and repressive. That the Mexican government return the Pilatus planes, used to bombard our people, to the Swiss government. The refund money should be channeled to programs to improve the life of rural and urban workers. We also ask that the government of the United States of North America take back its helicopters, as they are being used to repress Mexicans.

**Twenty-fifth:** The Indigenous campesinos took up arms because they have nothing but their humble shacks. When the Federal Army bombarded the civilian populations, it destroyed these humble homes and all of their few belongings. For this reason we ask and demand that the federal government compensate families that have suffered material losses due to air raids and actions by federal troops. We also demand indemnity for widows and orphans of the war, both civilians and Zapatistas.

**Twenty-sixth:** We Indigenous campesinos want to live in peace and tranquility and want to be allowed to live according to our rights to freedom and a dignified life.

**Twenty-seventh:** That the penal code of the state of Chiapas be eliminated, as it does not allow us to organize, except with arms, because legal and peaceful struggles are repressed and punished.

**Twenty-eighth:** We ask and demand an end to the expulsion of Indians from their communities by the *caciques* who are supported by the state. We demand a guarantee that all expelled people may return freely and voluntarily to their lands of origin and that they be compensated for their lost goods.

**Twenty-ninth:** Indigenous Campesino Women's Petition

We, Indigenous campesino women, demand the immediate solution to our urgent needs, which the government has never resolved:

**A:** Childbirth clinics with gynecologists so that campesino women receive necessary medical attention.

**B:** That child care facilities be built in the communities.

**C:** We ask the government to send sufficient food for the children in all rural communities including: milk, cornflour, rice, corn, soy, oil, beans, cheese, eggs, sugar, soup, oats, etc.

**D:** That kitchens and dining halls be built for the children in the communities, which have all the necessary services.

E: We demand the construction of community corn dough mills and *tortillerías* based on the number of families in each community.

F: That they give us poultry, rabbit, sheep and pig farm projects, and also that we be provided with technical assistance and veterinarians.

G: We ask for bakery projects, which include the provision of ovens and ingredients.

H: We want artisan workshops to be built, equipped with machinery and raw materials.

I: Markets in which to sell our crafts at fair prices.

J: That schools be built where women can get technical training.

K: That there be preschools and maternal schools in rural communities, where children can play and grow in a morally and physically healthy way.

L: That as women we have sufficient transportation for the products we produce in our various projects.

**Thirtieth:** We demand that Patrocinio González Blanco Garrido, Absalón Castellanos Domínguez and Elmar Setzer M. be tried politically.

**Thirty-first:** We demand that the lives of all EZLN members be respected and a guarantee that there will be no penal process or any repressive action brought against any EZLN members, combatants, sympathizers or collaborators.

**Thirty-second:** That all organizations and commissions for the defense of human rights be independent or non-governmental, because government human rights organizations only hide the arbitrary actions of the government.

**Thirty-third:** That a National Commission for Peace with Justice and Dignity be formed, composed primarily of people who are not in the government or any political party. And that this National Commission for Peace with Justice and Dignity oversee the fulfillment and implementation of the accords that the EZLN and the government arrive at.

**Thirty-fourth:** That the humanitarian aid for the victims of the conflict be channeled through authentic representatives from Indigenous communities.

While these just demands of our people are still unresolved we are prepared and committed to continue with our struggle until we obtain our goals.

For us, the smallest of these lands, those without face or history, those who arrived with truth and fire, those of us who come from the night and the mountain, those true men and women, the dead of yesterday, today, and always...for us nothing. For everyone, everything.
Justice!
Democracy!
Freedom!

Respectfully,
From the Mexican Southeast.
CCRI-CG of the EZLN

# 9. CONCLUDING THE DIALOGUE

## COMMUNIQUÉS AND LETTERS

*[As the dialogue ended the EZLN prepared itself to move into the next phase, that of bringing what the delegates had discussed to the communities. Many of these early responses show hope as well as realism about the possible outcome of the talks.*

*These letters and interviews also show that the EZLN would not compromise for peace: "If they deny us a just and dignified peace, then we, somber men and women, will dress ourselves once again for war."]*

### A THANK-YOU TO THE NGO's

March 1, 1994

To the people of Mexico:
To the peoples and governments of the world:
To the non-governmental organizations:
To the national and international press:

Brothers and Sisters:

The Clandestine Revolutionary Indigenous Committee-General Command of the EZLN addresses all of you with respect and honor:

We have explained many times the great importance that we give to the disinterested and honest work of non-governmental organizations. Now we want to speak to them again, to say thank you for having been around us all those days in the "peace belt." Good and true people came from different parts of Mexico and the world, sacrificing

245

their time, work and rest to accompany us along the first phase of the road to peace with justice and dignity.

In our dreams we have seen another world. A sincere world, a world definitively more just than the one in which we now move. We saw that in this world armies were not necessary; peace, justice, and freedom were so common in it that no one spoke of them as far-off things, but as one mentions bread, birds, air, water, as one says book and voice, that's how the good things in this world were spoken of. And in this world, the government of the majority was fair and followed the will of the people, and those who directed the people thought well; they directed while obeying. That sincere world was not a dream of the past, it was not something that came from our ancestors. It came from ahead, it was from the next step that we had taken. Thus it was that we began to move to make that dream sit at our table, illuminate our house, grow in our corn fields, fill the heart of our children, clean our sweat, restore our history, and be for all.

We want this. Nothing more, but nothing less.

Now we continue our steps toward our true heart to ask it what we will have to do. We will return to our mountains to speak with the same language and at the same time as our own [people].

Thanks to the brothers and sisters who cared for us all those days. Take our path. Farewell.

Freedom! Justice! Democracy!

Respectfully,
From the Mexican Southeast,
CCRI-CG of the EZLN

# On the Outcome of the Dialogue

March 1, 1994

To the people of Mexico:
To the peoples and governments of the world:
To the national and international press:

Brothers and Sisters:

The Clandestine Revolutionary Indigenous, Committee-General Command of the EZLN addresses itself to all of you with respect and honor.

**First:** The Zapatista National Liberation Army came to this dialogue table with the sincere intention of listening and explaining all the reasons that obliged us to rise up in arms in order not to die unworthily. We arrived to dialogue; that is, we came to talk and to listen. We addressed ourselves to the supreme government and to all the good and honest people there are in the world. We also spoke to the bad people so that they would hear the truth. Some listened to us; others continued on the road of contempt for our voice and our race.

**Second:** We found attentive ears ready to listen to the truth that came from our lips. The San Cristóbal dialogue was real. There was no underhandedness or lies. Nothing was hidden from our hearts or from the reasonable and kind people. There was no buying and selling of dignity. There was equality in speaking and in listening. There was good, real dialogue.

**Third:** Now we have responses that reflect the real interest of the man commissioned to find peace. Now we have the obligation to reflect well on what his words mean. Now we need to speak with the collective heart that governs us. We need to listen to its voice in order to walk again. The next signal to take the next step on this road whose destiny will or will not be peace with justice and dignity, will come from them, from our side, from the Indigenous in the mountains and ravines.

**Fourth:** We have found in the commissioner for peace and reconciliation in Chiapas a man ready to listen to our reasons and demands. He was not content with listening to and understanding us; moreover, he looked for possible solutions to the problems. We hail the attitude of Commissioner Manuel Camacho Solís.

**Fifth:** We have seen in the National Commissioner for Mediation, the Bishop Samuel Ruiz García, real and permanent concern for overcoming all the obstacles that intervene along the road to peace. Good men and women worked with him day and night so that nothing would interrupt the development of the dialogue. Sacrificing their personal security, well-being and health, the mediators completed their work, not between peace and war, but between two voices that try, still, to find themselves at peace.

These men and women welcomed us. If some tranquillity blossoms in these lands it will be due, above all, to their pacifying work. We hail the sacrifice and dedication of the National Mediation Commission, and especially Bishop Samuel Ruiz García.

**Sixth:** Now this phase of the dialogue has ended and its direction is good, we brush aside all obstacles to keep on going.

Freedom! Justice! Democracy!

Respectfully,
From the Mexican Southeast,
CCRI-CG of the EZLN

# A Conversation with Subcommander Marcos After the Dialogue

March 3, 1994
Julio Moguel and Hermann Bellinghausen, correspondents, San Cristóbal.
[La Jornada, 3/4]

Subcommander Marcos keeps up a loose and informal conversation after the last interviews that he granted in San Cristóbal de las Casas. Visibly tired, but with the nimble speech that characterizes him, he contemplates the military experience of the Zapatista

247

uprising, expressing his first impressions after the dialogue, reflecting on the period of consultation that the EZLN now has to carry out in its communities.

It is the end of a period, unexpected and surprising, that the rebels didn't count on. The insurgent subcommander evaluates the insufficiencies of the negotiations, as much on the part of the EZLN as the negotiators for the government. He shows himself to be skeptical about the promises, and outlines scenarios for the immediate future. Peace or war? A flare-up of repression and authoritarianism? Or effective transition to democracy?

The man of a thousand words takes his leave of the forum, and, before returning to the mountains, settles into a chair for one more conversation.

*"Do you feel more secure now that you are returning to the jungle?"*

"There we are in our element. When we enter the city we start to make errors, but while we are in the mountains and in the communities it is very difficult for anyone to mess with us, including the regular forces of the Federal Army."

*"You are asking journalists to go with you to the jungle. What does this invitation consist of? Does this mean that perhaps your encampments will not be clandestine any more?"*

"The idea is not to take them to places where the situation is delicate. There is a civilian section where the consultations will take place. Yes, some visits can be arranged that imply a certain risk, and these—like those before, will be conducted with a lot of security, blindfolding the journalists who are decided on. It is not a secret for anyone anymore which zones are Zapatista."

*"Are you thinking of continuing the war, or do you think the negotiations went well?"*

"We thought that the war would continue. What held it up on January 12 was that the Federal Army might enter the communities and start razing, that we would be drawing them toward the jungle, to the mountains. That was what stopped it. We were prepared for that type of combat: That was what we rehearsed for 10 years, not the attacks on San Cristóbal and the other main townships. For the past nine years we prepared for defense, for defense only.

"But our calculations were not, and are not, that everything will be decided by means of weapons. What we think and calculate is that it will be more expensive in political terms to annihilate us than to tell us that they will fulfill all our demands. Because right now they are only talking about that: what they will give us. And perhaps there may be some large investment, except in order to solve the problem of taking away the Zapatista Army's social base. And to take away the social base of the war, the government will have to combat its past to convince the communities that it will now fulfill its promises. Why would the people believe its promises now?

"The expectation we have is that the war will remain averted through the pressure exerted by the civil society of the whole country to complete the accords. I don't think that depends on the results of the San Cristóbal talks. A problem will arise if civil society becomes exhausted, tires, becomes deflated. In that case, everything would remain open and then, yes, they would move on us militarily. What I am trying to explain is that the problem is not with us, but with the country. Our cycle ended already, however many flashes and photos keep on going."

*"You counted on war and that it was going to be long. Did you think there was going to be a big military clash, or did you not count on that?"*

"Yes, we counted on a big military clash. We thought that the biggest military clash would be in San Cristóbal. Our calculations were that the military response would be immediate, to avoid a greater stir. We calculated that they would not hesitate. That is why we concentrated greater forces here, with the idea of holding off the Army's entrance. Our largest military core was around Rancho Nuevo, on the Tuxtla Road.

"With good reason we thought that there must have been a big clash when we saw that the main townships did not fall at the same time. We took San Cristóbal and realized that we were alone, that the other main townships had not fallen. The attacks in Altamirano and Ocosingo began at 7 in the morning and were not resolved in military terms until 4 in the afternoon. In Las Margaritas the attack started at 3 in the morning, and it fell in an hour. We started at 1 in the morning and at 2 we already had the city. Therefore we decided to give ourselves the necessary time in San Cristóbal to detain and hold up the Army, and give ourselves time for an orderly retreat, while we figured out what was happening and carried out an armed propaganda action. Then came the attack on Rancho Nuevo to recover arms and supplies, and it is there we failed in a sorry way. We lost people and, furthermore, we became scattered. That broke up an entire column, the one that came from San Cristóbal to Rancho Nuevo, and also the one that was descending from Altamirano to San Cristóbal.

"I repeat that we were not sure of what was happening. The quick way in which we went from armed action to the negotiating table in San Cristóbal took us by surprise. We have already said before that our relative delay in organizing ourselves for arriving at the peace table was precisely because we didn't expect it so soon."

*"Yes, the way in which the events grew took you by surprise, and you had to improvise and discuss the change of course immediately. Are you now prepared to discuss the terms of the accords in the jungle in as short a time as the one announced?"*

"There is not and will not be improvisation in the discussion of the accords, though. We know how to do that. That is how we decided on war. Let me tell you. First there emerged some voices that said not to wait anymore; later there appeared nuclei that said that they would go to war alone, on their part. Then the Command started to detect this situation. It analyzed it and decided to have consultations. An explanation of the pros and cons of the uprising was organized, taking into account the circumstances: the North American Free Trade Agreement, the fall of the socialist system, what happened in El Salvador, in Nicaragua, in Guatemala. And on the other side was the logic of death and misery: the increase in infant mortality, the cancellation of agrarian distribution through the reform of Article 27, the shock of the commissions that went to ask for resources and only returned with a heap of papers.

"Then the General Command explained it to the ethnic committees. Those committees to those of the regions and ravines, those ones to the local committees—which are in and cons were argued until the community said it was time to vote. Records were taken that show how many said yes, how many no, how many did not know, without distinction for age, men, women and children. Then came the reverse process: The local committees passed the basic resolves to the regions, the regions to the zone, the zone to the committees and these to the Command. That was when it appeared that we had been watching another television channel: While we thought no, that it appeared that everything at the international level was against it, that military action would be annulled as a result, it ended up that the immense majority was inclined toward it. Only a small handful of *compañeros* said any more than that it still was not time."

*"You said before that in order to win the accords at the table in San Cristóbal it would require something more than the express will of both sides. Did you mean that only with the support—or the addition—of civil society would it be possible to win the Zapatista demands? Could you explain this idea better?"*

"The government will only comply if it is forced to, by the force of rifles or through the pressure of society. To depend on that pressure being applied is the right way. The only possibility for peace that we see now is if there are other forces that will commit themselves to forcing the government to comply. That is the bet on this consultation process: It doesn't depend on what goes down, but on what goes to the rest of the country.

"We have received many letters that suggest a process of transmutation. First we got letters of surprise, from some who said that everything was beautiful but that they were going to smash us; later came letters that said we should search for the way of peace, of negotiation, so that we would not let ourselves be killed; the third phase was when we were told—are told—not to turn in our weapons, not to sell out, not to give in to what they are asking for. Solidarity committees are being formed not with the Chiapaneco people but with the EZLN. They come from many sides, above all from Indigenous groups. You will remember the letter that the marchers from Guerrero sent us; but we have also gotten letters from the Yaqui, Mayo, Tarahumara, from the Yucatán and Campeche Maya, from Colima, Puebla...

"We do not assume the head of this movement; rather we assume the tail. Now any other movement has more opportunity than us, because they can say: There are the radicals; I want the same as them, and if you do not comply with me, too, I will become radicalized. Now the field is open for that and we say: Come on in! But we do not see ourselves as propitiatory victims, because, yes, we are going to get back our dead, not with other deaths, but with benefits for the Indians in general and the state in particular. Right now the danger is that the movement will remain resigned to the level it grows to locally and will not aspire to contribute to a national movement."

*"In the document that came out of the discussions between you and the commissioner in San Cristóbal, some demands that the EZLN put forward at the federal level did not have positive responses, like the reform of Article 27 or Article Four of the Constitution. But a first reading gives the impression that you achieved things that, although they were not formally accepted, push toward a reform of important parts of the Constitution or, if the figure is permitted, won things that are too large for the narrowness of the legal and institutional frame-*

*mitted, won things that are too large for the narrowness of the legal and institutional framework currently in force.*

"There are responses that do not formally respond to some of the national demands, but that opens the door to developing a national movement that would end up smashing or modifying the current constitutional framework. They do not respond, for example, to the demand for reform of Article 27, but the established concessions make possible the coming together of other sectors and movements, with demands of that type and by other means, that would end up reforming it before the six-year term ends or at the start of a new government.

"According to our analysis and the consultations we held with lawyers, San Cristóbal necessarily begins to raise the necessity of a national forum, with a national dialogue, where, in addition to us, other forces would participate.

In any case, if they do not find a solution quickly and clearly, it is to maintain the principle of authority, with the idea that they do not have a reason to concede to these people. The neoliberal project is already indefensible."

*"You were really lucky not to be found. What was the formula or the conditions that made that possible?"*

"The government first thought that we were not a guerrilla group. They said that if we were a guerrilla group, we would already be attacking, because there is no guerrilla group that prepares itself first, grows and then attacks. Then they thought that we were Guatemalans, bases of support for the Revolutionary National Guatemalan Union (Unión Revolucionario Nacional Guatemalteca, URNG), or they thought other things, like that it was a question of some organizations' land invasions. The information that they had does not check out with the sketch on the Department of Defense's computer or the Department of Government's, if it does then the Department of Government still hid that information.

"Since 1985, we have thought that we would be discovered. Then, our entire military plan was defensive, waiting to be discovered. We were already growing too much: Entire communities spoke about us, helped us with the load, fed us."

*"What question would you have liked to hear? What is it that nobody has asked you and you would like to say?"*

"I would ask: What are the Zapatistas going to do, in one or another possibility? What are they going to do if the people say no to peace and yes to war? What are they going to do if the people say yes to peace and no to war? What are they going to do with their military units and 'professionals in violence' in one case or another? In case the choice is peace, we will not fight, since our Army is campesino. The incorporation into civilian life would be almost natural, although we would not turn in our arms for defending ourselves in case of a threat. Anyways, if we achieve peace we will have to remain as an army for a while to guarantee compliance with the accords. The problem is what, in that time, will our relationship to the Power be like, with that which we confronted, whose objective was to exterminate us, or take away our social base and undermine our prestige so that it could annihilate us with the least political cost."

251

*"In case the peace offer advances and the Zapatista demands are complied with, what will happen with the ranchers?"*

"I think that they are going to have to be sacrificed. If the government wants to arrive at an accord it has to sacrifice them. A process of coordination can grow among the ranchers, in the sense that they themselves would decide to sacrifice some of their number—those of these territories—so that others aren't touched. That is going to happen in Altamirano, in Ocosingo, in Las Margaritas, where the conflict was.

"A phenomenon similar to that of San Juan Chamula occurred there. The political machine of San Juan Chamula is promoted by the State in exchange for votes. By fulfilling this function of securing votes, they started to get more power, and that provoked the situation that we know. To such a point that now the government cannot touch the *caciques*. They become governors, and at high social costs; they cannot be touched. Perhaps they do not realize what a monster they have created, equal to the ranchers, when they gave training to, armed, funded, and covered them up in the mess that they made.

"And the government knew. Just like they discovered our training camps in '93, they knew at least since '90 that the ranchers were armed and preparing themselves. It was their officials who taught in the training camps of the *guardias blancas*, on the Castillians' [Spanish speakers'] ranches, in the municipal auditorium of Altamirano.

"The military hypothesis we had contemplated is that a bullring would be made called the Lacandona Jungle. The federal government and the Army are in the *burladero* [barrier to let bullfighters escape from the bull]; civilian society above; we are the bullfighter and the bull is the ranchers. The government says: Let them tear themselves to pieces and I will manage to get the rest. And then the aggressive army on human rights becomes a pacifying army and restores order. That is a probable scenario, which reproduces, in military terms, the detention of the Ricardo Pozas caravan: It is a lynching environment and the soldiers just stand by.

"The ranchers are already out of control. We threatened several times to break off the talks due to the situation in Altamirano, and the government could not control them. The ranchers are playing at breaking up the talks."

*"What is going to happen in Altamirano? Is there going to be a breakthrough? What happens if this plan of confrontation extends to other parts of the country?"*

"It appears that this also is going to play out with ranchers nationally. There they will see what support they have. But if these guys have the support of the ranchers, then its no good, because they are going to go from lynchers to martyrs of the small property cause. If the other ranchers start to make noise about this, well, they are going to create a contra. But the responsibility is the State's. In the same way, they are responsible for what happened on January 1, because they were told before that this would happen; we demanded that they correct things. Now they are told this is going to happen, to leave the doors open."

*"If this has been the response of the government, how do you now see the response or attitude of Camacho?"*

"Camacho's discovery was that, in reality, the leadership of this movement is Indigenous. It was a big surprise to them to have to address themselves to those speakers and not to the forces that were supposedly behind everything. That is when the world opened up to us, and then Camacho said that yes, there is a way out, although we are hidden behind a face mask, that we have nothing to do with foreign forces."

*"One of your conquests at the table in San Cristóbal is that conditions were created for clean and democratic elections in Chiapas. If this is accomplished, would the EZLN partici-pate in the electoral process as a force in some way, with its own candidates?"*

"We are not going to do that. We do not have the necessary organizational structure. But furthermore there is a fear among our people that one of us would do it. For example, all the leaders are prohibited from holding public office, under threat of expulsion. They also do not have the possibility of owning property. But, moreover, the structure of the EZLN is strictly military. Furthermore, we would need squadrons experienced in open struggle, mass struggle. We have the ability to organize ourselves in communities, to sur-vive, to maintain ourselves there, inside, but not to go into the public light yet, because we do not have the experience. That is where we could get muddled up."

*"But you, with the sympathy you generated, couldn't you have influence in the nomina-tion of municipal presidents? Isn't part of your objective to influence the naming of democra-tic authorities?"*

"That is without a doubt one of our objectives. That is definitely a near-reality in the rural areas, as the entire rural territory of the state is ours. But I see that more in the sense of bow-ing to the nomination, the candidacy of someone, and not launching a candidacy on our own account, which is another way you loose prestige, moral authority, and your social base."

## PROFESSIONALS IN HOPE

[*La Jornada*, 3/6]
March 5, 1994
Manuel Henríquez, corespondent, La Paz, Baja California Sur.

At 1:30 a.m. on Saturday, February 26, Francisco de los Santos, auxiliary of Bishop Samuel Ruiz, looked for Marina Valtierra at a hotel in San Cristóbal de las Casas, Chiapas, to give her a letter that Subcommander Marcos wrote in response to the message that Miguel A. Vázquez—13 years old—had written and sent via his mother, Marina.

Briefly, Miguel said to Marcos:

"I think that you did what was necessary, because there was no alternative to rising up in arms, since the government did not listen to the needs of the Indians; it was not interested in the misery or the hunger of the Chiapaneco population.

"Admired subcommander: Sometimes it is necessary, as in this case, to rise up in arms to be heard and paid attention to by the corrupt government. I would have liked for there to have been peace from the start. I send you this letter to tell you that since the armed conflict in Chiapas began, I have kept informed of it."

The young man decided to extend the message of the subcommander to all of the children of Mexico by sharing his letter with *El Financiero, Proceso* and *La Jornada*:

To the child Miguel A. Vázquez Valtierra:

Miguel:

Your mother gave me your letter, along with the photo of you and your dog. I'm taking advantage of the fact that your mother is returning to your land to write you a few hurried lines which you may not yet understand. Nevertheless, I am sure that one day, as I write to you here, you will understand that it is possible that men and women exist like us—faceless and nameless, who have left everything, even life itself, so that others (children like you and those who are not like you) can wake up every morning without words that silence and without masks to face the world. When this day comes we, the faceless and the nameless, will be able to rest, finally, under the ground... quite dead, certainly, but happy.

Our profession: Hope.

The day is almost dead-dark as it dresses in night and the next day begins to be born, first with its black veil, then with gray or blue, according to the taste of the sun, whether it will shine or not, dust and mud in our path. The day is almost dead in the nighttime arms of the crickets, and then this idea of writing you comes to me, to tell you something that comes from one of those "professionals in violence," which they have called us so often.

It turns out that yes, we are professionals. But our profession is hope. We decided one fine day to make ourselves soldiers so that one day soldiers would not be needed. That is, we picked a suicidal profession because it is a profession whose objective is to disappear: Soldiers who are soldiers so that one day nobody will need to be a soldier. This is clear, right? And then it turns out that these soldiers who want to stop being soldiers, us, have something that the books and speeches call "patriotism." Because that which we call country is not a vague idea found only in letters and books, but a great body of meat and bone, of pain and suffering, of sorrow, of hope that everything will change in the end, one fine day. And the country that we want will have to be born also from our errors and missteps. From our dispossession and our broken bodies a new world will have to rise up. Will we see it? Does it matter if we see it? I think that it does not matter as much as knowing for certain that it will be born and that, in the long and painful birth of history, we contributed something and everything: life, body and soul. Love and pain, not only do they rhyme [in Spanish, "*amor y dolor*"] but they unite and march together. Because of this we are soldiers who want to stop being soldiers. But it turns out that in order for soldiers to no longer be necessary, one has to become a soldier and prescribe a discrete quantity of lead, hot lead writing freedom and justice for all, not for one or for a few, but for all, everyone, the dead of before and of tomorrow, the living of today and always, all of those who we call people and country, those without anything, the losers of always before tomorrow, the nameless, the faceless.

To be a soldier who wants there to be no need for soldiers is very simple. It is enough to respond firmly to a small piece of hope that everyone else deposits in each one of us, those who have nothing, those who will have everything. For them and for those who have kept to the path, for one unjust reason or another. For those who try to really change and become better every day, every evening, every night of rain and crickets. To accumulate hate and love with patience. To cultivate the fierce tree of hate for the oppressor with the love that struggles and liberates. To cultivate the powerful tree of love that is wind that cleans and cures; not the small and egotistical love—the large one, the one that improves and makes one grow. To cultivate among us the tree of the hate and of love, the tree of duty. In this cultivation to put one's whole life, body and soul, breath and hope. To grow, then, crow and grow step by step, pace by pace. And in that climbing and falling of red stars, to not fear, to not fear until surrendering, sitting down in a chair to rest while others continue, to catch our breath while others struggle, to sleep while others stay up.

Abandon, if you have it, the love of death and the fascination with martyrs. Revolutionaries love life without fearing death, and seek a life that is dignified for all, and if for that they need to pay with their death, they will do it without drama or hesitation.

Receive my best hug and this tender pain that will always be hope.

Health, Miguel.
From the mountains of the Mexican Southeast,
Insurgent Subcommander Marcos

**P.S.** Here we live worse than dogs. We had to choose: to live like animals or die like dignified people. Dignity, Miguel, is the only thing that one should never lose...never.

# On Charging Conac-LN with Legal Matters

[*La Jornada*, 3/17]
March 15, 1994

To the people of Mexico:
To the people and governments of the world:
To the national and international press:

Brothers and Sisters:

The Clandestine Revolutionary Indigenous Committee-General Command of the Zapatista National Liberation Army addresses all of you with respect and honor to speak its word:

Since the stage prior to dialogue in San Cristóbal, the CCRI-CG of the EZLN asked for legal advice to be able to consult with several problems that the process of war and the process of peace presented to our Army. We did not receive any immediate response. The justice of our struggle was lost among slander and mistrust. Only one response came to us at that time, and that was from the response of the brothers and sisters of the National Coordinating Committee of Civic Action for National Liberation (Coordinadora Nacional de Acción Cívica para la Liberación Nacional, Conac-LN), who offered the support of their legal commission.

We thanked them for this gesture and placed our trust in these people. They will do all that is in their power to support us in the legal aspects, since our needs are large. We salute the commitment and altruism of the brothers and sisters of the Conac-LN and we address the Mexican people to ratify what we have written to them on previous days: All of the legal matters of our Zapatista National Liberation Army will be entrusted to the Legal Commission of the National Coordinating Committee of Civic Action for National Liberation.

Freedom!

Justice!

Democracy!

Respectfully,

From the Mexican Southeast,

Clandestine Revolutionary Indigenous Committee-General Command
 of the Zapatista National Liberation Army.


# THE STRUGGLE WILL CONTINUE

[*La Jornada* 3/17]
March 15, 1994

*"Like shadows of tender fury, our passing will shelter those who have nothing."*

To the State Council of Indigenous and Campesino Organizations (Consejo Estatal de Organizaciones Indígenas y Campesinas, CEOIC):
To the people of Mexico:
To the peoples and governments of the world:
To the national and international press:

Brothers and Sisters:

The Clandestine Revolutionary Indigenous Committee-General Command of the EZLN directs itself to you, with respect and honor, in order to say the following:

The federal government that yesterday usurped the will of the people is lying about what has occurred in the dialogue in San Cristóbal de las Casas, Chiapas; the evil government says that there are "agreements," when only dialogue took place. Do not let them lie to us, brothers and sisters. The powerful now usurp the truth and are trying to deceive us by saying that peace is only a question of a signature.

How can there be peace if those who caused the war continue demanding that we live in perpetual misery? The arrogance that inhabits the government palace and the homes of businessmen and landowners is still crying for war and the death of our people; they will not tolerate our Indigenous blood becoming equal to white people's blood. We are trying to become a part of the country and they won't let us. They pay us with contempt and mock the march of our dead.

256

If they speak with contempt, if they silence and murder our brothers and sisters, how can there be peace in these lands? How can we ask our collective heart if it is the hour in which peace will enter through the doorways of our poor land with dignity in hand?

Once again they want to corner us in order to extract our surrender. They want to drag us back, over the death of our dignity, to a peace which is war against our people.

We will not do it, we will not surrender. If they deny us a just and dignified peace, then we, somber men and women, will dress ourselves once again for war. Our fury will come from this deceit, once again our just machetes will be sharpened and our lands will smell of gunpowder. We are shadows of tender fury—our passage will cover the sky, it will shelter with its protective cloak the dispossessed and the good men and women who understand that justice and peace can slip through one's fingers. If they deny us our rights, then our tender fury will enter the mansions of the arrogant. There will not be a wall that can't be jumped, a door that can't be opened, a window that can't be broken, a wall that can't be brought down—our shadow will bring pain to those who demand war and the death of our people. There will be more crying and more blood in order that peace may sit at our table with kindness. Shadows of tender fury, we will once again raise up our voice so that it is heard and the lies are silenced. It is enough already! Our first voice wasn't enough. The land didn't flower with the blood of our dead. The men and women of tender fury will have to walk once again, our dead will again rise up. The history of our pained heart will speak again in order that the deception and the lies end, so that the arrogance will finally disappear from these Mexican lands, so that men and women will come to us again with the dark robes of tender fury in order to speak as one and to silence the many lies.

Do not let the mouths of the powerful speak. Only venom and rot leave their lips. Silence their lies and deceitfulness.

Now it is the time that our brothers and sisters speak, those brothers and sisters who walk on other paths, taking our pain to new suns. The time that the voice of our brothers and sisters of the CEOIC speaks, that every Indigenous person in these lands has their say. Do not let the poor campesino stay silent—let the worker in the city cry out. This warrior song should not forget the voices of the students and the teachers, the working people and every other oppressed person.

Do not leave this heavy flag in our hands alone—it should be raised by everyone. Let's all change the land that embraces this flag; brother Mexicans, don't forget this voice from the mountains; already the light that our dead give off is very small. Let's all join our lights together, let's break this shameful night. It is time that it dawned.

Let the truth speak. Let its voice speak now, let it walk forward with resolution. We, without faces or pasts, listen with our hearts and with open words for everyone's voices, but our men and women are still silent and there is still silence in the shadows of tender fury.

Let our dream guard your passage so that nothing bad happens to you, so that black shadows don't threaten you. Our hearts and our fire are alert for you, brothers and sisters, so that you can march forward. Let this furious tenderness reign in these lands. Peace isn't possible with deception. Peace is born in freedom and grows in justice. Democracy is dignified for all.

Greetings brothers and sisters of the CEOIC!

Greetings Indigenous brothers and sisters!

Greetings fellow Mexicans, walk forward without fear, with your head held high—our weapons will guard your passage...

Freedom!

Justice!

Democracy!

Respectfully,

From the Mexican Southeast,

Clandestine Revolutionary Indigenous Committee-General Command
   of the Zapatista National Liberation Army

## Government Lies About the Outcome of the Dialogue

[*La Jornada*, 3/17]
March 15, 1994

To the people of Mexico:

To the peoples and governments of the world:

To the national and international press:

Brothers and Sisters:

The Clandestine Revolutionary Indigenous Committee—General Command of the EZLN directs itself to you, with respect and honor, in order to say the following:

**First:** The federal government that yesterday usurped the will of the people is lying about what has occurred in the dialogue in San Cristóbal de las Casas, Chiapas. The evil government says that there are "agreements" when only a dialogue took place. The powerful are now trying to usurp the truth and are trying to deceive the people by saying that peace is only a question of a signature.

**Second:** The fundamental causes of our uprising are being forgotten and the truth about the dialogue is being supplanted by the lie that there is an "agreement." The CCRI-CG of the EZLN hasn't made any agreement with the federal government. We haven't negotiated anything other than the form in which the dialogue is to be carried out. No agreement has been made with the evil government that has been lying for so long.

**Third:** The CCRI-CG of the EZLN points out that to end the first phase of the dialogue with lies is the best way to ensure that peace fails. We will not trust a government that, even in making propositions, lies. If the supreme government wants to present the documents of San Cristóbal as "agreements," then let's consider the EZLN's list of demands the "agreement," and guarantee democracy in the next elections with the resignation of the federal president.

**Fourth:** The CCRI-CG of the EZLN respectfully asks the honest national and international press to not play the usurper's cheating game, and to point out, with truth and objectivity, what has occurred in the current stage of the dialogue.

Freedom!

Justice!

Democracy!

Respectfully,

From the Mexican Southeast,

Indigenous Clandestine Revolutionary Committee-General Command
of the Zapatista National Liberation Army

## A Letter and Poetry from Marcos

**March 15, 1994**

To the national and International press:

Gentlemen:

Did you miss me? Well, here I am anew but with little new. It is difficult to consult about peace with the other shadows that come from San Cristóbal. We are attending more to the voices of our own desire than to those who want eternal privileges and injustice. It hurts to see that even the "authentic" things are corrupted. Do they want more war so that they can understand peace? Accept it, you were happier with our troops inside the walls of your proud and regal city, than now that you have to live in fear. Learn from this struggle that arms itself out of shame...

Greetings and good luck on the Ides of March.

From the mountains of Southeastern Mexico,

Insurgent Subcommander Marcos

### Post-script of Immediate Nostalgia
### Section: "Images of Yesterday—of the Guerrilla."

I. My work had the appearance of "transcendent history:" I was caring for a small howler monkey who, as all young things should do, did not respect any authority at all. Ignoring my gallant military bearing and the already discolored red star on my chest (this last signified to the other members of the already powerful EZLN–that is to say, the other six members–that I was an infantry lieutenant), the small howler monkey (we always suspected it was a she and not a he) used to carefully crawl up my chest to my right shoulder and hang there every time that she felt like it. Raúl, the largest of us in every sense, taught us. He fights while singing tangos in the afternoons, the best hours for tangos and crickets. The food is finished. We used to walk knowing what would come. We were already invincible and small. January was still far away. The year? 1984 (does this remind you of something?) The Mad Hatter and the March Hare used to sing:

"A very merry un-birthday to you (repeat)
If today is not your birthday we'll have to celebrate etc. (again)"

"Alice got up to leave. We are still here...and we sing...still..."

II. And it was 1987 and I was an infantry captain and the country was between us and it was, for example, a poem:

### Problems

This thing that is one's country is somewhat difficult to explain
But it is more difficult to understand what it is to love one's country
For example
they taught us that to love one's country is, for example,
to salute the flag
to rise upon hearing the National Anthem
To get drunk when the national soccer team loses
To get drunk when the national soccer team wins
Some etceteras that change little from six-year term to six-year term
And, for example,
they didn't teach us that to love one's country can be
for example
to whistle like one who is leaving, but
behind that hill there is also part of the country and nobody can see us
And we are frank with each other (because one always is frank when nobody sees them)

And we tell the country,
for example,
everything we hate about it
and everything we love about it
and it is always better to say it,
for example,
with gunshots and smiling
And, for example,
they taught us that to love one's
country is
for example
to use a campesino sombrero
to know the names of the child-heroes
to shout "Viva-arriba Mexico!" even though Mexico is down and dead.
Other etceteras which change little from six-year term to six-year term.
And, for example,
they did not teach us that
to love the country

could be,
for example,
to be quiet as one who dies,
but no,
below this earth there is also country
and no one hears us
and we are frank
(because one is always frank when no one hears us)
and we tell
(the country).
the short and hard history
of those who were dying to love it
and that they are no longer hear to give me the reasons,
but they give me them without being here,
those who taught us
that the country can be loved,
for example,
with gunshots and smiling.

A **P.S.** to say goodbye from within a loving gale: This March, like all of them, is unsettling. Care for yourselves, if you can. All right.

# 10. Returning to the Communities

*[These communiqués and interviews are from the period during which the Zaptistas brought the peace accord proposals to the communites to be discussed.]*

## The EZLN Denies That the Prisoners in Cerro Hueco are Combatants

[*La Jornada*]
April 7, 1994

To the national and international press:

The Clandestine Revolutionary Indigenous Committee-General Command of the EZLN declares the following:

**First:** In recent days we have learned that 21 civilians are prisoners in the Cerro Hueco jail, under the unjust accusation of being part of our Zapatista National Liberation Army.

**Second:** The CCRI-CG of the EZLN declares that, since the liberation of the imprisoned combatants in the state of Chihuahua, it has no known combatants in the jails of the evil government.

**Third:** The General Command of the EZLN has consciensiously checked the lists of combatants, and the names of those unjustly imprisoned in the jail in Cerro Hueco do not appear on them.

**Fourth:** The CCRI-CG of the EZLN denounces the evil government for trying to cover its arbitrariness in the indiscriminate detention of civilians during the conflict by accusing them, without any basis, of belonging to our glorious Army.

**Fifth:** Keeping these innocents in jail is one of the obstacles to the process of continuing the dialogue, since the EZLN cannot speak of peace if the government speaks of war through the mouth of its actions.

Respectfully,

From the mountains of the Mexican Southeast,

Clandestine Revolutionary Indigenous Committee-General Command of the Zapatista National Liberation Army

Mexico, April 1994.

# Interview with Marcos

[*La Jornada*, 4/10]
David Aponte, on assignment, Lacandona Jungle.

"The Zapatista National Liberation Army believes that the military-political conditions for resuming our internal consultation on the government's compromise for a dignified peace in Chiapas and the dialogue, with Commissioner Manuel Camacho Solís, do not exist," declared Insurgent Subcommander Marcos today.

In order to reactivate dialogue, the Clandestine Revolutionary Indigenous Committee-General Command of the EZLN requires that the Mexican Army "loosen" their presence in the region, and that the ranchers and farmers "lower" their attitude of belligerence.

The military strategist of the EZLN also assured us that the Zapatistas have not received any communication from Manuel Camacho Solís—neither confidential nor public—as the ex-chancellor [Camacho Solís] confirmed.

In an interview with three reporters in a clearing of the Lacandona Jungle, the subcommander made several commentaries about the public reappearance of Camacho Solís and his points of view on the peace process.

In the beginning, Marcos believed that the political-military conditions to restart the dialogue are not now present. There exist new Mexican Army troop movements towards other zones of the region, he argued.

**M:** What they did was take it out of the press route. They did the retreat on the side that the press covers—which is Tuxtla Gutiérrez, San Cristóbal de las Casas, Ocosingo, Altamirano and Las Margaritas—and they went around Arriaga, for one part, and by Villahermosa and Tenosique, for the other. Five days ago approximately 30 large trucks of 8 and 12 tons came down from Tenosique, with approximately 1,000, 1,200 soldiers, on the border highway.

*Q: Do you believe that the troop movements are for relief, or that they are increasing their troops?*

**M:** Within the relief. What they do is relocate the parachutists and minesweepers, they take them on a circle through the press, and they put them in the back. The parachutists are rangers, counter-guerrillas. And in military terms, that means to put the minesweepers and the parachutists there, and the functioning of the hammer and the anvil are reversed. Now [the hammer] will be on the border and the anvil here.

I think that here they play a lot, and the play is to get into the stream bed (the Lacandona Jungle), dominate the highways, and put the anvil there. I don't think that they will risk putting the anvil in Ocosingo, Altamirano, and Las Margaritas, because it would be noticed, and they don't want it to be noticed.

*Q: What is their plan then? Are they contemplating an offensive?*

**M:** Of isolation, of taking the guerrillas out of the social discourse, that we stop declaring, that we stop doing what we are doing now. Take us out of this stream bed. But the movement of troops here will have to be very fast for us to leave. What was once planned on this side is to put the minesweepers and the parachutists, who are the Green Berets, to deactivate the mines. They are counterinsurgency units that enter to clash and locate you.

The units that they use are 12 to 15 people. We are talking about around 5,000 soldiers, a division. One air-transported division now following the gringo model for a rapid intervention.

Then initially they move in this line—Ocosingo, Altamirano, Las Margaritas. In the landing strips here, the restored one at Altamirano, and the one of Las Margaritas, they took out the commercial flights and set up a barracks and they launch it and start to push us over there (the border with Guatemala) and there is the anvil. In this case it will be the Kaibiles [elite unit of the Guatemalan Army]. If the Mexican Army loosens there then we would face the Kaibiles. Then the Kaibiles make the anvil.

In that sense they would publish in the newspapers that the soldiers had left and the journalists would see them pass through San Cristóbal de las Casas, but they turn around and make a change of troops.

*Q: Does the government have a double politic? Camacho spoke of coordinating the interests of peace, an allusion to the ranchers.*

**M:** Yes, I think that he was going to try to incorporate the ranchers into some part of the dialogue because they had already proposed it to him, that they wanted to speak with us. And since they know that we have not yet invaded the farms, maybe they could take advantage of that—make an arrangement and resolve the problem of the ranches, because there was a war tax, and negotiate in some way the possessing of the land.

The Army publicly maintains that they are loosening their military position, but actually they are simply moving troops around—not increasing their troops but simply changing their placement and composition. This is the last report that came to me yesterday [Friday, April 7].

*Q: I don't understand. What does the government want: to continue the dialogue or prepare for a definitive offensive?*

**M:** No, they want to continue the consultations; the consultations are now suspended. What they want to know is what the people will say, and maintain the military position depending of the result of the consultations: loosen the military pressure to go on to the negotiation.

*Q: You don't know whether they will continue if the conditions are appropriate?*

M: No, definitely not under these conditions. It seemed possible, since the committee saw a military loosening, but then we saw that the exterior line did not check out with them leaving. Our reports from the exterior line told us that they [the soldiers] did not leave the state. And then reports came to us that they were entering on the other side, and since there was no other movement anywhere else in the country, then they must be the same soldiers moving from one side to another.

For the moment there is no change in the situation. What happened to Colosio caused the suspension of the consultations. We said, then, here is all of the pretext they need. It seems like now the paranoia is clearing up and that it was not about us, but an internal plot for power. We can carry out the consultations with this [military] positioning, as long as it does not have the political foundation to make an offensive...

*Q: Is it true that you met with Camacho a few days ago?*

M: No, we have not seen Camacho since the dialogue, and it is also a lie that they have sent confidential communiqués. Maybe they sent them but they have not arrived. We haven't heard anything from Camacho since the dialogue. He was waiting for the response of the consultations. We were continuing the process, and then the Colosio thing happened, and now we can do even less. Until now we knew that he was going to come [to Chiapas]. But I have had no contact with him, neither written nor public nor secret.

*Q: What do you attribute this to?*

M: To the fact that they are waiting until they regain their composure as well. They were going with the Colosio option, negotiating, and, with the change; they have to see how they can reposition themselves to see what they will offer or what they are negotiating.

*Q: What will be the conditions for returning to the dialogue, and will you go down to the cathedral?*

M: They will have to reproduce the military conditions previous to the dialogue: One, the Army will have to loosen its presence; Two, the belligerence of the ranchers, the merchants and the political class [will have to] decrease as soon as possible to the point before the dialogue. This appears to be very closely tied to the municipal presidents and the ranchers. That would be enough. Of course, it would be a positive signal if Salinas would resign.

*Q: Is it true that you want to speak with Zedillo?*

M: No, I have never said that. I can give him some suggestions on how to write text books, but I never said anything like that. The Committee has not met since he was named, but most likely they will not speak in favor of any candidate.

I have already stopped the candidates from coming. We are no longer going to invite them, but we are ready to speak with a representative of theirs. In that sense, we are prepared to speak to any representative. What concerns us is that they go in there, and if anything should happen to them, if any plane should fall on them... What I have said is that we were ready to speak to any candidate, but I already cut that off, them coming, since if anything happened to them, they would blame us. If it happened to Colosio, well then the worse for any other candidate.

# EMILIANO ZAPATA WILL NOT DIE BY DECREE

[*La Jornada*, 4/11]
April 10, 1994

*"The right to land, of those who work, it is inalienable."*

To the people of Mexico:
To the people and governments of the world:
To the national and international press:

Brothers and Sisters:

The Clandestine Revolutionary Indigenous Committee-General Command of the Zapatista National Liberation Army addresses you to say the following:

Today, April 10, is the 75th anniversary of the assassination of General Emiliano Zapata. His cry of "Land and Liberty!" appeared to be drowned by the treachery of Venustiano Carranza. Today the usurper Salinas de Gortari, who calls himself "President of the Mexican Republic," lies to the people of Mexico saying that his reforms of Article 27 of the Constitution reflect the spirit of General Zapata. The supreme government is lying! Zapata will not die by an arrogant decree. The right to land, of those who work it, is inalienable, and the war cry of "Land and Liberty!" continues to have a place in these Mexican lands, lands under the banner of neoliberalism, which shadows our soil and imprisons and kills all of those campesinos who struggle for their agricultural rights.

The Salinista reforms of Article 27 of the Magna Carta represent a treachery to country, and the one responsible for this crime must be judged as a usurper of the federal executive power in Mexico.

Brothers and sisters, today we mark 100 days of the new dawn of our voice, in the mouths of the rifles of faceless men and women, the voice of the landless campesinos, of the agricultural workers, of the small property holders, of the Indigenous Mexicans. The voice of those who have nothing and deserve everything had to follow the path of its smallest people, the most humiliated, the most persecuted, the most forgotten. The voice of the true people spoke, the voice of the Mexicans dispossessed of their lands, of their dignity and of their history. Everything seemed to be lost in the long night of our peoples. The earth gave nothing but pain and death. But 10 years before this day, in our sorrowful lands, some planted the hope of life, that it might return to the true people. In the Mexican mountains, the seed of their word found a good place to be born. Their silence was cultivated. Their step was the night, to become dawn later.

Then, in our dawn, "Enough!", the land gave the fruits of that planting. Instead of pain was born rage; instead of humiliation came dignity; instead of laments, weapons were reaped. Thousands of men and women climbed out of the earth, from the same soil that only gave them poverty and the tender fire that would inhabit their hands, they covered their faces, they erased their pasts, they left behind their names and their lands, and began to walk the path of war. None of us, men and women of the night path, have a tomorrow. There will never again be any peace for our fears. Our bones and blood will never again find rest.

For whom do these men and women walk? Who drinks their blood? For who is the light of their words? For who is the death of their life? One hundred days. Ten years. Who will now join hands with these men and women who can't be here with you today. Who will now take the flag that their blood ripped out of the hands of the powerful? Who will add their steps to their dignified walk? Who speaks with them, with us, of voice and tender fury? Who will shout with us? Who will not abandon us? Who will struggle with us? Who will listen to our dead?

Not the usurper, whose arrogance is dispatched from the National Palace. Not he who sells us out. Not those who kill us. Not those who dispossess us? Not those who humiliate us?

You, brothers and sisters, yes. For you, our blood. For the night of all, our timid light. For your life, our death. Our war for your peace. For your ears, our words. Your pain, brothers and sisters, will find alleviation in our struggle. For you, everything, brothers and sisters; for us, nothing.

Brothers and sisters, in front of you, in that palace where today the lies reign, lives the man who denies everything to us and who has not been asked to be there. The powerful gentleman, who takes away our lives every day, should leave there. He must go, brothers and sisters. Nothing good comes from his doors. There are lies on his face and his word lives in deceit. He must go, brothers and sisters. This is the cry that comes from the mountains. This is what our blood says. This is what our dead ask. That he must go. Tell him this, brothers and sisters: That he must go!

Let no one else come to that palace that you have in front of you except through the mandate of the majority. Let the one who sits in that chair rule by obeying. Let the one who speaks from that balcony have truth in his words. Let the one who is our leader be so by obeying. Tell him this, brothers and sisters. This is what we want.

We cannot be with you this day, brothers and sisters. Our path is still in the night on the mountain. Our face is still gagged; our word is still far away. Take a moment, Mexican brothers and sisters! Give us a moment of your voice and let our words speak from your mouth. In that same instant, in the mountains of the Mexican Southeast, thousands of men and women with negated faces, nameless and with no past, renew in their breasts the first cry at the beginning of the year. Happiness is in our heart since Emiliano Zapata has come again, in your steps, to the Zócalo of Mexico. We, small and forgotten, raise the image of Zapata in the other heart of the country: that of the mountains of the Mexican Southeast.

Greetings Mexican brothers and sisters! May our cry be yours:

Viva Emiliano Zapata!

Death to the supreme government!
Freedom!
Justice!
Democracy!

Respectfully,
From the mountains of the Mexican Southeast.
Clandestine Revolutionary Indigenous Committee-General Command of the
   Zapatista National Liberation Army.


# THERE WILL BE NO PEACE UNTIL THERE IS JUSTICE

[*La Jornada*, 4/11]
April 10, 1994

To the bases of support of the EZLN:
To the regular and irregular Zapatista combatants in the various arms and services of
   the EZLN:

*Compañeros:*

Today, April 10, 1994, we mark 75 years since the assassination of general Emiliano
Zapata, and 100 days of our just war against the evil Mexican government.

As in 1919, we Zapatistas must pay with blood the price of our cry of "Land and
Liberty!" As in 1919, the supreme government kills us to stop our rebellion. As in 1919,
the land is not owned by those who work it. As in 1919, arms are the only means left
open by the evil government to those without land.

For this reason we have risen up in arms. For this reason our compañeros have died
in the last 100 days of our war. For this reason, today we dedicate our best homage to
those heroes and martyrs of the Zapatista struggle, to the dead of eternity, who live in
us. For this reason, today we say again that we do not surrender, that we will not hand
over our arms, that there will be no peace until life is just and dignified, that we will not
stop fighting until all of the people of Mexico have democracy, freedom, justice, independence, dignified housing, well-paid work, health care and education. Until this is
accomplished our armed steps will continue and our flag will continue waving in the
Mexican mountains.

Greetings, brother and sister Zapatistas!
Death to the supreme government!
Viva the Zapatista National Liberation Army!

From the mountains of the Mexican Southeast,
Clandestine Revolutionary Indigenous Committee-General Command of the
   Zapatista National Liberation Army
Mexico, April 10, 1994

# VOTÁN ZAPATA LIVES IN OUR DEAD

[*La Jornada*, 4/11]
April 10, 1994

To the people of Mexico:
To the people and governments of the world:
To the national and international press:

Brothers and Sisters:

The Clandestine Revolutionary Indigenous Committee-General Command of the Zapatista National Liberation Army addresses you to speak its word.

In these moments, tens of thousands of men, women, children and old people, Indigenous Mexicans all of them, are meeting on hundreds of *ejidos*, ranches, and communities of the Mexican countryside. Our hands also reach the heart of asphalt. Together with these people, we are united in front of a tri-color flag, in whose center there is the image of an eagle devouring a serpent. We are united by our shared misery, by the collective oblivion into which we were relocated 501 years ago, by the useless death that we suffer from, by our lack of faces, by having our names stripped from us, by wagering our life and death on an unknown future. Together with all these people, we are brought together by a collective desire in front of this flag: to change, once and for all, this sky and soil, which is now oppressed. To do this, we, the nameless and the faceless, the self-called "professionals in hope," the most mortal of all "transgressors of injustice," those of us who are mountains, those who walk in the night, those who are without voice in the palaces, who are the foreigners in their own land, who are eternally dying, who are the dispossessed of history, who are without a country and without a tomorrow, those of the tender fury, those of the unmasked truth, those of the long night of disdain, those men and women of truth... The smallest... The best... We must open again the door of your filial heart that you can receive our words.

We must speak truth from our mouths; we must put our heart in our hands. Brothers and sisters, we want you to know who is behind us, who directs us, who walks in our feet, who dominates our heart, who rides in our words, who lives in our dead.

We want you to know the truth, brothers and sisters, and it is like this:

From the very beginning of that long night in which we died, according to our most ancient grandparents, there was someone who collected our pain and our oblivion. There was a man who, his words coming from far away, came to our mountain and spoke with the language of the true men and women. His walk was, and was not, of these lands. In the mouths of our dead, in the voice of the wise elders, his words walked towards our heart. There were, and still are, brothers and sisters, those who are and are not the seed of this soil, who came to the mountain, dying, to live again, brother and sisters. Those who lived lived by his heart dying from this walk, his own but foreign, when he made his house in the mountain of the nighttime roof. His name was and is of many things appointed. His tender word waits and walks in our pain. He is, and is not, of these lands: Votán Zapata, guardian and heart of the people.

270

Votán Zapata, light from afar, came and was born here in our land. Votán Zapata, the appointed name again, always among our people. Votán Zapata, timid fire who lived 501 years in our death. Votán Zapata, name that changes, faceless man, tender light that gives us shelter. Coming, Votán Zapata came. Death was always with us. Dying, hope died. Coming, came Votán Zapata. Name without name, Votán Zapata watched in Miguel, walked in José María, was Vincente, was named in Benito, flew in a bird, mounted in Emiliano, shouted in Francisco, visited Pedro. Dying, he lived, named without name, in our land. Name without name, living, came Votán Zapata to our land. Speaking, his word fell into our mouths. Coming, he is. Votán Zapata, guardian and heart of the people.

He is and is not all in us... He is underway... Votán Zapata, guardian and heart of the mountain... Us... Votán, guardian and heart of the people. He is one and many. None and all. Living, he comes. Votán Zapata, guardian and heart of the people.

This is the truth, brothers and sisters. You should know it. He will never die again in our life, and in our death he lives now and forever. Votán, guardian and heart of the people. Without name he is named, face without face, all and none, one and many, living dead. Votán, guardian and heart of the people. Tapacamino bird, always in front of us. Nothing walks behind us. Votán, guardian and heart of the people.

He took a name in our existence without name. He took the face of those without faces. He is the sky in the mountains. Votán Guardian and heart of the people. And in our unnameable, faceless path, he took a name in us: Zapatista National Liberation Army.

With this new name, the nameless are named. With this flag gagging our faces, all of us have faces again. With this name, the unnameable is named: Votán Zapata, guardian and heart of the people.

The Zapatista National Liberation Army. Tender Fury that is armed. An unnameable name. Unjust peace is transformed into war. Death that is born. Anguish made into hope. Pain cries. Quiet shout. Our own present for an unknown future. Everything for everyone, nothing for us. The unnamed, us, the always dead. Us, foolish dignity, forgotten corner of our country. Us, Zapatista National Liberation Army. Us, black and red flag beneath the tri-color eagle. Us, the red star finally in our sky, never the only star, but one more, the smallest. Us, only a look and a voice. Us, Zapatista National Liberation Army. Us, Votán, guardian and heart of the people.

This is the truth brothers and sisters. This is where we come from. This is where we are going. Living, he comes. Dying, death lives. Votán Zapata, father and mother, brother and sister, son and daughter, large and small, us, we are coming...

Receive our truth with a dancing heart. Zapata lives, for now and forever, in these lands.

Greetings, fellow Mexicans!

Greetings, campesinos of this country!

Greetings, Indigenous people of all countries!

Greetings, Zapatista combatants!

Zapata, living he comes!

Dying, he lives!

Viva Zapata!

Democracy!

Freedom!
Justice!

From the mountains of the Mexican Southeast
Clandestine Revolutionary Indigenous Committee-General Command of the Zapatista National Liberation Army.

# Morelos Declaration, Tradition of Campesino Struggle

[*La Jornada*, 4/13]
April 10, 1994

To the signers of the Morelos Declaration [Declaración Morelense]:
Attention: Lieutenant Colonel Estanislao Tapia Sánchez:

From The Clandestine Revolutionary Indigenous Committee-General Command of the Zapatista National Liberation Army, Mexico

Brothers and Sisters:

We have received the historical document called the Morelos Declaration, sent out March 27, 1994 to the Mexican territory in struggle.

We, small and forgotten men and women, have seen how your words open our heart with truth and dignity. In the greatest tradition of campesino Mexican struggle, the Morelos Declaration follows the word of free dignity of the Plan de Ayala and the Plan de Cerro Prieto which, in different times, were put forth by our greatest historical leader and supreme general, Emiliano Zapata, and General Rubén Jaramillo. For that, we want you to accept the military ranks that our Army truly recognizes.

Our walk is lightened and our flag flies higher when we read your words of support for our Declaration of the Lacandona Jungle. For years, the supreme government, which is now headed by the usurper in the National Palace, has strangled in jail and blood the just word of all of the campesinos and the Indians together. We have been dispossessed of land and water; even the air no longer belongs to us. Our death is mute in these days. We die by dying, Zapata and Jaramillo, in the Salinista reforms of Article 27 of the Constitution. Hope walks without rest, hope that our people have left to us, hope to live and govern ourselves. Our strides are strange on our first soil. Any foreign stride would offend our earth. Lying papers stain our legitimate history. Our dignity is imprisoned in statues and museums. Foreign vacations take our voice, and their poison kills our words of truth. We have been alone, far from our people, and forgotten to each other. Our death was deaf to the ears of the poor life that lives in us.

The two-faced ones thought that they had forever silenced our shouts. They thought, the usurpers of the truth and givers of darkness, that our dead were already dead. They were already celebrating our defeat and their victory, in the arrogant loneliness of their palaces. Their lies danced on the trampled truth. The world looked without looking. The country and our hope were in a corner. Nothing moved inside of so much oppression. Silence died, living in silence.

But in the absence of anything happening, our path led through nights and mountains. Tender was the care we took with our fierce word. In near-silence we spoke. The night was patient; a *compañera*, a lover and an accomplice. Small, we grew, and again we were new. Our path had good direction, it was mute and coming, it was. For 10 years it was silent; broken hope slowly maturing without speaking; only our word spoke.

In the dawn of the year, we without names had a new name, we without faces had a face. Emiliano Zapata, our father, gave us his last name. Our brother was the armed example made by Emiliano Zapata. Our child Zapata asked us for a new future. A flag is what clothes our war path. Emiliano Zapata, of the soil of our land, is the dignity of our history, the light of our night, and always the clean morning of our hope.

Brothers and sisters, the evil government is still deaf to our voice. Other voices are needed to open its ears. Your words make strong our shouts.

Viva Emiliano Zapata!

Death to the supreme government!

Greetings, brother and sister Zapatistas and Jaramillistas of Morelos!

Democracy!

Justice!

Freedom!

Respectfully,

From the mountains of the Mexican Southeast,

Clandestine Revolutionary Indigenous Committee-General Command of the
    Zapatista National Liberation Army

April, 1994


# THE STORY OF DURITO AND THE DEFEAT OF NEOLIBERALISM

*[This story was written by Subcommander Marcos for a 10 year-old girl who sent him a drawing.]*

[*La Jornada*, 4/11]
**April 10, 1994**

To Mariana Moguel:

From: Insurgent Subcommander Marcos

Subcommander Mariana Moguel:

I greet you with respect and congratulate you for the new rank acquired with your drawing. Permit me to tell you a story which, perhaps, you will understand someday. It is the story of...

## DURITO

I am going to tell you a story that came to me the other day. It is the story of a small beetle who wears glasses and smokes a pipe. I met him one day as I was looking for tobacco to smoke, and could not find any. Suddenly, on one side of my hammock, I saw that a bit of tobacco had fallen and formed a small trail. I followed it to see where my tobacco was, and to see who the hell had taken it and was spilling it. A few meters away, behind a rock, I found a beetle sitting at a small typewriter, reading some papers and smoking a diminutive pipe.

"Ahem, ahem," I said, so that the beetle would notice my presence, but he paid me no heed.

Then I said:

"Listen, that tobacco is mine."

The beetle took off his glasses, looked me up and down, and told me, quite irritatedly:

"Please, captain, I beg you not to interrupt me. Don't you realize that I am studying?"

I was a bit surprised and was going to give him a kick, but I calmed myself and sat down to one side to wait for him to finish studying. In a little while, he gathered up his papers, put them away in the desk, and, chewing his pipe, said to me:

"Well, now, what can I do for you, captain?"

"My tobacco," I responded.

"Your tobacco?" he said to me. "You want me to give you a little?"

I started to get pissed off, but the little beetle handed me the bag of tobacco with its little foot, and added:

"Don't be angry, captain. Please understand that tobacco cannot be found here, and I had to take some of yours."

I calmed myself. I liked the beetle, and I said to him, "Don't worry about it. I have some more over there."

"Hmm," he answered.

"And you, what is your name?" I asked him.

"Nebuchanedzar," he said, and continued, "But my friends call me Durito. You can call me Durito, captain."

I thanked him and asked him what it was that he was studying.

"I'm studying neoliberalism and its strategy of domination for Latin America," he told me.

"And what good is that to a beetle?" I asked him.

He replied, very annoyed: "What good is it? I have to know how long your struggle is going to last, and whether you are going to win. In addition, a beetle should care enough to study the situation of the world in which it lives, don't you think, captain?"

"I don't know," I said. "Why do you want to know how long our struggle will last and whether we are going to win?"

"Well, nothing has been understood," he told me, putting on his glasses and lighting his pipe. After exhaling a mouthful of smoke, he continued:

"To know how long we beetles are going to have to take care that you do not smash us with your boots."

"Ah!" I said.

"Hmm," He said.

"And to what conclusion have you come in your study?" I asked him.

He took out the papers from the desk and began to leaf through them.

"Hmm...hmm," he said every so often as he looked through them.

After having finished, he looked at my eyes and said, "You are going to win."

"I already knew that," I told him. I added, "But how long will it last?"

"A long time," he said, sighing with resignation.

"I already knew that, too... Don't you know exactly how long?" I asked.

"It cannot be known exactly. We have to take into account many things: the objective conditions, the ripeness of the subjective conditions, the correlation of forces, the crisis of imperialism, the crisis of socialism, etcetera, etcetera."

"Hmm," I said.

"What are you thinking about, captain?"

"Nothing," I answered. "Well, Mr. Durito, I have to go. It was my pleasure to have met you. You may take all of the tobacco that you want, whenever you like."

"Thank you, captain. You can be informal with me if you like." [In Spanish, this is an invitation to use the familiar form of address, *tu*, instead of the formal *usted.*]

"Thank you, Durito. I am now going to give orders to my *compañeros* that it is prohibited to step on beetles. I hope that helps."

"Thank you, captain. Your order will be of much use to us."

"Whatever happens, take much care, because my young men are very distracted, and they do not always look where they are putting their feet."

"I will do so, captain."

"See you later."

"See you later. Come whenever you like, and we will talk."

"I wil,l" I told him, and went back to the headquarters.

That is all Mariana. I hope to know you personally someday and be able to trade ski masks and drawings. All right.

Health and other colors, because on the ones that you used, the ink must have run out.

Insurgent Subcommander Marcos,
Mountains of the Mexican Southeast.
April, 1994

# THE EZLN PROMISES JUSTICE

[*La Jornada*]
April 12, 1994

To the people of Mexico:
To the people and governments of the world:

Brothers and Sisters:

The Clandestine Revolutionary Indigenous Committee-General Command of the Zapatista National Liberation Army addresses you to denounce the following:

**First:** On the day of April 7, 1994, as he led a clearing of land for the planting, the *compañero* Francisco Mena López was cowardly assassinated by armed ranchers. The crime was committed near the Venustiano Carranza *ejido*, Altamirano township, Chiapas.

**Second:** Francisco Mena López was killed from two shots, one to the head, and the other to the mouth, both of them from a .38-special revolver.

**Third:** The ranchers named Arturo Espinoza, Juan Espinoza, and Jorge Espinoza, owners of the El Miradero Ranch, Altamirano township, Chiapas, are accused of this attack.

**Fourth:** The *compañero* Francisco Mena López was, at the time of his death, leader of the local committee of our EZLN, and had been threatened with death by ranchers of Altamirano before January 1, 1994, for his participation in the struggle for agrarian justice.

**Fifth:** After the assassination, the now-accused took flight and hid in the properties of their accomplices, ranchers of Altamirano, to escape the Zapatista action of justice. As of today, they are still fugitives.

**Sixth:** With the complicity of the governmental authorities, the arrogant ranchers of Altamirano have told the lie that the Espinoza family has been kidnapped by elements belonging to our EZLN. Accustomed to exercising arbitrariness and arrogance, the ranchers and the government think that our EZLN conducts itself with the same injustice that we fight against. They try to injure the prestige of our forces among the population, and a good number of small property holders want to end up breaking the already-weak process of dialogue and begin a military action against us.

**Seventh:** The EZLN, as opposed to the evil government, does not carry out arbitrary detentions. The CCRI-CG of the EZLN has taken up the case in the Zapatista tribunal of justice so that they may carry out an investigation and allocate responsibility to those responsible for this crime. No Zapatista judicial action will be carried out until the investigation underway has real results.

**Eighth:** We reiterate that we are not affected by poor argumentations that try to justify a military action against us. We are prepared to respond to any attack, and to resist the aggression that the supreme government prepares, to the last person.

**Ninth:** The process of consultation continues to be suspended. We will not speak of peace while the signs of war continue.

**Tenth:** The EZLN reiterates to the people of Mexico their commitment to conduct themselves with dignity, truth, and honesty, three weapons that the usurper government will never be able to acquire.

Respectfully,

From the mountains of the Mexican Southeast,

Clandestine Revolutionary Indigenous Committee-General Command of the Zapatista National Liberation Army

Mexico, April 11, 1994

# 11. The Consultations

## The EZLN Orders a Partial Deactivation of the Red Alert in its Territories

[*La Jornada*, 4/22]
April 20, 1994

To the people of Mexico:
To the people and governments of the world:
To the national and international press:

Brothers and Sisters:

The Clandestine Revolutionary Indigenous Committee-General Command of the Zapatista National Liberation Army addresses you to declare the following:

**First:** The EZLN recognizes the honest and dedicated efforts by the Commissioner for Peace and Reconciliation in Chiapas, Mr. Manuel Camacho Solís, and of the mediator, Bishop Samuel Ruiz García, to create conditions favorable for the continuation of the dialogue, whose objective is to achieve a just and dignified peace. In the last few days, both the commissioner and the mediator have worked on the solution of several obstacles that oppose the peace process. The EZLN salutes this true willingness of these two Mexicans.

**Second:** The EZLN salutes the liberation of some civil prisoners, unjustly accused of belonging to our troops, and sees in it a good signal for the beginning of the continuation of the dialogue for a just and dignified peace.

**Third:** With respect to this, the CCRI-CG of the EZLN orders the partial deactivation of the red alert in its territories and the return of part of its troops to their communities and *ejidos,* beginning April 23, 1994.

**Fourth:** If this climate, favorable to dialogue, is maintained, the EZLN will restart the consultation with its bases, in a progressive manner, starting with the least vulnerable territories, as soon as possible.

**Fifth:** The EZLN reiterates its real desire for a political solution to the just demands that animate its struggle, and it salutes the sincere effort of civil society and Mexican personalities to find dignified solutions to the large national problems through reason, and not through force.

Holding high the popular demands of freedom, justice and democracy for all Mexicans. Freedom!
Justice!
Democracy!

Respectfully,
Clandestine Revolutionary Indigenous Committee-General Command of the Zapatista National Liberation Army.
General Headquarters, The mountains of the Mexican Southeast, Chiapas Mexico, April, 1994

# WE ARE SURROUNDED

[*La Jornada*, 4/22]
April 21, 1994

To the national news weekly *Proceso*:
To the national newspaper *La Jornada*:
To the national newspaper *El Financiero*:
To the local newspaper of San Cristóbal de las Casas *Tiempo*:
To the national and international press:

Gentlemen:

We hereby communicate to you about those freed, about red alerts, and about consultations.

We are touched by the stupidity of those who declare, with solemnity and without reservation, that we are purposefully delaying the re-initiation of the dialogue. They say we are looking for pretexts and trying to extend the solution to the conflict. To reach a solution, perhaps we should greet with complacence the assassination of our *compañero* in the "peaceful" lands of Altamirano; perhaps we are pleased by the arbitrary detentions of civilians carried out by the military troops in Ocosingo? Maybe it is the federal troops and the government, and not us, who are surrounded; perhaps we enjoy not having food or medicine, nor any way of acquiring them; perhaps we are enthused by the inexorable asphyxiation of the civilian population of our territory (to whom the supreme government impedes the arrival of humanitarian aid; the federal troops, unhappy with their duties, argue that the food is not for the civilians, but is meant only to "fatten the little Marcoses"); perhaps our doubt about the supposed exit of governmental troops from the area is without foundation; perhaps the nighttime airplane is ours (the Zapatista Air Force?) and is only watching to see that nothing happens to us?

I am sorry to inform you, brilliant analysts, that we are surrounded. However, in order to not contradict you, we have resolved to follow in the footsteps of "the lords of the Central

American guerrilla" and follow the example of a "foreigner," "transgressor of the law," and a "professional in violence" from the days of yore called José María Morelos y Pavón. About this man and his troops, the "legal" General Félix María Calleja del Rey wrote:

"If the constancy and activity of the defenders of Cuautla had morality, and were led by a just cause, they would deserve a distinguished place in our history some day. Stretched by our troops and afflicted by necessity, they express happiness in all of the events. They bury their cadavers with peals of celebration in their glorious death, and they celebrate with clamor, dances, and drunkenness the return from their frequent trips, whatever the particular success happens to be, imposing pain or death on anyone who speaks of disgraces or surrender..." (recited in the book *Siglo de Caudillos: Biografía política de México* (1810-1910) [*A Century of Caudillos: A Political Biography of Mexico* (1810-1910)]. Tusquets Editorial. February, 1994.) The author is suspected of being "an apologist for violence," Enrique Krauze, who I read with the same, and sane, critical spirit with which he sees us).

In sum, we confirm that this is "the last Central American guerrilla group," and we celebrate 100 days of military encirclement and 112 days of war with a great dance to which, of course, you are not invited (rigorous-evening-gown-ski-mask-etiquette-we-reserve-the-right-to-limit-admission). There will be no dinner, and not because we are surrounded, but because we are on diets. The Zapatista orchestra has plenty of guitars with no strings, tambourines, harmonicas and one or two violins. Its repertoire is one of "delicious foreignism," and includes the Marcha de Zacatecas and the one that goes:

"For a bit, two reales
for a sergeant, a tostón;
for my general Morelos
I give all of my heart."

That is all. I promise to send the chronicle for the "Social" section. All right.

Health and history, remember it points towards the future.
From the mountains of the Mexican Southeast
Insurgent Subcommander Marcos

# TO THE WORKERS OF THE REPUBLIC

[*La Jornada*, 5/2]
May 1, 1994

To the people of Mexico:
To the people and governments of the world:
To the national and international press:

Brothers and Sisters:

The Clandestine Revolutionary Indigenous Committee-General Command of the Zapatista National Liberation Army directs itself to you to declare the following:

Today, May 1, 1994, we celebrate one more day for the workers. All over the world, rural and urban workers celebrate their rebellion against exploitation and reaffirm their aspirations for a more just world. In Mexico this is a day of struggle. Ever since the evil government, which now oppresses us from the Zócalo in Mexico City, usurped the just demands of the Flores Magón brothers, a chain now strangles the best of the Mexican workers. False and corrupt leaders, some for more than nine decades, traffic in the pain of the Mexican workers. They are the sustenance of the supreme government that now offers our history and our soil for foreign money. The struggle of the workers for organizational independence has revealed the triple alliance between the evil government, the corrupt leaders, and the powerful men of money.

Businesses of evil wealth have a new etiquette. Another mask hides our pain from our own eyes. A new name has been given to injustice, to slavery, to the usurpation: neoliberalism.

The workers that build this country bleed from three wounds. The powerful bleed them with unjust salaries, humiliations, and threats. The heads of the great central government unions bleed the workers with extortions, beatings, and death. Those who sell the country bleed the workers with the dispatches of usurpation, writing the laws that their treason dictates.

The workers die three times in the factory for the history of the country. They die of poverty because they are not paid fairly according to their work. They die of humiliation because their words of rebellion are silenced by the treachery of those who claim to represent them. They die of slavery because the evil government ignores their will and their efforts.

The Mexican workers struggle three times on land and on asphalt. They struggle for justice so that there can be bread and truth in their houses and on their tables. They struggle also to speak and walk freely and to not bequeath shame to their children. They struggle for democracy because it is their power to transform matter, and also their power to govern and to govern themselves.

The future has three lives that we all desire for the whole country. The life of their own strength in their brothers and sisters in recognized labor. The life of the workers and campesinos, hand in hand. The life of their embrace that includes all of the people, so they can march together again with a new, good direction.

Faceless, the worker lives and dies three times. Without a clean face because of the hunger that dirties it. Without a free face because of the treachery that kills it. Without a true face because of a will usurped.

They die three times, they struggle three times, they live three times. Faceless, they walk three times, those who make the riches of the country into something located, something measured, something changed.

Brothers and sisters:

From another history, the same and different, another faceless being looks with hope on this day. From the mountains of the last corner of Mexico, faceless hope, tender voice and fire walking alone greet the workers.

Three times the false masks which rob us today must fall.

Injustice at work and in pay must fall. The treachery that leaves us speechless must fall. The government that usurps our will must fall.

Justice! Freedom! Democracy! These are the three keys to the three chains. Justice in the right to a dignified job and to be well paid. Freedom in the right to organize ourselves with independence from the powerful and their spokespeople. Democracy in the right to demand that the government obey us in its mandate.

This is what we, the smallest of these lands ask for. We want this: three rights, three struggles, three suns. A tomorrow of a new Mexico.

Mexican workers of the city and the country:

Let your voice run together with ours. Let your shout sound strong and hard on this soil. Accept this hand that your smallest brothers and sisters offer you. Three forces should unite their paths: the force of the workers, the force of the campesinos, the popular force. With these three forces there will be nothing to detain us.

Our blood is already losing itself in history. Let the brothers and sisters of the machine not let their brothers and sisters of the country die in vain. Let all of the people unite. Let the curse that divides not come again to our skies.

Receive our voice, which, although far away, says: "Greetings, workers of the sea and of the land! The Zapatistas follow you in their struggles! With you there will be a country and future for all some day! Without you, night will continue to rule these lands!"

Freedom!

Justice!

Democracy!

Respectfully,

Clandestine Revolutionary Indigenous Committee-General Command of the Zapatista National Liberation Army

General Barracks, Mountains of the Mexican Southeast, Chiapas, Mexico

May 1, 1994

# INTERVIEW WITH THE CLANDESTINE REVOLUTIONARY INDIGENOUS COMMITTEE

[Transcribed from the original tape]
May 11, 1994

Interviewers: Eugenio Aguilera (Nightcrawlers Anarchist Black Cross), Ana Laura Hernández (*Amor y Rabia*/Mexico), Gustavo Rodríguez (*Amor y Rabia*/Mexico), Pablo Salazar Devereaux (Haitian Information Bureau)

*Q: You are members of the regional committee of the General Command?*

CC: The Clandestine Revolutionary Indigenous Committee. Yes.

*Q: The Tzetzal Committee?*

CC: Tzetzal? Yes.

*Q: What is your name? Or what name do you want to give?*

CC: Manuel

*Q: Manuel, what is your role in the Committee?*

M: What do we do in the Committee?

*Q: No, but, do you also have a military rank, are you a commander, or is it simply civilian work that is carried out by the Committee?*

M: Yes, civilian work. The political and economic work.

*Q: What are you specifically responsible for, as part of the Clandestine Committee?*

M: Well, seeing what goes on in the region. If there are any problems within the towns, the communities.

*Q: What type of problems?*

M: Whatever type of problem that may arise. Then we go around as the Clandestine Revolutionary Indigenous Committee to resolve these problems.

*Q: Are you also responsible for finances?*

M: Yes, to raise funds in the community, as well as throughout the zone.

*Q: How does that function? Do you charge taxes to the civilian population? How does the raising of funds take place?*

M: Well, in the civilian population, no. Only, also from some farmers. What's being done now is that there are some farmers, or ranchers, actually, who come to talk to us, who want, for example, to take some livestock. So we'll say: Yes, you can, if you leave some money. No, no it's not like a tax so much as a collaboration with the EZLN.

*Q: And the farmers collaborate, or are there farmers who are against the EZLN, who are in favor of the government and things like that?*

M: Up until now, no. They have always been...supporting as well.

*Q: They're not large landowners?*

M: No they're not large landowners. They are small.

*Q: And many of them are Tzetzales, Tzotziles...*

M: They also speak Tzetzal.

*Q: How long have you been in the EZLN?*

M: Ten years.

*Q: Have you always been in the Clandestine Revolutionary Indigenous Committee or did you first enter into the militias?*

M: Yes, first we entered into the militias.

*Q: Were you an insurgent?*

M: Me? No.

*Q: You were never in the...*

M: No. I'm in the militia.

*Q: You always worked in the communities?*

M: Yes, we've always done work here with these towns where you have to look at whatever problems occur.

*Q: You are from here? You are from this ejido, this zone?*

M: No. I'm from another town.

*G: Far from here?*

M: Yes, about five hours from here to there.

*Q: I also wanted to ask you, the work that the Clandestine Committees do in the regions, is there also, for example, security of the ejidos, where there are problems like in the case of alcoholism, people that drink, that don't respect the laws of the EZLN regarding alcohol, or when you find that a man is beating his wife or their kids? Do you have to act in these cases, do you have to intervene?*

M: Yes, that yes, here inside the EZLN we don't permit that *compañeros* go around getting drunk, and even if they're not members of the EZLN. We don't permit alcoholism. Yes, that is prohibited throughout the zone.

*Q: And as I was saying in the case of a campesino who hits his wife? What do you in this case? If there were such a case?*

M: Yes, depending, we go out as a Committee to see about these problems among the people. Then the people decide what kind of problem it is, and the nature of the problem. And if the people say so, we'll punish. Then the people are the ones to decide. It's not just up to the Committee. We talk as a Committee. As a Committee we go to see that this is OK. If they can be punished in this way. There it remains.

*Q: What means do you use? Do you fine people?*

M: Yes, a fine. What's being done now is that if a *compañero* has a drink we fine him 10,000 pesos. Or give him a job to do. Cutting wood or other things. That's what's been done in the past.

*Q: We interviewed Major Benito, as well as asking others in charge. They told us that in the Army there didn't exist laws against homosexuality but that it was the Committees, due to tradition, that don't permit for there to be homosexuals. How do you understand... As a Committee, why don't you permit it? And if there are lesbians or gays, what methods do you take...how do you...do you punish them? Can they be gay freely? Are they expelled from the community for that? How do you manage this?*

[Another member of the CCRI answers the question: Joaquín]

J: Well, if there's a *compañero* who, as you've asked about alcoholism, also if someone gets drunk or begins to fight with his woman. Well, we...are going to call to attention [to the fact] that a *compañero* is doing this. To make it clear...or to make them understand that it can't be this way. Because it shouldn't be that you will do whatever you want. Even if it's not their wife but another *compa*. We have to make it so that they have to obey, have to carry out an order that we give.

We are going to criticize...conduct a self-criticism. This is what we are doing. Some, who have a very grave problem, where you have to punish—well, the punishment is not very severe. Nothing more than so that the people will see. Since we are the Zapatisa Army we have to demonstrate our heart in the struggle, not fuck with *compañeros*. It's to call to attention—to tell someone how a certain job can get done, that people shouldn't be getting drunk, better, there's time.... We are trying to carry out collective work. That is what we are explaining to the *compañeros*. That they shouldn't be getting drunk...

*Q: Your name is...?*

J: Joaquín

*Q: How long have you been [in the CCRI]?*

J: It's been about 10 years now.

*Q: Well, the question I was asking, when you responded about alcoholism and about how people are punished when someone mistreats their woman or their children. But I had asked the* compañero *Manuel... I don't know if you understand the question...homosexuals.... They were telling us that the Army doesn't have any law against that. They respect it, but that the ones who, in fact, don't permit it are the Committees. It is because of the Indigenous tradition. In the communities there is no tradition of homosexuals; that is of men who like men, who go with men and not with women. Or women who go with women and not with men. Therefore since you are members of the Committee, I want to ask you: In this case, if this exists, is there punishment? How do you proceed? Is it prohibited?*

[They talk to each other in their native language.]

J: Well, what you are asking about, well, the law...like ourselves who work throughout the zone...this can be decided in the communities...if they have their plan, they have their...an agreement, in each town. A *compañera* who wants to get married... has to decide to do so...and if she doesn't want to we are not going to oblige her if she....

*Q: Yes but, the case that I was talking about was, if there is a* compañera *who is a lesbian or a* compañero *who is gay—who doesn't like women but likes men or a woman who doesn't like men but likes women ...the Army explained to us that they, for example, don't have any law against this. But, that the Committees, depending on the region, have laws, or actually agreements, that don't permit it. So, the case that I'm speaking of, for example, if a man likes other men, if he goes with another man, if he has sexual relations with another man, has sex with another man. Or a woman that doesn't like men, but likes other women and has a relationship with a woman. Is this punished? Are they expelled from the community? How do you proceed in this sense?*

[More discussion in their native language.]

*Q: Do you not understand what I'm saying?*

M: Yes...this... We are not really familiar with that. Because here in the region, throughout the zone, this almost does not exist. Therefore we don't really know about this.

*Q: It almost doesn't exist?*

M: Better said, it doesn't exist. Maybe in other places, but, around here we're not familiar with it.

*Q: Then you don't know what you would do...*

M: No, nothing more than as the *compañero* said, what happens to these people is that... We see it depends on the man or woman. If a woman wants a man, that is on her part, if the man also wants it....

*Q: Since it doesn't exist here...no law exists against it, because it hasn't happened?*

M: No, it doesn't exist because it hasn't happened.

*Q: The work that Joaquín does, I imagine that it is similiar to yours. To try to raise and collect funds, to try and economically help the EZLN in their regions?*

M: Yes, yes.

*Q: Do you also dedicate yourselves to recruitment in the regions where you work?*

J&M: Yes, we also do that.

*Q: You recruit* compañeros *and* compañeras *in the towns?*

M: Yes, it's up to the towns. If they want to join our struggle. They have to report that they want to visit our community. If we go to visit it's because a *compañero* wants us to talk with the people. We are going to meet with all the people—to call out all of the people to explain what the struggle is about. Because there are *compañeros* in other communities who don't even know how the struggle began, and now the struggle has been clarified. Or they are seeking out the Committees because they want to speak to them. If he comes, we are going to reach an agreement with all the *compañeros* of the Committees. Not only is one Committee in charge, but there has to be an agreement between all the *compañeros* of the various Committees. And all the *compañeros* of the Committee say you have to go to that town because we need you to fulfill your responsibilities, to get to know those *compañeros*, to discuss and see how the struggle is going there. That is the work that we do.

*Q: For example, in towns that are not like these villages and towns here in the liberated territories—towns like Ochuc? For example...where there are a lot of people who don't understand the struggle...who are on the side of the Federal Army. Are there* compañeros *there as well who do work as Clandestine Committees?*

M: Yes.

*Q: The only thing being that they have to be careful...*

M: Yes, they have to be more careful because it's not very close to here. In various places there are *compañeros* from the Clandestine Committees. Then there are various areas where the Committees can't reach because you can't reach there, you can't do it.

Q: *In San Cristóbal, for example, do you have Committees?*

M: Yes.

Q: *Because there are zones, especially colonies like Hormiga, that are almost a majority Tzotzil, Tzeltal. Do you work within these communitites in San Cristóbal?*

M: Possibly yes, I don't know in which places... But yes, it exists. The same in Ocosingo, everywhere.

Q: *Are you working in other states outside of Chiapas as Committees?*

M&J: [They speak to each other in their native tongue.] We can't speak about that...for security reasons.

Q: *OK. Thank you; that's all that I have... I don't know if the other* compas *have questions?*

Q: *To follow up on the other interviews we did with the* compañeras *and* compañeros, *they all told us about the equality that women have within the Zapatista Army. But, we also discussed with them the fact that in the communities this equality hasn't been completely arrived at yet. I imagine that you want this equality to extend to the civilian population.*

M: Uh-huh.

Q: *What are the methods that you use so that the* compañeros *accept this equality for the* compañeras, *the same that exists within the EZLN? Has it been difficult, does it take a lot of work?*

M: Well, yes. Right now it's been more work, it has required more work. There are *compañeros* in the towns who need to have things explained more about our struggle so that they will understand, so that they will begin to understand that there needs to be equality. So as a committee we struggle more so that they will understand more about the organization.

Q: *What is the position of the Clandestine Committees regarding abortion?*

M: I don't understand too well.

Q: *Is it prohibited by the CCRI that in the towns, is abortion permited...abortion being when a* compañera *in the town is pregnant but doesn't want to have more children, but she wasn't taking care of herself [on the pill] and she became pregnant. If she wants to end her pregnancy, if she doesn't want to continue her pregnancy...is it permited or is it the same as in federal territory, outside of Chiapas where abortion is not permitted?*

M: Yes, that depends on the conscience of the *compañera* or the *compañero*. If they come to an agreement and they want to cancel that, have an abortion, that's that. In those times it depends on the *compa*..

Q: *But, it's a personal decision, you don't get involved in that?*

M: No, not us. There are no laws against it. No, we are not going to give an order, we are explaining, educating... If someone wants to plan...but it's a question of whether they want to, it's up to them.

Q: *You have to respect the decision of the woman.*

M: There it is. Yes, in this case, now, the *compañeros* and *compañeras* are understanding the situation here with us—we were very fucked. So now it's being limited, pregnacies among the woman in each town. There has been a little advance regarding this. Some women have five or six children and now as we've explained, it depends on the father, whether or not he can sustain so many—well then, no more. But we also don't require it either.

Q: *The Revolutionary Women's Law says the woman has the right to choose.*

M: Right. She has to say, she has to choose.

Q: *Thank you* compañeros, *it was very interesting.*

# INTERVIEW WITH SUBCOMMANDER MARCOS

[Transcribed from the original tape]
Wednesday, May 11, 1994
Somewhere in the Lacandona Jungle

Interviewers: Eugenio Aguilera (Nightcrawlers Anarchist Black Cross), Ana Laura Hernández (*Amor y Rabia*/Mexico), Gustavo Rodríguez (*Amor y Rabia*/Mexico), Pablo Salazar Devereaux (Haitian Information Bureau)

Q: *Much has been written and said about the Zapatistas, but little is concretely known about your ideology. There are many who are trying to claim your struggle as their own. The Maoists say that you are Maoists, the Trotskyists say that you are Trotskyists, and the list goes on...*

M: The anarchists say that we are anarchists...

Q: *No, we have never been able to say for sure [laughter]. We need proof. However, you have insisted that you are Zapatistas. Even now we remember the words of an EZLN Major who affirmed: "We are not Marxists, nor are we guerrillas. We are Zapatistas and we are an army." Anti-authoritarianism is felt in each of your words and actions, in the manner in which you are organized, in the structure of the Clandestine Committees, in the collective participation [within the EZLN]. In Mexico, the only precedents for your actions and attitudes go back precisely to those whose names you constantly evoke: Zapata and Magón. Has Magonismo permeated your ideology?*

M: This is a question?

Q: *[laughter]. No, a presentation.*

**M:** I thought it was a speech.

*Q: No, no, a presentation.*

**M:** Well then, I'm going to explain. The EZLN was born having as points of reference the political-military organizations of the guerrilla movements in Latin America during the '60s and '70s: That is to say, political-military structures with the central aim of overthrowing a regime and the taking of power by the people in general.

When the first group of the EZLN arrived here, in the jungles of Chiapas, it was a very small group with this political-military structure that I am talking about. It began to adapt itself to the surroundings, to try to survive—that is to say, to permeate the territory, to make it survivable. But, above all, it began to forge in the combatant, in that initial group of combatants, the physical and ideological strength needed for the guerrilla process. I mean by this that the mountains served as a school for cadres, inflexible and constant, day and night. But things were taking shape. In this period there were no cameras, there were no recorders, there was no press, nor were there military actions. The only thing that lets you stay in the mountains and endure is hope, because there isn't any payment. I'm not referring to monetary payment, of course there never was any of that, but to some moral reward, to something that would serve as some sort of assurance that it is all worth it.

Ten years ago, we were clinging to the hope that everything that we were learning, with much suffering and many problems, was going to have results someday. In that period, there was a double learning process: the learning process of the mestizos (the inhabitants of this area call everyone who lives in the city "mestizo") and the process of the Indigenous peoples. The process of the Indigenous people includes learning the very basics—to speak Spanish, the history of Mexico, reading and writing, basic notions of mathematics, geography, biology, chemistry—in all, everything that we mestizos have as our basic culture. And we, for our part, had to learn and understand not only the world view of the Indigenous peoples of this zone, but also learn a series of physical aptitudes that are not innate to the Indigenous peoples, but that they learn when they are small: to handle a machete, to carry large loads over long distances, to reduce their food intake to the minimum required—in this case corn and sugar.

In this interplay, this exchange, this give and take, we both went to the mountains changed. What I mean is that, for the Indigenous people, the mountains are something sacred, something special, something magical, and ultimately something terrible. No, the Indigenous peoples do not go to the mountains. In fact, when we entered the mountains, many of them feared that something would happen to them before they could accomplish anything. The mountains are the place of the dead, of the gods, of good gods and bad gods, and because of this there was nobody who had experienced, not even on their part, life in the mountains. The Indigenous people were only used to living in their villages, to going hunting, to searching for land where they could plant. We should talk about this "romantic vision," if you understand me, of guerrilla war, with its references to grandiose military actions: the taking of power and triumph, all of those things that could be references to the triumphant guerrilla wars of that era, the Cuban and Nicaraguan revolutions.

This environment brings you back to reality and makes you understand that all revolutions have a cost and only those who are willing to pay it can carry out the revolution. To begin with, at that time you had to be crazy or stupid to try to carry it out. I think that we were both stupid and crazy. There was nothing that would tell us that we were fine and that the venture was going to have a future or that it had a chance. There was the fact that we had tried to bring about change—not necessarily revolutionary change—by other methods and in different places. But all of our struggles, our struggles in the university, campesino struggles, workers' struggles, collided with the State, with Power. It is better to speak about Power, because there are places in which the action of the State is not perfectly definable as such, and it makes more sense to speak of Power—in this case, the Power of a dominant class that spreads to other areas—culture for example. Then you arrive at the conclusion, intuitively or scientifically, that another road is necessary, the road of armed struggle.

We then confronted the common belief that an armed revolution was possible in any country other than Mexico. That is to say, Mexico was considered the country of solidarity, but never the country of the revolution. When we proposed a revolution, we were considered heretics among the left. The left said that revolution wasn't Mexico's role, that we were too close to the United States, that the regime in Mexico resembled the European model, and that because of this a "revolutionary" change was only possible by electoral methods, by peaceful methods, or, in the most radical scenario, by insurrectional methods. This means that the unarmed masses, with broad mobilizations, would disrupt the economy and create a crisis in the State apparatus, which would then fall and a new government would take power. When we proposed a guerrilla war, an armed struggle, we broke with this tradition, a tradition that was very strong during that time. With what was happening in Nicaragua and what was beginning to happen in El Salvador, well... Similar things had always been happening there, but they were becoming more intense. The struggle in Guatemala was rejuvenating itself a second time, a third, a fourth. I don't know. Eventually someone said, "And why not here in Mexico?" Immediately, there was a sense of caution, of prudence, as if to say, "Not here; here our role is to help those peoples that are liberating themselves and only later, eventually, Mexico might aspire to revolution." The fact that we broke with this idea implies that we also broke with other theoretical schema.

We were always confronted with the mountains. Let's say we survived that first stage, that this first stage was, in effect, about two things: surviving and beginning our political work. In this initial political work, a connection began to take place between the proposals of the guerrilla group, the initial group of the EZLN, and the communities. This means that there are different expectations of the movement. On one hand, there were those who hoped that armed action would bring about a revolution and a change of power, in this case the fall of the governing party and the ascension of another party, but that in the end it would be the people who took power. On the other hand, there were the more immediate expectations of the Indigenous people here. For them, the necessity of armed struggle was more as a form of defense against groups of very violent, aggressive, and powerful ranchers. In addition, there was an approaching storm—no, let's not say approaching storm—as if there was a wall, a wall that was the same mountain that separated the jungle from the city and that separated the Indigenous peoples from political power.

It was this wall that permitted the EZLN to grow so scandalously without anyone realizing to what point it had grown. The Indigenous peoples realized the necessity of learning to defend themselves. They had weapons, but they used them only for hunting or to protect their homes from animals or thieves. Then, we found each other and we began to speak in two different languages, but in this common point of necessity of armed struggle a relationship began to develop. They needed military instruction, and we needed the support of a social base. And we thus tried to convince them of the necessity of a broader political project. That didn't occur until elements of the community entered the Army. In that moment the difference between combatant force and civilian force began to disappear, until it reached the point you see now, when whole communities are Zapatistas, when there is no line that separates the civilians from the Zapatistas.

Then, when this began to occur, there began a confrontation, a relationship of convenience, between two ways of making decisions. On one hand, there was the initial proposal of the EZLN: a completely undemocratic and authoritarian proposal, as undemocratic and authoritarian as an army can be, since an army is the most authoritarian thing in this world, and also the most absurd in that one single person can decide the life and death of his subordinates. On the other hand there was the Indigenous tradition that before the Conquest was a way of life, and that after the Conquest became their only way of surviving. In other words, the communities, isolated, cornered, saw themselves as obligated to defend themselves collectively, to live collectively, to govern themselves collectively.

Since the internal life of the communities was totally separated from national and local political forces, the important thing was the work done by the communities, and because of this, a collective government came about. No, it was always there: a way of making decisions in common about problems that affect the entire community. These decisions included decisions about work that had to be done in common, judicial problems at an internal level—because it isn't possible to appeal to the judicial power of the State. What I mean to say is that the isolation of the Indigenous communities provoked the development of another type of "state," a state to deal with the survival of the collective, of a democratic collective with these two characteristics: The leadership is collective and it is removable.

In any moment, if you hold a position in the community (first, the community has to have appointed you, independent of your political affiliation), the community can remove you. There isn't a fixed term that you have to complete. The moment that the community begins to see that you are failing in your duties, that you are having problems, they sit you down in front of the community and they begin to tell you what you have done wrong. You defend yourself and, finally, the community, the collective, the majority decides what they are going to do with you. Eventually, you will have to leave your position and another will take up your responsibilities.

So, on one hand, there is this form of organization. I'm going to make a reference so that you understand better—student assemblies. Student assemblies are better as forms of protest or for analyzing problems. In the case of the Indigenous communities, it is a way of life. On the other hand, we have the authoritarian form of the Army, of a political-military organization, but a military organization above all. One began to see a confrontation between these modes of decision-making until people from the communities began to join the EZLN and the Indigenous form of decision-making began to take precedence.

I want you to understand me; we didn't arrive and say, "It is necessary that the collective and democracy guide us." That isn't true, of course. This wasn't our conception. Our conception was vertical: "What is necessary is a group of strong men and women, with ideological and physical strength, with the resistance to carry out this task." Our conception was that we were few but of high quality. Well, I'm not saying that we were of that high quality, but we sure were few.

Finally, I can't say exactly when—it's not something that's planned—the moment arrived in which the EZLN had to consult the communities in order to make a decision. At first, we only asked if what we were doing was going to cause problems for the *compañeros*. And later, when we left the jungle and entered the mountains, we also entered the assemblies and discussions of the communities. A moment arrives in which you can't do anything without the approval of the people with whom you work. It was something understood by both parties: They understood that we wouldn't do anything without consulting them, and we understood that if we did anything without consulting them, we would lose them. And this flow, this increase of men and women who left the communities in order to enter the mountains, made us realize that we couldn't draw a solid line between combatant forces and civilian forces. Even geographically this line had broken down. There were military units that didn't live in the mountains but that instead lived in the communities and participated in communal labors. They gave military instruction, but they also participated in the work of the communities. When we reflect on this now it isn't a question of "us" and "them"—now "we" are the entire community. It was necessary to organize, to establish this collective authority alongside the absurdity of a vertical, authoritarian structure. Then it was possible to divide the process of making decisions. I mean by this that strategic decisions, important decisions, have to be made democratically, from below, not from above. If there is going to be an action or series of actions that are going to implicate the entire organization, the authority has to come from below. In this sense, even the Clandestine Revolutionary Indigenous Committee isn't able to make every decision. You could say that the EZLN is different because in most political-military organizations there is only one commander, and in the EZLN the Clandestine Committees are composed of 80 people, 100 people, 120 people or however many. But this is not the difference. The difference is that even the Clandestine Committees cannot make certain decisions, the most important decisions. They are limited to such a degree that the Clandestine Committees cannot decide which path the organization is going to follow until every *compañero* is consulted. In the EZLN a decision cannot be made until everyone is consulted, even if it appears that the majority of the *compañeros* have already decided for one of the options. Only after consulting everyone can the Committee say, "We have asked everyone, and this is the result." The Committee cannot say, "We consulted the majority and..." This could cost you your life. You can't play games here.

293

In this way, we were not a guerrilla group, but an army, an army with territory, with troops, with a general strategic plan. Our initial plan was a defensive plan, a plan in which the *compañeros* could participate in one of three different ways: as part of the regular combat force that lives in the mountains, as part of the irregular combat force that lives and works in the communities, or as part of a reserve force composed of the elderly and children. These last also receive military training. At last, we arrived at the point where we were able to mobilize 5,000 people and concentrate them in a village as part of a military exercise.

What was it that made this possible? A centralized command? No! Rather, it was that decisions of this kind were made by consensus or consultation. It is more than consultation; it is not a consultation to see what you think, but more to ask, "What do you want to happen?" The purpose of this is to give power to those who should have power.

Then, in this interweaving, in this exchange between two different forms of decision-making, the most orthodox proposals of Marxism or Leninism, theoretical concepts or historical references—for example, that the vanguard of the revolution is the proletariat, that the taking of state power and the installation of the dictatorship of the proletariat is the aim of the revolution—were confronted by an ideological tradition that is, how can I say this, somewhat magical. It is magical in one sense, but very real in another. What I mean by this is that it is an ideological tradition born of war—in this case, the war of the Conquest that began, well, not exactly five hundred years ago, and that continued through different historical periods. It continues... It continues, and it grows. If we had been orthodox leftists, we would never have worked with Indigenous peoples. Now, today, I believe there are many theories in crisis. Who would have thought that it would be the Indigenous peoples who would provoke all of this? Not even in the Leninist conception of the weakest link was it thought that it might be the Indigenous people, right? I told you that there was a learning process at the beginning of our work here, albeit a forced one. It's not like we said, "Well, we are going to learn and see what happens." No! We were closed-minded, like any other orthodox leftist, like any other theoretician who believes that he knows the truth.

*Q: Even in "pure" Marxism there is discrimination against Indigenous people.*

M: Yes! Definitely. The events of this last January will bring changes at the theoretical level as well. We arrived here and we were confronted by this reality, the Indigenous reality, and it continues to control us. Ultimately the theoretical confronted the practical, and something happened—the result was the EZLN. Therefore our combatants are right when they say, "We are not Marxist-Leninists, we are Zapatistas." They are referring to this synthesis, this coming together, this compatibility that incorporates—I'm going to be very schematic—the historical traditions of struggle and resistance of Indigenous people and the necessity of a national revolution.

*Q: Excuse me for interrupting. This is exactly the meaning of the initial question: whether you believe that Magonismo has permeated the Zapatista movement. Let's look at the history of the Mexican revolution, in which Magón, who was also a descendent of Indigenous people, of Indigenous parents in Oaxaca, had a similar vision. He took into account the needs of the Indigenous peoples and didn't limit himself to saying, "Those poor*

*Indians!" but also assumed the responsibility of analyzing how to create an army with Indigenous bases, an army with a collective participation in the command structures. This is the point of the first question: Do you believe that Magonismo has permeated the ideological formation of the EZLN?*

M: Look, I have to be honest. When we talk about Magonismo, it also makes me think of the orthodox line, closed-minded and stupid. This is the truth. The Magón brothers are only talked about in the context of the labor movement, although we know that they developed many other important projects as well. But, ultimately, the unintentional result is that they are spoken of in this way. We referred to the Flores Magón brothers in order to highlight the need for the workers to participate in the revolution, and in order to highlight an important force that existed during the time previous to the outbreak and spread of the armed struggle in 1910-21.

Ultimately, this synthesis or confrontation that I am speaking of occurred in such a way that the EZLN was born without any links to the workers. I think that perhaps the synthesis was not enough. Probably it could have used more influence from Magón. It probably lacked more input from the history of the Mexican workers' movement so as to be able to truly incorporate the workers into the armed struggle. I'm not saying that we didn't consider this on a theoretical level, but evidently in practice nothing happened. This is to say that there was an error, not in the reality—I can't say, "Reality is stupid because it doesn't suit what I am thinking." It means that we were stupid because we didn't understand reality.

*Q: In this sense, the Zapatista movement and the Zapatista revolution have been called the first post-modernist revolution. Now, let's analyze the fact that many current theories of the new left, of an anti-authoritarian left with a definite tendency toward libertarian communism, break with the blueprint that sees the working class as the vanguard of the social revolution. Many of these new theories even see the working class as a class in decline, a class that does not recognize itself as a class, a class that less and less wants to be considered the working class. Is this conception of the working class one that you have adopted during your experiences?*

M: No, definitely not. Those idols against which we were fighting were different. The idea that armed struggle was possible in all places except Mexico was so omnipresent that we were obligated to confront it first and leave the rest for later. Beyond this, in historical or theoretical terms, who would have speculated before December 31, 1993 that it wasn't going to be the proletariat leading the revolution? Then who? Who was it going to be? They could have speculated that it would be the teachers, they could have speculated that it would be the unemployed, they could have speculated that it would be the students or some sector of the middle class, they could have speculated that it would be leftist or democratic factions within the Federal Army or within the supposedly democratic faction of the PRI. They could have speculated many things, including that the United States would become socialist and then they would invade us and make us socialists [laughter]. This was the reasoning then. Even in the university this idea had taken root.

It didn't occur to anyone that the Indigenous peoples were going to play this role and that they would manage to demand their place in the nation, or that they would demand that the nation recognize that they have a proposal, that they have a proposal for the nation. The same or better or worse—it's open for discussion—as any other proposal that intellectuals or political parties or social groups have for this country.

*Q: We don't want to deviate much from the questions that we planned to ask you, but now that you have brought up the term "nation"... There have been many discussions regarding this concept. Even within the discussions of post-modernism the term "nation" continues to be marked by a petit-bourgeois conception. The "nation" is used as an abstract feeling of a patriotism that ultimately does nothing more than pit us against one another, country against country. And in this sense, we have felt a certain distance, for example, between points such as the autonomy of the Indigenous peoples and the national proposals of which you speak. We would like it if you could tell us a little of the vision of which you speak. When you refer to your national proposals, is it with this bourgeois vision of the nation-state-fatherland, or are you merely using a language a little, well, we could say, more common—something more direct and easier to understand?*

M: When we speak of the nation we are necessarily speaking of history, of a history of common struggle with historical references that make us brothers to one group of people without distancing us from other groups. But what more do we have in common with the history of what is today called Mexico? I say this because the first accusation against Zapatismo is that it is aligned with Central America. Therefore it has to delineate itself and explain that its vision is not directed towards the South, but rather towards the North. That is to say, to that historical tradition that has brought it together with a group of people—in this case with the Mexican people, not with the Central American peoples. Because... remember that the other thing being said is that this revolution is the last Central American revolution. Some say it is the first post-modern revolution, others say that it is the last Central American revolution, even geographically speaking.

What occurs as a result of this insistence... When the concept of autonomy is brought up, the state understands it in this way: "Well, what the Indigenous peoples want are reservations, like the ones North American Indians have." This is where the *compañeros* say, "No, if we are going to end up like the North American Indians on reservations, no." This is not the concept of autonomy that we want, rather, that they recognize, for example, this structure of government that I have explained, a structure that gives us validity. We don't want them to operate as if they were conquering territory. When the Federal Army entered the communities before the war, or the judicial police or the Public Security police, or the municipal police, they entered as an invading army in enemy territory, even physically. When an army invades a country, everyone from that country is an enemy. When they entered the communities, they entered acting as if everyone were an enemy. At that point, the *compañeros* said, "We have our own forms of government, we have traditions of community decision-making that must be respected by the government. And not only that—these traditions are a good example for the national government, for the government of this country, for any government that pretends to be a democracy."

For this reason we speak of Mexico, of the Mexican nation, because we must mark our boundaries, we must say, "It is not nostalgia for Central America, it is not nostalgia for Nicaragua, nostalgia for El Salvador." On the other hand, when they speak of autonomy they are speaking as sectarians. They don't look to the future but to the past, the nostalgia... They look to ethnicity in a pejorative sense, as if we wanted to create a bubble, a bubble like the one in the movie, a bubble that isolates you from contamination or from what happens outside it. Therefore, any concept that you put out there... We must make clear what we are speaking of in all senses.

*Q: From our point of view... We felt a little shocked by the discrepancy in your positions. For example, what is put forward as the "nation" of Mexico we understand to be very similar to what Indigenous peoples understand to be the "nation" of the United States. It is a large nation that dominates a large number of Indigenous peoples, of small Indigenous nations. In this case they may be Choles, Tzotziles, Triquis, Yaquis. The same thing happens in the case of the United States. It is a large nation that has oppressed a large number of small nations, such as the Yaquis, the Pomos, the Apaches, the Dakotas, etc. And in this sense we understand Mexico to be an imperialist nation that has kept all of these peoples oppressed without recognizing their culture, their traditions, their identities, a nation that has imposed a culture and an identity and that is trying to maintain the entire territory under its control without the least respect for cultures, traditions, identities, or anything of the kind. This then we see as a kind of contradiction, speaking of a national project... Well, we can see it in history with the example of Lázaro Cárdenas when he was in the Army. He went to war against the Yaqui, no? And this was to massacre and oppress the Yaqui people, a people who were in rebellion, and who had not allowed themselves to be oppressed, a people who were one of the bastions of resistance against the so-called "new nation." Therefore, we see a contradiction. I don't know if you have given thought to this, if you have come across this contradiction in your experiences.*

M: No, this is your position, but since this is my interview, I am going to explain ours. Look, we believe that today's Mexico, the Mexico that we are fighting against, is not a Mexico in the abstract but rather a project of a certain class, of a certain social group. This project was born of the disorder or of the internal agreement provoked by the revolution at the beginning of this century. The implementation of this project has brought about a series of things as you indicate: domination, questions of land, of forms of government. For example, the lie that there is a federation when in reality the states depend upon the central government, or the lie that there are free townships when in reality the townships are dependent. We believe that it is possible to have the same Mexico with a different project, a project that recognizes not only that it is a multi-ethnic state—in fact, multi-national—but also that new concepts are needed in order to reform the Constitution. But, since there isn't a just relationship between the Federation and its parts, we are proposing autonomy. We are proposing this because we are mostly Indigenous people, but what we say with respect to the need for autonomy could be applied equally to the townships, to the unions, to social groupings, to campesino groups, to the governments of the states or to the states that are nominally free and sovereign inside the Federation.

*Q: Could it be said that you view the future society for which you are fighting as one in which the free township, the autonomous township, will be put into practice, a society in which a federation will be put into practice based upon a citizens, confederation?*

M: No, before this we have to complete the other revolution. The EZLN... The revolution that we are proposing isn't an Indigenous revolution. The EZLN was born with Indigenous demands due to how it developed, but it aspires to organize the workers, non-Indigenous campesinos, students, teachers, and all of the other social sectors in order to carry out a broader revolution, not just an Indigenous revolution.

We don't believe that the result of this revolution that we are proposing will be a new world, a new country; it will only be a first step, an antechamber that you enter before you enter this new country. We are proposing a space, an equilibrium between the different political forces, in order that each position has the same opportunity to influence the political direction of this country—not by backroom deals, corruption, or blackmail, but by convincing the majority of the people that their position is best. I mean by this... If there is a neoliberal proposal for the country, we shouldn't try to eliminate it, but confront it. If there is a Trotskyist proposal, a Maoist proposal, an anarchist proposal, or proposals from the Guevaristas, the Castristas, the Existentialists or whatever "ists" that you may think of, they shouldn't be eliminated. They shouldn't be discussed in the way we are discussing them now, in small groups. In this discussion, we are demonstrating that we know a lot, that we speak very prettily, but in the discussions that we are proposing... The rest of the country shouldn't be spectators, like they will be for the debate tomorrow [On May 12, for the first time in Mexican history, the presidential candidates of the major Mexican political parties engaged in an open, televised debate—trans.]The people have to decide what proposal to accept, and it's the people whom you have to convince that your opinion is correct. This will radically change the concept of revolution, of who the revolutionary class is, of what a revolutionary organization is. Now, the problem isn't in fighting against the other proposals, but instead, in trying to convince the people. It's because of this that the Zapatista revolution isn't proposing the taking of power, it isn't proposing a homogeneous ideological concept of revolution. We are saying that yes, we do have our idea of how the country should be, but something is lacking before we talk about this. We cannot replicate the same logic as the government. They have a vision for the country that they have imposed on the people with the weapons of the Federal Army. We cannot reverse this logic and say that now the Zapatista vision is going to be imposed on the people with the weapons of the Zapatista Army. We are saying, "Let's destroy this state, this state system. Let's open up this space and confront the people with ideas, not with weapons." This is why we propose democracy, freedom, and justice—justice in order that certain material conditions are satisfied so that people have an opportunity to participate in the political life of the country. We are saying, "We don't want this new world yet. We are not talking about a new world yet. We aren't talking about what form Article 27 should take. We aren't talking about what form the Federation agreement should take. We aren't talking about what form Indigenous autonomy should take. We are talking about a democratic space where the political parties, or groups that aren't parties, can air and discuss their social proposals."

*Q: Marcos, in analyzing the way in which you are organized—at least what you have let us see—it's evident that when you speak of democracy, you are referring to direct democracy, to total participation, to a participation in which each and every person who makes up this country, everyone that is living at this time in Mexico, can participate. Is this interpretation accurate?*

M: Yes. Definitely. Look, what we are trying to do... We are a clandestine organization that has taken up arms against the government, and still we are very careful to try and maintain this democracy. By this I mean the direct vote, everyone's vote. Yes, because only the Zapatistas can vote. It's not the kind of process where you arrive and ask the people, "Are you for war or are you for peace? Well, I'm for war. And you? Peace." And you go adding up the votes.

No, I tell you that it must be the logical outcome of community discussion. The people meet in assemblies and the representatives put forth, for example, in the case of the consultations, the demands of the EZLN and the response of the government. They're explained. What is it that we asked for and what has the government said in response? And they begin to debate, "Well, this is bad, and this is good." After the community says, "We have already debated, we already understand, now we can vote,"—this could take days. In fact, almost all the consultations have gone on for two, three days now and they haven't yet reached the point of voting. They arrive and say, "Well, okay, we are in agreement, let's vote if we are ready to vote, if we already understand what it is we are going to decide." It's not about raising your hand or putting a check-mark for one option or the other. You have to debate and analyze the pros and the cons.

In this case, you're not voting for a governor where he could turn out to be a son of a bitch, you're voting for your life or death as an organization. If you're at war you already know that you could live or die. But, if you err in a decision and you vote for war when it is time for peace or you vote for peace when it is time for war, you disappear as an organization. You might disappear because they destroy you, because you lose prestige or moral authority, or because you become a traitor to yourself by signing a fictitious peace that nobody wants. You can't leave decisions of this magnitude to a group of leaders, no matter how collective they are or how large the group is. Not even the Clandestine Revolutionary Indigenous Committee can decide these things. The Committee can't meet and decide, "We analyzed what Camacho said and we are going to decide yes or no." They can't do that.

*Q: Do you strive for consensus in the general assemblies?*

M: No, there is direct voting. It isn't the sort of voting where at the end they say, "The majority of the people voted yes and therefore it's yes for all the people." No, it has to be known how many said yes and how many said no, because these yeses and nos are added up proportionally. It's not the consensus of the government, for example, that says, "Well, nobody said no [laughs] so we have consensus. Are you in agreement? Nobody said they didn't agree so that means that you agree." No, it has to be a direct vote.

*Q: We want to ask you another question that deals with ground that's already been covered to some extent, since it's been made clear during the interview that the EZLN has never considered itself to be the vanguard of the Mexican revolutionary movement. Nevertheless, I need to ask this question directly because other groups, specifically the Revolutionary Worker's Clandestine Party-Union of the People [Partido Revolucionario Obrero Clandestino-Unión del Pueblo, PROCUP], have said that they are the vanguard of Zapatismo, that they, as a party, are the vanguard of Zapatismo. PROCUP recently circulated a document in which they implied that the EZLN is one of their "belligerent groups," and that all the recent events in Mexico are part of PROCUP's national plan, of which, logically, they are the vanguard. Is this true? Do you have some connection?*

**M:** The left is very closed-minded. The traditional left is very closed-minded. They say, "Well, these people don't draw from any of the known ideologies, so they must not have one. I will lend them one." [laughs]. Or they say, "They are good people but they don't know what they want. I'm going to tell them what they want." Or "They're good people but they need a leader. I'll be their leader." This is the reality not just in the case of PROCUP, but with groups of Trotskyists and Maoists who say, "What the EZLN needs is... ME!" [laughs].

*Q: My leadership...*

**M:** Yes, ultimately, "my leadership." What upsets the Pentagon is that when you punch "Zapatista" into the computer, nothing comes out that says, "Moscow," or "Havana," or "Libya," "Tripoli," "Bosnia" or any other group. And the left, accustomed to the same way of thinking, says, "Well, they don't fit in anywhere." It doesn't occur to them there might be something new, that you have to re-theorize. And they say, "Well then, these poor people don't know what they want, we need to help them." And furthermore, we are talking about an armed force at war, surrounded, that isn't able to receive all the declarations or the newspapers. Eventually, we find out what is said after a week or maybe 15 days. So, they know that we will not be able to deny it. We can't stop it. But, we believe that... We have confidence in the people, in the community, in that we have been clear about our positions, and that people will have difficulty swallowing that we are the armed arm of PROCUP or of any other organization of any type. But I have seen various magazines...

*Q: Very insidious... the commentaries.*

**M:** ...of Trotskyists and Maoists, of all of the orthodox leftists and of the old dinosaurs who say, "Well, the EZLN is very good and what they've done is very good and all, but they lack a program, so here's a program. They lack a party, so here's a party. They lack a leader, so here's a leader." This attitude is held by everyone from Aguilar Talamantes to the left.

*Q: Yes, he already wanted you to be a candidate for president, right?*

**M:** No, first he wanted to be our candidate for the presidency. [laughs].

*Q: Later he wanted you to be the candidate.*

**M:** Yes, but he made it very difficult. First I had to prove that I was more intelligent than he was.

*Q: Really? Imagine! Impossible.*

300

M: Evidently it was impossible.

*Q: Going back to the previous discussion, Dr. Armando Quiroz Alejandre of the National Assembly for Human Rights [Asamblea Nacional de Derechos Humanos, ANDH] met with comrades of the Zapatista Solidarity Committee in New York City. During the visit, he insinuated in private discussions with these comrades that PROCUP has a link to the EZLN and furthermore that the EZLN is following the same political line as PROCUP.*

M: It's not true. Those people need to be publicly denounced. It can't be. Why should the Zapatistas provide the dead bodies and the other groups collect the dollars and fool people into thinking that they're providing solidarity for an organization that never receives any of this aid? We don't subscribe to their ideologies—in this case the ideology of PROCUP. We definitely don't subscribe... If we subscribed to the ideology of PROCUP, well, we would be PROCUP. We are not, we are not in any way in league with them, we have not even entered in any kind of conversation with them since our inception, since their inception. There is absolutely no type of alliance. Well, in the sense that we are all human beings, you could also [laughs] link us to Clinton or to Reagan, to Perot, to Che, to Zapata.

*Q: With anybody... Now that we are clearing some things up. There have been other groups that have manipulated things in a different way. Specifically in the case of CLETA, who said, for example, that you are their vanguard. This is the opposite of PROCUP. CLETA needed a vanguard and put you in that position. Furthermore, as we are talking about the problem of solidarity, they are one of the groups that has organized concerts and collected funds saying that they are for you, saying that it is for...that this aid reaches you, that this money reaches you.*

M: Well, we're going to wait until it arrives. But, up until now nothing has arrived [laughs].

*Q: Nothing has arrived. A number of very biased press sources have tried to equate the EZLN with the Shining Path [Communist Party of Peru-Shining Path, Partido Comunista de Peru-Sendero Luminoso]. Making a simply objective analysis you can see that both groups are very different. For example, while the Shining Path has committed innumerable executions, you [the EZLN] tried a criminal like Absalón and you put him to work in the corn fields and in the end you freed him. We would like it if you could expound on this because there are Maoists who say that you part of the international Maoist revolution, that there is a link between the Shining Path and the Zapatista Army, etc., etc.*

M: No, there is no link. Look, if the Mexicans couldn't accept that an armed revolution was possible in Mexico, definitely foreigners couldn't accept the possibility. Come on, everyone saw, or still sees, Mexico as the rearguard for political solidarity work. Now I'm remembering something; let's see if this relates to the question—it will make the tape recorder jump. We just received a feminist magazine that says that we are sexists because we chose war and war is sexist, armies are in and of themselves sexist, so therefore the EZLN is sexist. Therefore, what the EZLN needs is to be feminist. The article was brilliant—it moved me to tears. I don't remember what it was called—it was written by "pure" feminists. The article goes beyond anything I've seen.

*Q: La Fem?*

M: No.

Q: *Is it national?*

M: No, it appeared to be...

Q: *Well, on that note, I'm going skip around in the order of the questions.*

M: No, it's that the article says... the foreward says, "Only for Zapatista women." And I disobeyed and read it, but I will pass it along to the *compañeras*.

Q: *Well, one of the things that we are most concerned about—specifically the com-pañeras—are the gender politics within the EZLN. You facilitated our being able to inter-view a number of* compañeras *and we have seen—to the point that you have allowed us to see [laughs]—that there exists an equality. This can be seen clearly. The women say it them-selves: "My partner,"—or in the case of those who are married—"My husband washes his things, does his work, does his part." And when you ask her if she has children, she says, "Yes, I already have mine, my M-16." Things like this show that yes, there is an equality that exists, at least in practice. The single* compañeras *that we've interviewed also tell us they do the same work as the men, that they aren't limited to working as nurses or in the kitchen as a result of being women. We would like you to tell us, as spokesperson of the EZLN: What are the politics of the EZLN towards gender issues?*

M: Look, there are many problems. I am speaking for the *compañeras*... Above all in the civilian population, the civilians have continued practicing many ancestral customs that don't belong in even a pre-revolutionary situation. For example, many still believe that the man should choose the woman that he wants to marry, but that the woman should have no choice in the matter. The difference, including the physical difference, between the civilian women and the combatant women is very clear. At the age when many of the com-batant women have, as you say, an M-16, many civilian women already have four or five children, are beaten by their husbands; they don't know how to read or write, they have no opportunity to develop themselves as people. What the *compañeras* say is that they cannot have their equality decreed from above, they have to achieve it through struggle. They say, "You can like it or not, but now we are going to change these things." By force. That's why in our list of demands to the government, it doesn't mention anything about gender. The *compañeras* say, "We aren't going to ask the government to give us freedom, nor are we going to ask you male fools. We are going to ensure our freedom, our respect, and our dig-nity as women and as human beings." I'm speaking of the *compañeras*... They also criticize us, the men, for our sexist or authoritarian attitudes. For example, in relationships between combatants, many things have changed, things that haven't changed in the civilian popula-tion. For example, in the civilian population, when a woman marries, she is no longer allowed to dance. She is married, and dances are places where single people meet and decide to get married. If she is married, then she doesn't dance because now she is some-body's "property." Among the civilians it is still this way. Among the combatants, no, the combatants dance whether they are married or single, and it is very common that the woman chooses her dancing partner. They dance just to dance, to have fun, without any other motive such as to sleep with someone or have a relationship.

The politics of gender in the EZLN, among the regular forces... There isn't a politic of gender, there are only combatants. There are women soldiers and there are men soldiers, but in the end they are soldiers. In order to rise to a command position, in order to rise in rank or to carry out actions and missions, we take into account the soldier's aptitudes; it doesn't matter whether they are male or female. Many times, in our daily life as combatants, in couple relationships, sexist attitudes are reproduced, and because of this our laws tend to favor the woman. It is very common for couples to fight physically when they fight. Let's say that the difference between the women combatants and civilian women is that the women combatants hit back. [laughter]

*Q: They defend themselves.*

**M:** Yes, it's common that it's the man who comes to us complaining that his partner hit him. We have to be very cautious in this respect because both are armed; if it occurs to one of them to shoot the other... A blow is much different than a gunshot. For us—for me it's very clear, and I believe that it's clear to many *compañeras* as well—that equality isn't something that's conceded. You can't say, "I as a man am going to give you your freedom and now we are going to be equal." That's not true, of course. In the same way, the government can't concede us our rights as Indigenous peoples; we have to fight for them. The women are also fighting for them, many times in very radical ways. I believe that they've achieved many things inside the combat forces and inside the civilian population. For example, men who had never received orders from a woman, who couldn't stand it when women would give them orders in the mountains... When they saw them fighting, they saw that the *compañeras* knew how to fight. They look on them with respect now because they realized that the women knew how to fight, and they didn't. They saw them facing death, and they stopped being women. They stopped being women in the classic sense of the term, weak and unable to...

*Q: Women in the pejorative sense.*

**M:** It could be also that you see a woman and you think that she's only there to sleep with. But when it changes to, "She's going to give me orders and I have to obey her," or, "I'm going to give her orders and she is going to obey me," in that moment you stop being a female combatant or a male combatant and you become a soldier, equal. I'm not saying that the women stop being women and become men, but that both women and men stop being what they are and become combatants. Since we are soldiers all the time—we aren't able to take vacations—it is very difficult to tell when one is acting in the role of combatant and when one is off-duty. I believe that this has brought more benefits to the *compañeras* than to the sexists, to us men, in the sense that this equality in combat, in work is transmitted to other aspects of life.

*Q: Do you accept the analysis that we live in a patriarchal society, that men have controlled society for centuries, and that this is also part of the system that feeds Capital, that feeds the bourgeoisie?*

**M:** Definitely!

*Q: We must rise above this and the sexist attitudes that we hold.*

M: Definitely! There are *compañeros* who are very revolutionary politically, but who are real assholes in relationships, in marriages, in relationships between men and women. But, I believe that changes in this aren't going to be our concession—I'm speaking as a man. The women are going to change things whether we like it or not, despite our closed-mindedness. It is the same thing we are doing with respect to the government. The government doesn't like the fact that the Indigenous peoples have risen up, but we did it. The sexists don't like the fact that the women are doing what they are doing, but they are going to do it and that's that. They have fought in combat, they haven't even won. Some of them led successful missions, they won, they defeated men. They commanded entire units of men. The EZLN is composed of about two-thirds men and one-third women. It is very common to have military units where the only woman is the commander. The entire unit, all of her subordinates, are men. This caused many problems before January 1.

*Q: And these problems were eliminated?*

M: They finally saw that yes, what was important wasn't that they were women but that they had learned during their years in the mountains to lead the same as any man.

*Q: We have seen this. We have met many women captains during our stay here in the liberated territories. We have met many female captains and this demonstrates the truth of what you are saying...*

M: The male captains hide themselves [laughter]. No, that's not true.

*Q: Continuing along this same subject... We have seen that there is also a cultural difference, a difference in tradition. You said this also, at the beginning when you spoke of your links to the Indigenous communities. Many of the* compañeras *have told us that they aren't allowed to have sex until they are married, that there is a regulation that says that they must be married. If they like a man and they want to sleep with him, it's easier to marry him. We're not speaking of a religious marriage, but that you, the EZLN, expedite some form of marriage... But we feel this to be a little puritanical, as if to say, "You can't have sex because you are a woman and you have to be married."*

M: No, no, it's that marriage for us means that you are a couple and you have permission. Let me explain. When you are going to have a sexual relationship... During the day you can't have sex, you're working. The most logical thing is that you are going to sleep with someone at night. You have to advise the commander that you are going to be having sex somewhere, because if you are attacked the commander has to look for you and... We tell the combatants, "You have to trust the commanders to tell them that you are sleeping with someone." Why? It doesn't matter to me, I'm not going to watch you, I'm not a voyeur. It isn't like that. What I'm interested in is that I have someone covering your position. If we are attacked, we can't have the entire defensive line having sex. Well, it could happen, but it shouldn't happen. We don't demand that they are married.

*Q: You mean a woman can have sexual relations freely?*

M: Yes, what she is told is to follow a birth-control method. That's why she is told to let us know, so that she can follow a method. Because if you become pregnant... you can't stay in the mountains pregnant, you have to go to town, go get an abortion there. It has already happened; there are *compañeras* who abort on the long walks that... Then, the method has to be followed, you have to look after yourself. Only when the Army says, "Now it's possible to have children and remain in the mountains or at some positions," only then will it cease to be an issue. But, yes, the nurses are asked to be checking for pregnancy. But there is no formal procedure. You do have to ask the commanders for permission, but it's not as if...

*Q: As if it's mandatory to be married to have sex, or anything like that.*

M: No, no.

*Q: Simply put, it's more a matter of coordination, to...*

M: Yes, a military question. You let the commanders know, but generally no, they don't get married to have sex.

*Q: They can have sexual relations freely?*

M: In fact, they have sex and then they say, "Well, not this one." Or "Yes, this is the one I want to marry. Or maybe I don't want to marry this person, but I just want it to be clear that we are a couple." They say this to avoid gossip—like that he or she gets in bed with one person and then another, and so on.

*Q: That involves culture and tradition as well.*

M: Yes, we are talking about Indigenous people that come from the villages...

*Q: Who hold different concepts than we who come from the cities.*

M: But it is a rule that you have to let the commanders know.

*Q: Now, when you were explaining this to us, something else came to mind, another question. You spoke of the possibility... well, of pregnant* compañeras *who risk abortion while engaging in maneuvers. In the Women's Revolutionary Law it is stated explicitly that a woman has full rights over her body and her life. Radical feminists have been fighting throughout the world to truly have control over their lives and bodies. However, the issue becomes very confused when an article appears in the media, in a paper like* La Jornada, *saying that the EZLN has presented a law proposal to the governor of Chiapas in which abortion is addressed, but at no time does it make clear in the media the position of the EZLN concerning the issue. I don't know if it was intentional or if there really was no in-depth knowledge about your position, but the media assumed that the EZLN is opposed to abortion. Thus, I would like to divide the question in several parts. The first question would be: What is the proposal of the Zapatistas in relation to the legalization of abortion? And the second question is: At this time, if a* compañera *becomes pregnant because her contraceptive method fails and she does not wish to carry the pregnancy to term, if she wants to interrupt it, does she have authority over her body in order to decide if she aborts or not? And the third question...*

M: Wait, wait, let's start with the first question.

*Q: Well, yes, let's go question by question. The first one is: What does this law proposal consist of?*

**M:** The EZLN demands that the state's penal code be modified because there is no political freedom. The government, taking advantage of the fact that we are tied up in talks and that we are surrounded, is taking the opportunity to reverse the decriminalization of abortion that existed in the penal code. They say that this is at the EZLN's request, but the EZLN did not request the modification of the Code in that respect. The stupidity of this article is based on the argument that this is a position of Samuel Ruiz García, that it is evidence of the influence of the Church on the EZLN, and since the Church is against abortion they want it to be penalized. Then, according to the argument, the Church directed us to present this law proposal. We have not presented any law proposal or anything of the kind—nor an electoral reform proposal or anything like that either. The proposal says contextually: "We demand that the penal code of the state be eliminated." We don't say that it should be reformed or replaced by a more just one. We demand that it be removed because it leaves us no other form of political participation other than taking up arms. That's what it says. I sent a letter to *La Jornada* because of that stupid article that was published.

*Q: Very insidious!*

**M:** Yes. That answers the first question. Question two: The *compañera* not only has the right to terminate the pregnancy, but the organization also has the obligation to provide the means for her to do it with total safety.

*Q: Well, that was the third question, you already answered it.*

**M:** If she says, "I have become pregnant"—it could even be that she became pregnant on purpose, not just that the birth-control method failed—"but I don't want it anymore," this is fine, as long as her life is not in danger; I mean, if a certain number of months have gone by it can't be done. Then she can demand by the right of Zapatista law that the EZLN give her the means to terminate the pregnancy under the best health conditions that the EZLN can ensure. It is the obligation of the commanders that she be given these means. If the pregnancy can't be stopped, aborted, then the commanders have to find the way to resolve the problem.

*Q: In this case, for free.*

**M:** It is not, in the strictest sense, control over their bodies, and the *compañeras* demonstrate this very clearly, "We are not free in this sense because, for example, I can't become pregnant and continue to serve in the Army. In this sense, I am not free. I am free in that, if I am pregnant, I can stop the pregnancy, but if I am not pregnant, I can't decide to become pregnant, because if I become pregnant, I have to leave the Army." And yes, we do tell them they have to leave the Army, because of the conditions we face. That's why the *compañeras* say, "There is no freedom over my own body." In the case of the female combatants, it is only half-freedom, the other freedom is lacking. Right now they can't decide to carry a pregnancy to term and remain in the Army. It is only fair to point this out, and the *compañeras* continue to fight for their right to become pregnant. The other side of the issue has already been resolved for many years, and we deal with abortions with the means we have at our disposal. Up to now, no one has died during an abortion. In the communities, abortion is practiced to the extent that our resources allow.

*Q: Then it exists also for the civilian population, for the women in the civilian community. There is that possibility, in case she needs it, if she so wishes.*

M: Yes. In general, they don't seek it because of their beliefs; also for health reasons, since in their nutritional conditions an abortion can be deadly. Sometimes it is best to let the pregnancy be carried through, even if there is still time for an abortion. But we do facilitate the use of contraceptives and all that, for example.

*Q: The compañeras we met also had access to contraceptives. The question has been raised of whether there is the possibility for the organization of women's groups within the Army, where women could organize as women of the Army, but also autonomously, as women. By this, we mean self-help collectives, where they could gain and acquire more knowledge about their bodies, and could even get to the point... for example, in the case of abortions in the first weeks, there are methods that have been proposed by radical women's groups, like abortion by menstrual extraction, one of the first methods for aborting early in the pregnancy. Is autonomy given in this sense or not?*

M: No, I didn't know about this method. The situation here is not so advanced. The most we managed to achieve some time ago—when I was captain—many years ago, was to have sex-education classes, explaining the man's body, the woman's body, what was the mechanism of pregnancy, what things were going on in their bodies. This was received with much enthusiasm from the men, and much embarrassment from the women. The men came to see how a woman's body was. For example—look, this town has a power plant project that breaks down all the time, but when it works... Some months ago it worked for a few days. One of the *compañeros* told us, very enthusiastically, that at last he had "seen" his wife. He said, "I finally saw all of her." And they have 10 kids. He had 10 kids and he didn't know his wife's body. He didn't know his wife's body! Until there was electric light, and they thought of making love with the light on, then yes, he could see everything that was going on. And he talked about it as if it had been his first time. He already had 10 children, one of them fully grown, already an insurgent, an 18-year-old, a member of a combat unit.

We organized these classes in order to combat the diseases that afflict the women, so that they understand the necessity of hygiene. It is a problem for them; the men don't take it into account. They think that when a *compañera* has a urinary-tract infection, from lack of cleanliness, for example—or if she has her period—that she is just lazy, that she doesn't want to work. We need to sensitize the men to this so that they understand that a woman's body is not like a man's, in many senses. And that's why we organized these classes. We try in the talks and lectures to address these issues.

*Q: Is there an education as far as the use of the condom—not only as a contraceptive but also to avoid diseases, to avoid contracting and spreading them?*

M: No, in reality, no. In reality, we teach about the condom as a contraceptive when the *compañeras* can't use the pill, when they get sick from the pill. There are many who get ill from the pill, they are very young; when they use pills with high estrogen content they get sick. With all the heavy work they do already, they get nauseated, get headaches and all that—it's very hard on them. They can't always get IUDs, the rhythm method is really

307

prehistoric, so then there is the use of condoms. But we should say that the Zapatistas' sexual horizons are very limited. I mean by this that gonorrhea, and things of this sort... Well, we didn't get a chance to catch them in the cities, since we fled before attacking the whorehouses. We are in the mountains, we are at war—within the regular troops, I'm saying, it is very, very difficult to spread diseases. In fact, we have not seen one case. And we can instill fear, in fact we did it, and they tell you, "Not me, I have never been with a woman, where am I going to become infected, or in what whorehouse am I going to catch this?" It's more pragmatic in that sense. I am not saying it is good, because I do think that it would be good to promote their use... but no, we haven't done it, I would lie to you if I said that we were doing it. It is recommended when...as a contraceptive, not for sexual hygiene.

*Q: Well, in case this kind of sexual education could be resumed... Do you believe that it would be acceptable that the problem of disease, in the case of AIDS, etc., be included in the instruction?*

M: I believe so. Let's say that we understand, for example, about AIDS. Well, according to the information that we were getting when we were in the mountains, AIDS is a homosexual's disease, and therefore, if you weren't a homosexual, nothing would happen to you. In fact, we just found that you can get AIDS in other ways, it can be transmitted even in heterosexual relationships. I am talking about the basic sexual culture here, because in this case all references to AIDS are in the context of homosexuality: "If I'm not homosexual I have nothing to worry about." The main worry here is different: "What I have to worry about is to not get anyone pregnant, or that no one gets me pregnant." No, we don't have a sexual culture based on fear of disease due to our isolation, but yes, we do need educate about it.

*Q: Well, let's relate this to another question... We want to ask another question relating to immediate solidarity. Have you received or do you have access to condoms? Would it be feasible to bring them?*

M: Yes, but unfortunately they would be very hard to eat [laughs]. But yes, we do get contraceptives, condoms and all that.

*Q: So, as I was saying...*

M: These things are allowed through by the Mexican Army so that the Zapatistas don't reproduce [laughs]. They have enough problems with the ones that already exist for us to make even more.

*Q: Now, relating the answers with other questions... One of the questions that we were asked to ask by* compañeros *Mateo and Robin is: what is the EZLN's policy, in the Army and in the liberated communities, toward sexual preference, in this specific case, homosexuality and lesbianism? Is the EZLN given to the "satanization" of homosexuality that has sometimes been found in other leftist groups? Or is it simply unknown what you are talking about when you attempt to address these issues?*

M: No, let's say that at a level of, well, of basic culture, it is not punished. I mean, they don't say, "He's a homosexual, put him in jail, kill him." On one hand, they laugh, make jokes, but homosexuals have a normal life in the community. Our position as an Army is that—let me put it to you in a general way—there are many minorities that will have to say, "Enough!" Just as the Indigenous people said, "Enough!" other minorities not tolerated by the powerful will have to say it also. In that sense, then, there is no sexual policy in the Zapatista Army.

*Q: That is, there is no law—in the communities either—that forbids lesbianism or homosexuality?*

M: No.

*Q: Not even in the Army?*

M: No, not even in the Army.

*Q: There is no policy in the Army that says, "We found two girls fucking or two guys fucking," and well... They are jailed, suspended, expelled—I don't know...*

M: No, there is nothing like that. They go ask the commanders, the same as when it is a male-female couple. That means, they let us know they are not going to be at their posts, because that is what the commanders are concerned about, that their position is covered.

## COMMUNIQUÉ ABOUT THE END OF THE CONSULTATIONS

[*La Jornada*]
May 28, 1994

To the national magazine *Proceso*:
To the national newspaper *La Jornada*:
To the national newspaper *El Financiero*:
To the local newspaper *Tiempo*:

Dear Gentlemen:

This communiqué is about the end, finally, of the consultations. In addition, we have sent several letters to various addresses.

We are totally surrounded. We have been "heroically" resisting the avalanche of reactions to the event of May 15. Three days ago, helicopters joined the airplanes that watch us from overhead. The cooks complain that there won't be enough pots to cook all the food we will need if they all fall at the same time. The superintendent argues that there is enough firewood to have a barbecue, and that we should invite some Argentinian journalist to it because the Argentinians know how to barbecue. I think about it, but it's useless: The best Argentinians are guerrillas (for example, Che), or poets (Juan Gelman, for example), or writers (for example, Borges), or artists (Maradona, for example), or chroniclers (for example, Cortázar). There aren't any famous Argentinian barbecuers. Some ingenious person proposes that we wait for the improbable hamburgers from the University Student Council (Consejo Estudiantil Universitario, CEU). Yesterday we ate the XEOCH's control console and two microphones. They had a rancid taste, like something rotten. The medics are giving out lists of jokes instead of analgesics. They say that laughter is also a cure. The other day I surprised Tacho and Moi as they were crying...of laughter. "Why are you laughing?" I asked. They couldn't answer because their laughter had left them short of breath. A medic explained, "It is because they have bad headaches." Day 136 of the military blockade. Sigh.

To top it all off, Toñita asks me to tell a story. I tell her a story as it was told to me by old Antonio, the father of the Antonio that appears in "Chiapas: The Southeast in Two Winds, a Storm and a Prophecy":

"In the time before the world came into being, the gods came together and decided to create the world and to create men and women. They thought to make the first people very beautiful and very strong. So they made the first people of gold, and the gods were very content because these people were strong and shining. Then the gods realized that the golden people never moved; they never walked or worked because they were so heavy. So the gods came together again in order to figure out a way to solve this problem. They decided to make another group of people and they decided to make this group of people of wood. The wooden people worked and walked and the gods were again content. Then the gods realized that the golden people were forcing the wooden people to work for them and carry things for them. The gods realized that they had made a mistake, and in order to remedy the mistake, they decided to make some people of corn, a good people, a true people. Then the gods went to sleep and they left the corn people to find a solution to the problem. The corn people spoke the true tongue to find an agreement among themselves, and they went to the mountains in order to find a path for people..."

Old Antonio told me that the golden people were the rich, the white-skinned ones, and the wooden people were the poor, the brown-skinned ones, who forever work for the rich. They are both waiting for the arrival of the corn people. The rich fear their arrival and the poor hope for it. I asked old Antonio what color the skin of the corn people was, and he showed me several types of corn with different colors. He told me that they were of every sort of skin color, but that nobody knew exactly, because the corn people don't have faces...

Old Antonio has died. I met him 10 years ago in a community deep in the jungle. He smoked like nobody else I knew, and when he was out of cigarettes he would ask me for some tobacco and would make more cigarettes. He viewed my pipe with curiosity, but the one time I tried to loan it to him he showed me the cigarette in his hand, telling me without words that he preferred his own method of smoking. Two years ago, in 1992, I was travelling through the communities attending meetings to decide whether or not we should go to war, and eventually I arrived at the village where old Antonio lived. While the community was discussing whether or not to go to war, old Antonio took me by the arm and led me to the river, about 100 meters from the center of the village. It was May and the river was green. Old Antonio sat on a tree trunk and didn't say anything. After a little while he spoke, "Do you see? Everything is clear and calm. It appears that nothing will happen..." "Hmmm," I answered, knowing that he wasn't asking me to answer yes or no. Then he pointed out to me the top of the nearest mountain. The clouds lay gray upon the summit, and the lightning was illuminating the diffuse blue of the hills. It was a powerful storm, but it seemed so far away and inoffensive that old Antonio made a cigarette and looked uselessly around for a lighter that he knew he didn't have. I offered my lighter. "When everything is calm here below, there is a storm in the mountains," he said after inhaling. "The mountain streams run strongly and flow toward the riverbed. During the rainy season this river becomes fierce, like a whip, like an earthquake. Its power doesn't come from the rain that falls on its banks, but from the mountain streams that flow down to feed it. By destroying, the river reconstructs the land. Its waters will become corn, beans, and bread on our tables here in the jungle.

"Our struggle is the same," the older Antonio told me. "It was born in the mountains, but its effects won't be seen until it arrives here below." He responded to my question about whether he believed the time had come for war by saying, "Now is the time for the river to change color..." Old Antonio became quiet and supported himself on my shoulder. We returned to the village slowly. He said to me, "You [the Army] are the mountain streams and we are the river. You must descend now..." The silence continued and we arrived at his shack as it was growing dark. The younger Antonio returned with the official result of the meeting, an announcement that read, more or less:

"We, the men, women, and children of this village met in the community's school in order to see if we believed in our hearts that it is time to go to war for our freedom. We divided ourselves into three groups, one of men, one of women, and one of children to discuss the matter. Later, we came together again and it was seen that the majority believed that it was time to go to war because Mexico is being sold to foreigners and the people are always hungry. Twelve men, 23 women and eight children were in favor of beginning the war and have signed this announcement."

I left the village in the early morning hours. Old Antonio wasn't around; he had already gone to the river.

Two months ago I saw old Antonio again. He didn't say anything when he saw me and I sat by his side and began to shuck corn with him. "The river rose," he said to me after a bit. "Yes," I answered. I explained to the younger Antonio what was happening with the consultations and I gave him the documents that outlined our demands and the government's response. We spoke of what had happened in Ocosingo during the offensive, and once again I left the village in the early morning hours. Old Antonio was waiting for me at a turn in the road. I stopped alongside him and lowered my backpack to look for some tobacco to offer him. "Not now," he said to me as he pushed away the bag of tobacco that I was offering him. He put his arm around me and led me to the foot of a tree. "Do you remember what I told you about the mountain streams and the river?" he asked me. "Yes," I responded, whispering as he had when he had asked me the question. "There is something I didn't tell you," he added, looking at his bare feet. I answered with silence. "The streams..." He was stopped by a cough that wracked his entire body. He took a breath and continued, "The streams, when they descend..." Once again he was stopped

311

by a cough and I went for a medic. Old Antonio turned down the help of the *compañero* with the Red Cross. The medic looked at me and I made a sign that he should leave. Old Antonio waited until the medic left and then, in the penumbra of the dawn, he continued, "The streams...when they descend...have no way of returning...except beneath the ground." He embraced me rapidly and left. I stayed there watching as he walked away, and as he disappeared in the distance, I lit my pipe and picked up my backpack. As I mounted my horse I thought about what had just occurred. I don't know why, it was very dark, but it seemed that old Antonio was crying.

I just received a letter from the younger Antonio with his village's response to the government's proposals. He also wrote me that old Antonio had become very ill and that he had died that night. He didn't want anyone to tell me that he was dying. The younger Antonio wrote me that when they insisted that I be told, old Antonio said, "No, I have already told him what I had to tell him. Leave him alone, he has much work to do."

When I finished the story that old Antonio had told me, six-year-old Toñita solemnly told me that yes, she loves me, but that from now on she won't kiss me because "it itches." Rolando says that when Toñita has to go to the medic's area, she asks if the Sup is there. If she is told that I'm there she doesn't go. "Because the Sup only wants kisses and he itches," says the inevitable logic of a six year old, which, on this side of the stream, we call "Toñita."

The first rains have begun here. We thought that we would have to wait for the arrival of the anti-riot water cannons in order to have water.

Ana María says that the rain comes from the clouds that are fighting on top of the mountains. They do it this way so that men and women will not see their disputes. On the summits of the mountains, the clouds fight their ferocious battles with what we call lightning. Armed with infinity, the clouds fight for the privilege of dying and becoming rain to feed the land. We Zapatistas are similar to the clouds, without faces, without names, without any payment. Like the clouds we fight for the privilege of becoming a seed for the land.

All right. Health and a raincoat (for the rains and the riots),

From the mountains of the Mexican Southeast,
Subcommander Marcos
May, 1994

P.S.: The majority disguised as the untolerated minority. About all of this whether Marcos is homosexual: Marcos is gay in San Francisco, a black person in South Africa, Asian in Europe, a Chicano in San Isidro, an anarchist in Spain, a Palestinian in Israel, an Indigenous person in the streets of San Cristóbal, a gang-member in Neza, a rocker on [University] campus, a Jew in Germany, an ombudsman in Department of Defense (Secretaria de Defensa, Sedena), a feminist in a political party, a communist in the post-Cold War period, a prisoner in Cintalapa, a pacifist in Bosnia, a Mapuche in the Andes, a teacher in National Confederation of Educational Workers (Confederación Nacional de Trabajadores de Educación, CNTE), an artist without a gallery or a portfolio, a housewife in any neighborhood in any city in any part of Mexico on a Saturday night, a guerrilla in Mexico at the end of the twentieth century, a striker in the CTM, a sexist in the feminist movement, a woman alone in a Metro station at 10 p.m., a retired person standing around in the Zócalo, a campesino without land, an underground editor, an unemployed worker, a doctor with no office, a non-conformist student, a dissident against neoliberalism, a writer without books or readers, and a Zapatista in the Mexican Southeast. In other words, Marcos is a human being in this world. Marcos is every untolerated, oppressed, exploited minority that is resisting and saying, "Enough!" He is every minority who is now beginning to speak and every majority that must shut up and listen. He is every untolerated group searching for a way to speak, their way to speak. Everything that makes power and the good consciences of those in power uncomfortable—this is Marcos.

You're welcome, dear gentlemen of the Attorney General's Office, I'm here to serve you...with lead.

**Postscript** for the PRD—About the logic of the dead: The *compañeros* read what you wrote about "having had more casualties than the EZLN," and immediately they started to count up the casualties. They added and multiplied the casualties starting from more than 10 years ago when we began to lay ambushes along the footpaths and roads "against bandits." The *compañeros* say that when it comes to counting the dead, nobody beats them. "We are well trained in this," says Gabino. The discussions among the different "tendencies" in the EZLN have become more heated: The most radical *compañeros* want to start counting from when the Spanish began their violent advance toward the jungle and the mountains, but the more discreet and prudent *compañeros* want to start counting from when we formed the EZLN. Some ask whether we should count those who have died during the 136 days that the military has had us surrounded. They ask if we should count Amalia, 25 years old and with seven children. She began to become "a little ill" at 6 p.m. on day 125 of the military blockade. Then began the fever, the diarrhea, the vomiting, and the bleeding between her legs, and at midnight we were asked for an ambulance. The ambulance said that it couldn't make it, and at 4 in the morning we managed to get some gasoline and we went to get her in a three-ton truck. One hundred meters from the medical compound, where Lieutenant Elena was, she said, "I'm going to die." And she did die, 98 meters from the medical compound and Lieutenant Elena, the life and blood flowing out from between her legs. When I asked if she was dead, Lieutenant Elena said yes, she died "at once." The morning of day 126 of the military blockade, Amalia's second daughter looked upon the body of her mother on the stretcher and told her father that she was going to ask the neighbors for some stew, "because mother can't make it anymore." The *compañeros* ask if they should count Ibarra's daughter, who died "as if she had become bored with coughing." Everyone is counting up the dead. Some are using a calculator taken from the town hall in Ocosingo. They are still doing this when Juana comes to ask them to count old Antonio, "who died of sorrow." Later Lorenzo comes and asks them to count his son Lorenzo, "who died during the night." By radio they transmit the names of dead men and women. Soon people stop and take out their calculators or pencils, and they

313

look at each other. They're confused; they don't know whether they're adding...or sub-tracting. Of pontificators. Magnificent self-criticism is always opportunistic.

Finally, you might accuse us of not taking into account the scale of the different political forces, you might accuse us of political clumsiness, of not having a satellite [dish] so that we could view the debate ourselves, of not having subscriptions to the principal newspapers and magazines so we could read the post-debate analysis. You might accuse us of not being friendly, of being discourteous, of not recognizing possible allies, of being sectarians.

All right. Remember that all we have done is get hope started. We wish you health and hope that you leave the animosity for the lazy fools.

A hug from this side of of the military blockade,

The impertinent subcommander, just like a tornado.

# 12. REJECTING THE GOVERNMENT'S OFFER

## EARLY RESULTS OF THE CONSULTATIONS

[from a photocopy of the original, signed communiqué
received via the Nicaragua Solidarity Network]
June 1, 1994

To the national news weekly *Proceso*:
To the national newspaper *La Jornada*:
To the national newspaper *El Financiero*:
To the local newspaper of San Cristóbal de las Casas *Tiempo*:

Gentlemen:

The following communicates to you the early results of the consultations. The wind and the gray already inhabit their June, some shreds of May will come for several of its days. The wind, the real captain of the world, rules again in these lands. We, as is appropriate, obey it.

The jump from the fifth to the sixth month was with memorable rain and wind. I did not know it, and now I read it. It was *Juntacadáveres* [gather cadavers] coming through for the last time...

From the mountains of the Mexican Southeast,
Insurgent Subcommander Marcos
June of 1994

**P.S.** of Torricelli [US Senator (D, NJ) who went to Chiapas but was denied meetings with the EZLN and other campesino groups]: We discussed whether we were going to receive him or not. What happened is that the "tendencies" in the EZLN faced off again:

Some said that we should receive him and we could trade him for an aircraft carrier (to carry those water cannons in the anti-riot trucks). Others said that he could remain captive and that Lieutenant Serapio could have dart competitions with him to see how many dollars he could get out of him (this tendency was defeated almost immediately when we wondered in what exchange bureau we could change the dollars). Some others said that he could stop by and we could detain him for a few years (let's say 30) so that he could see what it feels like to be surrounded (or blockaded, as the case may be: "it is not the same thing, but it's the same.") The minority said that he should stay and, when the airplane fell, he should be the first to taste the hard aluminum, to make sure that it is not poisoned. The discussion was at the tastiest part (in other words, when they were serving the meal), but then, after lighting my pipe, the lit match fell on the two pieces of fax paper and, in the face of the flame, the enthusiasm spread; they brought tostadas to heat up, stale cookies and a guitar. They started to sing, and of course, to dance. The "tendencies" were diluted in the dance of a *cumbia*, and the first drops of the first rains put out the embers... So went the 133rd night of the encirclement, and the moon was a red and large hole in the wounded nighttime of May. I set myself to one side. That was the last dry match...

P.S. of "THE OTHER CONSULTATION": I have looked over the portion of the external correspondence addressed to my ski mask. There is everything: drawings, famous people (of the mind and others), death threats, and challenges to duels. These are the preliminary results:

—97.98% of those consulted think I am a big fool. 2% think I am not a fool, but a clown. 0.02% did not answer (they were telling a *pepito* joke).

—87.56% think that I will end up selling myself to the government. 12% asked the price. 0.44% looked in their wallets for change.

—74.38% say that I don't write the letters and communiqués, and that with this face, they doubt I could put together a pair of coherent ideas. 25% indicate that I do write them, but that they are dictated to me. 0.62% preferred to read "el chahuistle."

—69.69% say what they say. The rest don't say it but think it. Several did not answer, but turned their eyes away and sighed noticeably.

—53.45% say that I have never been in the mountains and that I send things out from a public desk where theses and letters are typewritten [untranslatable word play follows here]; 46% said that I had been in the mountains, but those of Vail, Colorado, Iuesei [Spanish phonetic for USA]. 0.55% are lining up for the ticket to the roller coaster.

—49.99% say that I have never picked up a weapon, and that I am "a desk soldier." 50% say that the only weapon that I have picked up is the one god gave me, and who knows about that, they say. 0.01% maintained a prudent distance. (Hey! Don't splash!)

—33.71% say that "I lost ground" with the criticism of the PRD and the veto of "important newspapers"(?) . 66% say that I never had any ground at all, and that they would surely evict me. 0.29% did not bring their land tax ticket.

—26% said that my ski mask was too loose, and that it showed EVERYTHING. 73% told me to close my zipper. 0.38% went to get their binoculars.

—13.64% said I am egocentric. 86% said I am very vain. 0.36% switched newspapers and now read Nexus.

—99.99999% say to hell with meetings and consultations. 0.00001% went to the bathroom and are coming back (note: They took the consultation sheet, don't leave with it).

Well, that is how things are going. To stop the adverse tendencies I need to support the "serious" work that they are doing, such as the polls rating the popularity of Zedillo, or a voter register which they will use in August, or a carousel with the most loyal troops. Benito says that instead of tamales we can try "operation tostada." Mario cuts shells and says that "the crazy rat" is not necessary, that he will take charge of purifying the voter register. Pure modernity, then.

All right. Health, and (please) advice for the downfall of this system of computation. (Hurry! The Committee threatens with an "ad hoc" consultation on the sup-consultations.)

From some sup-electoral laboratory in the Mexican Southeast,
Subcommander Marcos
The sup, trying some alchemy to resuscitate even dinosaurs.

# On Groups Claiming Connection to the EZLN

[*La Jornada*]
June 3, 1994

To the people of Mexico:
To the peoples and governments of the world:

Brothers:

The Clandestine Revolutionary Indigenous Committee-General Command of the EZLN addresses itself to you in order to declare the following:

**First:** It has come to our attention that people who say that they are members of the organization Revolutionary Workers Clandestine Party-Union of the People (Partido Revolucionario Obrero Clandestino-Unión del Pueblo, PROCUP) have declared in certain places in the United States that PROCUP has links with the Zapatista National Liberation Army, and that the EZLN is the "armed wing" of PROCUP. These people have gathered funds implying that "they are for the EZLN."

**Second:** The Zapatista National Liberation Army declares that it has absolutely no relationship or link with the PROCUP. The EZLN has never had any contact with PROCUP, it is not part of PROCUP's structure, it does not have anything to do with PROCUP. The funds gathered by PROCUP were in no way gathered for the EZLN.

**Third:** In several townships in the state of Chiapas, members of the organization called Workers Party (Partido del Trabajo, PT) have tried to convince the campesinos to vote for them in the upcoming elections in August by saying that the PT is in contact with the EZLN and that "they have an agreement from Insurgent Subcommander Marcos," to support the PT in August.

319

**Fourth:** The Zapatista National Liberation Army declares that it has absolutely no relationship or pact with the PT. Leaders of the PT have never met with Insurgent Subcommander Marcos, nor with members of the Clandestine Revolutionary Indigenous Committee of the EZLN. We do not support the PT in the upcoming elections in August.

**Fifth:** We urge these different organizations not to use the EZLN's name for their benefit, and we ask them not to lie about supposed relationships that they do not have with the EZLN.

**Sixth:** We call on the Mexican people and on the peoples of the world to not let themselves be deceived. When the EZLN has contact or a pact with an organization, we will let it be known publicly in a communiqué, as we have done before with CEOIC and Conac-LN.

Democracy!

Freedom!

Justice!

Respectfully,

Clandestine Revolutionary Indigenous Committee-General Command of the
Zapatista National Liberation Army Mexico

# First Communiqué on the Results of the Consultations

*[La Jornada]*
June 3, 1994

To the people of Mexico:

To the peoples and governments of the world:

To the different non-governmental organizations:

Brothers:

The Clandestine Revolutionary Indigenous Committee-General Command of the Zapatista National Liberation Army addresses itself to you in order to declare the following:

**First:** The CCRI of the EZLN, as we have have recently reported, has finished its consultations in all of the communities that make up the EZLN.

**Second:** In order to inform the Mexican people about the details of the internal and external consultations that we have carried out regarding the peace accords that the federal government presented to us during the dialogue in San Cristóbal de las Casas, the CCRI of the EZLN wants to report the following figures from the internal consultations:

—The consultations took place in every community and *ejido* where there are members of the EZLN.

—The study, analysis, and discussion of the peace accords took place in democratic assemblies. The voting was direct, free, and democratic.

—After the voting, official reports of the results of the assemblies were prepared. These reports specify: the date and place of the assembly, the number of people who attended (men, women and children older than 12 years old), opinions and principal points discussed, and the number of people who voted.

—Of the Zapatista population who took part in the consultations, 100% were Indigenous, 49.54% were adult men, 42.13% were adult women and 8.32% were children over 12 years old.

—After studying, analyzing, and discussing the peace accords, those in attendance could vote on whether to sign the peace accords or not sign them.

—In addition, after voting yes or no to the peace accords, proposals were made about what actions we should take.

**Third:** At this time we are counting the votes of the internal consultations and analyzing the results of the external consultations. We will continue to inform the Mexican people about the results.

Democracy!
Freedom!
Justice!

Respectfully,
Clandestine Revolutionary Indigenous Committee-General Command of the
    Zapatista National Liberation Army

## RESULTS OF THE CONSULTATIONS

[*La Jornada*, 6/12]
June 10, 1994

To the people of Mexico:
To the peoples and governments of the world:
To the different Non-governmental organizations:
To the commissioner for peace and reconciliation in Chiapas:
To the national and international press:

The Clandestine Revolutionary Indigenous Committee-General Command of the Zapatista National Liberation Army addresses itself to you in order to report and declare the following:

**First:** The CCRI-CG of the EZLN, as we have recently reported, has finished its consultations in all of the communities that make up and support the EZLN. By means of official reports from assemblies in the *ejidos* and communities, we have learned the opinions that are in our people's hearts.

**Second:** The CCRI-CG of the EZLN has now counted the votes concerning the peace accord proposals presented to the EZLN by the federal government during the dialogue that took place in San Cristóbal de las Casas, Chiapas.

321

**Third:** The result of the free and democratic voting in the assemblies is as follows:

In favor of signing the government's peace accord proposals—2.11% of the total

Against signing the government's peace accord proposals—97.88% of the total

**Fourth:** The result of the voting about what actions we should take in case it was decided not to sign the government's peace accords is as follows:

In favor of renewing the hostilities—3.26% of the total.

In favor of continued resistance and the convening of a new national dialogue to be attended by all of the independent and honest forces in the country—96.74% of the total.

**Fifth:** Therefore, in accordance with the majority of the Zapatistas, the CCRI-CG of the EZLN wishes to inform you that:

It rejects the peace accord proposals presented by the federal government.

It considers the Dialogue of San Cristóbal to have ended. It calls on the Mexican people to attend a new national dialogue to be attended by all of the progressive forces in the country. The central themes of this dialogue will be democracy, freedom, and justice for all Mexicans.

In order not to impede the search for a political solution to the conflict and so as to not interfere in the electoral process that will take place this coming August, the CCRI-CG of the EZLN orders its regular and irregular forces in national territory and outside of Mexico to respect a unilateral offensive cease-fire.

The EZLN guarantees that it will take no offensive military action against the Federal Army.

The EZLN will not interfere with the upcoming elections in the territories under its control. It will permit the installation of electoral polls in these territories under the supervision of the different non-governmental organizations and the International Red Cross.

The EZLN will accept absolutely no aid from the municipal, state or federal governments. It will resist the military siege by its owns means, and with the help of the Mexican people.

**Sixth:** The CCRI-CG of the EZLN thanks the Commissioner for Peace and Reconciliation in Chiapas, Manuel Camacho Solís, for his true efforts in search of a political solution to the conflict. Unfortunately, the historic blindness of the supreme government kept it from seeing that its unwillingness to give in to the democratic impulse will bring about painful conflicts and unforeseen consequences.

**Seventh:** The CCRI-CG of the EZLN thanks the National Mediator, Bishop Samuel Ruiz García, and his working group, for their efforts and sacrifices in attempting to mediate between the parties involved in the conflict, their integrity in withstanding pressures and threats, and their willingness to listen. We hope that in the new dialogue that we are calling for today we can count on his honest participation in search of political solutions to the national demands for democracy, freedom, and justice.

**Eighth:** The CCRI-CG of the EZLN thanks the honest and independent media for its commitment to the truth, and for having presented the truth to the Mexican people despite threats, pressure, and blackmail. We would like to publicly apologize if we have doubted your profession at any point with our clumsy media policy. We hope that you understand that this is the first time that we have tried to carry out a revolution, and we are still learning. We would like to reiterate that, thanks to the efforts of the press, it was possible to stop the military phase of the war. We sincerely hope that you understand the difficult conditions we found ourselves in, and our unfair selection of media that we allowed to approach us. We hope that you continue publishing the truth.

**Ninth:** The CCRI-CG of the EZLN especially thanks the different non-governmental organizations, the vanguard of civil society. The NGOs have carried out a selfless work in order to bring about a peace with justice and dignity for our people. The government's siege keeps us, for the moment, from arriving at a pact with these organizations. We are still open to dialogue and are willing to continue down the path that the NGOs have pointed out to us with their commitment: a political route in the transition to democracy.

**Tenth:** The CCRI-CG of the EZLN thanks all those men, women and children, people without faces, throughout the country and outside of Mexico, who have given us their solidarity and who have joined our just cause. Our struggle and death is for you, brothers and sisters. We will not take off our masks until every Mexican—the Indigenous peoples, campesinos, workers, students, teachers, housewives, squatters, artists, intellectuals, retirees, the unemployed—men and women without voices or faces—have everything they need for a dignified and true life. Everything for everyone, nothing for ourselves.

While the national flag waves without democracy, freedom and justice above Mexican soil, we, our tender fury, will continue fighting.
Democracy!
Freedom!
Justice!

Respectfully,
Clandestine Revolutionary Indigenous Committee-General Command of the Zapatista National Liberation Army
From the mountains of the Mexican Southeast

# ON THE ZAPATISTA RESPONSE TO
# THE PEACE ACCORD PROPOSALS

[*La Jornada*, 6/12]
June 10, 1994

To the people of Mexico:
To the people and governments of the world:
To the national and international press:

Brothers and Sisters:

The Clandestine Revolutionary Indigenous Committee-General Command of the Zapatista National Liberation Army respectfully addresses itself to you to make known its response to the peace accord proposals presented to us by the supreme government during the Dialogue for Peace and Reconciliation in Chiapas.

**First:** The Zapatista National Liberation Army, the majority of whose members are Indigenous peoples, rose up against the supreme government on January 1, 1994. The demands of the EZLN can be found in the Declaration from the Lacandona Jungle: work, land, shelter, food, health, education, independence, freedom, democracy, justice, and peace. These demands are supported by the majority of the Mexican people, and the EZLN is fighting for the fulfillment of these demands for all Mexicans.

**Second:** After bloody fighting between our troops and government forces from the police and Federal Army, a national civil movement obligated us to stop the fighting and enter a dialogue with the supreme government. This dialogue took place in San Cristóbal de las Casas at the end of February and beginning of March, 1994.

**Third:** During the dialogue, the EZLN presented a list of 34 demands whose resolution would lead to a peace with justice and dignity.

**Fourth:** The list of 34 demands addressed national and state concerns, some of which affected the entire population, and some of which only referred to campesinos and Indigenous peoples. The supreme government tried in vain to reduce the importance of our just struggle to local, Indigenous concerns. They even tried to reduce its importance to concerns in four townships in the southeastern state of Chiapas.

**Fifth:** Among the national demands that affect the entire population:

**A:** Free and democratic elections. These should be held with equal rights and obligations for all political forces.

**B:** In order to guarantee freedom and democracy, we demand the resignation of the head of the federal executive power, as well as the resignations of the illegitimate heads of the state executive powers. Upon the resignation of the president of the Republic, a transitional government should be formed that will organize free and democratic elections. We also demand the passage of legislation to guarantee the rights of citizens and groups of citizens, regardless of their party affiliation, to participate in the electoral process, as the highest political authority.

**C:** We demand a new federal agreement that will end centralism and permit autonomy for Indigenous communities and townships.

**D:** We demand a review of the North American Free Trade Agreement signed with Canada and the United States because the agreement doesn't correspond with Mexico's reality.

**E:** We demand dignified work and a just salary for all workers in the country and in the cities. We also demand that the Federal Labor Law be applied and respected for the benefit of the workers in the country and in the cities.

F: We demand an end to the looting of our national resources.

G: We demand the cancellation of all debts brought about by credit, loans, or taxes.

H: We demand solutions to the national problems of hunger and malnutrition that affect the Mexican country and cities.

I: We demand immediate and unconditional freedom for all political prisoners and poor people unjustly held prisoner in jails throughout the country.

**Sixth:** The supreme government avoided responding positively to these national demands of the EZLN, demands that are shared by broad sectors of the Mexican people. The events that happened after the dialogue in San Cristóbal have shown the reason behind the EZLN's demands for democracy. The cowardly murder of Colosio, the imposed designation of Zedillo as the PRI's candidate, and the new enterprise with which the government hard-liners have been advancing, demonstrate that it would have been best for the nation if Salinas de Gortari had resigned as head of the federal executive after January 1. His keen desire to stay in power has kept our country in a permanent state of insecurity. His desire to continue his usurpation through election fraud, and now with Zedillo, has pushed our nation to the brink of civil war.

The electoral reform was incomplete. The continuing existence of a corrupt electoral process allows electronic fraud, and reinforces the usurpation of the people's will.

The reinforcement of the government's repressive apparatus, and the attempt to force the Federal Army to assume police duties, allows us to see very clearly that the goal of Salinas's group is not a transition to democracy, but to fraud.

The Zapatista National Liberation Army confirms what reality points out: There is no democratic impulse on the part of the supreme government. The state-party system must be destroyed. The EZLN reiterates the demands expressed in points one and two of the list presented in San Cristóbal:

**One:** Free and democratic elections.

**Two:** The overthrow of the usurpers in the federal government and in the governments of the states of the Federation.

The EZLN broadens its demands:

A democratic transitional government and a new legislature are necessary. These new bodies should ensure, in law and in fact, that the fundamental demands of the Mexican people are carried out: the demands for democracy, freedom, and justice, demands that have been voiced by those without a voice, that have taken on a face in those who have no faces, and have taken on life in our deaths.

The government tried to reduce the demands for autonomy to the Indigenous communities, and thereby leave intact the centralist power structure that magnifies the power of the federal executive in a dictatorial manner. The demand for the autonomy of the townships was tossed aside. The law promised by the government to recognize the political, economic, and cultural autonomy of the Indigenous communities follows the usual line: a law that doesn't resolve the deep-rooted problems, that isn't consensed upon within the Indigenous movement, and that is to be approved undemocratically. Violating its own offer that the General Law of the Rights of the Indigenous Communities would respond to "the demands, opinions, worries, and political consensus of the Indigenous communities," and that it would be enhanced by "a group of specialists," the law merely focuses on an expedient application of Article Four of the Constitution.

To the demand for a review of the North American Free Trade Agreement, the government responded by continuing with an economic project that has done nothing but increase poverty in our country and deceive their foreign business partners by promising them economic stability and social peace in Mexico. The government agreed to make a "careful evaluation of the effects of NAFTA" within 90 days. This "evaluation" hasn't been carried out, but the government doesn't have to spend time or money on an "impact evaluation commission." The impacts of NAFTA can be observed in any poor household in Mexico.

As a response to the national demand for dignified work and a just salary, the government continued with its economic policies; these policies increase unemployment and underemployment and reduce workers' purchasing power. The corruption of the unions is still the base that sustains the neoliberal economic project. The demand for an end to the looting of our national resources is tossed aside, and the government's response tries to reduce it to an ecological problem. A national policy to defend our country's natural resources does not exist. To the demand for the cancellation of all debts incurred by the impoverished classes of the nation, the government responded with a promise for a study, the result of which would surely be to postpone the problem.

As with the aforementioned points, the government tried to reduce the demand for a solution to the problem of hunger and malnutrition to certain regions of Chiapas. As if hunger only affected the Indigenous peoples of the mountains and the jungle, and as if social programs could be eaten, the government promised infant nutrition programs.

They laughed at our demand for freedom for all political prisoners and for all poor people unjustly held in jails throughout the country. They promised to set up a commission that would study the cases. The unjust Mexican judicial system, a system that only favors the rich, will remain intact.

In all, the EZLN's just national demands were not in any way answered by the federal government. Therefore, the EZLN rejects points 1, 2, 4, 7, 18, 29, 21, 22, and 23 of the government's peace accord proposals.

**Seventh:** Among the EZLN's demands on the part of Mexican campesinos were:

A: A demand that Article 27 of the Constitution respect the original spirit of Emiliano Zapata: The land belongs to those who work it.

B: A demand for the construction of hospitals and clinics with doctors and medicines in every rural community in the country.

C: A demand for a just price for products from the countryside, an end to the current middle-man arrangement and an end to the direct exploitation of campesinos as rural workers.

**D:** A demand that the Army and police stop acting for the benefit of landlords and *caciques* in rural communities.

**Eighth:** The supreme government refused to answer the campesinos' national demands. The government's refusal to change Salinas's reforms to Article 27 of the Constitution, and to return the right to land to the Constitution, was repudiated by broad sectors of campesinos throughout the country. The current reforms to Article 27, the base of neoliberal policies in the countryside, should be changed. The Political Constitution of the United Mexican States should reflect Emiliano Zapata's struggle.

The government's response to our demand for hospitals, clinics, doctors, and medicines for the Mexican countryside was limited to offers that only would have affected the conflict zone. The rest of the Mexican countryside would have been forgotten.

To our demand for just prices for products from the countryside and an end to the current middle-man arrangement, the government responded by offering the services of Procampo, an agency that is only efficient at corrupting campesino leaders and buying their votes for the state party. The government's solution to the problems of Mexican campesinos, campesinos who are fighting for survival, is promises of projects.

To our demand that the police and military leave rural areas, the government responded by promising changes in the justice system. These changes would mean an increase in troops in the countryside and an increase in repressive measures. They still intend to force the Federal Army to assume police powers. The power of ranchers, backed by the economic strength of the government, is holding campesinos and Indigenous peoples hostage.

In all, the EZLN's just demands on the part of Mexican campesinos were not satisfactorily answered by the government. Some of their responses pointed to partial or local solutions. Therefore, the EZLN rejects points 8, 9, 19, and 24 of the peace accord proposals.

**Ninth:** Among the EZLN's demands on the part of Indigenous peoples were:

**A:** The right of Indigenous peoples to timely and true information by means of an independent Indigenous radio station.

**B:** Complete and free education for all Indigenous peoples.

**C:** The official status of Indigenous languages. They should be taught at all levels of education.

**D:** Respect for the culture and traditions of Indigenous peoples.

**E:** An end to discrimination and racism against Indigenous peoples.

**F:** Cultural, political, and judicial autonomy for Indigenous peoples.

**G:** Respect for the Indigenous peoples' right to freedom and a dignified life.

**H:** Social and economic support for Indigenous women.

**Tenth:** The supreme government partially answered these demands on the part of Indigenous peoples.

Although the government promised Indigenous peoples their own independent radio station, their response to our demands for education was limited to offers of selective scholarships that would leave most Indigenous peoples without an education. The rest of their response to our demands was limited to promises of studies and programs. These were to be carried out in time-frames that have, for the most part, already passed.

In all, the partial responses of the government to our demands and their failure to carry out previous agreements lead us to reject points 10, 12, 13, 14, 15, 16, 17, 27, and 29 of the peace accord proposals.

**Eleventh:** Among the EZLN's demands at the state level were:

**A:** General elections in Chiapas and legal recognition of all political forces in the state.

**B:** Electricity for rural Chiapas and the use of a percentage of state profits for the commercialization of oil.

**C:** Indemnities for victims of the war.

**D:** Elimination of all limitations on political movements in the Penal Code of the State of Chiapas.

**E:** An end to evictions and the free and voluntary return of those who have been evicted to their land, along with compensation for damages suffered.

**F:** Political trial of Patrocinio González Garrido, Absalón Castellanos Domínguez and Elmar Setzer.

**Twelfth:** The supreme government failed to respond satisfactorily to the EZLN's demands at a state level.

Electoral reform in Chiapas doesn't permit groups that are not parties to organize and take part in the elections. To our demand for electricity for rural Chiapas, the government responded with programs and promises. Evictions continue and those responsible are still not punished. There are only promises of economic support for Indigenous peoples in the state, and when some of these promises are carried out, it is in exchange for votes. A political trial of the three ex-governors who are responsible for forcing us to take up arms was omitted from the proposals.

In all, the government's unsatisfactory answers, and our lack of trust in the government's willingness to carry out their promises, lead us to reject points 5, 6, 25, 27, 28, 29, and 30 of the peace accord proposals.

**Thirteenth:** Finally, the EZLN demanded its recognition as a belligerent force by the government. The Mexican people, by means of different organizations, has given us this recognition.

To our demand for recognition as a belligerent force and for the recognition of our troops as true combatants, the government responded by offering respectful and dignified treatment for all members of the EZLN. It also offered us legal registration as a political force.

The government can't even guarantee the security of those who are part of the government. We cannot hope for a respectful and dignified treatment of those who have taken up arms in a just struggle for democracy, freedom, and justice. The EZLN was formed as an army to demand respect for the will of the people. The usurping government still refuses to respect this will.

The reasons behind the birth of the EZLN still exist. The EZLN will continue its armed struggle until our demands for democracy, freedom, and justice are achieved. The EZLN agrees to follow international treaties that regulate combat and warfare. The EZLN has held true to these treaties and we will continue to do so.

The EZLN reiterates its demand that it be recognized as a belligerent force, and that its troops be recognized as true combatants. To this end, the EZLN will go to different international forums to demand this recognition from the peoples and governments of the world.

The recognition of the EZLN as a belligerent force is necessary for the dialogue process to have a firm base to develop from.

**Fourteenth:** The supreme government presented its peace accord proposals during the dialogue in San Cristóbal de las Casas. The EZLN responded by explaining that it had to consult all of its members; the people who make us up are those who gave us the order to go to war and only these people can order us to make peace. After a period of time, we have finished with the consultations. This is our response to the government's proposals.

**Fifteenth:** Through the foregoing communiqué, and in light of the free and democratic vote of those who are part of the EZLN, we say NO to the supreme government's peace accord proposals. We see this as a close to the dialogue of San Cristóbal. We reiterate our disposition to continue in search of a political solution that will lead to a peace with justice and dignity. We call on all progressive and independent sectors of society to attend a national dialogue for a peace with democracy, freedom, and justice.

We will not surrender!
Democracy!
Freedom!
Justice!
Respectfully,

From the mountains of the Mexican Southeast,
Clandestine Revolutionary Indigenous Committee-General Command
    of the EZLN


# Second Declaration from the Lacandona Jungle

[*La Jornada*, 6/12]
June 10, 1994

*"Today we say: We will not surrender!"*

*"... Those who bear swords aren't the only ones who lose blood or who shine with the fleeting light of military glory. They aren't the only ones who should have a voice in designating the leaders of the government of a people who want democracy; this right to choose belongs to every citizen who has fought in the press or in the courts. It belongs to every citizen who identifies with the ideals of the Revolution and who has fought against the despotism that has ignored our laws. Tyranny isn't eliminated just by fighting on the battlefield; dictatorships and empires are also overthrown by launching cries of freedom and terrible threats against those who are executing the people... Historical events have shown us that the destruction of tyranny and the overthrow of all evil governments are the work of ideas together with the sword. It is therefore an absurdity, an aberration, an outrageous despotism to deny the people the right to elect their government. The people's sovereignty is formed by all those people in society who are conscious of their rights and who, be they civilians or armed, love freedom and justice and who work for the good of the country."*
—Paulino Martínez, Zapatista delegate to the Revolutionary Sovereignty Convention, Aguascalientes, Mexico, on behalf of Emiliano Zapata.
October 27, 1914

To the people of Mexico:
To the peoples and governments of the world:

Brothers and Sisters:

The Zapatista National Liberation Army, on a war footing against the government since January 1, 1994, addresses itself to you in order to make known its opinion:

Mexican Brothers and Sisters:

In December, 1993, we said, "Enough!" On January 1, 1994, we called on the legislative and judicial powers to assume their constitutional responsibility and to restrain the genocidal policies that the federal executive imposes on our people. We base our constitutional right in the application of Article 39 of the Political Constitution of the United Mexican States:
"National sovereignty essentially and originally resides in the people. All political power emanates from the people and its purpose is to help the people. The people have, at all times, the inalienable right to alter or modify their form of government."
The government responded to this call with a policy of extermination and lies. The powers in Mexico ignored our just demand and permitted a massacre. However, this massacre only lasted 12 days. Another force, a force superior to any political or military power, imposed its will on the parties involved in the conflict. Civil society assumed the duty of preserving our country. It showed its disapproval of the massacre and it obliged us to dialogue with the government. We understand that the ascendancy of the political party that has been in power for so long cannot be allowed to continue. We understand that this party, a party that has kept the fruits of every Mexican's labor for itself, cannot be allowed to continue. We understand that the corruption of the presidential elections

330

that sustains this party impedes our freedom and should not be allowed to continue. We understand that the culture of fraud is the method with which this party imposes and impedes democracy. We understand that justice only exists for the corrupt and powerful. We understand that we must construct a society in which those who lead do so with the will of the people. There is no other path.

This is understood by every honest Mexican in civil society. Only those who have based their success on the theft of the public trust, those who protect criminals and murderers by prostituting justice, those who resort to political murder and electoral fraud in order to impose their will, are opposed to our demands.

These antiquated politicians plan to roll back history and erase the cry from the national consciousness that was taken up by the country after January 1, 1994: "Enough!"

We will not permit this. Today we do not call on those weak powers in Mexico that refuse to assume their constitutional duties and which permit themselves to be controlled by the federal executive. If the legislature and the judges have no dignity, then others who do understand that they must serve the people, and not the individual, will step forward. Our call transcends the question of presidential terms or the upcoming election. Our sovereignty resides in civil society. Only the people can alter or modify our form of government. It is to them that we address this Second Declaration from the Lacandona Jungle.

**First:** We have respected the international conventions of warfare while we have carried out our military actions. These conventions have allowed us to be recognized as a belligerent force by national and foreign forces. We will continue to respect these conventions.

**Second:** We order all of our regular and irregular forces, both inside national territory and outside the country, to continue to obey the unilateral offensive cease-fire. We will continue to respect the cease-fire in order to permit civil society to organize in whatever forms they consider pertinent toward the goal of achieving a transition to democracy in our country.

**Third:** We condemn the threats against civilian society brought about by the militarization of the country, both in terms of personal and modern repressive equipment, during this time leading up to the federal elections. Without a doubt, the Salinas government is trying to impose its will by fraud. We will not permit this.

**Fourth:** We propose to all independent political parties that are suffering from intimidation and repression of political rights—the same intimidation and repression that our people have suffered for the last 65 years—that they declare themselves in favor of a government of transition toward democracy.

**Fifth:** We reject the manipulation and the attempts to separate our just demands from the demands of the Mexican people. We are Mexicans, and we will not put aside our demands nor our arms until we have democracy, freedom, and justice for all.

**Sixth:** We reiterate our disposition toward finding a political solution to the transition to democracy in Mexico. We call upon civil society to re-take the protagonist's role that it first took up in order to stop the military phase of the war. We call upon civil society to organize itself in order to direct the peaceful efforts towards democracy, freedom, and justice. Democratic change is the only alternative to war.

**Seventh:** We call on all honest sectors of civil society to attend a National Dialogue for Democracy, Freedom and Justice.

For this reason we say:

Brothers and Sisters:

After the start of the war in January, 1994, the organized cry of the Mexican people stopped the fighting and called for a dialogue between the contending forces. The federal government responded to the just demands of the EZLN with a series of offers that didn't touch on the essential problem: the lack of justice, freedom, and democracy in Mexican territory.

The offers with which the federal government responded to the demands of the EZLN are limited by the system of the political party in power. This system has made possible the continuation of certain sectors in the Mexican countryside that have superseded the power of the Constitution, and whose roots have maintained the party in power. It is this system of complicity that has made possible the existence and belligerence of the *caciques*, the omnipotent power of the ranchers and businessmen, and the spread of drug-trafficking. Just the fact that the government offered us the so-called Proposals for a Dignified Peace in Chiapas provoked tremendous agitation and an open defiance by these sectors. The single-party political system is trying to maneuver within this reduced horizon. It can't alienate these sectors without attacking itself, yet it can't leave things as they are without having to face the anger of the campesinos and Indigenous peoples. In other words, to go through with the proposals would necessarily mean the death of the state party system. By suicide or execution, the death of the current Mexican political system is a necessary precondition, although it is not sufficient, for the transition to democracy in our country. There will be no real solutions in Chiapas until the situation in Mexico as a whole is resolved.

The EZLN understands that the problem of poverty in Mexico isn't due just to a lack of resources. Our fundamental understanding and position is that whatever efforts are made will only postpone the problem if these efforts aren't made within the context of new local, regional, and national political relationships—relationships marked by democracy, freedom, and justice. The problem of power is not a question of who rules, but of who exercises power. If it is exercised by a majority of the people, the political parties will be obligated to put their proposals forward to the people instead of merely relating to each other.

Looking at the problem of power within the context of democracy, freedom, and justice will create a new political culture within the parties. A new type of political leader will be born and, without a doubt, new types of political parties will be born as well.

We aren't proposing a new world, but something preceding a new world: an antechamber looking into the new Mexico. In this sense, this revolution will not end in a new class, faction of a class, or group in power. It will end in a free and democratic space for political struggle. This free and democratic space will be born on the fetid cadaver of the state party system and the tradition of fixed presidential succession. A new political relationship will be born, a relationship based not in the confrontation of political organizations among themselves, but in the confrontation of their political proposals with different social classes. Political leadership will depend on the support of these social classes, and not

332

on the mere exercise of power. In this new political relationship, different political proposals (socialism, capitalism, social democracy, liberalism, christian democracy, etc.) will have to convince a majority of the nation that their proposal is the best for the country. The groups in power will be watched by the people in such a way that they will be obligated to give a regular accounting of themselves, and the people will be able to decide whether they remain in power or not. The plebiscite is a regulated form of confrontation among the nation, political parties, and power, and it merits a place in the highest law of the country.

Current Mexican law is too constricting for these new political relationships between the governed and the governors. A National Democratic Convention is needed from which a provisional or transitional government can emerge, be it by the resignation of the federal executive or by an electoral route.

This National Democratic Convention and transitional government should lead to the creation of a new constitution, and, in the context of this new constitution, new elections should be held. The pain that this process will bring to the country will be less than the damage that would be caused by a civil war. The prophecy of the Southeast is valid for the entire country. We can learn from what has already occurred so that there is less pain during the birth of the new Mexico.

The EZLN has its idea of what system and proposal are best for the country. The political maturity of the EZLN as a representative of a sector of the nation is shown by the fact that it doesn't want to impose its proposal on the country. The EZLN demands what is shown by their example: the political maturity of Mexico and the right for all to decide, freely and democratically, the course that Mexico must take. Not only will a better and more-just Mexico emerge from this historic synthesis, but a new Mexico as well. This is why we are gambling our lives: so that the Mexicans of the future can inherit a country in which it isn't shameful to live...

The EZLN, in a democratic exercise without precedent in an armed organization, consulted its component bases about whether or not to sign the peace accords presented by the federal government. The Indigenous bases of the EZLN, seeing that the central demands of democracy, freedom and justice have yet to be resolved, decided against signing the government's proposal.

Under siege and under pressure from different sectors that threatened us with extermination if the peace accords weren't signed, we Zapatistas reaffirmed our commitment to achieve a peace with justice and dignity. In our struggle, the dignified struggle of our ancestors has found a home. The cry of dignity of the insurgent Vincente Guererro, "Live for the country or die for freedom," once again sounds from our throats. We cannot accept an undignified peace.

Our path sprang out of the impossibility of struggling peacefully for our elemental rights as human beings. The most valuable of these rights is the right to decide, freely and democratically, what form the government will take. Now the possibility of a peaceful change to democracy and freedom confronts a new test: the electoral process that will take place this August, 1994. There are those who are betting on the outcome of the elections and the post-election period. There are those who are predicting apathy and disillusionment. They hope to profit from the blood of those who fall in the struggles, both violent

333

and peaceful, in the cities and in the countryside. They found their political project in the conflict they hope will come after the elections. They hope that the political demobilization will once again open the door to war. They say that they will save the country.

Others hope that the armed conflict will restart before the elections so that they can take advantage of the chaotic situation to keep themselves in power. Just as they did before, when they usurped popular will with electoral fraud, these people hope to take advantage of a pre-electoral civil war in order to prolong the agony of a dictatorship that has already lasted decades. There are others, sterile nay-sayers, who reason that war is inevitable and who are waiting to watch their enemy's cadaver float by...or their friend's cadaver. The sectarians suppose, erroneously, that just the firing of a gun will bring about the dawn that our people have waited for since night fell upon Mexican soil with the death of Villa and Zapata.

Every one of these people who steals hope supposes that behind our weapons are ambition and an agenda that will guide us to the future. They are wrong. Behind our weapons is another weapon: reason. Hope gives life to both of our weapons. We won't let them steal our hope.

The hope that came with the trigger came about at the beginning of the year. It is precisely now that the hope that comes with political mobilizations takes up the protagonist's role that belongs to it by right and reason. The flag is now in the hands of those who have names and faces, good and honest people who have the same goal that we yearn for. Our greetings to these men and women. You have our greetings and our hope that you can carry the flag to where it should be. We will be standing there waiting for you with dignity. If the flag should fall, we will be there to pick it up again...

Now is the time for hope to organize itself and to walk forward in the valleys and in the cities, as it did before in the mountains of the Southeast. Fight with your weapons; don't worry about ours. We know how to resist to the end. We know how to wait... And we know what to do if the doors through which dignity walks close once again.

This is why we address our brothers and sisters in different non-governmental organizations, in campesino and Indigenous organizations, workers in the cities and in the countryside, teachers and students, housewives and squatters, artists and intellectuals, members of independent political parties, Mexicans.

We call all of you to a national dialogue with the theme of democracy, freedom, and justice. For this reason, we put forward the following invitation to a National Democratic Convention:

We, the Zapatista National Liberation Army, fighting to achieve the democracy, freedom, and justice that our country deserves, and considering that:

**One:** The supreme government has usurped the legality that we inherited from the hero of the Mexican Revolution.

**Two:** The Constitution that exists doesn't reflect the popular will of the Mexican people.

**Three:** The resignation of the federal executive usurper isn't enough and that a new law is necessary for the new country that will be born from the struggles of all honest Mexicans.

**Four:** Every form of struggle is necessary in order to achieve the transition to democracy in Mexico.

Considering these things, we call for a sovereign and revolutionary National Democratic Convention from which will come a transitional government and a new national law, a new constitution that will guarantee the legal fulfillment of the people's will.

This sovereign revolutionary convention will be national in that all states of the federation will be represented. It will be plural in the sense that all patriotic sectors will be represented. It will be democratic in the way in which it will make decisions by national consultations.

The Convention will be presided over, freely and voluntarily, by civilians, prestigious public figures, regardless of their political affiliation, race, religion, sex, or age.

The Convention will be launched by local, state, and regional committees in every *ejido*, settlement, school, and factory. These committees of the Convention will be in charge of collecting the people's proposals for the new constitution and the demands to be completed by the new government that comes out of the Convention.

The convention should demand free and democratic elections and should fight for the people's will to be respected.

The Zapatista National Liberation Army will recognize the National Democratic Convention as the authentic representative of the interests of the Mexican people in their transition to democracy.

The Zapatista National Liberation Army is now to be found throughout national territory and is in a position to offer itself to the Mexican people as an army to guarantee that the people's will is carried out.

For the first meeting of the National Democratic Convention, the EZLN offers as a meeting-place a Zapatista settlement with all of the resources to be found there.

The date and place of the first session of the National Democratic Convention will be announced when it is appropriate to do so.

Mexican Brothers and Sisters:

Our struggle continues. The Zapatista flag still waves in the mountains of the Mexican Southeast and today we say: We will not surrender!

Facing the mountains we speak to our dead so that their words will guide us along the path that we must walk.

The drums sound, and in the voices from the land we hear our pain and our history.

"Everything for everyone," say our dead. "As long as this is not true, there will be nothing for us.

"Find in your hearts the voices of those for whom we fight. Invite them to walk the dignified path of those who have no faces. Call them to resist. Let no one receive anything from those who rule. Ask them to reject the handouts from the powerful. Let all the good people in this land organize with dignity. Let them resist and not sell out.

"Don't surrender! Resist! Resist with dignity in the lands of the true men and women! Let the mountains shelter the pain of the people of this land. Don't surrender! Resist! Don't sell-out! Resist!"

Our dead spoke these words from their hearts. We have seen that the words of our dead are good, that there is truth in what they say and dignity in their counsel. For this reason we call on our brother Mexicans to resist with us. We call on the Indigenous campesinos to resist with us. We call on the workers, squatters, housewives, students, teachers, intellectuals, writers, on all those with dignity, to resist with us. The government doesn't want democracy in our land. We will accept nothing that comes from the rotting heart of the government, not a single coin nor a single dose of medication, not a single stone nor a single grain of food. We will not accept the handouts that the government offers in exchange for our dignity.

We will not take anything from the supreme government. Although they increase our pain and sorrow, although death may accompany us, although we may see others selling themselves to the hand that oppresses them, although everything may hurt and sorrow may cry out from the rocks, we will not accept anything. We will resist. We will not take anything from the government. We will resist until those who are in power exercise their power while obeying the people's will.

Brothers and Sisters:

Don't sell out. Resist with us. Don't surrender. Resist with us. Repeat along with us, "We will not surrender! We will resist!" Let these words be heard not only in the mountains of the Mexican Southeast, but in the North and on the peninsulas. Let it be heard on both coasts. Let it be heard in the center of the country. Let it cry out in the valleys and in the mountains. Let it sound in the cities and in the countryside. Unite your voices, brothers. Cry out with us: "We will not surrender! We will resist!"

Let dignity break the siege and lift off of us the filthy hands with which the government is trying to strangle us. We are all under siege. They will not let democracy, freedom, and justice enter Mexican territory. Brothers, we are all under siege. We will not surrender! We will resist! We have dignity! We will not sell-out!

What good are the riches of the powerful if they aren't able to buy the most valuable thing in these lands? If the dignity of the Mexican people has no price, then what good is the power of the powerful?

Dignity will not surrender!

Dignity will resist!

Democracy!

Freedom!

Justice!

From the mountains of the Mexican Southeast,

Clandestine Revolutionary Indigenous Committee-General Command of the
    Zapatista National Liberation Army

Mexico

June, 1994

# TIMELINE

**January 1** The North American Free Trade Agreement (NAFTA) takes effect. The Zapatista National Liberation Army (EZLN) emerges from the Lacandona Jungle, occupies the Chiapas highland towns of Ocosingo, Las Margaritas, Altamirano and San Cristóbal de las Casas, resulting in two police dead in Ocosingo. The EZLN takes over municipal buildings, frees prisoners from jails, opens government shops to the populace. The EZLN issues the *Declaration from the Lacandona Jungle*, denouncing NAFTA as a "death sentence" for Mexican Indians, demanding legal recognition as a legitimate belligerent force against the Federal Army, announcing their intent to comply with the Geneva Conventions and international law, and calling upon the world community to pressure the Mexican government to do likewise.

**January 2** Fighting ensues as police and the Federal Army attempt to take occupied towns, leaving scores dead. General Absalón Castellanos Domínguez, former governor of Chiapas, is seized at his ranch by the EZLN, charged with crimes against campesinos and Indians.

**January 3** The EZLN retreats from San Cristóbal, engages the Federal Army at the Nuevo Rancho Base outside town; fighting escalates in Ocosingo, Las Margaritas and Altamirano.

**January 4** The government begins aerial bombardment of San Cristóbal's poor, outlying areas. Fierce fighting in Ocosingo's central square. Bishop Samuel Ruiz García of San Cristóbal calls for a cease-fire.

**January 6** The EZLN retreats from Ocosingo, Las Margaritas and Altamirano.

**January 7** A car bomb explodes in Mexico City's University Plaza.

**January 8** Power lines and other targets are bombed elsewhere in the country, including a federal building in Acapulco. An ultra-left cell, PROCUP-PDLP, claims responsibility, "in solidarity" with the EZLN. The EZLN denies any connection.

**January 10** The Mexican stock market plunges. Demonstrations against the repression mount in Mexico City and around the country. President Carlos Salinas de Gortari fires former governor of Chiapas Patrocinio Gonzalez Blanco Garrido from his post as Interior Minister for denying the existence of the guerrilla threat.

**January 12** A massive march on Mexico City in protest of the repression. The government declares a cease-fire, offers limited amnesty to the EZLN.

**January 16** The National Human Rights Commission investigators uncover a mass grave in Ocosingo.

**January 20** Accounts mount of summary executions and torture by government troops during the fighting.

**January 25** President Salinas visits Chiapas state capital Tuxtla Gutierrez to meet with campesino leaders; gets angry response from them. The government promises dialogue, names Bishop Ruiz as mediator and former Mexico City mayor and federal Environment Minister Manuel Camacho Solís as government peace spokesman.

**January 29** The government begins freeing Zapatista prisoners.

**February 1** An Americas Watch report accuses the Mexican government of grave human rights violations in putting down the uprising.

**February 7** Campesinos occupy a municipal building in the highlands town of Teopisca, beginning a wave of militant protests and land occupations by unarmed Indians and campesinos throughout the highlands of Chiapas. Campesinos march on Tuxtla Gutierrez to demand land reform.

**February 12** "Secret" meeting between new Interior Minister (former Attorney General) Jorge Carpizo and CIA chief James Woolsey in Mexico City.

**February 16** The EZLN releases General Absalón Castellanos to Ruiz and Camacho at Guadalupe Tepeyac, on the edge of the Lacandona Jungle.

**February 27** EZLN-government Dialogue for Peace and Reconciliation in Chiapas begins at the Cathedral of San Cristóbal. The EZLN team includes Subcommander Marcos and Commander Ramona, who wow the press. Death threats mount against Bishop Ruiz, who is accused of being a spokesperson for the EZLN.

**March 2** The EZLN dialogue team ends the "first phase" of the dialogue and returns to the Lacandona Jungle to bring the government proposals to the communities for discussion and decision-making.

**March 6** The newly-formed State Council of Indigenous and Campesino Organizations (CEOIC) holds the first open, pro-EZLN rally in San Cristóbal. The Municipal Palace is occupied; "¡VIVA EZLN!" is painted on walls throughout the city.

**March 9** Mariano Perez Diaz of the Emeliano Zapata Campesino Organization (OCEZ) is murdered in the highlands village of Simojovel, escalating the wave of terror against campesino leaders by presumed *guardias blancas*.

**March 23** Luis Donaldo Colosio, presidential candidate of the long-ruling Institutional Revolutionary Party (PRI), is assassinated at a campaign stop in Tijuana, just five months before the scheduled elections.

**March 24** The EZLN declares a state of "Red Alert" throughout their Lacandona Jungle stronghold; they claim that the Federal Army used the assassination as a cover to violate the cease-fire with an aerial bombardment of a road in Zapatista-held territory. They declare the consultations of the communities temporarily suspended.

**March 29** The PRI names former education minister Ernesto Ponce de Leon Zedillo as their new presidential candidate.

**April 4** The government announces seven suspects in Colosio's death, including members of his security team. The Mexican stock market takes another plunge.

**April 10** Thousands march on Mexico City in solidarity with the EZLN's demands, and to commemorate the 1917 assassination of Emiliano Zapata. Clashes with the police are reported in the city of Puebla.

**April 28** Tijuana police chief Federico Benitez is killed in an ambush by unknown assailants. Left and right opposition parties accuse the government of a cover-up in the Colosio assassination.

**May 1** Traditional Mayday celebrations bring out thousands in Mexico City, and elsewhere, in support of the EZLN.

**June 12** The EZLN announces that, after consulting with their communities in the Lacandona Jungle villages, the government peace proposals have been rejected. They urge "civil society" to take up the struggle.

# GLOSSARY

This glossary is intended to help you identify people, places, and ideas that would be difficult to look up in standard reference books. We are not professional glossary writers, and this glossary is not comprehensive or perfect. Some readers will probably wish we had been more political, and others less. Overall, we have tended towards caution.

**10 Points**—the EZLN's basic demands, these are often cited partially in the text; they include some or all of the following: work, land, housing, food, health care, education, independence, freedom, democracy, justice, and peace

**1846 (the Yankee Invasion of 1846)**—known in the US as the Mexican War, this was touched off by the forcible US annexation of Texas

**1968**—the year of an incident in which the Mexican Federal Army sprayed machine-gun fire into a plaza in which students were protesting; more than 300 students were killed; the government denies the incident

**1988**—the year of the most recent Mexican presidential elections; it is widely believed that Cuauhtémoc **Cardenas** won the popular vote, although the official results were in favor of the ruling **PRI**. Public outrage at the alleged fraud resulted in riots, marches, and other protests.

**31st Military Zone**—the Mexican Army command area that includes Chiapas

**Agrarian Reform**—the redistribution of land from large-landowners to the landless, based on **Zapata**'s idea of returning the land to those who work it. Agrarian reform has been undertaken at various times throughout the recent history of Mexico, especially during and after the **Mexican Revolution**. The plans for reform have consistently been weakened, and were effectively dismantled by Carlos **Salinas de Gortari**'s re-definition of **Article 27** of the Mexican Constitution.

**Amuzgo**—an Indigenous ethnicity

**ARIC/Union of Unions (Asociación Rural de Interés Colectivo, Rural Association of Collective Interest)**—an association of Indigenous campesinos, many of whom have been relocated to the Lacandona Jungle; the EZLN denounced elements of the ARIC for collaboration with the government

**Article 27 of the Mexican Constitution**—refers to the **Agrarian Reform** portion of the Constitution, which **Salinas** altered, effectively ending the redistribution of land

**Article 39 of the Mexican Constitution**—states that "National sovereignty essentially and originally resides in the people. All political power emanates from the people, and its purpose is to help the people. The people have, at all times, the inalienable right to alter or modify their form of government."

**Article 4 of the Mexican Constitution**—defines Mexico as a multi-ethnic country and reserves the right of Indigenous people to preserve their language and culture

**Banrural (Banco de Crédito Rural)**—a national bank that provides credit to rural areas; the EZLN decries the Banrural as a tool of economic control over campesinos

**Boggie el Aceitoso**—an Argentinean cartoon character by Fontanarosa, he is a mercenary with no ideology except his love of money

**Cabañas, Lucio**—the founder and *caudillo* of PROCOUP and PDLP

**Cacique**—a member of a local ruling class, frequently Indigenous, who maintains political power by supporting and maintaining the power of a particular political party

**Camacho Solís, Manuel**—a PRI party official, former mayor of Mexico City, and anticipated-but-passed-over candidate for the presidency, Camacho acted as **Commissioner for Peace and Reconciliation in Chiapas** in the government negotiations with the EZLN

**Campesino**—a person who works the land and lives in the country

**Cardenas, Cuauhtémoc**—the PRD candidate for the Mexican presidency, he is widely believed to have won the popular vote in **1988**

**Carranza, Venustiano**—a major figure in the **Mexican Revolution**, he was seen as representing the interests of the national bourgeoisie

**Castellanos Domínguez, Division General Absalón**—a Mexican Army General, Castellanos Domínguez was captured by the EZLN, put on trial for his oppression of Indigenous peoples during his term as governor of Chiapas, and condemned to life in prison. The sentence was commuted to life working in the fields of Chiapas. Castellanos Domínguez was released just before the beginning of the **Dialogue for Peace and Reconciliation in Chiapas.**

*Caudillo/caudillismo*—the practice of an individual becoming, or being seen as, the supreme leader of a political movement, especially a guerrilla movement

**CCRI-CG**—see **Clandestine Revolutionary Indigenous Committee**

*Charro*—a labor boss

**Chiapaneco**—of Chiapas, or from Chiapas

**Chol**—a Mayan Indigenous ethnicity

**Clandestine Revolutionary Indigenous Committee-General Command of the EZLN (Comité Clandestino Revolucionario Indigena-Comandancia General, CCRI-CG)**—the leadership of the Zapatista National Liberation Army, the CCRI-CG is composed of delegates from various Indigenous Committees, and is responsible to the Committees, which are in turn responsible to the local communities

**CLETA (Centro Libre de Experimentación Teatral y Artistical, Free Center of Theatrical and Artistic Experimentation)**—a leftist arts and culture group in Mexico City

**CNPA (Coordinadora Nacional Plan de Ayala, National Plan de Ayala Coordinating Committee)**—named after Emiliano **Zapata**'s 1914 land redistribution manifesto, and oversees it's implementation.

**Colima**—an indigenous ethnicity

**Colosio, Luis Donaldo**—the **PRI** candidate for president, Colosio was assassinated on March 23 while making a campaign speech; the social crisis caused by the assassination caused the EZLN to suspend its community **consultations** about the results of the **Dialogue for Peace and Reconciliation in Chiapas**

**Commissioner**—refers to Manuel **Camacho Solís**

*Compañero*—companions and comrades, partners in life and in struggle

**Corralchén**—a town in the township of Ocosingo. In May, 1993 the Federal Army discovered an EZLN training camp there, and began to deploy troops to crush the movement. The military operation was quickly called off, to the confusion of many commentators.

*Coyotes*—profiteering middle-men

**Díaz, Porfirio**—Dictator of Mexico from 1876-1880 and 1884-1911, whose rule began with the Revolution of Tuxtepec, after Díaz lost his bid for the Mexican presidency. He brought capitalist development to Mexico and also encouraged the concentration of wealth in the hands of an elite. He was overthrown by the **Mexican Revolution**.

*Ejidos*—collectively held land, mostly for farming. Provided for by **Article 27** of the Mexican Constitution.

**Federation**—the Republic of Mexico

**Fernández de Cevallos, Diego**—the **PAN**'s presidential candidate

*Finquero*—a farmer or rancher (see *Ganadero*)

**Flores Magón Brothers**—Mexican anarchists who organized workers during the **Mexican Revolution**

**FMLN (Frente Farabundo Martí de Liberación Nacional, Farabundo Martí National Liberation Front)**—an armed liberation group in El Salvador; they accepted a government amnesty and disarmament in 1992

**Foco**—a kind of guerrilla cell common to Latin American revolutionary movements; also a theory of guerrilla warfare associated with Ché Guevarra; it involves forming a liberated zone in the mountains and then expanding the liberated area towards the cities

**Franco, Aguirre**—bishop of **Tuxtla Gutierrez**

**FSLN**—see **Sandinistas**

*Ganadero*—a rancher; someone who holds a large amount of land as an individual

**Geneva Conventions**—a series of conventions signed in Geneva, Switzerland between 1864

and 1949 that provide for the humane treatment of combatants and civilians during wartime

**Gobernación**—the Mexican Department of Government

**Godínez, General Miguel Angel**—the Mexican Army commander for the Southeastern Zone, which includes Chiapas

**Gonzáles Blanco Garrido, Patrocinio**—a former governor of the state of Chiapas, Garrido was Interior Minister until January 10, 1994, when he was dismissed from that post

**de Grijalva, Juan**—a Spanish explorer of the Yucatán in 1518; there is also a river in Chiapas named after him. During the Conquest, Indigenous people resisting the invasion became trapped between the river and the Conquerors; they drowned themselves in the river rather than face defeat.

*Guardias Blancas* (White Guards)—armed guards hired by the ranchers to protect their property

**Guerrero, Vincente**—a revolutionary from the time of **Hidalgo** and **Morelos**, he joined forces with Morelos

**Hectare**—a unit of land equivalent to 10,000 square meters, or 2.47 acres

**Hidalgo y Costilla, Father Manuel**—a creole revolutionary, who, in the early 1800's, when his plans to liberate Mexico from Spanish rule began to fall apart, called on Indigenous people and mestizos to join the struggle. His *Declaration of 1810* ignited the Wars of Independence.

**Jaramillo, General Rubén**—a major figure in the **Mexican Revolution**

**Kamarrada**—a satirical reference to a traditional communist guerrilla

*La Fem*—a Mexican feminist magazine

*Ladino (latino)*—another term for *mestizo,* though it refers specifically to people of primarily Spanish descent, or those associated with Spanish-derived bourgeois culture

*Latifundista*—wealthy large-land owner

**Magna Carta**—refers to the Mexican Constitution

**Magonismo**—the political theory of the **Flores Magón** brothers

**Mam**—an Indigenous ethnicity

**Mayo**—an Indigenous ethnicity

**Menchú, Rigoberta**—Indigenous Guatemalan activist and Nobel Peace Prize winner

**Mestizo**—a person of mixed Indigenous and European descent; people in the Indigenous communities of Chiapas frequently refer to anyone living in the city as mestizo

**Mexican Revolution**—the revolution that overthrew Porfirio Díaz, dictator of Mexico from 1876-1911, it also transformed Mexican society; many modern-day groups claim to be the true heirs of the Revolution, including the ruling **PRI**

*Milpas*—corn fields

*Montoneros*—a band of mounted rebels

**Morelos y Pávon, Father José María**—a *caudillo* who, when he heard of **Hidalgo**'s revolt, organized local troops for the struggle; known for his populist politics, demanding the abolition of privilege and the return of stolen lands to the Indigenous people

**Náhuatl**—an Indigenous language

**Neoliberalism**—the political ideology of the PRI; a free-market, anti-state approach to economics and international relations, it encourages privatization of state enterprises, reduction of state subsidies, and fewer constraints on business

**Nexos**—a Mexican journal with extensive coverage of **campesinos**

**Padrón, Father Joel**—a Catholic priest from the Parish of Simojovel who was arrested for initiating and taking part in land takeovers

**PAN (Partido de Acción Nacional, National Action Party)**—a political party, founded by Manuel Goméz Morín, embraced by Catholics

**PARM (Partido Auténtico de la Revolución Mexicana, Authentic Party of the Mexican Revolution)**—a conservative satellite party of the **PRI**

**PDLP (Partido de los Pobres, Party of the Poor)**—a guerrilla group founded in the early '70s that subsequently joined forces with **PROCUP**

**PDM (Partido Demócratica Mexicano, Mexican Democratic Party)**—a Mexican political party

**Pemex**—the Mexican national oil company

**PFCRN (Partido Frente Cardenista de la Reconstruccion Nacional, Party of the Cardenista Front of National Reconstruction)**—an opposition party which offered to be the political arm of the EZLN, but was quickly refused; led by Aguilar **Talamantes**

**PGR (Procurador General de la Republica, Attorney General's Office)**—keeps records of personal information concerning opposition groups and their leadership

**Plan de Ayala**—the land reform plan proposed by Emiliano **Zapata**, as a condition for his laying down arms during the **Mexican Revolution**

**Porfirista**—of or refering to the rule of Porfirio **Díaz** or his regime

*Pozol*—corn meal soup

**PPS (Partido Popular Socialista, Popular Socialist Party)**—a satellite party of the **PRI**

**PRD (Partido de la Revolución Democratica, Party of the Democratic Revolution)**—a center-left opposition party, whose candidate, Cuauhtémoc **Cardenas**, is widely believed to have won the presidential election in **1988**

**PRI (Partido Revolucionaria Institucionalizada, The Revolutionary Institutional Party)**—the ruling party in Mexico for 65 years

**PRM (Partido Revolucionaria de Mexico, Mexican Revolutionary Party)**—precursor to the **PRI**

**Procampo**—a national aid program similar to **Pronasol**

**PROCUP (Partido Revolucionario Obrero Clandestino-Unión del Pueblo, Revolutionary Workers Clandestine Party-Union of the People)**—a revolutionary group started in the 1960's by Luis **Cabañas**

**Pronasol (Programa Nacional de Solidaridad, National Program of Solidarity)**—a national solidarity program of rural-aid programs aimed at capitalizing small farms

**PT (Partido del Trabajo, Workers' Party)**—one of the socialist-oriented opposition parties founded in 1991

**Rancho Nuevo**—a city in Chiapas; the location of an important military barracks unsuccessfully attacked by the EZLN on January 3

**Reform Laws**—see **Agrarian Reform**

**Republic**—the Republic of Mexico

**Ruiz García, Bishop Samuel**—the Bishop of the Diocese of San Cristóbal de las Casas, long-time supporter of Indian rights, liberation theologist, and intermediary between the **Commissioner for Peace and Reconciliation** and the representatives of the EZLN

**Salinas de Gortati, Carlos**—the president of Mexico

**Salinista**—of or referring to Carlos **Salinas de Gortari** or his regime

**Samuel, Don**—see Bishop Samuel **Ruiz García**

**Sandinistas (Frente Sandinista de Liberacion Nacional, Sandinsta National Liberation Front, FSLN)**—a Nicaraguan revolutionary movement that seized power in 1979. The Sandinistas were later voted out of power, and are now an opposition party.

**Sedesol**—a Mexican government aid and development project

**Setzer Marseille, Elmar**—former governor of Chiapas

**Shining Path (Sendero Luminoso, Communist Party of Peru)**—a Maoist guerrilla army in Peru

**Solidaridad**—see **Pronasol**

**Superbarrio**—a tenant organizer in Mexico City who dresses in a costume reminiscent of the great Mexican wrestlers, including a trademark ski mask. He is thought of as a "superman with class consciousness."

**Talamantes, Aguilar**—the head of the PFCRN and its presidential candidate, he offered to be the EZLN's candidate for the presidency and was quickly refused

**Tarahumaras**—an Indigenous ethnicity

**Televisa**—a privately owned television station, the largest in Mexico; known for parroting government opinion

**Televisión Azteca**—a television station; it's reporters offended the EZLN when they offered money to EZLN combatants in exchange for interviews

*Tierra y Libertad*—"Land and Freedom"; slogan of Emiliano **Zapata**

**Tlapanecos**—an Indigenous ethnicity

**TLC**—the Spanish initials for **NAFTA**

**Tojolabal**—an Indigenous ethnicity

**Tupamaros**—an Uruguayan armed-struggle group, they faced serious repression in 1972, resurfaced in the late 1980s and became a legal opposition party.

**Tuxtla Gutierrez**—the capital of Chiapas

**Tzeltal**—one of the Mayan ethnicities that is widely represented in Chiapas

**Tzotzil**—one of the Mayan ethnicities that is widely represented in Chiapas

**Union**—the Republic of Mexico

**UNO (Unión Nacional Opositora, National Opposition Union)**—a Mexican political party

**URNG (Unión Revolucionario Nacional Guatemalteca, Revolutionary National Guatemala Union)**—a Guatemalan guerrilla group

**Villa, Pancho**—a major figure in the **Mexican Revolution**

**XEOCH**—a radio station created by the government "for" the Indigenous people of Chiapas

**Yaqui**—an Indigenous ethnicity

**Zedillo, Ernesto Ponce de Leon**—the **PRI** presidential candidate who was nominated after **Colosio** was assassinated

**Zócalo**—town square; capitalized, it refers to the square in front of the Presidential Palace in Mexico city

**Zoque**—an Indigenous ethnicity

# CONTACT LIST

The uprising in Chiapas is not over. We had to stop collecting information at an arbitrary point in time to get this book to the printer, and already (before it has gone to press) there has been a lot of new information. Below are several useful sources of information about the Zapatistas, as well as some contacts for solidarity work.

## The Diocese of San Cristóbal de las Casas

The Diocese of San Cristóbal has been acting as a center for information about the Zapatistas, especially during the Dialogue for Peace and Reconcilliation. They are also a good way to send support to the Zapatistas.

Diocese de San Cristóbal de las Casas
Calle 5 de Febrero, Colonia Centro
29200 San Cristóbal, Chiapas, Mexico
Tel: 011-52-967-80053
Fax: 011-52-967-83138

## Institute for Agriculture and Trade Policy

IATP produces the *Chiapas Digest*, which has given timely and useful information about the uprising. IATP is an organization that seeks to understand and educate the public on links among community development, the environment, and international trade policy. The digest is available via email through Hannah Holm: hholm@igc.apc.org or you can write them at:

Institute for Agriculture and Trade Policy
1313 Fifth St. SE #303
Minneapolis, MN 55414
Tel: (612) 379-5980
Fax: (612) 379-5982

## Equipo Pueblo

This organization works closely with popular movements and civilian coalitions in the promotion of democracy, the defense of human rights, and the advancement of economic jus-

tice. You can subscribe to their news bulletin, *La Otra Cara de Mexico*, available for US$10 in Latin America and US$15 in North America and Europe. Individuals in this organization have also been an ongoing source for primary materials concerning the Zapatistas.

Equipo Pueblo
Apartado Postal 27-467
06760 México D.F. México
Tel: 011-525-539-0015
Fax: 011-525-627-7453
email: pueblo@laneta.igc.apc.org

### Love and Rage

This is a revolutionary anarchist newspaper that has had consistent, thoughtful coverage of the Zapatistas from an anarchist perspective. The same federation also publishes *Amor y Rabia* in Mexico City.

Love and Rage
PO Box 853
New York, NY 10009
(718) 834-9077
email: lnr@blythe.org

### Weekly News Update on the Americas
### Nicaragua Solidarity Network

The *Weekly News Update* has been one of the best ongoing sources for news of the situation in Chiapas. It is available directly through Nicanet or, for email users, is regularly posted to the ACTIV-L list (see below), and is archived by New York Transfer News Collective Online Library. You can reach NYT at nyt@blyhte.org

Nicaragua Solidarity Network
339 Lafayette St.
New York, NY 10012
(212) 674-9499

### Resource Center of the Americas

A US-based group that works to connect people throughout the Americas. They are monitoring the situation in Chiapas, and are a good source of information.

Resource Center of the Americas
317 17th Ave SE
Minneapolis, MN 55414
Tel: (612) 627-9445
Fax: (612) 627-9450

# THE ZAPATISTAS IN CYBERSPACE

As suggested in the Introduction, one of the fastest ways to keep up with what is happening in Chiapas is through the use of computer communications. The following is a brief description of some sources of information and discussion available in cyberspace.

We realize that not everyone has easy access to email, and thus to cyberspace. If you don't have email, you can try getting access through universities and some libraries. There are also cheap, private email suppliers in many cities.

## ANTHAP Archives (Internet)

The Applied Anthropology Computer Network has an ftp/gopher site that includes an archive of "Chiapas-Zapatista News" in its home computer at Oakland University, Rochester, Michigan. This archive contains all kinds of materials downloaded from just about everywhere. The archive contains a great deal of material from January-March 1994. Very little has been added since. "Chiapas-Zapatista News" can be accessed via gopher to Michigan/Oakland University/Applied Anthropology Computer Network/Chiapas_news. The archive can also be accessed via ftp vela.acs.oakland.edu (anonymous login, then cd pub/anthap/ls). This material can also be accessed through UT-LANIC (see below) at gopher lanic.utexas.edu /Latin America/Mexico/Chiapas-Zapatista News.

## CHIAPAS-L and MEXICO94 (Internet)

The Chiapas Discussion List was created in the wake of the uprising. The Mexican Elections List was created later to focus on the August 1994 elections. They are maintained by PROFMEXIS at CETEI-UNAM (Center of Technology and Information at the National Autonomous University of Mexico, Centro de Tecnologia e Informatica at UNAM). Both have archives (Correspondencia) that can be accessed via gopher lanic.utexas.edu Subscribe by sending the command "subscribe chiapas-l (or Mexico94-l) your_name" to listproc@listas.unam.mx (leave "SUBJECT:" line empty).

## NATIVE-L and NATCHAT (Internet)

These two "lists"—Aboriginal Peoples: News and Information List and Aboriginal Peoples: Discussion List—are part of the NATIVENET series of lists and contain information and discussion (respectively) of struggle among a wide variety of Indigenous peoples. The NATIVE-L archives are maintained at Texas A&M University (listserv@tamvm1.bitnet). Subscribe by sending the command "subscribe native-l (or natchat) your_name" to listserv@tamvm1.tamu.edu (leave "SUBJECT:" line empty).

## CENTAM-L (Internet)

The Central American Discussion List covers the other countries of Central America as well as Chiapas, especially struggles in Guatemala, El Salvador and Nicaragua. Subscribe by sending the command "subscribe centam-l your-name" to listserv@ubvm.cc.buffalo.edu (leave "SUBJECT:" line empty)

## MEXICO-L (Internet)

The Mexico Discussion List covers anything and everything about Mexico besides Chiapas, cultural as well as political. Originating in Mexico, much of the discussion (but not all) is in Spanish. Subscribe by sending the command "subscribe mexico-l yourname" to majordomo@udlapvms.pue.udlap.mx (leave "SUBJECT:" line empty)

## ACTIV-L (Internet)

The Activist Mailing List regularly posts news stories/analyses on the Zapatistas. They also post stories on a vast array of other activist issues, but you can subscribe to a once-a-day index of articles that only gives you a listing of stories available, and then order the ones on Chiapas that you want. Subscribe by sending the command "subscribe activ-l" to listserv@mizzou1.missouri.edu (leave "SUBJECT:" line empty). To get only the daily list, send the command "set activ-l index" to the same address. Activ-l's discussion group is on USENET, and has the name "misc.activism.progressive", which also includes the articles.

## PEACENET

There are several "conferences" (discussion groups) on Peacenet that have contained a large amount of information about the situation in Chiapas, including eai.news, reg.mex.news, trade.news and especially gen.nativenet and reg.mexico.

## AMDH

The Mexican Academy for Human Rights (Academia Mexicana de Derechos Humanos, AC) has issued irregular but very detailed "Special Bulletins, Chiapas Conflict" in both Spanish and English. They contain day-by-day chronologies as well as other kinds of information—including e-mail addresses to other human rights organizations active in Chiapas. You can get on their mailing list and obtain previous bulletins by posting to: amdh@laneta.apc.org The bulletins have also been placed in reg.mexico (PEACENET) and show up in the ANTHAP Archives.

## NAFTA & INTER-AM MONITOR

Published by the Institute for Agriculture and Trade Policy (IATP) in Minneapolis, the *MONITOR* is the result of the merger of the *Inter-American Trade Monitor* and the *NAFTA Monitor*. A weekly bulletin, the *MONITOR* contains news briefs and information on resources and events in the struggle against "free trade." The *MONITOR* has carried both news of the Chiapas uprising and other information on NAFTA—which the Zapatistas have called a "death sentence" to Indigenous peoples and campesinos. The *MONITOR* is posted on ACTIV-L and on PEACENET (eai.news). The IATP produces a number of other trade-related bulletins on PEACENET and ECONET, including trade.news and trade.library. Direct subscriptions to any of these can be obtained from the IATP at kmander@igc.apc.org

## LADB

The Latin American Data Base at the University of New Mexico in Albuquerque issued a series of special reports called *CHIAPAS NEWS,* and continues to produce a number of regular electronic publications that often contain information about Chiapas and the Zapatistas, i.e., *NotiSur, SourceMex, Chronicle of Latin American Economic Affairs,* and *Central America Update.* Information about subscriptions to LADB can be obtained from ladbad@unmb.unm.edu Subscriptions can also be obtained from places with site licenses, such as ladb@lanic.utexas.edu

## SOC.CULTURE.MEXICAN and SOC.CULTURE.LATIN-AMERICA (Usenet)

These are two discussion groups (among thousands) distributed to computer sites all over the world. Each computer site accumulates the articles and distributes them to its own users. Exactly how you access Usenet groups depends on your local setup. If you are modem-connected to a mainframe with a personal computer, access is facilitated with client software such as Nuntius (Mac) or Trumpet (DOS).

## UT-LANIC

The University of Texas at Austin-Latin American Network Information Center provides access to a wide variety of academic databases and information services around the world. Besides the sources mentioned above, it includes access to over 200 databases and over 200 libraries (including the UT Benson Latin American Collection, the "largest repository of Latin American materials with an electronic catalog accessible via Internet." UT-LANIC can be reached via gopher (or telnet) lanic.utexas.edu Questions can be addressed to info@lanic.utexas.edu

## The Web

The Web is another cyberspace location (a site for information exchange). There has been a lot of information about the EZLN and Chiapas on the Web.

# INDEX

This is a highly selective index. The selections were partially controlled by time and space constraints and partially controlled by our sense of what we thought you might want to look up. The Table of Contents may also be useful for finding information about specific subjects, events, ideas, and people.

# COLOPHON

A colophon is an explanation of how a book was designed, typeset, and printed. Colophons were common when printers (who often were also authors, designers, and typesetters) had pride in and ownership of their work. As book production has become more corporate and alienating, colophons have disappeared. A small and diminishing number of publishers still occasionally include colophons in their books, often providing a look into the design process and the interesting (if occasionally esoteric) world of typesetting and printing.

Many of the people involved in the production of this book are typesetters and designers; some of us for capitalist bosses, but all of us for political projects. We are printing this colophon because we have pride in and ownership of the work we do, and believe that the form and process of the production of a book have political implications, in addition to the content.

**Pre-Press Production:** The computer this book was produced on is a Comtrade EISA 486 66-DX2 with 16 MB of RAM, has a Conner 545MB SCSI hard drive, a ViewSonic 20 monitor and a Diamond Viper video card. The typesetting and page design was done using Quark Xpress 3.3. The index was produced using Sonar's Bookends extension to Quark. The pages were output on a LaserMaster Winprinter 600XL onto Hammermill Laser Plus paper. The pages were output larger than normal, then camera-reduced to increase sharpness. This inexpensive method (most printers do not charge for camera reductions when making film) dramatically increases the quality of type output on low- and medium-resolution (300-800 dpi) printers. The photos were veloxed (screened) conventionally, because scanning them digitally turned out to take too long and be too much work, and the conventional results looked better.

**Printing and Binding:** The book was printed and bound by Wickersham Printing in Lancaster, Pennsylvania on 50# offset paper. The cover was printed by Cosmos Communications in Long Island City, New York.

**Typefaces:** The headlines are set in the Font Company's **FC-NUELAND INLINE** and **FC-NUELAND**. The text is set in Adobe's Garamond, 10-point type on a 12-point line. The text on the cover is set in Adobe's **Frutiger 55**. We chose Nueland and Nueland Inline (historically known as Neuland) because they seem to us to have Mexican and Indigenous design elements, and because such Indigenous periodicals as Vancouver's *Oh-Toh-Kin,* and groups such as New York's Amanaka'a Amazon Network, have used them for apparently the same reason. Garamond is a fairly popular typeface for body text, and we think it is pretty readable.

# MORE AUTONOMEDIA / SEMIOTEXT(E) TITLES